A HISTORY OF

GEORGETOWN UNIVERSITY

VOLUME 3

Past and present success in collegiate, legal and medical training and research provide the model to make Georgetown complete its being—to add the doctoral research faculties that will make us what the nation's capital much needs, a great university.

TIMOTHY STAFFORD HEALY, SJ, *ANNUAL REPORT,* 1989

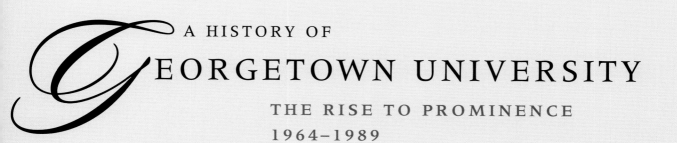

A HISTORY OF
GEORGETOWN UNIVERSITY

THE RISE TO PROMINENCE
1964–1989

VOLUME 3

ROBERT EMMETT CURRAN
Foreword by John J. DeGioia

Georgetown University Press | *Washington, D.C.*

This text of this book is set using the Meridien typeface family with Myriad as the supporting sans serif typeface and Sloop for the script elements that appear in the front matter.

The ornamental images used in the chapter opening pages are details of the stained glass window in Healy Hall (photographed by James Schaefer).

The book is printed on 70# Somerset matte paper by R.R. Donnelly and Sons, Willard, Ohio.

Cover and interior design and composition by Naylor Design, Inc., Washington, DC.

Library of Congress Cataloging-in-Publication Data

Curran, Robert Emmett.
    A history of Georgetown University / Robert Emmett Curran ; foreword by John J. DeGioia.
        v. cm.
    Includes bibliographical references and index.
    Contents: v. 1. From academy to university, 1789-1889—v. 2. The quest for excellence, 1889-1964—v. 3. The rise to prominence, 1964-1989.
    ISBN 978-1-58901-688-0 (v. 1 : cloth : alk. paper)—ISBN 978-1-58901-689-7 (v. 2 : cloth : alk. paper)—ISBN 978-1-58901-690-3 (v. 3 : cloth : alk. paper)— ISBN 978-1-58901-691-0 (set : alk. paper)
    1. Georgetown University—History. I. Title.
    LD1961.G52C88 2010
    378.753—dc22

                                                                                    2009030489

∞ This book is printed on acid-free paper meeting the requirements of the American National Standard for Permanence in Paper for Printed Library Materials.

15 14 13 12 11 10   9 8 7 6 5 4 3 2
First printing

Printed in the United States of America

FSC
Mixed Sources
Product group from well-managed
forests, controlled sources and
recycled wood or fiber

Cert no. SCS-COC-000648
www.fsc.org
© 1996 Forest Stewardship Council

Lord, teach me to number my days aright that I may gain wisdom of heart.

PSALM 90

In memory of Michael Foley and all his heart-wise companions through Georgetown's two centuries.

TITLES IN THIS SERIES

CONTENTS

FOREWORD

From the Jesuit tradition of education and the American spirit of independence, Georgetown has grown from the Catholic academy founded by Archbishop John Carroll that first educated six students, into a global research university with more than 1,300 faculty members that today welcomes 15,000 students from more than 130 countries to our campuses each year. *A History of Georgetown University,* volumes 1–3, captures the compelling narrative of the people and the traditions that have made this remarkable transformation possible.

Georgetown's first hundred years saw great change in Archbishop Carroll's academy. From the very start, we had assets of incalculable value: the extraordinary vision of our founder, and a commitment to pluralism, inclusiveness, and support for the highest ambitions of this country. In the decades leading to the Civil War, Georgetown transformed itself from something not much more than a high school—our first student, William Gaston, was only thirteen years old when he entered—to a full college. In 1851, Georgetown established the nation's first Catholic medical school. And at the close of Georgetown's first century, the leadership and extraordinary vision of Patrick Healy, SJ, laid the foundation for our emergence as a university. Perhaps the most symbolically significant step was Father Healy's decision to construct the building that would bear his name, and to reorient the college to have it positioned away from the river and directly facing the city of Washington, DC, thereby permanently linking our campus and community. Over the next hundred years, Georgetown expanded in enriching ways by becoming a more diverse community committed to educational excellence in each of our nine schools. In the early twentieth century, as a direct response to the tragedy of World War I, Georgetown opened the nation's first school dedicated to the study of international affairs and to the preparation of a new type of public servant. After World War II, in response to the nation's new, international economy, we founded a school of business.

Georgetown has seen immense growth and change in the size and diversity of our community, in the breadth of scholarship, and in the physical expansion of our campus. We have seen the university grow from an outstanding regional university that is recognized for superior undergraduate teaching and highly regarded for our schools of medicine and law, to an exceptional national research university, and now as an aspiring global university. Yet we know that the Georgetown University of today is only possible because we move forward in the traditions espoused by John Carroll and animated by our identity as a Catholic and Jesuit university. The commitment to education, service, and academic freedom that brought the first Georgetown community together in 1789 continues to inspire and motivate our faculty, students, and alumni today.

In over two centuries, our university has become something that John Carroll and our other early leaders could never have imagined. Sometimes, when I see the Gilbert Stuart portrait of John Carroll that hangs on the wall in my office, I wonder what he would think of his little "Academy." I suspect that he would marvel at how far we have come, how much we have accomplished, and how much we have contributed to the educational and social landscape of our city and our nation. I also think that he would remind us of our continuing responsibility to fulfill our promise and potential and to strive to become the university we are called to be.

We are deeply grateful to Robert Emmett Curran for creating this wonderful record of our work as a community to fulfill this mission over the past two centuries. In the words of the 28th Superior General of the Society of Jesus, Father Pedro Arrupe, we seek to foster a community of "women and men for others"—individuals who are committed not only to intellectual inquiry, but to advancing human knowledge in service to others and, in turn, advancing the common good.

—John J. DeGioia
President, Georgetown University

PREFACE

When the first volume of this history, titled *The Bicentennial History of Georgetown University: From Academy to University, 1789–1889*, was published in 1993, I noted that it was appearing much later than the bicentenary of the university that had originally occasioned it. Little did I realize that it would not be until the end of the first decade of a new century before the companion volumes would be in print, two decades removed from the event it was supposed to commemorate. Lateness, however, can bring some benefits.

Father Timothy Healy had envisioned a bicentennial history that would carry Georgetown's story up to 1964, with the retirement of Father Edward Bunn, who is commonly considered to be the university's second founder. To go beyond that, Father Healy reckoned, would be to plunge into historical waters that were still making their way to shore and carrying along many persons still very much part of the Georgetown scene. Even in the 1980s that constricted coverage of the university's past made little sense to me. Ending Georgetown's history in the middle of the 1960s was to miss a great, if not the greatest, part of the narrative that was the university's by the end of its second century. My intention early on was to carry the history to 1989. From the prespective of another fifteen years I decided finally to bring it—through an epilogue—as close to the present as I could, knowing that recent history is always quite different from the older kind to which there is paradoxically greater access with less of a tendency to bring presuppositions to the weighing of people and events. Georgetown as a vital institution should have a living history that tries as best as it can to tie past to present. However realized, that has been my aim.

This edition consists of three volumes. Volume 1 is a revision of the 1993 volume that covers Georgetown's initial century. The second volume traces Georgetown's history through its next seventy-five years, from 1889 to 1964. Two very strong presidents bookended its second hundred years: Joseph Havens Richards and Edward Bunn. Richards, in his ten-year tenure

(1888–98), renewed Patrick Healy's aspirations to make Georgetown a full-fledged American Catholic university in the nation's capital. "Situated as we are at the nation's Capital, and enjoying an exceptionally fine reputation," he wrote in September 1894, "we have an admirable field for development into one of the greatest, perhaps the greatest institutions of the country." Richards's efforts to create a broad cadre of academic specialists to direct advanced studies, do research in the arts and sciences, as well as develop the facilities and funding to support them, failed in great part but they set the standard for Georgetown's quest to become an elite research university over the course of its second century.

With Richards's departure, that quest was essentially put on hold for the next twenty years while his successors concentrated their attention on the college, and the professional schools of law and medicine reverted to their separate spheres. In that interim the configuration of the university changed as the professional schools of dentistry, nursing, and foreign service were added piecemeal, and the preparatory school, which had been the heart of Georgetown during its first century, was finally unlinked from the university and relocated in Maryland. In the 1920s "The Greater Georgetown" campaign was a formal attempt by a new president, John Creeden, to create an endowment to enable the university to develop the centralized facilities and faculty that would make it a bona fide comprehensive institution of higher education. That campaign proved to be a crushing disappointment and Creeden's successor had little interest in pursuing his plans. The Depression, however, ironically proved to be a catalyst for the effective resumption of "The Greater Georgetown" as the next president, Coleman Nevils, took advantage of the favorable building conditions to construct a new home for the medical and dental schools, a classroom building, and a student residence.

The second "Great War" of the twentieth century transformed the main campus of Georgetown into a testing center for the Army; most of the medical, dental, and nursing students became members of the training corps of the various services. To compensate for the loss of male students, females were admitted to the graduate school and the school of foreign service for the first time. In the immediate postwar era enrollment nearly doubled as the GI Bill opened the university's doors to many who earlier could not have considered such an education.

Edward Bunn (1952–64) brought the university into the modern world of higher education by centralizing the administration of its schools, introducing planning as a mechanism for shaping the development of the university, by recruiting, particularly in the medical center, a faculty who was more committed to research and publication, and by overseeing an unprecedentedly ambitious building program largely funded by the federal government. By the time he stepped down as president at the end of 1964, "Doc" Bunn had earned the title of "founder of the modern Georgetown."

The third volume, with the exception of the epilogue, covers the shortest part of Georgetown's history, barely a quarter of a century, yet arguably its most important one in terms of its development as a university. Edward Bunn's immediate successor, Gerard Campbell, completed the modernization of the university in the 1960s and brought it into the mainstream of American university life by restructuring the governance of Georgetown and allowing, for the first time, participation of faculty in the process; establishing the first comprehensive capital development campaign; and completing the democratization of student enrollment by admitting African Americans and women into all the schools of the university.

The last three decades of the twentieth century have proved to be the most dynamic in Georgetown's history as the institution acquired national and international stature. Its enrollment at both the undergraduate and professional levels not only doubled but the diversity and quality of the student body increased dramatically as well. The caliber of the faculty improved impressively across the three campuses. Strong administrative leadership in those decades developed the institution's academic and financial strengths. No one was more responsible for Georgetown's rise to prominence as a university than Timothy Stafford Healy, who as president from 1976 to 1989, gave the university an unprecedentedly national voice as he became one of the most influential leaders in higher education by articulating its ideals and challenges, as well as defining the unique Catholic and Jesuit traditions that inform Georgetown. Healy personally led the university in becoming more diverse in both the student body and faculty, and he was highly instrumental in sextupling the institution's endowment during his tenure. By the time he stepped down from office at the end of Georgetown's second century, he had brought the university to the brink of becoming a truly great institution.

The organization of the three volumes is partly chronological, partly thematic. Volume 1 follows a broadly chronological pattern, with the exception of chapters 7 and 8, which deal with student culture and education, respectively, during the antebellum era. In volume 2 the chronological approach prevails, aside from chapter 4, which covers the development of intercollegiate sports at Georgetown from the 1890s through the 1920s. Volume 3 employs a topical approach within the larger timelines of the period we have come to know as "The Sixties," as well as that of the fifteen years following the "Sixties" that has yet to receive a distinguishing label. In organizing the volumes in this way, I have tried to minimize the repetition inherent in such a treatment.

ACKNOWLEDGMENTS

In the course of nearly a quarter century of work on this history, I have amassed many debts. The board of advisors that Father Healy established to supervise the project was very helpful in the early planning. Several members were especially invaluable: John Rose was an unfailing resource for the history of the medical center. Brian McGrath generously shared with me over the course of many hours his extensive knowledge of Georgetown's history from the 1930s to the 1980s. Dorothy Brown, Paul Mattingly, and James Scanlon read all three manuscripts. The published text has profited immensely from their critiques. I told them, when the first volume came out, that had they been the authors, Georgetown's history would have been the richer. Having benefited from their comments on the second and third volumes, I can repeat that with even more assurance. Georgette Dorn provided invaluable help in the translation of documents in Italian and Spanish. Hubert Cloke, John Hirsh, John Farina, Christopher Kauffman, Dolores Liptak, Timothy Meagher, and Paul Robichaud, CSP, have also generously read and responded to various chapters.

I would like to thank also the following archivists and historians for their assistance: Sister Felicitas Powers, RSM, the Reverend Paul Thomas, and Dr. Tricia Pyne of the Archives of the Archdiocese of Baltimore; Francis Edwards, SJ, of the English Province Archives of the Society of Jesus; Edmond Lamalle, SJ, of the Roman Archives of the Society of Jesus; Henry Bertels, SJ, librarian at the Roman Curia of the Society of Jesus; John Bowen, SS, of the Sulpician Archives of Baltimore; Hugh Kennedy, SJ, and John Lamartina, SJ, of the Maryland Province Archives of the Society of Jesus at Roland Park, Baltimore; and Paul Nelligan, SJ, of the Archives of the College of the Holy Cross.

The university has been consistently generous in supporting this project. A university leave from 1985 to 1987 allowed me to begin the research in Europe and in this country. The university also provided research assistants for the project: Keith Allen, Mark Andrews, Anne Christensen, Katherine Early,

Tracy Fitzgerald, Bruce Fort, Patricia Jones, Ellen Kern, James Miller, Mark Sullivan, and Yang Wen put in countless hours, largely in the tedious task of compiling and entering information for the student-faculty databanks. Sally Irvine and Barbara Shuttleworth, my two original assistants, were marvels at organizing the research and setting high standards in coordinating it. Anna Sam, my research associate for several years, was virtually a coauthor of the first volume. Grants from the Graduate School in recent years have assisted me significantly in bringing the project to a close.

At the Joseph Mark Lauinger Library, several persons were especially instrumental in the preparation of these three volumes: Artemis Kirk, university librarian; John Buchtel, head of special collections; Jon Reynolds, university archivist from 1970 to 2000; Lynn Conway, his successor; Lynn's assistant, Ann Galloway; and David Hagen, Gelardin New Media Center. Patrick J. McArdle, associate athletic director, was a rich source of information for the history of Georgetown sports. At Georgetown University Press, director Richard Brown and his staff have provided a steady and resourceful hand in shepherding this edition through its long and twisting path toward publication, and the entire staff has my appreciation.

It is with added pleasure that I acknowledge the photography of James Schaefer, associate dean for academic affairs and financial aid in the Graduate School of Arts and Sciences. Jim has photographed the campus over many years and we acknowledge with gratitude his permission to use many of his photographs throughout the three volumes.

Finally, to my wife, Eileen, whose patience and support over the years have meant more than she can ever realize, I owe so very, very much.

ABBREVIATIONS

AVP	Academic Vice President
B	McDonough School of Business Administration alumnus
C	College of Arts and Sciences alumnus
CAS	College of Arts and Sciences
D	Dental School alumnus
F	School of Foreign Service alumnus
G	Graduate School alumnus
GM	*Georgetown Magazine*
GT	*Georgetown Today*
GUA	Georgetown University Archives
GUSC	Georgetown University Special Collections
GVA	Georgetown Visitation Archives
L	Law School alumnus
M	Medical School alumnus
N	Nursing School alumna
SBA	School of Business Administration
SFS	School of Foreign Service
SLL	School of Languages and Linguistics

PART ONE

THE ACADEMY IN THE 1960s

CHAPTER 1

Into the Groves of Modernity

Tradition, however glorious, is useless, even detrimental, if it serves as an anchor; it is of inestimable value as a rudder. And the first to rise up and condemn us, should we keep our gaze anywhere but forward, would be those very forebears whom we would dishonor by resting on *their* laurels. For if we are heirs of the past, we are no less the trustees and brokers of the future. . . . She has to adapt, to examine, to restate, to alter her methods and her machinery, while holding fast to fundamental principle and purpose.

GERARD CAMPBELL, SJ, APRIL 9, 1967

"A New Breed of Jesuit Priest"

In many ways the Bunn presidency laid the groundwork for the extraordinary rise of the university during the next generation. But in some ways, by its 175th anniversary in 1964, the university had outgrown itself while still exhibiting the strong strains of paternalism and familialism that, as one critical observer—Andrew Greeley—thought, were not disappearing nearly fast enough as Jesuit schools became more professional and collegial. Indeed, Georgetown was not above Greeley's charges of lay faculty that were valued as auxiliaries rather than colleagues, of a theology department that was cause for embarrassment, and of students who were heavily censured and controlled in their social and religious lives.[1]

The manner by which Bunn's successor was designated was one indication of the continuing familial nature of the institution. Gerard Campbell had spent the 1962–63 academic year as a research fellow at Princeton, where he had earned his doctorate in history six years earlier. He was a young (forty-four years old) historian of great promise who had deeply impressed the Princeton faculty during his doctoral studies. Upon his graduation he was appointed to the history department at Loyola College. In the early summer of 1963, while still at Princeton, Campbell learned by accident that several weeks earlier President Bunn had announced Campbell's appointment to a new position, that of executive vice president. When he called Bunn to find out just what the position entailed, the president informed him that, since he anticipated being on the road fund-raising during much of the coming year, he wanted someone to cover for him on campus. In fact, the provincial had assigned Campbell to Georgetown in order to relieve the president of many of his ordinary responsibilities and, apparently, to test Campbell's presidential aptitude.[2] Once at Georgetown, Campbell read a description of his new position that not only made him the acting president in the president's absence but also gave him all the powers of the president, even when the latter was at home. Gradually he began to suspect that he was Bunn's heir apparent. Months later, in early 1964, a Jesuit superior informed him that he would be the next president of Georgetown.

Gerard Campbell, SJ, president of Georgetown, 1964–68. (© Georgetown News Service; Georgetown University Archives)

In early December, at the same convocation that closed the anniversary year, Campbell's inauguration as Georgetown's forty-fourth president took place.[3] The *Washington Post* noted that the tall, angular, soft-spoken Campbell represented "a new breed of Jesuit priest whose style might be described as Ivy League Catholic." At his initial news conference he paid implicit homage to Edward Bunn by noting that only recently had Georgetown become a true university rather than "a college with professional school satellites grouped unevenly around it." With the institution now elevated, Campbell saw that a key mission of his presidency would be to continue to build upon his predecessor's efforts to attract "the best faculty possible"—both excellent teachers and scholars—to Georgetown, for a strong faculty was the cornerstone upon which to construct the first-rate university that Georgetown aspired to become. Faculty expansion, he indicated, would be greatest in the area of graduate education, leaving unsaid that that area was still among the weakest of Georgetown's divisions. He had great hopes for what the Consortium of Washington Universities could do to improve graduate education in the DC area by pooling resources. Georgetown was ready to embark on the joint financing of certain facilities for graduate research, particularly in the sciences. He also pledged that Georgetown would play a wider community role under his administration by fostering student volunteer activities in the city and providing educational opportunities and other services for the city's residents. All these commitments would require a great deal of money to achieve, he added, and implied that fundraising at Georgetown would have to reach an unprecedented scale in order to support the envisioned academic growth. Georgetown, he concluded, was not yet a university in the first academic rank, but it had already taken sizable steps toward "taking our place among the great public and private institutions in the country." He intended to do everything possible to aid the university on that journey.[4]

His tenure, it turned out, was hardly longer than Hunter Guthrie's, a little more than four years. Campbell clearly would have preferred to remain a scholar and teacher. As many observed, he did not enjoy being president. Declining health in a position he found uncomfortable, especially in the mounting turbulence of the late sixties, forced him to submit his resignation in 1968. But as one who served under him has remarked, "in some ways he remade the place," moving it completely from its familial and paternalistic province into the mainstream of American university life.[5] Campbell in fact took several important steps to complete the modernization of the university, including the reform of its charter, the establishment of a formal process for the appointment of faculty and department heads, the creation of the first comprehensive capital development fund, the remaking of the undergraduate curriculum, the transformation of an internal board of directors into an autonomous governing body, and the legal separation of the university from the Jesuit community. The faculty, partly through his initiative, gained its first involvement in university governance through the establishment of a senate. Under Campbell the university democratized student enrollment by admitting African Americans to all the undergraduate schools and women to the College of Arts and Sciences. At a time when in loco parentis was collapsing everywhere as a rationale for student governance, the seminary-inspired regimen of residential life at Georgetown was replaced by structures that gave students more responsibility and freedom in organizing their culture. Campbell even contemplated the complete severance of the university from the provision of room and board for students in order to concentrate on strengthening academic life. During his presidency no dormitories were built on campus. The main priorities were academic, especially the construction of a new library and law center.

Constructing an Autonomous University

One of the first things Campbell did after arriving at Georgetown, as a way of getting a sense of the place, was to acquaint himself with the institution's founding documents. He discovered that the charter and bylaws "had no reality to what was going on" in the actual workings of the university.[6] So he began to work on a set of bylaws that would both sanction the operations that had come into existence over the past several generations and provide authorization for changes in structure and governance that Campbell felt Georgetown badly needed to make. Specifically he amended the Act of Incorporation in the District of Columbia to enable the institution's directors to borrow money and construct or reconstruct facilities, as well as to grant them "all such powers conferred upon nonprofit corporations by the District of Columbia." He also greatly enlarged the bylaws of the university by making a distinction between the corporation and the board of directors (which had previously been one) and creating for each body a set of articles that laid out the membership limits and powers. The corporation was to be a five-person body, the successors to the original incorporators and the legal owners, whose sole, explicit duty was to meet annually to elect its own members as well as the members of the board of directors. The latter group was to be a body ranging from ten to twenty-five persons who would be the chief policymaking and governance authority within the university.

Getting the articles of incorporation and bylaws officially amended was a complicated process that involved the existing board of directors, the provincial and superior general of the Society of Jesus, and the federal government. For the first two parties, the board and the Jesuit superiors, the restructuring of the board of directors under the amended constitution was a controversial element. The board that Campbell inherited was a completely in-house one, composed of the president and the chief Jesuit administrators. Convinced that such an internal board made for bad governance, because the same persons were "making policy, going out and implementing it, and then coming back to evaluate it," the president intended to transform it gradually into an external one that included both Jesuit and lay members and functioned as a policymaking body rather than as a group of consultants.[7] As Campbell explained to the superior general in Rome, if Georgetown was to develop into a "high-grade American academic institution," it needed the "breadth, depth, and variety of experience" that only laypeople could provide. The public image of the university was also something Campbell and his fellow Jesuits had in mind in making a change.[8] Involving the laity in sharing ultimate authority within the institution was clearly related to fund-raising and public support, both individual and governmental.[9]

The creation of an external board that had ultimate authority in operating the institution, including the appointment of its president, meant that

Georgetown University would be an autonomous institution, legally independent of any outside authority, including that of the Society of Jesus. Campbell first secured the support of Edward Sponga, the provincial superior, but had more difficulty in persuading Roman authorities to approve the restructuring. The superior general was understandably concerned about the impact of an external board upon the traditional control that the Society had exercised over the institution since John Carroll had effectively turned the college over to the restored Jesuits in America in 1805. "Why," the superior general asked the Maryland provincial, "should the Society of Jesus permit its name to be identified with an institution in which the responsible superiors of the Society can exercise no authority?" Sponga admitted that, under American corporation law and educational practice, the president of a university, despite being a Jesuit, was a chief executive officer who served at the pleasure of the board. Nonetheless, Sponga contended, "the Society of Jesus should permit its name to be identified with an institution which adheres to the Jesuit Education Association, and in which it is able to place responsible Jesuits, even Jesuit subjects rather than superiors, since a group of such responsible men can exercise a truly Jesuit apostolic influence within the institution." Sponga's argument eventually prevailed, as Rome allowed the creation of an external board in 1966 and a year later the addition of laymen to it.[10]

Campbell's own board was divided about the wisdom of the proposed changes. Campbell slowly introduced the concept of an external board, first raising the prospect of adding Jesuits unconnected with the university, and much later the possibility of non-Jesuits, including laypersons. In July 1966 the board, after a final discussion in which some members expressed their lingering fears about the consequences of what they were considering, unanimously approved the new act of incorporation and by-laws. At that same meeting they chose five Jesuits—Campbell, Brian McGrath, Mark Bauer, and two outside of Georgetown—to make up the new corporation.

The amended act of incorporation still needed congressional ratification. Just as Georgetown had turned to an alumnus, William Gaston, to secure the original charter from the government, now another alumnus, James R. Jones, appointments secretary for President Lyndon B. Johnson, shepherded the new act through the Congress, where it became Public Law 89-631 on October 4, 1966. Two weeks later the corporation met for the first time and elected five new members of the board of directors, all outside Jesuits.[11] The following May the corporation added to the board the writer and labor activist Monsignor George Higgins and three laymen from the president's council who had been nominated by their fellow members.[12] Gradually outsiders replaced Georgetown administrators on the board; by 1970 laypersons had become a majority.[13]

Separate Incorporation and the End of the Familial University

With the establishment of an external board in 1965, the separate incorporation of the Jesuit Community at Georgetown in 1968 was a logical addition to the new university structure. "I thought it was important to divide the office of president from that of rector [head of the Jesuit Community]," Campbell remembered. There was a need to make a clear legal distinction between the university and the Society of Jesus that would remove the notions that the Jesuits "owned" the institution and that the university's autonomy was conditioned by the will of religious superiors.[14] Indeed, there was a legal opinion emerging that found that "educational institutions' charters as corporations under American law are not owned by the sponsoring body" and advised that "the administration of the institution should be separated from the government of the religious community" involved with the institution in order to protect the latter's identity and possessions.[15]

At Campbell's initiative, a committee of Jesuits headed by Dexter Hanley, a law center faculty member, drew up a rationale for, as well as a preliminary draft of, a document of separation of the Jesuit Community from the university. The committee wrote that the new understanding of the apostolic life for a local religious community that both the Second Vatican Council and the Thirty-First General Congregation of the Society of Jesus had fostered called for "a re-evaluation of the structure of the Community which is now identified with the corporate educational institution. A separation of the Jesuit community, carried out through a legal incorporation, can serve to give a sense of identity to the Community, an independence to the individual Jesuit, and a flexibility in adapting to modern needs and apostolic missions." "Prudence and good government," they concluded, "dictate a separation of the offices."[16]

After a series of meetings within the Jesuit Community at Georgetown, the provincial asked Campbell in late November 1967 to join with him to appoint a task force to work out the details of separate incorporation. The task force met several times over the next four months, and in March they issued their report. Separation, they concluded, was a recognition of the reality that "today's increased size of the University . . . the increased number of the lay faculty, the complexity of academic administration—all have conspired to lessen the influence of the old family-style of government." "If the Jesuit Community at Georgetown University is to subsist," they found, "it must possess assets which are peculiarly and specifically its own, and this possession must be licit and valid in accord with American civil law." Legal incorporation of the community was the best means to ensure its perpetuation.

Among the provisions of the agreement signed by the community and the university was the grant of several campus properties, including the Mulledy, Ryan, Gervase, and Ryder buildings, to the Jesuit Community. It also provided for members of the community who were part of the faculty, administration, or staff of the university to receive salaries, which would be the chief support of the community. It was the mutual responsibility of the provincial superior and the president to cooperate in ensuring "the continuance, effectiveness, and strength of the Jesuit presence at Georgetown University." There was an expectation that the board of directors would "regularly appoint qualified members of the Society of Jesus" to the offices of academic vice president and deans "in the spirit of the Georgetown tradition." There was recognition that "the Society, through the Community," had the responsibility and "mission" of making the university Catholic and Jesuit. To this end the office of university chaplain was to be raised to a higher rank and report directly to the president. Finally, recognizing the incomparable role of the president in shaping the character of the institution, especially in preserving "the Jesuit traditions of Georgetown University," the agreement declared the desirability of having a Jesuit as president.[17]

The separation very much embittered some Community Jesuits. To one who had been at Georgetown for nearly four decades, the community had effectively bartered away its birthright for "the crumbs . . . of a few of the oldest buildings, that the Jesuits may occupy as an appendage to the University."[18] It was, in fact, the legal recognition that the familial university was no more. It was also a recognition of the need of a sense of identity and mission for the Jesuit Community in a university that had long since transcended it.[19] The separation, Thomas Fitzgerald acknowledged, had made the position of the Jesuits at Georgetown a different one from what they had historically enjoyed. No longer could a Jesuit provincial superior simply appoint men to positions in the university. He could merely assign to the Jesuit Community those who had successfully gone through the same processes of hiring that laypersons did. The Jesuits, Fitzgerald concluded, still had a distinctive role to play at Georgetown as the chief purveyors of the Ignatian tradition of liberal education and as witnesses to their faith and religious commitment.[20]

University Planning and Capital Fund-Raising

During his first semester as executive vice president, Campbell called a three-day retreat of the board at an off-campus site to review the schools and academic programs of the university, as well as its governance, finances, building needs, development, land acquisition possibilities, endowment, and enrollment goals. The self-evaluation and planning that Edward Bunn had done in a more informal way and with a more limited focus during his initial year in office Gerard Campbell now more deliberately structured to cover the entire university. Not since Patrick Healy had gathered his consultors together in 1874 to consider the steps necessary for Georgetown to become a university had the top university officials gathered to assess and plan in such a comprehensive fashion. In the course of the meeting the board heard reports from all the schools and areas of the university. They ranked the building projects, with a main campus library being the top priority, followed by a library and an administration building for the medical center as well as unspecified facilities for the Law School. They committed the university to maintaining the Dental School. They set enrollment targets for the various schools, with the exception of the Graduate School. They made the School of Foreign Service an exclusively day institution for undergraduates and charged the regent and dean of the school to "reenunciate clearly" the objectives of the school and the means by which its objectives should be attained. They appointed a committee to determine the status of the Business School and mandated a study of the feasibility of making the Graduate School strictly a daytime operation. They dropped the practical nursing program in the School of Nursing. They set a goal of increasing the endowment by $9 million, with $5 million to endowed chairs and $4 million for scholarships. They approved raising between $1.5 and $2.5 million for the acquisition of land, most probably the Archbold estate on the northern border of the university.

At a second, three-day meeting in March 1964, they developed a master plan for the three campuses to be submitted to the National Capital Planning Commission. In addition, they took up issues regarding student life and the student personnel office, the expansion of the medical center, and a review of the faculty handbook.[21]

"The university was in a time of enormous change," Thomas Fitzgerald recalled. "It was becoming much larger and outgrowing itself." Reorganization of the administration, including certain changes in personnel, was a necessity for the efficient management of what was effectively a new institution.[22] In the spring of 1965, there was a reorganization of the financial and business operations of the university, which had been under Joseph Haller and Bryon Collins. Haller remained as the treasurer of the university, and Collins was named vice president for planning and physical plant. Because there was no qualified Jesuit available, John Pateros was brought in to act as vice president for business and finance. The following year there was a further administrative restructuring. A new position of administrative vice president was created to oversee the changes being made in the governance of the university and the relationship of the Jesuit Community to the institution, as well as the direction of the university's self-evaluation for the next Middle States examination. Brian McGrath, SJ, assumed this position, and Thomas Fitzgerald, SJ, with a doctorate in classical languages from the University of Chicago, succeeded McGrath as academic vice president. Royden Davis, SJ, became dean of the college; Daniel Powers, SJ, was named director of public affairs; and Daniel Altobello (**C** 1963), who had been working in the alumni office, was appointed assistant to the president.

Faculty and Faculty Senate

Campbell had stated at his initial news conference that a top priority for him would be to continue to upgrade the faculty that had begun with his predecessor. He more than delivered on that promise, particularly on the main campus. Nearly a decade later, when Thomas Fitzgerald was leaving Georgetown to assume the presidency of Fairfield University, he found himself leafing through the faculty section of the 1964 yearbook, the year Campbell had become president. It surprised Fitzgerald how much the faculty had improved in that nine-year period. "Generally speaking," he reflected, "we had brought in a young faculty that had been better trained professionally, large numbers of them were producing scholars, and in retrospect I felt that the improvement of the faculty, while it had been gradual and not particularly noticeable[,] was one of the major changes in the campus during that period. The improvements had already occurred in the sciences before 1964, but in the humanities and social sciences that [major] change came after 1964."[23]

From the middle sixties well into the seventies it was very much a seller's market for academics seeking faculty appointments. The faculty at research universities such as Georgetown expanded by 50 percent in just six years, from 1968 to 1974. Georgetown made serious efforts to compete in this market to bolster its faculty. Under Campbell, organized and advertised faculty searches increasingly became the norm for departments that previously had hired faculty in a random, familial manner in which the chair, dean, or president found a candidate (sometimes the candidate found him by walking into an administrator's office and inquiring about the chance for an appointment) and made the decision to hire.

Left: Paul Betz, professor of English. (Georgetown University Archives) *Right:* Michael Foley, associate professor of history. *(Ye Domesday Booke)*

In addition, the new faculty tended to be very active scholars, as the dramatic rise of scholarly production at research universities clearly showed.[24] New hires included Paul Betz (1965), Joel Siegel (1966), John Glavin, Roland Flint (1968), Eusebio Rodrigues (1970), John Hirsh (1970), Bruce Smith (1972), John Pfordresher (1973), Jason Rosenblatt (1974), and Penn Szittya (1974) in the English department; Clifford Chieffo (1967) in fine arts; John Brough (1966), Wilfried Ver Eecke (1967), Tom Beauchamp (1970), Henry Veatch (1973), and Terry Pinkard (1975) in philosophy; Gilmour Sherman (1969), Daniel Robinson (1971), Norman Finkel (1971), Robert Ruskin (1971), and Steven Sabat (1975) in psychology; Murray Gendell (1966) and William McDonald (1970) in sociology; John Haught (1970) in theology; Bruce Douglass (1973), Roy Godson (1970), and John Bailey (1970) in government; Thomas Dodd (1966), Richard Duncan (1967), Michael Foley (1967), David Goldfrank (1970), and Ronald Johnson (1972) in history; and William McElroy (1966), Bradley Billings (1971), Ibrahim Oweis (1967), Stanislaw Wasowski (1971), and Douglas Brown (1972) in economics. Although the sciences had made great improvement in their hires of the early sixties, there were important additions here as well: Richard Blanquet (1967), David Robinson (1972), and Donald Spoon (1972) in biology; Richard Bates (1973) in chemistry; and Wesley Matthews (1968) in physics. Business administration added Ali Fekrat (1970), William Droms (1973), Stanley Nollen (1973), Harvey Iglarsh (1976), and Douglas McCabe (1976). Languages and linguistics brought in Roger Bensky (1966) in French; William Cressey (1971) and Michael Gerli (1972) in Spanish; Roberto Severino (1973) in Italian; and Roger Shuy (1968) and Michael Zarechnak (1968) in linguistics.

Federal nondiscrimination legislation and policies put pressure on universities and colleges to develop affirmative action plans for the hiring of minorities, including women and African Americans. In 1969 the university drew up its first affirmative action program and hired a director, Robert E. Richardson, to implement it. It essentially called for a diverse mixture of minorities and women among the faculty and staff. It pledged not only to provide minorities and women with equal opportunity in securing available positions but also to seek out appropriate minorities and women and encourage them to apply.[25] In 1973 the university established a committee to develop programs to meet the university's commitment to affirmative action for faculty and staff positions. There were five black faculty members on the three campuses (.6%). In contrast, African Americans comprised 23 percent of the university's employees, most of whom were in clerical, maintenance, housekeeping, and hospital aide positions. The ad hoc Committee on Affirmative Action established specific goals and timetables for each campus; for example, the main campus was committed to hiring four minority (those of African, Hispanic, or Asian origin) faculty over the next five years.[26]

Georgetown began to hire women in significant numbers in the late sixties and early seventies. Dorothy Brown (MA 1959, PhD 1962) was the runner-

up for a position in the history department in 1966, but when the leading candidate (a male) turned down Georgetown's offer, she received the appointment and went on to prove that alternates can sometimes prove to be extremely felicitous choices. In 1967 Jeane Kirkpatrick received an appointment as associate professor in the government department. In 1970 Selma Mushkin joined the economics department, and Margaret Hall was appointed to the sociology department. Two years later Jeanne Ridley and Darlene Howard joined sociology and psychology, respectively. Joan Holmer became an assistant professor of English in 1973. Monika Hellwig (1967) and Elizabeth McKeown (1972) joined the theology department. Sandra Horvath-Peterson (1974) became the second full-time, female faculty member in the history department. Women hires in the School of Languages and Linguistics included Michele Morris (1966) and Dorothy Betz (1972) in French, Clea Rameh (1967) and Barbara Mujica (1974) in Portuguese, and Margareta Bowen (1972) in the Division of Interpretation and Translation. By 1974 women on the main campus (exclusive of nursing) comprised 22.1 percent of all full-time faculty, slightly above the national average. Their largest presence was in the School of Languages and Linguistics, where they made up 38 percent of the faculty. In the two largest undergraduate schools, the college and foreign service, they were only 11 percent of the full-time faculty at a time when those two schools were rapidly approaching gender parity in enrollment.

Left: Monika Hellwig, professor of theology. (Georgetown University Archives)
Right: Margaret Hall, professor of sociology. (Georgetown University Archives)

Jesuits, now no longer automatically appointed to Georgetown faculty positions by religious superiors but having to compete with other candidates for openings, ironically began receiving appointments at a greater rate than they had when they were simply assigned to the university. The Jesuit chair of the board in 1970 suggested that the university give Jesuits an advantage, that is, in hiring "where their credentials are of sufficient value to merit favorable consideration."[27] The board never adopted an affirmative action program for Jesuits, but several departments, at least, seemed to have informally exercised such a preference when qualified Jesuits became available. The Maryland Province in 1968 had made Georgetown University its top educational priority, which meant that Georgetown would have first claim on Jesuits seeking academic positions. To Thomas Fitzgerald, then academic vice president, fell the responsibility for recruiting Jesuits and coordinating their applications with relevant departments. He proved to be a very effective recruiter and just as effective a lobbyist for their placement with individual departments. "We brought them in three or so . . . a year [in the late sixties and early seventies]," he recalled.[28] So Robert Baumiller (1970) joined the Medical School Department of Biochemistry; Thomas King (1968), Paul Cioffi (1968), Francis X. Winters (1972), Otto Hentz (1973), and James Walsh (1974) helped to remake the theology department; Aloysius Kelley (1969) came in to chair the classics department; Eugene Poirier joined the economics department; Emmett Curran (1972) and John Witek (1974) received appointments in history; Walter Cook (1965) and Solomon Sara (1969) joined the linguistics department; and G. Ronald Murphy (1974) became the first Jesuit in the German department.

By 1974 about 70 percent of the full-time faculty on the main campus held a doctoral degree. A PhD had become a virtual sine qua non for appointment. Not only had the doctorate become a prerequisite for faculty appointment, but also research was becoming integral to, if not paramount in, the work of those in the academy. By the late sixties, as Daniel Bell has observed, the predominant concern with research was transforming American universities. Washington was becoming one of the nation's research and development capitals, ranking second behind Los Angeles among all metropolitan areas in the receipt of federal research and development funds.[29] And the DC universities were sharing fully in that growth. By 1973, 791 persons within Georgetown were involved in sponsored programs or research. From 1971 to 1973, the grants given to the university for research grew from $12.9 million to $21.9 million, despite the fact that the grant cow the federal government had become since the late fifties had cut back on its production sharply since the end of the sixties, as federal funding shifted from defense and space to biomedical and energy.[30] A year later Georgetown's total amount of grants for research and general education rose to $54.4 million, with $38.5 million of it going to the medical center, which put it within the top one hundred universities for research monies received from foundations, government agencies, and private industry.[31] The center clearly benefited from the emergence of the National Institutes of Health as the chief source of federal funding by the seventies.

On the main campus, among the sciences the faculty of the chemistry department became the most active publishers, led by Daniel E. Martire (1964), Jacinto Steinhardt (1962), Joseph E. Earley (1958), Michael Pope (1963), and Richard Bates (1973). In biology, Irving Gray (1964), Otto Landman (1963), and Joseph Panuska, SJ (1963) continued to be among the most productive, joined by Richard Blanquet (1967) and David Robinson (1972). In physics, Wesley Matthews (1968) published widely on his research into superconductors, as did James Lambert (1964) and Paul Treado (1962) on nuclear and particle physics. Professor William Thaler (1960) had probably the most important experimental success. Into the seventies, Thaler and his collaborators in the physics department continued to receive $200,000 annually from the U.S. Air Force for Project Themis, which involved basic research in the field of lasers.[32] In 1967 he managed to produce true frequency modulation of a laser beam through the invention of a device that provided an inexpensive but efficient way of making a beam the bearer of thousands of messages, or one hundred thousand times as much information as microwave beams could convey.[33]

In the social sciences William McElroy (1966), Selma Mushkin (1970), and Bruce Davie (1963) were three important publishers in economics. In government Victor Ferkiss (1962) was the author of two wide-selling volumes, *Technological Man: The Myth and the Reality* (1969) and *The Future of Technological Civilization* (1974). George Carey (1961), William O'Brien (1950), Jeane Kirkpatrick (1967), and John Bailey (1970) were other political scientists who had a broad output of scholarship. In 1965–66 three senior historians published important volumes on twentieth-century developments: Carroll Quigley's sweeping study *Tragedy and Hope: A History of the World in Our Time* (1941), Jules Davids's *The United States in World Affairs* (1946), and Hisham Sharabi's *Nationalism and Revolution in the Arab World* (1953).

In the English department, John Hirsh (1970) had a singular scholarly niche in producing studies of both medieval and American literature. Jason Rosenblatt and Penn Szittya both joined the department in 1974 and quickly distinguished themselves by their scholarship in medieval and early modern English literature. Eusebio Rodriquez (1970) became a leading critic of contemporary American literature through his journal articles. In philosophy, Wilfrid Désan (1957) and Louis Dupré (1958) led the way, most notably Désan's *The Marxism of Jean-Paul Sartre* (1965) and Dupré's *Philosophical Foundations of Marxism* (1966) as well as his *The Other Dimension: A Search for the Meaning of Religious Attitudes* (1972). Henry Veatch, already a much-published metaphysician, was brought in to chair the department in 1973 and the following year published *Aristotle: A Contemporary Appreciation*. Wilfried Ver

Eecke's (1967) scholarship ranged from studies of phenomenology to commentaries on Hegel and Keynes.

Monika Hellwig (1967), John Haught (1970), Thomas King, SJ (1968), and Francis X. Winters, SJ (1972) introduced serious scholarship to the newly established theology department. In the newest department of psychology, Daniel Robinson (1971) and Steve Sabat (1975) published widely on the history of psychology and physiological bases of psychology, respectively. Another new department, sociology, housed several highly productive scholars: Murray Gendell (1966) and Margaret Hall (1970) on the family, William McDonald on criminology, and Jeanne Ridley (1972) on fertility and women.

In linguistics, Walter Cook, SJ (1965) and Roger W. Shuy (1968) were the leading producers in a highly productive division of the School of Languages and Linguistics. In the other divisions of the school, Irfan Shahid (1963) and Wallace M. Erwin (1964) had important publications in the Division of Arabic. Michael Gerli (1972) and Stefan Fink (1969) were exceptionally active publishers in the Spanish and German divisions, respectively.

Institutional research in its most concentrated form was found in the academic centers of the university. In addition to the Center for Strategic and International Studies and the Center for Population Studies, the university established or brought to campus four other centers during this period: the Kennedy Institute Center for Bioethics, the Jesuit Center for Social Research, the Center for Contemporary Arab Studies, and the Woodstock Center for Theological Reflection. The Kennedy Institute originated in the fall of 1971 when the Kennedy Foundation pledged $1,350,000 to found a center for the study of human reproduction. Its mission was to conduct coordinated research into the ethical and scientific aspects of human reproduction and development. The new field of joint research involving theologians, social scientists, and physicians, they labeled "bioethics." Andre E. Hellegers, forty-five years old, became the first director. Hellegers had come to Georgetown from Johns Hopkins in 1967 to join the Department of Obstetrics and Gynecology, where he became involved with the Center for Population Studies. That center was now folded into the Kennedy Institute. Among those to accept initial appointments as Kennedy Research Scholars were Bernard Haring, professor of moral theology at the Lateran University in Rome; Charles Curran, president of the American Society of Christian Ethics; Leroy Walters, Mennonite minister and ethicist; and Richard McCormick, SJ, president of the Catholic Theological Association and an ethicist. Over the next four years, the Kennedy Foundation contributed an additional $2 million for the funding of two chairs and general operations.

In the fall of 1975, under the auspices of the School of Foreign Service, the Center for Contemporary Arab Studies (CCAS) opened at Georgetown. On the occasion of a trip to Egypt two years earlier, Dean Peter Krogh of the School of Foreign Service realized the virtual absence of contemporary Arab studies in American higher education. Upon his return, Krogh, together with some faculty members, began charting out plans for the establishment of an operation that would address this lacuna.[34] The center was designed to provide for the study of Arab development and international relations. Fields of study included comparative politics, economic development, diplomatic history, and Arabic language and literature. An interdisciplinary master's program in contemporary Arab studies and an Institute of Arab Development and International Relations were the centerpieces of CCAS. Its original faculty consisted of economist Ibrahim Oweiss; historians Hisham Sharabi, John Ruedy, and Thomas Ricks; Arabic professor Irfan Shahid; and political scientist Michael Hudson, who became the director of the center. Dean Krogh and others sought funding from Arab countries as well as from U.S. foundations. Initial support for the center came from the Sultanate of Oman, with a gift of $200,000.[35] Other early supporters were the United Arab Emirates and Egypt, as well as the Mobil Oil Corporation.

Some centers that developed in the seventies were independent but affiliated with Georgetown. One such was the Woodstock Center for Theological Reflection, established on campus in 1974 by the Society of Jesus. Jesuit officials had decided to locate the center in Washington, as it was the capital and the home of many economic and social agencies. In announcing the decision to house the center at Georgetown, President Henle noted that establishing the think tank, together with its extensive library, at Georgetown would instantly make the Washington area one of the nation's great hubs of theological resources. The center, he said, would better enable the university to pursue its special interests in bioethics, as well as the ethics of public policy and business administration.[36] Edward Glynn, SJ, was named its executive director. The first permanent members of the research staff were Walter Burghardt, SJ, professor of historical theology; Avery Dulles, SJ, professor of systematic theology; and Richard A. McCormick, SJ, professor of Christian ethics at the Kennedy Institute. Its first major project was a joint study of the issue of ethics and nuclear strategy, in collaboration with Georgetown's Institute for the Study of Ethics and International Affairs, directed by Francis X. Winters, SJ.[37] Perhaps its most influential contribution was the "Preaching the Just Word" project that Burghardt initiated in 1977. Over the course of the next three decades, he led 7,500 priests and deacons in dioceses around the world in five-day retreats on homiletics and social justice.

Faculty Salaries and Morale

Concern about the inadequate level of faculty salaries was acute by the middle sixties. What aggravated the situation was the growing number of faculty as new academic programs were launched, while the major source of revenue, tuition, remained relatively fixed, because the university lacked the facilities to increase enrollment.[38] In 1967 the American Association of University Professors (AAUP) gave Georgetown a B ranking for the salaries of its three lower ranks (associate, assistant, and instructor) and a C for its top rank (professor). Average salaries were actually rising significantly at Georgetown, from $8,796 in 1965 to $10,441 in 1967. But fringe benefits, mainly the Georgetown retirement plan, were considered below the acceptable level, which seriously affected the ratings.[39] The administration made sincere attempts over the next two years to raise salaries at all levels, and Georgetown switched from its own retirement plan to TIAA/CREF. In 1968–69 salaries on the whole were one-fifth higher than they had been the year before.[40] By 1970 the average faculty compensation had risen from $8,300 in 1963 to $13,400, an average increase of 7 percent per year.[41]

By the end of the academic year 1972–73, Georgetown's faculty (not counting those in the Medical School) had risen above the AAUP's eightieth percentile of average salaries at comparable institutions for associate professors, above the sixtieth percentile for full professors, but below that benchmark for assistants and instructors.[42] In new AAUP ratings for 1975, Georgetown ranked B at the professorial rank, A at the associate, C at the assistant, and B for the instructor.[43] For the faculty on the main campus, the ratings did not reflect their salaries, because the faculty rated included both those at the Law Center and in the School of Dentistry. In reality, the scale of main campus salaries fell below the eightieth percentile at every rank. The Senate Committee on Faculty Salaries reported in 1975 that their research showed that Georgetown's main campus faculty were not only failing to reach the eightieth percentile but were actually slipping relative to the salary scales of other comparable institutions. They also reported that there was an enormous salary difference among disciplines on the main campus. Salaries at the full professorial level ranged, according to discipline, from $17,000 to $30,499, and similar disparities existed at the lower levels.[44] The Middle States team of evaluators acknowledged that faculty salaries were much better than they had been a decade before but still fell short of the salary scales of comparable institutions. That situation had to change, it warned, if Georgetown hoped to attract and, more important, retain high-quality faculty.[45]

When Campbell became president, one administrator remembered that "relations between the faculty and university administration were not very good. . . . The centralized organization [had] made the faculty very restless."[46] "I felt that we needed something like a faculty senate," Campbell recalled. He was aware that a number of faculty, especially Valerie Earle and the dean of the college, Thomas Fitzgerald, were raising the issue of a faculty body. In early 1965 the officers of the Georgetown chapter of the AAUP invited the president to address their next meeting on the issue of a faculty senate. Campbell subsequently informed the chapter that Dean Fitzgerald and three faculty members would shortly be representing the university at a Danforth meeting in Aspen, Colorado, that would, among other things, take up the issue of faculty governance. Adopting a suggestion of Fitzgerald's, he proposed that this quartet use the occasion to draft the constitution of a senate and bring it back for a faculty vote. When Campbell asked the AAUP chapter whether they were in favor of the proposal, many in the audience seemed stunned. To Campbell's question of whether their silence indicated that they disapproved, one member replied, "We've never been asked to vote on anything before." They readily endorsed Campbell's plan, and the process of forming the senate began.[47]

When the group returned with their report that called for a faculty senate, the faculty voted to approve the proposal, and the board of directors gave their support in the early fall of 1965. The faculty subsequently elected a provisional assembly to draw up a constitution and bylaws for a faculty senate. The ensuing constitution created an elected senate of fifty members from the three campuses to ensure "full Faculty participation in matters of general University interest by sharing responsibility with the University Board of Directors and Administration in the conduct of University affairs." In the spring of 1967, the faculty and the board approved the permanent formation of a senate.[48] The faculty was now a formal, university-wide participant in the governance of the institution.

A formal system for regulating faculty sabbaticals was begun in the 1967–68 academic year. Applications for a semester of paid leave could be made after the completion of six years of service. Approval of applications by the academic vice president was dependent, he warned, on the merit of the proposed endeavor of scholarship and the ability of the department to release a member.[49] Faculty who qualified could take a semester's sabbatical at full pay or a year's sabbatical at half pay. At the same time, the university introduced annual contracts for faculty. As the numbers and quality of the faculty increased and new departments were created, the chairs of departments began to be selected, not through the mere appointment by the president, but at the recommendation secured from a departmental election. The academic vice president decentralized the reporting structure for the chairs who now reported to deans, not the academic vice president himself.

In 1968 Campbell established a university-wide rank and tenure committee, consisting of faculty from the three campuses, which reviewed applications for tenure and promotion and made recommendations to the president. Initially a twelve-person committee, with half its members appointed by the president and half by the faculty senate, it eventually grew to seventeen, in order to better represent the various academic units within the university.

The Library Renaissance

From Gerard Campbell's first semester at Georgetown, new libraries for the main campus and medical center had topped the building priorities for the university; library facilities were among its weakest academic resources. Edward Bunn had begun the movement to improve and develop the main campus library. In the fifties and early sixties he had opened up much of the Healy and Maguire buildings for its necessary expansion. He also initiated the planning for a new library that the assistant librarian, Joseph Jeffs (**C** 1950), carried out. A search committee chose the renowned Carl Warneke as the architect for the building.

The university had actually committed itself to building a new library for the main campus as early as the spring of 1963 but decided to defer a formal announcement until after the 175th celebration. Within his first month as president, in January 1965, Campbell set in motion the funding of a library for the main campus. The university applied for partial federal funding of the project. Selecting a site proved to be a long and difficult process that involved securing the approval of several municipal groups, including the National Capital Planning Commission, the Fine Arts Commission, the Board of Zoning Adjustment, and the Georgetown Citizens Association. Initial plans to locate it on the southeast corner of 37th and O streets had created immediate problems with the reviewing groups that forced the university to re-site it

Lauinger Library, 1971.

(Georgetown University Archives)

within the walls on the southeast corner of campus where tennis courts had been. Finding an appropriate design that would win the favor of the Fine Arts Commission added to the complicated, tedious process that stretched well over a year.[50] The university finally broke ground for the facility during the spring of 1968 and completed it in October 1971. Through Title Three of the Higher Education Facilities Act, the university received grant and loan money from the federal government totaling $4.6 million for the library's construction, with the university funding the remaining $1.5 million of the costs. The five-story structure completed in striking style the Edward Douglas White Quadrangle first planned in the 1920s. Its modernistic spires and exposed granite chip concrete echoed the forms and stone facades of the other buildings that form the quadrangle: Healy, Copley, and White-Gravenor.[51] Six months before breaking ground, the administration informed the planners that the first two floors of the building had to be redesigned to accommodate faculty offices, classrooms, and the bookstore. Pressing space needs had temporarily transformed the building from a library facility to a multipurpose one.[52]

Inside the completed structure was potential shelf space for one million volumes, more than double what the university then possessed. On the outside perimeter of the second, fourth, and fifth floors were 180 study carrels for faculty and graduate students. The audiovisual department that housed tapes, records, slides, films, videotapes, and microtexts occupied much of the first floor. Circulation and reference departments were on the third, or entrance, floor. The university's special collections and archives took up much of the fifth floor. With ample storage space, special collections personnel began serious efforts to acquire relevant collections. The library of the American Friends of the Middle East was an early acquisition, as were those of the American Political Science Association and the Center for Applied Linguistics. In 1972 the photographic archives of the Quigley Publishing Company, which comprised more than thirty-five thousand photographic prints and negatives related to the film industry, were acquired. The Woodstock College archives came in 1973, along with the 160,000 volumes in theology and related fields of the Woodstock Library, which came to Georgetown along with the Woodstock Center. Ironically, the core of that collection had originally been part of Georgetown's library but was sent to Woodstock when it opened as a theologate in 1869 in Maryland. Now more than a century later, it returned to the university to become a permanent part of the university's holdings. The archives of the Maryland Province of the Society of Jesus followed in 1976. An aggressive nationwide solicitation of the private libraries and collections of individuals brought some very valuable acquisitions over the next thirty years. The establishment of the Georgetown University Library Associates in 1975 provided occasions for further gifts and funds for the acquisition of books and manuscripts.

The new librarian, Joseph Jeffs, with a dramatically larger budget than the library had had in its Riggs location, greatly expanded his staff and set out to utilize the suddenly available space to double the main campus's holdings from the approximate 500,000 volumes in 1970 to 1 million within the next decade. The government documents depository, housed on the ground floor of the building, increased its holdings sixfold during the decade. The periodical collection also greatly expanded before it became a prime victim of the stagflation of the late seventies that caused a severe reduction in the budget.

The end of the sixties proved to be a renaissance era for the university's libraries. The main campus library, Lauinger Memorial Library (named for an alumnus, Joseph Lauinger [x**C** 1967], who had been killed in Vietnam), was but one of three libraries that the university opened within a two-year period at the beginning of the seventies (Lauinger in April 1970, the four-story John Vinton Dahlgren Library in the medical center a few months later, and the law library the following year). University officials noted the unique accomplishments of a university erecting three libraries within a two-year period.

Finances and Fund-Raising

The sixties were a time of remarkable expansion for American institutions of higher education. Enrollments doubled, more construction occurred in the decade than in the previous century, and budgets consequently quadrupled.[53] In the ten-year period from 1962 to 1972, Georgetown's budget more than tripled, from $21,900,000 to $76,164,000. Unlike the national financial good times for higher education, from 1965 through 1969, the university experienced deficits that cumulatively amounted to more than $2 million. In an effort to secure revenue from a new source, the university appealed to the business community of Washington for support. More than eight hundred local firms and individuals contributed more than $200,000 to Georgetown's first community support program.[54] Nevertheless, in fiscal year 1966 the university operated at a deficit of $336,000, according to auditors. The vice president for business and finance, John Pateros, reported it at $207,000. For the following fiscal year, he estimated a deficit of $175,000.[55] In January 1967 the treasurer, Joseph Haller, SJ, realized that the deficit for fiscal year 1967 would be more than $1.2 million. He had to liquidate $400,000 of securities in order to keep the current fund operational. Fearing that the university might be on the brink of insolvency, Haller informed the president and the board at their February meeting. The board authorized Haller to use approximately $800,000 of endowment funds to meet the deficits.[56] Also the board set up a finance committee to oversee the budget. The university engaged a new accounting firm, Lybrand, Ross Brothers, and Montgomery. In March 1967, Pateros resigned at the president's request. The deficit proved to be $1.5 million. The following November, Dayton Morgan was announced as Pateros's successor.

The board charged the budget committee with producing a budget that would show a $900,000 surplus for fiscal year 1968, despite the protests of McGrath and Fitzgerald that the budget could not produce such a surplus because of the need to raise salaries for both academic and nonacademic personnel.[57] In his report to the university community in the summer of 1967, President Campbell noted the ubiquitous reports "citing the growing seriousness of financial problems facing American private higher education today" that constituted a "mounting crisis." The alarming situation they described, Campbell warned, was "not exaggerated" and was "particularly applicable to Georgetown University today." Inflation and the need to provide a much broader range of services for students were the two chief factors in the increase of expenses. During the previous fiscal year, expenses at the university had exceeded revenue by $1.5 million. "Georgetown will not long survive as the institution you and I know" unless substantial help was quickly on the way. Two specific targets had to be met for Georgetown's economic well-being: within the next year and a half, the Progress Fund had to reach its goal of $26 million, and a year and a half beyond that the annual alumni fund had to be producing a minimum of $1 million.[58]

In the fall of 1967, the new accounting firm reported that the university was on track for a deficit of $1.5 million for fiscal year 1968.[59] By January 1968, university planners were projecting a similar deficit for fiscal year 1969, even though the increase in tuition would produce nearly $1 million more in revenue. The board agreed that severe economic measures had to be implemented to avoid further deficits. They charged that every school within the university be held to a less than a 5 percent increase in their expenditures. They also ordered that every effort be made to reduce the number of unfunded fellowships and scholarships.[60] "The financial position of the University will be seriously threatened if these efforts at economy are not pursued vigorously," the president warned the institution's top administrators after the meeting.[61]

The tuition increase plus reduction in expenditures, largely met by deferring maintenance, resulted in a much smaller deficit than feared for fiscal year 1968, $220,000.[62] The board renewed warnings to the schools that they needed to be rigorous in controlling their expenses or find new sources of revenue if they wanted to avoid drastic increases in tuition.[63] On the main campus an ad hoc advisory and information committee on finances, consisting of deans, students, and faculty members, was set up to plan a provisional budget for their schools and programs. In the meantime it became necessary to obtain a loan of $2 million from Chase Manhattan Bank to meet the operating costs of the university.[64]

Departments

In 1966 two new departments, both in the social sciences, were established under the umbrella of the college—psychology and sociology. Dean Fitzgerald was supportive of the need to expand the academic programs related to the social sciences.[65] Initially, in 1964, the college administration considered creating a broad-based social science department that would include psychology, sociology, and anthropology. Further exploration of this idea found strong opposition on the part of both psychologists and sociologists. An opportunity to establish a separate department of sociology developed in the fall of 1965 in a roundabout way. In September the graduate studies board recommended the inauguration of a master's program in demography, to be offered by members of the Center for Population Studies. A problem arose as to where the demographers should be housed in the departmental structure of the university in order to satisfy the requirements of the Graduate School. The solution was the creation of a new department, sociology, which would be the academic base of the demographers as well as two sociologists who were already teaching undergraduate courses. A sociologist, Robert Hoggson, SJ, was named the first chairman, and the department was put under college administration. Several more sociologists were hired in the early 1970s. A year after adding sociology, the college created a psychology department.[66] Both disciplines became majors for college students. There were explorations into starting a department of anthropology as well, but this led only to the hiring of two anthropologists over the next decade, who then became part of the sociology department.

No department within the college underwent more change during the period than theology. Beginning in 1967 with the addition of Protestant and Jewish theologians, the theology faculty took on a highly diverse character in respect to traditions and approaches to theology. This enrichment enabled the department to offer a wide variety of elective courses. With the reduction of required theology courses from four to two in 1970, it was possible for students to take more electives. One of the most popular proved to be Introduction to Biblical Literature, which was first offered in 1973, when 200 students enrolled in it. Enrollment in the course, offered in several sections, continued to grow throughout the decade and reached 650 by 1980.[67] In 1968 theology was established as a major for students in the college. A relatively small but growing number of students chose theology as their major over the next two decades. Eventually theology majors were able to concentrate in five areas: Christian theology, biblical studies, Christian ethics, world religions, and religious studies.[68]

Fine arts became a department in fact as well as in name. When Royden Davis became assistant dean in the college in 1965, he found a "minuscule" department that consisted of one person—Paul Hume, whose main responsibility was the direction of the glee club. Davis, who considered the stimulation of the imagination to be a fundamental part of a liberal arts education, was keenly aware of the prominence of the fine arts in classical Jesuit education, a tradition that had been lost in the Society after its restoration in 1814. Once he became dean he set out, through slow, incremental steps, to restore that tradition at Georgetown. He introduced studio courses. He hired full-time artists as well as art historians. He brought in musicologists and drama people. He sponsored art shows. Simply, he created a fine arts department virtually ex nihilo.

"All the Dams Seemed to Burst at Once"

More change occurred in the curriculum in undergraduate education at Georgetown during this period than at any time previously. The integration of women and minorities into the student body, the rapid expansion and fragmentation of knowledge, and the questioning of the relevance of traditional staples of liberal education all produced pressures for a fundamental reform of the curriculum that would recognize the diverse and segmented character of modern intellectual culture. Dorothy Brown notes,

Georgetown was clearly moving in the direction of increased flexibility and student involvement before the deluge of the 1960s. Then all the dams seemed to burst at once. Academically, the knowledge explosion and the proliferation of fields and specializations challenged the old distribution requirements that still distantly echoed the 1828 Yale confidence that there was a certain body of knowledge that could be transmitted in the undergraduate years and was guaranteed to produce an educated person. By the 1960s, there was clear evidence that faculties radically disagreed on how to achieve a distribution that had unity, order, or coherence, or more significantly, produced a shared learning carrying on a Western Judeo-Christian tradition. There was no longer an accepted canon.[69]

"We are at a moment when some real academic planning is much needed at Georgetown," Thomas Fitzgerald told a group of students in December 1967. "All sorts of factors suggest that the moment for far-reaching change is upon us"—growing quality and numbers of faculty and students, new student freedom, new facilities, international involvements, and urban problems making an impact on the university. His desire was that each of the undergraduate schools engage in a radical reevaluation of its programs. "Lest we drift into a combination of specialization plus sheer eclecticism, we must seek to determine what a student should be doing outside his field of specialization"; the focus of one's academic life needed to shift from the classroom to a student's private study and research. The course of studies ought to be flexible enough to enable gifted undergraduates to complete their education in fewer than four years. The use of computers needed to become a standard part of the quest for an education. "The academic uses of computers are going to be almost without limit." (It would be another six years before the university established an academic computer center for faculty and student use.) "We are at a turning point in Georgetown's history. Let us see each problem as an opportunity for progress, if only we will seize it. Above all, let us have . . . the courage to make Georgetown a pioneer in the collegiate education of tomorrow."[70]

Vice President Fitzgerald appointed a curriculum committee in 1968 to examine the general education requirements in the five undergraduate schools and to make recommendations for change. The committee reported that the core curriculum, which mainly affected freshmen, was failing to challenge them. They were bored, seldom if ever used the library, and virtually never did research papers. Too many were repeating areas that they had already covered in high school. There was, in short, a curricular lag. The colleges had to catch up with the advances made by the high schools in the wake of post-Sputnik reform.[71]

By the middle seventies, all of the undergraduate schools, responding to administration prodding, student pressure, and curricular changes in the academy nationally, had completed a curricular revision that reduced the number of required courses and introduced greater flexibility to the curriculum in general.[72] The greater freedom for students in shaping their academic programs increased the need for an effective system of faculty advising. Schools struggled to find the format to accomplish this guidance, with some schools having more success than others. The increased share that electives had within the curriculum also tended to lead to grade inflation, in some departments more so than others, but nonetheless a general trend, as professors found a premium put on their ability to attract students to their courses. Inflated grades was one magnet many professors utilized.[73]

One way that students managed to exercise power in the shaping of curriculum was through course evaluations, which began at Georgetown in 1965 with *Georgetown Confidential*. This publication reported the results of questionnaires filled out by selected students in undergraduate courses that evaluated faculty according to their preparation for class, knowledge of their subject, effectiveness of presentation, fairness of examinations, and course requirements. By 1970 students were routinely utilizing evaluation forms for each course. In 1969 the university rank and tenure committee established its own student critique form for evaluating teachers and courses. Eventually the two forms were consolidated into one, with the expectation that all faculty seeking tenure and/or promotion would use it.

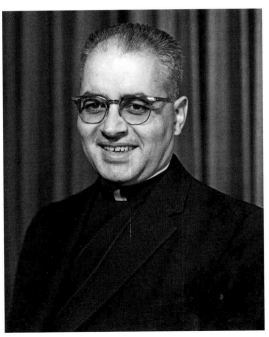

Thomas Fitzgerald, SJ, academic vice president, 1965–72. (Georgetown University Archives)

In Search of an Identity

The sociologist Andrew Greeley told a group of Jesuit academic administrators in 1966 that "Jesuit higher education at the present time is in desperate need of a new comprehensive rationale for its existence."[74] The modernizing process that Georgetown and other leading American Jesuit and Catholic institutions had embarked upon was inevitably raising questions about the identity of these universities, given that their identity had seemed interwoven with traditions that were now being cast aside or seriously modified. That summer a group of leading American Catholic educators at a meeting in Land O'Lakes, Wisconsin, attempted to address Greeley's challenge. The "Land O'Lakes statement" of 1967 declared that an American Catholic institution "must be a university in the full modern sense of the word," which meant that autonomy and academic freedom were absolute prerequisites for it to be "an institution, a community of learners or a community of scholars, in which Catholicism is *perceptibly present* and *effectively operative*." It embraced a limited collegiality in governance insofar as it recognized an "appropriate participation by all members of the community of learners in university decisions," which assumed different scales of participation by the various segments of the university. Thus the academic polity needed to become more democratic. In addition, every university, including Catholic ones, needed to serve as "the critical reflective intelligence of its society, as its critics and prophets, to both church and state." The first signatory of the document was Gerard J. Campbell, SJ.[75] In many ways the document affirmed the structural changes that Campbell had introduced at Georgetown. But it did not define what was precisely distinctive about a Catholic, not to mention a Catholic Jesuit, university.

The following summer the board of directors of the university recognized the need for such a definition about "the distinct character of a Georgetown education."[76] It created a task force on goals and priorities, which, among its aims, was an attempt to delineate Georgetown's distinctive characteristics. As the task force explained in its report in 1969, planning presupposes an understanding of the identity and mission of an institution. It identified six distinctive characteristics that shaped Georgetown: (a) Catholic but ecumenical in thrust, with a basis in worship and a recognition of the importance of theology as an academic discipline; (b) Jesuit in tradition focused on the individual's moral and intellectual growth as a person and in the participation of a critical core of members of the Society of Jesus involved in teaching, administration, or the pastoral life of the university community; (c) a commitment to excellence shown by its admissions policy, its faculty selection and retention, and its program selection; (d) urban; (e) national in the composition of its faculty and students and in its awareness of its location in the nation's capital; and (f) international in its faculty, students, and orientation of its programs. It was a university, at the heart of which was undergraduate education, that placed primary stress on teaching, an institution in which faculty and students shared in governance.[77] The task force marked the beginning of a discourse that sought to establish Georgetown's identity and mission that would continue over the next two decades.

"There's No There There": The Graduate School

In 1966, Rocco Porreco of the philosophy department succeeded James Horigan, SJ, as dean of the Graduate School. Porreco soon discovered how little authority he had as dean. Both those above and below him in practice exercised the power that formally belonged to the dean. On the one hand, the academic vice president in some ways, Porreco reported to the board of directors, was "effectively the Graduate Dean" insofar as he controlled all planning related to the school. On the other hand, the departmental chairs, as the board of graduate studies, controlled the policymaking of the school. "These act like feudal barons," he noted, unconcerned with the development of the school as such, but highly protective of their own departmental turf. The result was the pell-mell growth of the various graduate programs. Porreco, well aware of the glut of PhDs in many fields, saw the need for the "pruning" of graduate programs, but so long as the chairs were in the saddle, no real reform was possible.[78] "The role of the Dean," he pointed out in 1968, "is to provide academic leadership in stimulating and helping to formulate academic policy and in vigorously carrying it out. . . . What is good for the departments is not always good for the Graduate School."[79] The dean, he strongly felt, should have some say in forming the departmental budgets and in faculty appointments and development. At present he had virtually none. Nor was he in any way involved in the admission of students or the granting of fellowships beyond notifying applicants of the results of their applications. There was a need for quality control beyond that which departments themselves might or might not exercise. It was also crucially important to end the domination of the department chairs over the board of graduate studies.[80]

For a decade, from the late fifties to the late sixties, graduate education had grown by leaps and bounds, spurred by the availability of graduate fellowships from the National Aeronautics and Space Administration (NASA), the National Science Foundation (NSF), the National Institutes of

Rocco Porreco, dean of the graduate school, 1967–73.
(Georgetown University Archives)

Health (NIH), the Department of Health, Education, and Welfare (HEW), other federal agencies, and foundations in the wake of the educational armada that the shock of Sputnik had launched. Georgetown shared in this boom period. In 1967 and 1968 alone there were seven new master of arts programs introduced, most offering a master of art in teaching in several disciplines. From a postwar graduate school that numbered 9 departments, 47 faculty, and about 30 students, by 1968 there were 27 graduate departments and divisions, as well as 3 interdepartmental programs within the university offering various advanced degrees. There were 348 faculty and more than 1,800 students. History and government together accounted for more than 445 students.

The graduate programs of the Institute of Languages and Linguistics benefited greatly in this golden era. By the middle sixties they had become collectively the largest in the university. Graduate students in languages and linguistics tended to receive a disproportionate share of the National Defense Education Act (NDEA) fellowships that the university housed. In the academic year 1966–67, there were 19 fellows doing work in linguistics and languages. The number of doctorates awarded to languages and linguistics graduate students grew exponentially in the sixties, from 16 in 1962 to 82 five years later. Especially large was the number specializing in applied linguistics. By the early seventies applied linguistics, which originally had focused chiefly on teaching English to foreign speakers (the field of Lado's early work), now came to comprise psycholinguistics, mathematical and computational linguistics, and sociolinguistics, as well as English to foreign speakers. In 1970, with a grant of $460,000 from the NSF, the linguistics division began a program in sociolinguistics. The funding allowed the department the opportunity to support several new sociolinguists. The Ford Foundation granted $350,000 in 1961 for a five-year period to strengthen the school's doctoral program in linguistics, foreign languages, and applied linguistics, including English as a second language. Another grant of $266,000 from the foundation in 1966 supported other graduate programs of the institute.[81] In 1970 the NSF awarded Georgetown $1.5 million to study linguistic problems in inner cities.[82] That proved to be the last major federal grant the institute received for some years.

By then two ominous trends had emerged, a glutting of the academic market by the PhDs being produced and a precipitous decline in the number of fellowships available (as there was a major shift in federal support from the graduate to the undergraduate level).[83] In his report on the 1969–70 academic year, Dean Porreco wrote, "This last year . . . has been one of painful reckoning for the Graduate School." The oversupply of PhDs and the acute shortage of funds and fellowships for graduate education "have become increasingly visible to all of us."[84] By the close of 1970, Porreco felt that the situation was such that "the very survival of the Graduate School appears to be at stake."[85] Not only were fellowship funds drying up, but so was the pool of graduate applicants. From 1968 to 1973, there was a sharp decline in the number of students in many graduate programs, especially those in the social sciences, even though admission standards remained constant. In economics, for instance, enrollment fell from 117 to 84, in government from 270 to 146, in history from 254 to 162, in foreign service from 104 to 60. The economy, the draft, and the availability of fellowships were all factors in the decline. Whatever the reasons for it, the horizon for graduate studies seemed bleak.

This perceived crisis inspired Porreco to examine the presuppositions that presumably had undergirded Georgetown's sweeping development in graduate education over the prior fifteen years: to provide the academic credentials for faculty in Catholic colleges and universities; to qualify professionally Catholics interested in such areas as social work, journalism, and nursing; and to provide a faith-friendly intellectual environment in certain disciplines, such as history, philosophy, psychology, and social work, where Catholics could be in danger in non-Catholic institutions. "There is serious question today," Porreco went on, "whether Georgetown in its graduate programs can or should reflect a Jesuit and Catholic character."[86] In brief, religious concerns should not alone dictate the breadth or type of graduate education. Location should also be a prominent consideration. In Georgetown's case, this meant its presence in the nation's capital and its location in a major city. Being in the capital of a great world power meant that Georgetown should focus on programs of an international or national character as well as on those especially relevant to contemporary urban issues. Indeed, much of the recent growth in graduate education at Georgetown reflected a realization of these truths, with the development of programs in international relations and in area studies. But on the whole, the growth of the school's programs had not been consistently along lines that reflected the international and urban priorities that should govern development in graduate education. Prior commitments and the very governing structure were locking the school into a kind of institutional inertia that could prove fatal unless some very hard-headed evaluation and planning took place. "We should aim at selective excellence, building on our strengths," he wrote in 1968.[87]

In the summer of 1971 at a planning retreat, university officials agreed that the development of graduate programs should be determined by the extent to which they responded to local needs and opportunities, not by an ecumenical desire to preserve existing disciplines.[88] By that time the board of directors had already decided to terminate a major graduate program—astronomy. In 1965, President Campbell, concerned about the state and prospects of the Department of Astronomy and its programs, had charged the academic vice president, Thomas Fitzgerald, to make an informal investigation. Fitzgerald found, in talking with astronomers at other universities, that an undergraduate major in astronomy, as Georgetown had, was a dubious proposition. The departure of Vera Rubin had stripped the department of one of its best graduate-level faculty members. Fitzgerald's recommendations were to discontinue the undergraduate major and concentrate resources on reforming the graduate program through the hiring of at least three laymen, one of whom should chair the department and carry out the necessary changes, including active cooperation with the astronomy departments at the Catholic University of America and the University of Maryland, both of which were building strong programs. To give gravitas to such changes, Fitzgerald directed the department to conduct a self-study, including an evaluation by a committee of outside experts. The committee's report, in 1967, concluded that the present full-time staff was too small to operate a PhD program; its part-timers tended to be weak. There were crucial areas, such as in advanced astrophysics and in radio astronomy, that were either inadequately covered or not covered at all. The department needed a minimum of six additional full-time faculty and a sharp upgrade in the quality of its part-time faculty. Admission standards needed tightening, and students needed to be full-time, not part-time, as most were at that time. The department also needed to establish a field station, which would cost at least $300,000 to put into operation.[89]

With this dismal report in hand, in December 1967 the board of directors voted that the graduate program in astronomy be discontinued as soon as possible after June 1968.[90] Faced with this prospect, the board of graduate studies proposed that the astronomy and physics departments be combined, but the board of directors refused to approve such a consolidation, although it allowed further study of ways to preserve astronomy as a graduate program at Georgetown.[91] At the end of 1968, the university task force evaluating astronomy as well as other troubled programs at the graduate level reluctantly concluded that the cost of making the department a truly fine one was too prohibitive and supported its closure.

In October 1971, Dean Porreco, deciding to return to full-time teaching after eleven years in administration, submitted his resignation. In December the academic affairs committee of the board of directors concluded that the first step toward the reform of the Graduate School had to be the university's commitment to establishing "first-rate graduate education." That would entail many modifications: primarily, there would have to be a change in the attitude that Georgetown was principally an undergraduate institution in which effective teaching ability was the top prerequisite in faculty. Instead there would have to be a focus on the kind of faculty the university sought to appoint: first-rate candidates who would be attracted to an environment that fosters research and who would themselves attract funding. Finally there should be a distinct faculty for the school.[92]

Donald Herzberg, dean of the graduate school, 1973–81. (Georgetown University Archives)

The search for a dean to carry out this mission took more than a year. In February 1973, Donald Herzberg became the first dean of the school with no previous ties to Georgetown. Herzberg, forty-seven years old, had been a professor of political science and executive director of the Eagleton Institute of Politics at Rutgers when he received the Georgetown appointment. Although he did not possess a graduate degree, Herzberg was the author of several books on the American political system. President Henle expressed confidence that the new dean had "a strong background in scholarship and is eminently qualified to lead a graduate program."[93]

Herzberg recalled that his first impression of the school he now headed was, à la Gertrude Stein, that "there's no there there." President Henle's charge to him was essentially to change that condition—to create a representative structure of governance and put together a graduate faculty.[94] One of the first things he did as dean was to change the title of the school from the "Graduate School of Arts and Sciences" to simply the "Graduate School," to denote the reality that graduate education spanned the three campuses at Georgetown. Changing the structure of governance to give the school both cohesiveness and identity took longer. An ad hoc Committee on the Reorganization of the Graduate School took approximately a year to complete its task. As the committee reported, it aimed to create a structure that "would allow participation of all areas involved in graduate education and at the same time allow the Dean of the Graduate School sufficient authority to provide direction for the School as a whole." A three-tiered polity was the result, which consisted of four area councils, an executive council with two representatives from each council, and an assembly of all the area councils. At the departmental level it was now possible for graduate students to have representatives on the graduate committees. The new organization gave the dean the involvement in the formation of departmental budgets and the hiring and promotion decisions that Rocco Porreco had sought. Under the new dean, periodic reviews of graduate programs, including outside evaluations, began, which officials hoped would be the first step in a winnowing process toward achieving excellence in education at this level.

Among notable graduates of the school during the era were Warren Kimball (1968) and J. Albert Bailey (1969), who became professors of history at Rutgers and Michigan, respectively; Robert Gates (1974), who headed up the CIA in the Reagan administration and, later, the Department of Defense in the George W. Bush and Obama administrations; Kenneth L. Adelman (1970), who became the director of the Arms Control and Disarmament Agency under President Reagan; John J. O'Connor (1970), who became cardinal archbishop of the Archdiocese of New York; Rabbi David Novak (1971), who held the Chair of Modern Jewish Thought in the Department of Religious Studies at the University of Virginia; John-David Bartoe (1974), who became head of the spectroscopy section of the Naval Research Lab in Washington and in 1981 became one of the first noncareer astronauts to enter space; Pascale Cossart (1971), who became a professor at the Pasteur Institute of Paris; Chimansing Jesseramsing (1974), who became the ambassador from Mauritius to the United States; and Lawrence Biondi, SJ (1975), who became the president of Saint Louis University.

The School for Summer and Continuing Education

Shortly after Joseph Pettit became dean of the summer school in 1969, he proposed a new name for the school: the School for Summer and Continuing Education. The change indicated the enlarging scope of the programs that the school was operating, programs that were no longer confined to the summer months. Indeed, as enrollments in the traditional summer courses at both the graduate and undergraduate levels began to drop sharply in the early seventies, the school began to look more and more to adult education on a year-round basis. In 1973, Dean Pettit proposed establishing the first degree program for the school, the Liberal Studies Program, which would focus on enrolling nontraditional or mature students already in careers or beyond them in a humanities-centered curriculum that would involve much independent study through guided projects. The program would offer bachelor of arts and master of arts degrees. It would be a program not for professional advancement but personal fulfillment. "It is nonprofessional," Dean Pettit commented, "in the sense that the program will attempt to bring the knowledge and insights of a field of study to bear on timely or timeless problems, and not to train the student in that field. Moreover, the emphasis will rest on the human values implicit or explicit in the problems and fields."[95] Approved by the council of deans and the board of directors, the program admitted its first students in the summer of 1974. Among the first students in the program were a retired foreign correspondent for *Time* magazine, a managing editor of a professional journal, a local television producer, and the dean of the school. It was immediately apparent that the program had met a latent demand in the professional ranks in Washington. Within a

Joseph Pettit, dean of the summer school, 1969–81. (Georgetown University Archives)

year there were eighty-three nontraditional students (average age thirty-five) in the program.[96] As outgoing President Henle noted in 1976, "The rationale of the School, its basic plan, and its development have all been enormously improved during the last six years with the appointment of Dean Pettit as Dean of the combined operation of [the] Summer School and Continuing Education. The conjunction of these two related operations has proved to be extremely successful and mutually reinforcing."[97]

The Medical Center: Growth and Progress

The late sixties and the early seventies proved to be a boom period for the medical center, during which the size of the faculty, student body, administration, physical plant, and budget all grew enormously. All of this growth was related directly to the surge of government assistance to medical schools, beginning in 1963 and continuing through the mid-1970s. The Health Professions Educational Assistance Act of 1963 was the first of several acts intended to increase the supply of physicians in this country. In return for a school's increasing its enrollment, the government committed itself to contributing substantially to the construction of new facilities at the school. Two years later another assistance act made available major funding for the operating expenses as well as for construction on a "capitation" basis that tied the amount of money given to the size of a school's enrollment.

As noted in chapter 9 of volume 2, the medical center administration was all too conscious of the urgent physical needs of the medical center that would provide the foundation of a first-class medical institution: basic science building, dental clinic, critical care center, library, and pediatric facility. "We had some dire needs," Dean Rose recalled. "We had a threat to our accreditation because of the library. And we knew the bad state of our labs and classrooms."[98] Architects and administrators devised a master plan for the development of the medical center: basic science building, a library, and a dental clinic facility, as well as the renovation of the Medical-Dental Building. The educational assistance acts provided the opportunity to begin to implement it. Through the work of Byron Collins, federal funding under the assistance acts provided the majority of the funding to construct those three facilities. In return, the Medical School committed itself to increasing by stages the size of its entering class from 121 to 145 by 1971.[99] The university also sought federal funding for the critical care facility and a pediatric diagnostic center (Marcus J. Bles Building). The DC Medical Care Facilities Act, Public Law 90-457, written by Collins, called for $40 million in grants and a matching figure in loans.[100] This provided additional money as well for the basic science building, the dental clinic, and the John Vinton Dahlgren Memorial Library. Between 1970 and 1972, these three facilities, as well as the Bles Building, were completed.

Separate Incorporation

There was growing concern among the university's top officials about its ability to sustain the financial impact of the medical center's operations, particularly the spiraling costs of its building projects. As early as the summer of 1967, the board of directors had raised a red flag about the drain upon the university's resources that the center was having in attempting to realize its physical makeover.[101] At a time when many academic medical centers in the nation were in dire fiscal condition because of the drying up of federal funding and the generally poor economic conditions, Georgetown was very sensitive to its risks in carrying the fiscal responsibilities of its medical center. At the center of its concern was the largest construction project of the medical center, the critical care facility, or Concentrated Care Center (CCC). Planning for this experimental facility for the care of critically ill and postoperative patients and major disaster victims had been in the works since 1963. The Public Health Service provided a grant to proceed with the design of the experimental building. Federal funding furnished $7.2 million for the project, with the university responsible for raising the rest of the $10.8 million, the building's projected cost. By the summer of 1967, it became evident that the total cost of the CCC would be not $10.8 million but $19 million. Aggravating this situation was the fact that the university's share of the other medical center construction projects (basic science building, dental clinic, and library) was now going to be $9.3 million rather than the anticipated $5.5 million and that the cost for equipping these buildings was going to be about $2.5 million more than budgeted.

In October the board created an ad hoc medical center committee to determine how the university should proceed to address this staggering fund-raising challenge. The committee in its report offered three possible avenues for the university to take: (a) cancel the project, (b) proceed with construction and raise the needed funds, or (c) proceed with the construction but create a separate corporation for the medical center to insulate the university from any "adverse financial impact." The committee thought that the first option would be an academic disaster for the center, not to mention that the university would lose the $7.2 million federal grant and would have to repay the $1.7 million already spent on the project. The second option seemed impossible to fulfill—involving the raising of more than $8 million within the next two or three years. The third option, the committee implied, was clearly the best one to take.[102]

At its December meeting the board approved in principle the separate incorporation of the medical center and authorized the president to take the steps to "prepare for it."[103] The following month Campbell appointed a committee to explore the financial, educational, legal, and other factors involved in the setting up of a corporation that would be separate from, but retain an academic affiliation with, the university. The committee, headed by Dean John Rose, met for several months and issued its report in June 1968. After an examination that lasted five months, the committee, although charged with finding the means to realize separate incorporation, decided that it was "not advisable at this time." Separate incorporation would not provide the medical center with any funding that being part of the university was preventing it from acquiring. Conversely, separate incorporation would not protect the university from accountability for the center's fiscal losses. As Rose explained, "The lawyers told us that if there were any financial disaster incurred by the medical center the corporate veil would be pierced anyway because the corporation would clearly have been formed for the prevention of just that kind of a disaster." The committee recommended that certain steps be taken to ensure greater autonomy in planning and management of the center's finances. They called for the establishment of a separate development office for fund-raising, an advisory board for the medical center, and a "stronger executive organization." A minority of the committee urged that the vice president be given the power to set policy and manage the administration of the center.[104] The board accepted the report and abandoned plans for separate incorporation.

A New Vice President

A month after the committee presented their report, Mark Bauer, SJ, resigned as vice president for medical center affairs. Even though the committee had not formally supported the proposal for a powerful top executive officer of the center, the search committee, chaired by Edward Quain, SJ, was very deliberately seeking someone who could assume such a role as

Matthew McNulty, executive vice president for medical center affairs, 1968–82.

(Georgetown University Archives)

vice president of the center. They found one in Matthew McNulty. Several of the Georgetown faculty, including Dean Rose, knew McNulty, who was then head of the Washington-based Council of Teaching Hospitals, an affiliate of the Association of American Medical Colleges. He had had a long career in hospital administration for the Veterans Administration and at the University of Alabama. "Matt had managerial and administrative skills that were far better than anyone here," Rose later observed. And McNulty immediately began to utilize them in overseeing the immensely complex organization with a rapidly expanding budget that the medical center had become by the end of the sixties. One of his first moves was to form the school deans, the hospital administrator, and himself into a quasi council that met weekly to share information and coordinate policy and planning. He also began monthly faculty assemblies to improve communication between the administration and the faculty. When he arrived, rumors were swirling that the university was going to close the hospital and the Nursing School. McNulty utilized the assemblies during his first months at Georgetown to have Deans Rose and Murto assure the faculty that no one was going to close either part of the medical center.[105] He was also well aware of the broad possibilities that federal assistance legislation offered for medical schools. He became a very active participant in seeking and lobbying for further federal assistance.

Increased Enrollment and Federal Funding

By 1970 the medical center still lacked the funding to complete its ambitious building program. The passage in 1969 of the Physician's Augmentation Program by Congress, which provided special funding to any medical school that increased its enrollment by at least 10 percent, provided a new opportunity for Georgetown to use the expansion of enrollment as a means of acquiring funding for capital purposes. Georgetown committed itself to increasing its enrollment, not by 10 percent, but by 75 percent, within the next five years. It raised the size of its entering class to 205. To provide for the education of a much larger student body, the university also made plans to hire an additional 50 full-time faculty (there were currently 269 members) and to convert Kober-Cogan from a dormitory to offices for clinical faculty. In return it received a grant of $8.5 million from HEW, bringing the total amount that the university had received from the various physician-expansion laws to more than $15 million.[106]

As the costs of medical education soared, and tuition fees along with them, the school faced the daunting prospect of either pricing itself out of the market through ruinous tuition hikes or of risking enormous deficit. By 1970 the cost of educating a medical student had risen to $21,000 a year. Tuition covered barely one-seventh of the cost. Again Georgetown turned to the federal government for relief. The second major bill that Father Collins wrote, Public Law 91-650, the Medical-Dental Manpower Bill of the District of Columbia, proved even more crucial for the medical center's development. The medical and dental schools of the District were unique in the country in not having any government subsidies that state governments ordinarily supplied to such institutions. "We believe," Dean Rose commented in his annual report for 1972–73, that "the U.S. Congress must act as a state legislature with regard to private medical and dental schools of the District of Columbia."[107] The bill as crafted by Collins called for the federal government to provide up to $5,000 for each medical student in the District of Columbia and up to $3,000 for each dental student. As passed, the bill provided $6.2 million to Georgetown for 1971, and $6.75 million for 1972. Ultimately the bill was renewed for an additional five years, through the 1976–77 academic year; during that time the university was able to keep its tuition for medical school below $7,000. In sum, from 1971 to 1977, the federal government was a major underwriter of the educational costs of Georgetown dental and medical students. In the ten-year period from 1965 to 1975 the federal government had, through the various augmentation and student support bills, provided more than $22 million to the Medical School.[108]

The Lombardi Cancer Center and the CCC

In November 1970 the university announced the establishment of the Vincent T. Lombardi Cancer Center, named for the legendary football coach of the Green Bay Packers and Washington Redskins who had died of cancer at the Georgetown Hospital two months earlier. Robert Coffey, who performed the surgery on Lombardi's intestinal cancer, had mentioned to Lombardi that Georgetown was hoping to open a cancer institute. Planning for the center had been under way for two years. After Lombardi's death in September, his widow and an official of the National Football League came to see Dean Rose and agreed to help raise the funds for the establishment of a center to be named for the coach.[109] John F. Potter, professor of surgery, became its first director. A major mission of the center was to facilitate the collaboration of basic scientists and clinicians in the search for effective treatments and cures for the disease, to involve the basic scientist as well as the clinician in the care of cancer patients. The National Cancer Institute (NCI) was a major supporter of the center from its inception. Dr. Philip S. Schein, who had been chief of the clinical pharmacology section of NCI and on the staff of the Lombardi Center since its opening, in 1974, was named chief of the center's medical oncology section.

For four years the CCC project was dormant. In the spring of 1972 the chancellor of the medical center presented it anew to the board of directors. By now its estimated cost had risen to $21 million, but Georgetown lobbying had in the meantime secured passage of legislation that provided $15 million in grants and $6.7 million in loans at 2.5 percent. "This Center is critical to the future of Georgetown Hospital," Chancellor McNulty told the board. The board approved the project but stipulated that construction could not begin until the federal funds had been secured. That proved to be much longer than anyone figured. The Nixon administration refused to release the authorized funds as part of its campaign to contain spending. When a year passed with no funds in hand, the board authorized the university president to borrow the money from commercial sources. In September the secretary of HEW was still sitting on the funds. Board member Patricia Harris advocated suing the federal government to get the money.[110] Finally, in October, Byron Collins's patient but persistent pursuit of the appropriated funds through the federal labyrinth finally succeeded in getting the $15 million in grants delivered to the university. Ground was finally broken in November 1974, more than eleven years after planning for the building had begun. Dedicated in June 1976, the CCC was one of the most advanced facilities in the country for the care of the acutely ill and one of the nation's largest disaster care centers. At the heart of the eight-story building was Charles Hufnagel's revolutionary design: a series of care units, each in the configuration of a wheel, with the nurses' station functioning as a hub and the patients' rooms encircling the station like spokes. There were altogether 160 beds in these pods; in addition, there were twelve surgical suites, a spacious emergency department, and a disaster center able to handle as many as 120 patients simultaneously.[111] Its final cost was $23 million, with the federal government providing virtually all of it in the form of grants or loans. The CCC became a prototype for many other intensive care centers throughout the nation and beyond.

Faculty Development and Practice Plan

As the size of the student body, faculty, administration, and physical plant grew dramatically, so did the budget. In 1965 the medical center budget had been approximately $14 million. By 1972 it had more than doubled—to more than $35 million—far greater than the combined budget of the rest of the university. The center, thanks largely to its hospital producing large surpluses from high occupancy rates (better than 80%) and to the revenue realized from the clinical faculty who practiced there, had no overall deficit.

In 1965 there were 17,000 full-time medical faculty across the nation; by the end of the seventies they numbered more than 50,000. Georgetown shared in this expansion. In 1966 there were 232 full-time faculty in the center; by 1975, the full-time faculty had grown by a third to 344. Most of the growth at Georgetown, as was true nationally, occurred in the clinical field where faculty practice had become the major source of revenue for the medical center and, specifically, the Medical School.[112] The establishment of Medicare and Medicaid led to a great increase in the clinical service that the faculty gave in the university hospital and affiliated hospitals. On the hospital corridors, in the operating rooms, and in their on-campus offices, faculty members saw a dramatic increase in their private practice and in their income from that practice. To regulate this suddenly enlarged practice as well as to utilize some of the income for faculty salaries and for offsetting some of the costs of medical education, medical centers universally began introducing "faculty practice plans," by which a certain portion of the income of private practice went to the department or school for its discretionary use.[113]

At Georgetown most of the clinical faculty were "geographic full-time," which meant that while they were physically present at the medical center or its affiliates for their entire work week, they were allowed to keep all the income earned from patient care in their private practice. This arrangement had in fact been an attraction to physicians seeking a place where they could supplement their salaries with the revenue from private care (which in most cases dwarfed their salaries). The administration at first attempted to institute an annual confidential report by each faculty member of the amount of income he had realized from his private practice and the amount of time spent in private practice.[114] Its purpose, Dean Rose explained to one chair who reported "considerable resentment" from members of his department about

such a report, was to ensure that there was a proper balance between the teaching/research responsibilities of a faculty member and his private practice. The American Association of Medical Colleges (AAMC), which was the accrediting organization for the Medical School, insisted that limits be placed on the private care that medical school faculty could provide, precisely to make sure that they fully met their teaching and research responsibilities.[115] Since there was such consternation about individual reporting, Dean Rose offered the alternative of having departments or divisions submit group reports on the aggregate private practice and income from it.[116]

Two months later President Campbell wrote the dean that "in view of the continuing growth of the faculty of the School . . . in view of our plans for expansion, and in view of the changing character of medical practice in the United States, it is apparent that a control mechanism must exist which insures that the full-time faculty of the School . . . maintains a proper balance in its research, educational, and patient care activities, in line with the objectives of the School." The board of directors, Campbell informed him, had voted to establish "a regulatory mechanism . . . [for] income derived from private patients in the University Hospital and affiliated hospitals that will apply to all geographic full-time faculty." Campbell wanted the faculty themselves to draw up a plan mutually acceptable to the faculty and the administration. He gave them a year and a half to devise one and set a date of July 1967 for the plan to go into effect.[117]

There was much faculty opposition to such a change, especially in the Department of Surgery, where salaries were minimal but opportunities for considerable private income were the greatest. There was obviously strong suspicion that this was merely a first step that would inevitably lead to the school's claiming a substantial portion of that income for its own purposes. The opposition of the surgery department led to a special meeting with the dean, at which the department members informed him that if he insisted on the deadline he had set for receiving faculty reports, most of them, including the chair, would resign. Rose, aware that senior faculty in other departments also opposed the deadline for reporting, agreed eventually to the suggestion of the surgery department's chair to set up a committee, not to implement a faculty plan, but to consider the question of starting one.[118] The medical practice plan committee began to meet in the summer of 1965. A year and a half later, in January 1967, the committee submitted a preliminary proposal to Dean Rose, which assumed that most clinical faculty would continue to be geographic full-time and that previous arrangements regarding private care would be honored. That effectively removed a large majority of the faculty from any private practice plan.[119] The committee's recalcitrance stunned Rose, but he decided to push the matter no further. Instead he concentrated with some success on persuading certain divisions within the departments of surgery and medicine that were dominated by younger doctors to agree to a strict full-time status in which their salaries would be

Concentrated Care Center, 1976. (Georgetown University Archives)

John Rose, dean of the
Medical School, 1963–74.

(Georgetown University Archives)

their major source of income. A practice plan for all medical school faculty
was deferred for a later day.[120]

Research continued to become a more prominent part of clinical medicine
at Georgetown. In 1965 Clifton K. Himmelsbach was named associate dean
for research, to coordinate and supervise the various research projects within
the center. In 1966 Georgetown Medical Center pulled in more than $4.7
million in grants. That same year it ranked sixth among medical centers in the
number of research abstracts submitted to *Clinical Research,* a major compiler
of clinical investigations.[121] Robert Coffey and Thomas Lee continued their
pathbreaking research on hyperthyroidism in endocrine surgery.[122] Charles
Hufnagel performed the area's first successful kidney transplant in October
1965. In 1972, George E. Schreiner, director of the Division of Nephrology at
Georgetown, led one of the largest studies on kidney disease ever conducted
in a joint project, funded by the John A. Hartford Foundation, the Georgetown University Kidney Research Fund, and NIH.[123] Melvin Blecher and his
colleagues in biochemistry discovered a simple method of detecting diabetes
early in adults by analyzing through a blood test the interaction of glucagon
and insulin, the two hormones involved in diabetic problems, with white
blood cells. The results enabled them to determine which persons were dia-

betic or diabetes-prone and to treat them through medication or preventive medicine.[124] In September 1976 a team of doctors led by Michael C. Gelfand created an artificial liver for a thirteen-year-old in a deep coma from liver failure. The artificial liver, created by perfusion of the blood through a charcoal column, enabled the patient to regain consciousness and become healthy enough to receive a liver transplant.[125] Professor Robert S. Ledly and colleagues in the Department of Physiology and Biophysics invented the Automatic Computerized Transverse Axial (ACTA) scanner. The scanner captured in three dimensions tissue abnormalities throughout the body. In 1975 the department and the National Biomedical Research Foundation, of which Ledly was president, entered into a contract with Pfizer Medical System, Inc., to supply scanners to other medical centers. It marked the beginning of the commercialization of biomedical research at Georgetown through partnerships established between the medical center and biomedical businesses to realize the financial fruits of inventions and research discoveries.[126]

Medical School

The Medical School, which was the only school during the Bunn era to experience a decline in its enrollment, was, together with the Law School, the coleader in growth during the next decade (1965–75). In the 1964–65 academic year, total enrollment in the Medical School was 393. By 1975–76 it was 818. In that decade the school had become one of the largest medical schools in the country. That growth was the fruit of a plan to secure federal funding made available by legislation that rewarded medical schools for increasing their enrollment and thereby helping to eliminate the shortfall of doctors that the nation was experiencing. No school took better advantage of these incentive-filled laws than Georgetown.[127] In the admission of students into Medical School, it was very much a buyer's market in the latter sixties. In the fall of 1965, Georgetown enrolled 111 students. The school had 1,757 applicants; it accepted approximately 14 percent of them. It could afford to grow a great deal without diluting the quality of its students. And over the next decade the applicant pool continued to grow, as did the quality. By 1974 there were 42,624 applicants nationally for medical school, or nearly three applicants for every available place in medical schools.[128]

As early as 1971, there were more than 5,000 applicants for the 205 positions for the class of 1975 at Georgetown, an increase of 40 percent from the previous year. It was the largest pool of applicants that any medical school had ever received. Officials at the school attributed the massive rise in applications to the completion of the massive building campaign over the past decade. It probably also reflected the administration's ability to keep tuition at a reasonable level. The school continued to break its own records over the next four years, culminating in 1975 with more than 9,100 applications for the 205 spots in the first-year class. The quality of the accepted students continued to rise as well. Of those accepted in 1972, the average MCAT score was

600; in 1963 it had been 563. In 1972 the QPI was 3.32; in 1962 it had been 2.93. And the traditional dominance of Jesuit and Catholic colleges as feeder schools sharply declined as many more graduates of Yale, Stanford, Princeton, Dartmouth, Duke, the University of Pennsylvania, Johns Hopkins, and other elite institutions chose Georgetown for their medical education. That said, the ten schools, including Georgetown, that had traditionally accounted for a third of Georgetown's entering class continued to do so through the seventies.

In 1975–76, total enrollment was 818, of whom 134, or 17.4 percent, were women. This represented a nearly eightfold increase in the number of women in the school compared to 1965. Still, like minority enrollment, the proportion of women among medical students at Georgetown continued to lag behind the national percentage (which approached 25 percent by 1975) Catholics made up a slight majority of 53 percent in 1975, compared to more than 75 percent of the students in 1965.

In 1969 a task force of the AAMS recommended the establishment of a five-year goal of having the proportion of black students in the medical school population equal to their proportion within the general population. This would mean increasing the percentage of black medical students from 2.8 percent to 12 percent by 1975.[129] A number of medical schools had already established affirmative action programs for black students, and many more did so in the wake of the task force recommendation. Schools located in majority black areas, such as Georgetown, were particularly intent on increasing their minority enrollment as well as creating outreach programs in the community.

In 1970 there were five black students enrolled in the Georgetown Medical School. That year the school began an affirmative action program in which it admitted minority candidates who showed potential, despite academic credentials that were below the norm. That fall it admitted sixteen black students in the entering class, bringing the percentage of black students in the school to 3.9 percent. Early in the fall it quickly became apparent that virtually all of the students admitted under the new program were struggling academically. The school set up a group composed of faculty from the basic science departments and certain upperclassmen to assist and tutor these first-year students. Despite the special help, all of the students admitted under the new program failed at least two of their courses. Six, who failed five or more courses, were dismissed. The school gave the other eight the opportunity to redo the failed courses by participating in a summer academic reinforcement program funded by a grant from the Sloan Foundation. As a result of their successful completion of courses they had previously failed, two students advanced to the sophomore class. The rest were allowed to repeat freshman year. Two of the six originally dropped were allowed eventually to resume classes. Of the original sixteen admitted in the fall of 1971, twelve ultimately graduated. In 1972 the school, with a three-year grant from the Sloan Foundation, renewed the eight-week summer program of condensed courses in anatomy, histology, biochemistry, and physiology; in 1975 it was given a regular budget by the medical and dental schools.[130] By 1974, minority groups (African Americans, Hispanic Americans, and native Americans) represented 10 percent of the national medical student population; African Americans themselves made up 7.5 percent. Georgetown, despite its efforts, lagged well behind in these categories, with 5.7 percent of its student body consisting of minorities, and African Americans only 3.7 percent.[131]

The Physicians' Augmentation Program grant was in part dependent on the school's reform of its curriculum so as to make medical education more productive and cost-efficient. Georgetown had already been considering a substantial overhaul of its curriculum, which had been in place for more than two decades. The new curriculum went into effect in the 1970–71 academic year, coinciding with the opening of the basic science building and Dahlgren Library. Under it, first-year students began clinical work immediately. Fourth-year students now served 3 twelve-week electives, one of which was to be in an inpatient hospital and another in an ambulatory health service.

A significant number of graduates in the latter sixties, when the U.S. military commitment to Vietnam was peaking, made their careers as physicians in armed services, such as Joseph J. Bellanca and Albert B. Briccetti of the class of 1966 in the navy and air force, respectively, as well as Paul Kovalcik and Anthony Martyak of the class of 1969. Lt. Gen. Kevin C. Kiley (1976) rose to head the U.S. Army Medical Command. Andrew von Sechenbach (1967), Joseph D'Ercole (1969), Patrick Duff (1974), and Marie Landry (1974) were among those who made careers in academic medicine: von Sechenbach at the University of Texas, D'Ercole at the University of North Carolina, Duff at the University of Florida, and Landry at Yale. Andrew von Eschenbach (1967) was director of the National Cancer Institute before being appointed head of the Food and Drug Administration in the George W. Bush administration.

In 1973, John Rose stepped down after ten years as dean. John Philip Utz, a former member of the faculty and an internationally recognized authority in the field of fungus diseases who had been chief of the Division of Immunology and Infectious Diseases at the Medical College of Virginia, succeeded Rose. Rose had played a crucial role in bringing about the major changes in the center over the previous decade: the greatly enlarged student body that was better qualified and much more diverse; the reformation of the curriculum; the increased research, with the funding to support it; the remarkable progress of the ambitious building program at the center; the creation of the Lombardi Cancer Center; and the growing reputation of the school. As the self-study committee concluded in its report in 1971, the medical center was clearly now in "the big leagues and, though not the best, . . . much improved." John Rose had had much to do with the center's earning such an appraisal.

Dental School

At the end of 1965, Clemens Rault, who had served as dean of the Dental School for more than fifteen years, submitted his resignation. In January 1966, President Campbell announced that, upon the recommendation of a committee, Charles B. Murto (1932), a member of the faculty for more than three decades and chairman of the Department of Prosthodontics, had been appointed to succeed Rault. At the same time, in recognition of the need to expand the administration of the school, three new associate deans' positions were created: one for curriculum and graduate education, one for admissions and student affairs, and one as director of clinics and continuing education.[132]

The much anticipated dental clinic opened in the spring of 1971. The four-story facility of 128,160 square feet was a state-of-the-art clinics building that contained 294 private operatories for student use, as well as 11 x-ray rooms, 9 clinic laboratories, and 55 offices for faculty and staff. Junior and senior students treated on average 500 patients a day.[133] Dental administrators anticipated an increase of 25 percent in revenue in clinical services, owing to the increased efficiency it would provide with its larger and more central laboratories, the additional clinical areas that it would make available, and the expanded graduate program that it would make possible.[134]

In 1964 there were 369 students in the school. Sixty-three percent of the students were Catholic. Women made up 1 percent of the school. Eighty-two percent were from the Northeast (20.8% from the DC area). Seventy-three percent had college degrees, at a time when less than half of dental students nationally had degrees. Applications for the school were increasing in the middle sixties, and the percentage of college graduates increased as well. For the entering class of 1965 there was a 25 percent increase in applications. The school enrolled 87 out of 756 applicants.[135] The following year they accepted fewer than 20 percent of their applicants. By 1968, 88.6 percent had college degrees.

At the end of the sixties applications declined, which was a reaction to the loss of the deferment from the draft for dental students as well as to the growing cost of a dental education, this at a time when the school was increasing its enrollment. But any concern school administrators had about what they had committed themselves to quickly vanished the next year when the boom in applications returned, with a record 1,350 applications for the 131 places. Nor was it a temporary rise. By 1974 the school received 3,600 applications for its 147 places in first year. The sharp increase in applications was remark-

Charles B. Murto, dean of the Dental School, 1966–77. (Georgetown University Archives)

able, considering that there were 12 more dental schools in the country by 1974 (59) than there had been in 1963. In 1975–76 total enrollment was 575, of whom 5.2 percent (30) were women. Catholics made up 42.4 percent of the population, which had become much more geographically diverse. But 12.6 percent were now from the DC area, 48.8 percent from the Northeast, 18.7 percent from the South, and 18.1 percent from the far West.

In conjunction with the opening of the new dental clinics building in 1970, the school put into operation a revised curriculum for its first-year students. Instead of taking the traditional courses in anatomy, biochemistry, histology, physiology, and neuroanatomy separately, students were now taught them as interrelated subjects. From their first year on, students were given clinical experience.

The clinical curriculum of the junior and senior years became a highly contested issue by 1970. In May of that year the seniors protested against the "block system" under which they were required to perform successful operations in various fields to qualify for their degrees. "With our present system," they stated, "the student is forced to perform a mechanical technique not treatment. . . . This type of patient treatment does not bring into society the Dentist of tomorrow but merely just another 'tooth jockey.' . . . The Dentist of the future will be a preventive Dentist, not a mechanic. He must look at the total oral health of the patient." They called for more emphasis on preventive dentistry and less on the quantity of mechanical tests. In the past too many seniors had been unable to graduate because they had failed to complete their "block." They urged that May 22, three weeks before graduation, be the last day of clinical work on requirements and that all 91 members of the class receive their diplomas on June 6 rather than merely participate in the ceremony, as too many others in the past had been made to do.[136] A day after receiving this petition, the faculty and dean held a special meeting during which they rejected the proposals but voted to initiate a faculty-student liaison committee to improve communication.[137]

Two years later the students voted to boycott classes beginning on May 1 in protest of the curricular priorities and of their lack of representation on school committees. "The problems are manifold," the senior class president stated, "the major one being in the Department of Operative Dentistry." He cited the practice of telling seniors a short time before graduation that they lacked the proficiency in certain fields to graduate and requiring them to return after graduation to repeat the work. "It's ridiculous for a gifted or perfectly capable dentist to have to return to school

Dental students in clinic.
(Appollonian, 1972)

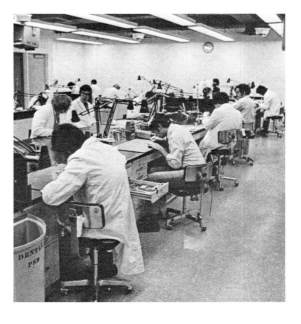

for 9 or 18 weeks just to satisfy a clinical number" of tooth restorations or extractions. "The whole archaic standard," he concluded, "is putting the emphasis on quantity, rather than quality."[138] This again brought the faculty into special sessions in which they determined that there would be no change of requirements for the graduating class. The dean reminded the students that senior requirements had been reduced by one-fifth in the past few years and that the number of clinical examinations had been cut in half. In the future, students would be represented on committees regarding clinical standing, admissions, and the curriculum. In addition, the faculty established an ad hoc committee of faculty and students to do a general evaluation of the clinical programs and to make recommendations concerning them to the executive faculty.[139] When the administration agreed to allow additional time for those seniors who had not completed their clinical requirements, the seniors called off their boycott.[140]

In its report issued in the summer of 1972, the ad hoc committee recommended that the block system be maintained but that additional clinical faculty needed to be appointed in order to ensure that all seniors would have the opportunity to complete their requirements on schedule. It also urged that the school institute evaluations of the faculty that students could fill out at the end of each course and clinical experiment.[141]

When the American Dental Association (ADA) visited the school in 1975, among its recommendations was a major reform of the curriculum. The evaluation committee singled out the "rigid 'block' structure of the third and fourth [year] clinical" curriculum for its failure to train students in treating their patients comprehensively. The examiners found that faculty teaching loads continued to be too heavy for most faculty members to have adequate time for research. There was also too much inbreeding among the faculty. There was still a shortage of clinical faculty, and their salaries remained low and noncompetitive.[142]

By the sixties the school had master of science programs in six fields: dental materials, oral pathology, oral surgery, orthodontics, periodontics, and prosthodontics, each involving a two-year residency. In 1966 there were thirty-four students in these programs, as well as forty-six special students from the army and navy dental corps. In 1968 an Institute of Preventive Dentistry was established at Georgetown to promote educational programs at dental schools and in communities throughout the nation on the ways to prevent dental disease. The institute was under the direction of Dr. Joseph Bernier, former chief of the U.S. Army Dental Corps and chair of the Department of Oral Pathology. Bernier as dental corps chief had organized the Army Preventive Dentistry Program.

Hospital and Community Outreach

In 1972, under Vice President McNulty's leadership, the university formed its own health maintenance organization (HMO), the Georgetown University

Community Health Plan, Inc. It was one of the first HMOs in the country to be part of a university. "It was an effort," McNulty commented, "to control costs, develop the group practice prepayment concept, and research the delivery of health care through HMOs," with Georgetown serving as the research subject.[143] The HMO was intended, for research purposes, to cover three distinct communities in the DC metropolitan area: one in the planned town of Reston, one in the inner city, and one in the community of Georgetown University itself. Not only was it intended to be a model program to demonstrate the provision of cost-effective, productive health care, but it was also another tangible sign of the university's outreach to the larger community in providing a vital service.[144]

The Medicare/Medicaid revolution plus the racial crisis of the cities in the latter sixties made urban medical centers much more sensitive to their responsibility to contribute more aggressively to public health. In the summer of 1971 Georgetown sent a mobile unit into the neighborhoods of DC, to block parties, supermarkets, and churches, where the medical team gave blood tests for the detection of hypertension, the most common cause of death in inner-city Washington. It was part of a national, seven-year program funded by the National Heart and Lung Institute of NIH to develop and evaluate different methods of detecting and treating hypertension.[145] Fourteen percent of the 6,480 persons examined had hypertension—36 percent of those over thirty—and they were given persistent personal medical care, which restored to normal the blood pressure of nearly 60 percent of those treated. Two years later Frank A. Finnerty, the cardiologist who directed the program, was able to expand it greatly by sending teams into homes in northeast Washington on a daily basis to check all residents between 20 and 69 for high blood pressure.[146]

A Resignation and a Search for a President

One day in the late spring of 1968 President Campbell called his assistant and his secretary into his office. Once the door was closed he said to them: "I've had it. I'm going to tell the board this afternoon that I'm resigning." His health had not been good recently. His assistant, Dan Altobello, had found him in "extreme pain" in his hotel room in New Orleans some weeks before, where they were on an alumni outreach and fund-raising tour.[147] The diverticulosis he chronically suffered from had gotten worse under the financial and social stress he had experienced during the previous year. For someone who had never wanted the position, it all proved too much to continue much longer. When he informed Paul Harbrecht, SJ, the chair of the board of directors, what he intended to tell the board, Harbrecht managed to persuade him to delay his announcement and reconsider. Two months later Harbrecht came to realize "how much [Campbell] wanted to be a teacher . . . rather than an administrator" and informed the board that Campbell was resigning but would stay on until a successor could be found.[148]

For the first time in the university's history, a committee selected by the board was to seek a new president. The board appointed five of its own, including the chair, Edward Quain, SJ; four faculty; and, under pressure, two students. The board charged the committee to look for a Jesuit, "with experience in teaching, . . . research, and administration, . . . someone [who had a] capacity for leadership . . . good judgement in choice of administrators, decisive, someone who could command the confidence and respect of faculty and students, . . . who could ensure fiscal responsibility, [who was willing and had the energy to fund-raise]." This person would have influence in every circle, from the federal to the academic to the municipal and to the larger Georgetown community.[149] As the search for this prodigy was being organized, faculty members expressed concern that it was being limited to Jesuits. The board responded that "the selection of a non-Jesuit president at this time would be destructive of the image of the university in the eyes of parents, alumni, potential benefactors, and the general public." Remove a Jesuit president and the uniqueness of Georgetown as the Jesuit institution of learning in the nation's capital would disappear with him. The *Hoya*'s editorial board agreed; it warned that "the selection of a Catholic layman as president would give the unmistakable impression that Georgetown will no longer remain Jesuit." As the living symbol of Georgetown's Catholic and Jesuit tradition, the president had to be a Jesuit.[150]

Robert Henle, SJ, president of Georgetown, 1969–76. (Georgetown University Archives)

From an initial list of forty-five candidates, nine were selected to be interviewed. Once the search committee reached this short list, the faculty senate again pressed the case for widening the search. "It is clear that the number of available candidates is small," Valerie Earle, the president of the faculty senate, reported to her colleagues. The faculty members of the committee, she announced, were ready to select any Jesuit who could hold his own in "inclusive competition." Without lay candidates, she went on, there could be no significant comparison, hence no confidence that choosing a Jesuit would represent their best option.[151] Despite the renewed plea, the search came down to three finalists, all Jesuits. Quain reported that the faculty members of the committee were now satisfied with the demonstrated quality of the Jesuit finalists, as apparently were the student members. The board interviewed the three at a special meeting on December 30, 1968, and chose Robert Henle as the forty-fifth president of Georgetown.

The new president was fifty-nine years old, of medium height, barrel-chested, and florid in complexion—the looks of one who could have been a guard on his high school football team. Looks were deceiving. Henle's background was filled with abundant scholarship but no athletics. He was the dean of the graduate school of Saint Louis University. He was the author of a series of Latin textbooks (*Henle's Latin Grammars*) that were in wide use in Jesuit and Catholic high schools. He had earned his doctorate in philosophy at the University of Toronto, where his professors had included Jacques Maritain and Étienne Gilson. He had joined the philosophy department at Saint Louis in 1943, where he published prolifically as a Thomistic scholar. His connections to Georgetown were nil. For the first time since Louis DuBourg in 1796, Georgetown had an outsider as its president.

VISITATION CONVENT

CANAL ROAD

POTOMAC RIVER

CHAPTER 2

A Time of Crisis and Challenge
Georgetown in the 1960s (1965–75) I

I certainly did not wish to preside over the University as it
slowly bled to death.

ROBERT HENLE, SJ

The Laicization of Administration

"When [Robert Henle, SJ] came here to become president," one who served
under him observed, "there was trouble in the country, church, and university. The university president had resigned, the chair of the board . . . had left
the priesthood. Everything seemed to be going wrong; . . . he took hold of
the place and began to push it. I thought that was a terribly important contribution to the history of the university. . . . He put the place on a proper
financial footing. . . . He had the courage to wade in and get that corrected."[1]

Henle, in his first year, brought about a sweeping change in top administration: the director of public relations, the treasurer, the director of building
and planning and business operations, the director of admissions—all Jesuits—were removed from their positions or left to take positions elsewhere.
Before Gerard Campbell there had been the assumption that Jesuits would
hold all or virtually all of the top administrative positions, including those in
the medical center and law center. In effect, they were appointments of the
provincial superior of the Society of Jesus. With separate incorporation that
protocol no longer held. Into all these positions—public relations, treasurer,

building and planning, business operations, admissions—Henle placed laymen. Henle instituted a mass laicization of high administrative positions.

In addition, he restructured the administration itself. In order to decentralize authority within the university, four executive vice presidents were created: a vice president for medical center affairs (Matthew McNulty), a vice president for university relations (Malcolm McCormack), and two new positions—a vice president for administrative affairs (James F. Kelly) and a vice president for educational affairs (Edmund Ryan, SJ). Also at this time the president established two other positions: a director of international affairs and a director of campus ministry.[2]

When James Kelly resigned in 1973, President Henle decided not to fill his position of administrative vice president. On his own, the president devised a new administrative pyramid. Rather than a top tier of four executive vice presidents, he created one of five administrators: the vice president for educational affairs (Ryan), the vice president for medical center affairs (McNulty), the vice president for university relations (McCormack), the treasurer of the university (Houston), and the secretary of the university (Altobello). As Henle himself admitted to the board, the plan did not have "unanimous support," referring presumably to his cabinet. Henle defended his decision not to directly replace Kelly by explaining that he did not wish to subject the university community to a drawn-out search and "the great unrest that a new Vice Presidential appointment from outside the institution would bring," although the prospect of the latter occurring seemed remote.[3] Three of the top five executives of the university were now nonacademic persons.[4] The treasurer became the chief financial officer, with the director of the budget, the comptroller, the director of sponsored programs, and the director of administrative data processing all reporting to him. The secretary of the university, whose prior duties had been mainly as assistant to the president and amanuensis of the board, now had under him, among others, the vice president for planning and physical plant and the director of personnel. The secretary and treasurer were now, aside from the president, the two most powerful people in the administration.

Daniel Altobello, secretary of Georgetown. *(Ye Domesday Booke)*

This restructuring seems to have given formal recognition to the power and influence that the secretary and treasurer had previously exercised informally with the president. Indeed, the idea to split Kelly's position between Altobello and Houston had come from Houston himself.[5] From early in his presidency, Robert Henle had met regularly with Houston; Altobello; the president of the Alumni Association, Jim Shannon, and his wife at Houston's home on O Street, just outside the gates of the university. The get-togethers were dinners prepared by Mrs. Shannon and were attended by some or all of the four children the Shannons had at Georgetown during that time. "They were great, off-the-record completely private family affairs," Shannon remembered. But the business of the university was also done. "I was one of the 'Kitchen Cabinet,'" Shannon remembered with pride. "We were intimately involved in the University in those days," he added. "Father asked our counsel . . . on almost everything. Certainly some of the great appointments I had something to do with . . . Danny [Altobello] . . . Dave McCarthy, George Houston, John Thompson, Peter Krogh. . . . An awful lot of the decisions in the University were made there in a relaxed atmosphere with a lot of give and take."[6]

George Houston, treasurer of Georgetown. (Georgetown University Archives)

Putting the Financial House in Order

By the summer of 1969, when the new president took office, the institution was bordering on a financial crisis. Georgetown was undergoing what American higher education in general was beginning to experience, after more than a dozen years of boom times—a new depression brought on by dwindling federal support, high energy costs, "stagflation" and its crippling effect upon endowments and fund-raising, technological necessities occasioned by the advent of the computer, and spiraling administrative costs from the profusion of new student services that had developed during the sixties. Fiscal year 1969 at Georgetown had ended with the university carrying a deficit of $455,458, more than twice the amount of the previous year. The operating budget had been in the red for the past five fiscal years, and the university was staring at a projected deficit of more than $1.2 million for fiscal year 1970. Long-term debt had swelled from $5.1 million in 1962 to nearly $30 million by 1972, costing the university $1 million a year just to meet the interest on the debt. The bearish market during 1969–70 aggravated the university's finances as its investments lost 20 percent of their value during the period to fall to about $26 million.[7] Before accepting the presidency, Robert Henle had asked to be allowed the opportunity to do a review of the university, particularly its finances. "I certainly did not wish to preside over the University as it slowly bled to death," he later wrote. He discovered that the cumulative debt over the past five years was nearly $3.5 million, that accounting procedures were poor, budgets not well monitored, and due revenue inconsistently invoiced and collected. But he saw opportunities to change that bleak financial picture and accepted the post.[8]

He set his immediate sights on getting the university's fiscal house in order: reorganizing the business and financial management of the institution to reflect the large and complex entity that Georgetown had become over the past quarter century. He asked for and received the resignation of the vice president for business and finance, who, Henle had concluded, lacked the managerial capability needed for the position.[9] He saw the need to integrate financial management through the creation of a vice presidential position with authority over the treasurer, the business manager, budget planning, and so on. A special committee of the board chose James Kelly, then assistant secretary and comptroller of HEW, to be the vice president for administrative affairs, with the greater jurisdiction that the title indicated.

To bring the budget under control, Henle saw several steps that had to happen: direct federal support for private higher education, a significant increase in tuition and fees, the making of university operations as economically efficient as possible, and the substantial increase in revenue from the private sector.[10] In order to balance the budget for fiscal year 1970, the board authorized the president to use the income from unrestricted gifts to the Progress Fund to offset the deficit.[11] Nonetheless, the deficit more than tripled from the year before, reaching the alarming figure of $1.4 million. In the fall of 1970, Henle reported to the board that he had lost confidence in the treasurer and his assistant. The board requested their resignations, and Henle appointed George Houston (SBA 1964) the new treasurer, with Altobello as his assistant.[12]

When Houston became treasurer, he discovered that decisions about faculty salary and tuition increases, which represented about 70 percent of the budget for fiscal year 1971, had already been made independent of any budget planning. "I told the president," Houston later remarked, "this is a crazy way to run a ship, to make major decisions before making a budget." So Houston got permission to begin a formal budget planning process in the summer of 1970 for fiscal year 1972. In a related move he got board authorization to change the university's investment portfolio. From an eighty-twenty mixture of stocks and bonds, Georgetown went to a more aggressive balance of stocks and bonds, with a goal of realizing a 12 percent return on investments in the course of a year, tripling the amount the university had been getting. Henle also moved management of the portfolio from the treasurer's office to Chase Manhattan Bank (where Hunter Guthrie had initially put it two decades earlier). Over the next two years, the new strategy succeeded, with returns exceeding the goal by nearly a percentage point.[13]

As the university budgeted for the 1971 fiscal year, Henle announced that, unlike the several previous years, there would be no increase in tuition for the following year. Nor would there be any further borrowing or use of endowment funds to eliminate deficits, both of which would simply worsen the university's financial position. "I have said repeatedly," he wrote to the faculty, "that, while the next two years will be financially very difficult for Georgetown, I will not engage in a comparable retrenchment. . . . Our academic and educational position must not only be maintained, but it must be strengthened." Salaries would not be frozen but financial equity would be preserved and merit rewarded with a significant increase in earnings. In fact, salaries on the main campus and law center increased by 10 percent, and those at the medical center by 8 percent.[14] He and the board realized that deciding not to further raise tuition might result in a dramatically larger deficit.[15] Still, he professed confidence that more intensive efforts at fund-raising could bring the budget under control. What also probably buoyed his confidence was the decision to increase enrollment sharply at both the undergraduate and professional levels.

By the end of the 1970–71 academic year, thanks to the influx of revenue from fund-raising and increased enrollments, the university enjoyed a budget surplus of $572,000. For the 1972 fiscal year, the university adopted an austerity budget: not only a virtual hiring freeze of both academic and nonacademic positions but also the consolidation of full-time academic positions to ensure that faculty carried full teaching loads and the reduction of certain nonacademic positions to part-time status. Tuition was raised to $2,400 for both undergraduates and graduate students.[16] At the same time, the board authorized the administration to recruit an additional 200 transfer students and 110 more freshmen for each of the following four years to increase revenue by more than a half million a year.[17] The result was a second year in the black for the university, with a surplus of $222,000. But the following year saw a return to the red, a deficit of nearly $550,000 that was reduced to $134,481 by applying undesignated gifts to operating costs.[18] The deficit seems largely to have stemmed from a miscalculation of revenue that had been made in preparing the budget, a miscalculation of approximately $1 million.[19] James Kelly, the vice president for administrative affairs who assumed responsibility for the miscalculation, left the university shortly afterward for a principal position at the State University of New York at Stonybrook. Henle subsequently divided Kelly's responsibilities between Houston, who now became vice president for financial affairs, and Altobello, who became vice president for administrative affairs (as well as secretary of the university). For fiscal years 1975 and 1976, the increased enrollments plus raises in tuition and increased income from the endowment enabled the university to balance its budget, an achievement that was replicated during the remaining fiscal years of the decade.

As a formal budget planning process took shape in the beginning of the seventies, other constituencies wanted to share in this strategic work. The faculty senate requested that the president empanel a budget committee of financial experts, including appropriate faculty members, to establish guidelines and parameters for the construction of budgets. At the same time, the deans of the undergraduate schools were voicing their displeasure that no academic officials or faculty were involved in the formation of the budget. There were dark suspicions, the deans told the board, that the academic side was being asked to bear the burden of a deficit due, not to academics, but to such factors as a large increase in administrative appointments and the exorbitant cost of the physical plant department. They were also upset that they had had no input into the financial decision to sharply increase undergraduate enrollment, even though they were the ones that had to deal with the effects of that decision.[20] In response the president established a budget advisory committee, which included faculty but which proved to be an unsatisfactory mechanism for academic participation in the formation of the budget because the group met at the initiative of the finance officials of the administration and was given insufficient data from which to make informed judgments.[21] In January 1975 a permanent main campus finance committee was formed, consisting of three academic deans, three other administrators, and seven faculty, with the academic vice president chairing the group.

Sherman Cohn, professor in the Law School. (*Res Ipsa Loquitor*, 21:3)

The law center community's dissatisfaction with the university's finances stemmed from something more fundamental than process. They wanted to control the use of their own revenue and determine their own budget. A single, university-wide budget was perennially exploiting the center by drawing off its surplus revenue to cover deficits in other parts of the university. In September 1972, Professor Sherman Cohn made a presentation at a faculty retreat that indicated that the law center was running a revenue surplus of about $1 million. When the executive vice president for educational affairs announced at a faculty meeting that the law center's budget for the 1973–74 year would be cut by some $200,000 from the requested amount, there was immediate resistance from the law center's faculty. In late February they set up a special faculty-student committee under Professor Jack Murphy to consider possible options to pursue in its budgetary dispute with the university. This "ad hoc committee of February 23" identified five options, including the separation of the school from the university and the unionization of the faculty. A student-faculty delegation from the center met with President Henle to push for the center to be able to retain its own income, but the president refused to change the centralization of revenue.[22] Professor Murphy commented that the dispute "is a question of why we have lost $1.6 million in surplus . . . when we have a crying need at the Law Center for more financial aid to students, more faculty members to improve our crowded classes, a change in our preposterous faculty-student ratio, and more money for library facilities."[23]

In April 1973 the student bar association passed a resolution urging the law center administration to refuse to turn over its tuition revenue to the university and use it to add faculty, purchase books, and increase student financial aid.[24] The following academic year there were further causes for distress about the use of the center's income by the university. In October 1973 Professor Murphy reported that his committee had determined that the university had previously badly underestimated the center's total surplus from the years 1971–74, that the correct amount should be around $2.3 million rather than the $1.5 million the university had acknowledged.[25] When university officials announced a tuition increase for the following year, students threatened to go on a financial strike by withholding 20 percent of their second semester's tuition and to sue the university.

Jack Murphy, professor in the Law School. (Photo by Jim Lawrence. Georgetown University Archives)

Henle, who had gotten to know Sherman Cohn from the latter's work on the budget advisory committee, at some point during the escalating dispute began to have private conversations with the law professor about the issues. "One day, Father Henle called me and asked if we might have a private dinner," Cohn recalled. That night the two met at a restaurant in Rosslyn, Virginia, just across the Potomac River from the university. Over dinner Henle said that he had to find a solution to the persistent problems between the university and the center. He wanted to know if Cohn had any suggestions. Cohn did and proceeded to lay out a model of three-campus budgeting under which each campus would control its own revenue and be responsible for producing a balanced budget. Cohn suggested that some formula should be devised for equitably sharing campuswide expenses. The main campus, which had been the one running a significant deficit, should be given a three-year period in which to eliminate it. They argued the idea back and forth for two hours.[26] Although Henle left the dinner uncommitted, shortly afterward the president made the idea his own when, at a faculty convocation, he announced a new, three-campus budgeting process, with each campus retaining its own revenue.[27] "This was an important step for GULC," Cohn later observed. Tuition increases could now be defended on the grounds that all additional revenue would stay at the law center to be used for the most critical needs. Fund-raising for the school also presented a powerful incentive to alumni: All gifts would remain with the law center and would benefit it alone.[28] This new budgeting plan also enabled the center to get a full-time fund-raising staff that would not only raise money from alumni but also get them involved with the center so that they would feel a vested interest in helping it develop.

"Imperial Georgetown" and a Master Plan

By the 1960s many local residents were referring to their academic neighbor as "imperial Georgetown." One resident, Edith Ray Saul of 3632 Prospect Street, complained to Archbishop Patrick O'Boyle, "The clock on Healy Hall strikes . . . pealing forth over our neighborhood the ominous suggestion that our days as a residential community are numbered and soon . . . Georgetown University will extend all the way to Rock Creek."[29] Despite President Bunn's public assurance that the university "had no intention of encroaching on anyone's property rights," the university had since the turn of the century committed to buying up any available dwellings in the area bounded by P, 36th, Prospect, and 37th streets, including the home owned by Mrs. Saul.[30] Indeed, in 1967 the university board of directors, looking to extend the campus, at a minimum, to 36th Street and to construct several major academic facilities in that area, authorized university administrators to acquire, if possible, thirty-one properties in the three targeted blocks.[31] Over the next six years the university successfully acquired a few of these properties but fell far short of gaining ownership of the entire area.[32] This failure in turn intensified efforts to secure two valuable portions of real estate lying to the immediate north and northeast of the campus.

One promising site for expansion was the sprawling forty-seven-acre Archbold estate immediately across from the medical center on Reservoir Road. For much of his presidency Edward Bunn had sought to acquire it. In the late sixties the university made provisional plans for the use of the property, which included residence halls for medical students, interns, and staff physicians as well as a nursing home, an outpatient facility, research laboratories, and a parking garage. The estate mansion would become a conference center.[33] When Robert Henle became president, the university renewed discussions with John Archbold about the acquisition of the estate and made presentations to him regarding the ways they intended to utilize the property. By February 1971 Henle reported to the board that the university would soon be making a final offer to Archbold and that all indications were that he would accept the bid within the next three to six months.[34] Unfortunately for Georgetown, Archbold in the meantime had remarried, and his new wife insisted on his keeping most of the estate.[35] Negotiations for purchasing a portion of the estate continued for another year, but when university officials concluded that Archbold could not be persuaded to lower his asking price, which they considered unreasonable, they redirected their focus toward the other target for expansion: the northern portion of the Visitation Convent grounds.[36]

The Sisters had, fifteen years earlier, sold a five-acre portion of their property to the university for the site of St. Mary's Hall. In 1971 the board of directors considered making an attempt to acquire the western and northern portions of the Visitation property for the future expansion of both the main campus and the medical center.[37] Serious negotiations began in 1975 about acquiring or leasing Visitation land. Henle reported at the beginning of 1976 that they seemed to be on the brink of an agreement with the Sisters; the latter's remaining concern was the use that the university had in mind for the property.[38] The university indicated its intentions of limiting any construction there to an extended care facility and a home for the Kennedy Institute. Despite these commitments, negotiations dragged on beyond the end of Henle's presidency.

The university did acquire a huge property at the end of the sixties. Unfortunately, it was more than twenty miles removed in Loudoun County, Virginia. A gift of Marcus Bles, out of gratitude for what he regarded as lifesaving surgery at Georgetown Hospital, the property consisted of some two thousand acres close to Dulles Airport. The university intended to lease the land for commercial uses and commit its revenue to the medical center. In the fall of 1969, Bles donated one-third of the property, with the rest to follow at an undefined later date. As it happened, the rental possibilities failed to develop, and by 1972 the university was ready to sell the tract and use the proceeds to support child treatment programs at the medical center.[39]

One of the things that Robert Henle noticed during his examination of the university as a candidate for the presidency in 1968 was a lack of institutional short- and long-term planning.[40] In fact, that very spring the board had approved the establishment of a University Task Force for Planning and Priorities, which the faculty senate had been lobbying for. The task force, in its report issued in the fall of 1969, recommended the establishment of a permanent planning body for the university, composed of board members, the academic vice president, and certain faculty members. It also called for the creation of an office of institutional research to generate and distribute information for planning. In the summer of 1970, Henle created the Office of Institutional Research, in large part to assist administrators in their planning. But he rejected the proposal of the permanent university-wide planning body

University Master Plan, 1971.
(Georgetown University Archives)

that the task force favored. As Henle wrote later, "The President must . . . be the chief coordinator of planning. . . . I can conceive of nothing more disastrous and more dangerous [than a] super university-wide committee . . . as the directing and coordinating body for university[-]wide planning.[41]

An architectural master plan for the university was another matter. In the summer of 1970, the vice president for planning, Chris Hansen, expressed to the board the need for the development of a master plan for the university that would cover its desired expansion over the next five years.[42] A year later, with the board's approval, Hansen and the university architect, Dean Price, presented a plan to the board that provided an additional 1.5 million square feet of space for villages containing academic facilities and housing that would enable the university to accommodate a student body of ten thousand, with 80 percent of its undergraduates, twice as many as at present, as well as 20 percent of its main campus faculty living on campus. These villages would be situated in descending podia from the medical center to the southern end of campus. Classrooms and offices would be located underground. On top would be townhouses for students and faculty. Thus George-town's new cluster of villages would symbolize the interconnection between living and learning. "They can't be separated," Price noted.

The architectural design of these villages would be in a vernacular, low-rise Georgetown style that would nicely integrate with the extant buildings on campus and those of the surrounding neighborhood.[43] Outside the walls, the plan called for a learning resources center containing classrooms, language laboratories, computation center, auditoriums, offices, and food services, to be built on the site of Annex II along the eastern side of 37th Street from O to N streets. The Board of Zoning and Adjustment subsequently approved the portion of the plan that covered university property west of 37th Street but rejected that portion dealing with property east of 37th Street. As a result the learning center was added to the intramural part of the plan, to be located in the area between Reiss Science Building and Copley Hall. The original planned site of the learning center now in the revised master plan became the locus for a complex of townhouses for students.[44]

The degreening of the campus accelerated in the sixties. Besides the new buildings, new parking areas were needed to accommodate the rapidly growing number of automobiles of the university community: students, faculty, administration, and staff. A multistoried parking deck for five hundred cars was erected in front of the hospital in the late sixties. In 1975 a second tiered parking garage was added in front of the Medical School. To control the usage of the parking sites, as well as to pay for construction of parking facilities, the university introduced fees in 1966 for parking on the lower campus and in the parking garages.[45] By 1975 the university had on-campus parking for 1,300 vehicles, but with additional growth imminent and an on-street parking ban going into effect throughout the surrounding neighborhood, its parking capacity still fell well short if its need.

"The Best Floor-walker Who Comes to the Hill"

Since 1959, Byron Collins, SJ, as vice president for business management, had been responsible for coordinating and supervising all business personnel and operations as well as planning and construction. Over the next decade Collins planned and funded, through federal grants and loans, foundation support, and private gifts, two dormitories (Harbin and Darnall), a new law center, a concentrated care center, two libraries, a children's diagnostic center (Bles Building), a basic science building, a dental clinic, and a power plant. In his five previous years as physical plant administrator, he oversaw the building of a wing for the hospital, a diagnostic center (Gorman Building), quarters for the School of Foreign Service (Edmund A. Walsh Building) and the Nursing School (St. Mary's), and dormitories for undergraduates (New South) and medical/dental students (Kober/Cogan). All told, more construction occurred in that fifteen-year period than over the university's previous 165 years. Collins's forte, as noted in chapter 9 of volume 2, was in initiating and piloting through the Congress earmarked monies for Georgetown projects. It involved meticulous planning and coordinated, persistent lobbying that made him legendary in the halls and staff rooms of Congress and the federal bureaucracy for more than thirty years. One of his congressional allies once described Father Collins as "probably the best floor-walker who comes to the Hill."[46] In the decade from 1965 to 1974, Collins secured approximately $33 million in grant money from the federal government alone.

The scope and complexities of construction and planning took its toll. By 1969, funding shortfalls, construction delays, cost overruns, and lack of coordinated planning on several major projects reached the critical point of causing university officials to question their ability to finance this ambitious building program without putting the university's credit in jeopardy. The costs of projects kept rising; completion dates kept being pushed back. The construction of the power plant that would supply heat and cooling for the new buildings was delayed by a year, partly because its original site, behind McDonough and abutting Glover-Archbold Park, aroused the neighboring community and certain preservation groups to such protest that the university had to relocate it to the east side of McDonough. For several of the major constructions, the board of directors was dismayed to discover that funding for equipment had not been included in the project budgets that they had approved, meaning that buildings, once completed, would sit idle for months, if not longer, while equipment was obtained. Part of the problem was the unpredictable nature of federal funding: that is, whether it would in fact become a reality for a particular project and when such funds, if authorized, would be appropriated and available. Another part was the custom of the university to act as its own contractor, with inadequate supervision and inspection of the work being done. Combined with this was a lack of design control and poor construction contracts.[47] In June 1969 acting president Edward Quain acknowledged to the board "his growing concern about the lack of reliable information on Planning and Plant Matters." The board authorized him to reorganize the area.[48]

The reorganization of the building and planning areas was one of the tasks Robert Henle inherited upon taking over as president. On Jim Kelly's recommendation, he brought in Chris Hansen as the new vice president of planning and physical plant, and he was charged with reorganizing the division. Dean Price was named director of planning under Hansen. Henle appointed Byron Collins to the new position of special assistant to the president for federal relations. As President Henle noted in making the appointment, he wanted to take advantage of Father Collins's "very special talent in Congressional and Federal Relation." The position, which evolved into the Office of Federal Relations, proved to be the perfect fit for Collins.[49]

Development and Fund-Raising

In 1966 Georgetown's endowment stood at $11 million. Out of the blue came the notice that the university was the beneficiary of a legacy worth nearly as much as their entire endowment—$9.6 million. The money was to be used exclusively to support student scholarships (by 1974 more than 1,100 students were being supported by this legacy). The benefactress was Florence M. Dailey of Rochester, New York, who had never had any contact or connection with Georgetown but had designated Georgetown and Notre Dame as her chief beneficiaries in a will she had made in 1933. Why she had selected the two universities as her main heirs was a question Georgetown officials could only speculate about. In the early thirties when she made her will, her bishop had been urging his subjects to send their sons either to Georgetown or to Notre Dame. More influential, perhaps, was Dailey's cousin, a lawyer who had drawn up her will. This cousin had graduated from Georgetown on a full scholarship in 1911. He had assured the president at that time, Joseph Himmel, that he would one day, when able, compensate the university for its support. It was nice to think, a Georgetown official observed in 1966, that her cousin had fulfilled his promise of 1911 by a thousandfold by recommending the university to Dailey when she was making her will.[50]

In 1964, John Vinton Dahlgren, Jr., the son of the donor of Dahlgren Chapel, bequeathed $2 million to the university for the enlargement of the chapel. In 1968 the university approached Mrs. Dahlgren about changing the construction of her husband's will to permit the application of the bequeathed funds to the general endowment of the university (the alternate use stated in his will). In exchange for this permission, the university promised to name a building in the medical center for John Vinton Dahlgren.[51] With that addition and the Daley legacy, the endowment passed the $23 million mark.

By 1972, with aggressive managing, the endowment reached $36.4 million, triple what it had been just six years before, but still, together with the annual fund, accounted for only 2.7 percent of the university's total income. The annual fund was particularly stagnant in the latter sixties. In 1964–65 it raised $389,190. Four years later the fund brought in $397,300. By 1972–73 it had increased to $525,000, far less than the university had expected the alumni would have contributed.[52] By June 1973 the endowment had shrunk to approximately $30 million. The oil crisis and its impact on the economy caused a reversal of fortune for the portfolio over the next year and a half, but by 1975 the university was again growing its endowment beyond the $34 million mark. This was still a minuscule sum compared with Yale's $600 million endowment, and more still Harvard's $1.4 billion. As Vice President Houston pointed out in 1973, Harvard's endowment contributed more than twenty-five times as much income to operations as Georgetown's.[53]

Henle also set out to complete the Progress Fund, which had been languishing.[54] James Egan was brought in to direct development and fundraising, specifically the newly launched Progress Fund, in the fall of 1963. He immediately increased the staff from one person to nine. They began to form soliciting committees in one hundred cities to raise the $26 million that had been set as a goal for the Progress Fund. Three years later they had raised barely $1 million. The Progress Fund showed that about $12 million had been raised, but most of that came from the Daley legacy (in itself about $10 million) and other gifts to the university unrelated to the development office.[55]

In November 1966 the board held a special meeting to discuss the faltering development campaign. They concluded that Egan, despite his rich experience, was not an effective director and requested his resignation.[56] Responsibility for directing the fund-raising campaign was formally assigned to a professional firm in New York City. At the time there was heavy sentiment among Georgetown officials and advisors, including the board of regents, that the university should discretely bury the campaign in order to avoid embarrassment. John Snyder, the former secretary of the treasury under President Truman and a member of the board, would have none of it. "I am not in the habit of associating with causes that fail," he told the board and assembled administrators. "If you can find me an office here, I'll make certain this one doesn't."[57] They did, and Snyder took charge of the campaign. Through Snyder's efforts, by December 1968 the campaign had raised more than $16 million, $2.5 million in the previous year, but still far short of the $26 million the campaign was to have raised by that date.[58]

That same month an alumnus, Malcolm McCormack (BSFS 1948, MSFS 1951) was named the new executive director of development and public relations.[59] When Robert Henle became president in the summer of 1969, the total stood at $17.5 million. Shortly afterward the new president decided to make a last effort to attain the goal by announcing that the drive would end the following June. Thanks to the Marcus Bles land gift, which was counted as $3 million, its appraised value, as well as several millions from the board of regents headed by Snyder, and federal grants that amounted to more than $15 million, Henle was able to proclaim in March that the $26 million goal had been surpassed. Counting the federal grants received, the special legacies, the gifts of the board of regents (approximately $5 million), and the funds generated by the development office, the university could claim to have raised $41.6 million in the period between March 1966, when the campaign had officially been announced, and its closing four years later.[60] But as the president admitted to the board of regents in an understatement a few months before the Progress Fund officially ended, "in general the private sector has not delivered the amount expected," although that had been the intended main target for funds when the drive was conceived.[61] As a result, many of the specific projects intended to be funded by the drive, particularly medical center construction and endowed chairs, fell far short of their goals. However, nearly three times as much money as had been sought was raised for endowing scholarships, some $11 million, largely because of the designation of the Daley gift.

Mandate 81

Even before university officials artfully concluded the Progress Fund, plans were afoot for a new ten-year campaign to begin in the fall of 1971. As it prepared to embark on a new campaign, the university laid the groundwork by taking steps to reorganize the university's fund-raising apparatus as well as the national alumni. Educating the alumni to the proper scale of giving essential for the development of a modern university was considered crucial in this preparation.[62] Henle announced in his first annual report that a new, long-range development program was in the planning stage, which not only would ensure Georgetown's survival in the 1970s but also "will thrust the university to a distinctively new level of achievement—a preeminent position in American higher education."[63]

Mandate 81, the development campaign for the 1970s, was to be conducted in two stages. The first stage, over five years, was to have a goal of $51.3 million that would allow the university to implement its master plan, including a multipurpose academic building, a concentrated care center, and an aquatic center ($15 million), as well as enlarge its endowment for scholarships by $10 million, establish chairs and lectureships ($11 million), create an endowment ($1 million) for the library, and raise $8 million in support of ongoing programs. The ambitious goal of the drive was to secure three thousand major donors.[64] The drive was officially announced in the fall of 1971. Compared with the Progress Fund, Mandate 81 had an excellent start. By October 1974, almost $27 million, or more than 50 percent of the goal, had been pledged, all from foundations, corporations, or individuals.[65] A year later, the drive reached the $35 million mark. By May 1976, it stood at $42 million.

Chairs and the "Tenure Crisis"

When Robert Henle became president, he was surprised to discover that the university had only one endowed chair, the Schering Foundation Chair of Pharmacology in the Medical School. For Henle there was a direct correlation between creating chairs and raising the quality of the faculty. So he made this a high priority in fund-raising. By 1975 ten chairs had been established, and six more were in the process of being funded. Of the established ones, three were in the medical center, two in the law center, and five on the main campus.

By the early seventies, administrators were becoming increasingly concerned about what they perceived to be a "tenure crisis." A large majority of the faculty either had tenure or were in the process of gaining tenure. Fears of a top-heavy, stagnant faculty locked into tenure forced administrators to look for ways to limit the reach of tenure within the faculty. The idea of establishing quotas for the four faculty ranks came up originally at a board of directors meeting in the summer of 1967. The board had no intention of intervening in the normal process of promoting and tenuring but hoped that the establishment of viable benchmarks might encourage departments to plan more efficiently to achieve balance in faculty ranks.[66]

Concern about overcrowding at senior ranks of the faculty resurfaced four years later. When the academic committee of the board met with department chairs about the issue, the faculty feared that tenure itself might be endangered. In December 1972 the board issued assurances that no such action was under consideration.[67] One dean, however, thought that the institution should be questioned, for the good of the university. Tenure, he was convinced, was "mortgaging the university to mediocrity, institutionalizing old age in the faculty, inhibiting innovation and creating departmental empires." Eliminating it, he granted, might lead the faculty to unionize, but, in that event, would the university be any worse off than it now was?[68] Indeed, the faculty senate had recently set up a committee to explore the feasibility and necessity of collective bargaining. Top administrators in general, thinking the faculty would respond favorably to departmental numerical quotas, favored such an objective norm that would establish the proportion of professors in any department that might hold tenure.[69] Further meetings with groups of faculty revealed to the academic committee of the board that there was near universal opposition to tenure quotas. Faculty members pointed out that fewer than half of the full-time faculty on the main campus and law center were tenured, much below the national average of 65 percent.[70] The way to ensure that the faculty would not become top-heavy with tenured members, some suggested, was to make the promotion and tenuring process rigorous. As for the issue of deadwood among the tenured faculty, although there was disagreement among faculty about it, a plurality seemed to believe it was a legitimate concern. There was little agreement about possible solutions. The newly imposed annual merit evaluation of faculty held promise for winnowing out some of the nonproductive members. Others favored a policy of selective early retirement incentives to free the university of unwanted faculty.[71]

In March 1973 the AAUP's commission on tenure issued its report, in which it stated that most institutions should not permit their tenured faculty to constitute more than one-half to two-thirds of their total full-time faculty. It recommended, however, that policies regarding a tenure ceiling should be flexible enough to accommodate "necessary variation" among departments.[72] The academic vice president let it be known that he favored a ceiling of 50 percent for tenured faculty but wanted advice from the executive committees of the schools before acting. At the ensuing meetings, there was continuing opposition to the imposition of any quota. In the executive council of the School of Foreign Service, it was pointed out that in the three departments that represented the core of the school's curriculum—economics, government, and history—the percentage of tenured faculty was already close to two-thirds, and many of them were relatively young. Future recruiting for tenure-track positions would be virtually nonexistent should the proposed ceiling be established. The School of Foreign Service executive council recommended that serious consideration be given to setting up a new category of faculty appointments, that is, new members would be given contracts for a number of years rather than put on the tenure track.[73]

President Henle, convinced that some form of tenure quotas was necessary, appointed an ad hoc committee on tenure, a group of faculty from all three campuses under Edmund Ryan, in the summer of 1973 to make an intensive study of the issue and come up with recommendations. The committee met throughout the summer and into the fall. It held town hall meetings with faculty to propound the economic and academic dimensions of the issue as well as to get their further views. The following April it issued its report, which hardly satisfied President Henle and his administration. The committee had concluded that, with no anticipated increase in the ranks of the faculty, and given the poor market conditions for faculty moving elsewhere, everything pointed to a very stable faculty in the foreseeable future. That prospect meant that there was little realistic hope that long-term, renewable contracts could be substituted for tenure-track positions. Moreover, even if they were feasible, contracts in themselves would not eliminate the problems connected with tenure. More important, tenure was the only way to ensure the protection of academic freedom. To say that the university was committed to preserving academic freedom while eliminating tenure was a contradiction in terms. Tenure was simply necessary, not only to protect the freedom of inquiry, but also to provide a continuity of mission and achievement that could only occur with a tenured faculty. Nor would setting a tenure ceiling address problems associated with the system of tenure.

Meeting the goal of creating a distinguished faculty had to begin with the strictest evaluation, not just by a chair or dean, but by the faculty of a department or school as a whole, of candidates for positions within the university. Such rigorous scrutiny should continue through annual formal reviews of tenure-track faculty (which the university had begun in 1971), culminating with the application for tenure, which should be judged according to how well the candidate met the three criteria governing the award of tenure: excellent teaching, significant and ongoing scholarship, and active service. Finally, the committee called for the establishment of a regular review system, activated at least once every five years, for tenured members of the faculty.[74]

A year and a half later, the president acknowledged the report and reluctantly accepted most of its recommendations, although not that of formally reviewing tenured faculty. He added, "Very frankly, I do not believe the Committee faced the major problems involved in the continuation of all current policies with regard to tenure." It had not, in his opinion, faced the grim economic realities of a largely tenured faculty or the deleterious academic consequences that would come from being "locked into totally or almost totally, tenured departments." He predicted that someday both faculty and administration would have no choice but to deal with them, at a price far greater than they would have borne, had they engaged them now.[75]

Retirement as a Mechanism for Regulating Tenure

The university's policy for the normal age of retirement for faculty was sixty-five, but in practice many continued teaching until the age of seventy, if not beyond. In the early 1970s, the administration, partly to open up faculty positions, began to apply the policy to those sixty-five or older. In June 1973, Gerard Yates, SJ, then sixty-seven, was informed that the university was not renewing his contract for 1974–75, as it had adopted the policy that faculty should continue beyond the age of sixty-five in only the most exceptional circumstances. Yates brought his case to the faculty senate who, in April 1974, passed a resolution calling for the establishment of a Committee on Continuation of Service, composed of six faculty, who would make recommendations, based on an evaluation of the needs of the department or school as well as on the qualifications of the individual, to the president regarding the retention or nonretention of faculty who wished to continue full time beyond the normal retirement date.[76] Later that month a presidential ad hoc committee on tenure issued its report in which it stated its belief that there should not be a mandatory retirement age at Georgetown, but that a faculty member, judged capable of fulfilling his obligations and desirous of doing so, should be allowed to continue on a year-to-year basis beyond the age of sixty-five.[77]

In his response to the senate about the matter, Henle contended that, in the past, many faculty had been allowed to continue beyond sixty-five because of financial need. With the new retirement plan going into effect and with the university contributing 10 percent of a faculty member's yearly salary to his or her retirement fund, this need should no longer be a factor.[78] The assumption in the future, for those faculty sixty-five or older, was retirement, not continuation of service. However, this was not a rigid rule to be mechanically applied. It was possible for the university, when appropriate, to offer year-to-year continuing appointments, but such cases should be confined to those individuals making "extraordinary and special contribution[s]" to the university. As he noted to the chancellor of the medical center, there were serious reasons for adhering to the policy. One was the pressure put on the university to meet its affirmative action obligations by appointing minorities to available positions. Another was the concern to infuse fresh blood into the faculty through appointing younger PhDs. Continuing older faculty would only make it more difficult to carry out both those goals.[79]

While Yates was challenging the university's imposition of retirement, the university was preparing a grievance code for faculty and administrators that was approved by the board of directors in March 1974. Since the code stated that it was to apply to all full-time faculty and that no faculty member should be dismissed except through the procedures the code itself set down, Yates invoked the code in filing a grievance against the university. The procedures involved the appointment of a four-member grievance committee, half appointed by the academic vice president and half by the faculty senate president. Henle, taking the position that the code did not apply to persons who had reached the age of sixty-five, appointed no persons to the grievance committee. The senate, whose Committee on Academic Freedom and Responsibility had found that the code indeed covered Yates's grievance, appointed two faculty to take up the matter. The two, Samuel Dash and Howard Penniman, issued their report in May 1976 in which they found that there was "probable cause" for the grievance, when one examined the past practice of the administration's continuing persons to seventy or beyond and the current practice of approving contract extensions for persons beyond sixty-five in other social science departments.[80] At this point the code called for a professional arbitrator to be selected by the university from a pool supplied by the Federal Mediation and Conciliation Service to adjudicate the grievance. By this time, however, Robert Henle was barely a month away from leaving the presidency, and the case went no further. Henle's successor deftly appointed Yates as his special assistant for alumni.[81]

Retirement continued to be decided on an individual, informal basis, but the late sixties and early seventies saw the retirement of a wave of faculty who had been major figures in their departments for decades: Josef Solterer in economics; Olgerd P. Sherbowitz-Wetzor, Cyril Toumanoff, Joseph Durkin, SJ, Frank Fadner, SJ, and Carroll Quigley in history; John Waldron, Bernard Wagner, and Franklin B. Williams Jr. in English; Stefan Horn in interpretation and linguistics; Francis Heyden, SJ, in astronomy; Roman DeBicki in government; and Richard Weber in biology. These retirements, along with unexpected deaths of tenured faculty members (four in the history department alone between 1976 and 1984), more rigorous vetting of tenure-track faculty at the departmental and university levels, and the expansion of faculty ranks from the late 1970s on, while not lowering the rate of tenured faculty to the level of 50 percent that Thomas Fitzgerald had sought, at least prevented the university from approaching a situation of tenure lock in its departments in general.

Changing Undergraduate Admissions Policies

In the fall of 1964 total undergraduate enrollment was 3,094. By 1975 it stood at 5,475, an increase of 77 percent in eleven years. Most of that growth occurred after 1970 when the university chose to increase revenue by raising sharply the quotas for freshman admissions and transfers. At the same time it decided to increase the diversity of the undergraduate population by three means: first, by extending recruiting beyond the Northeast, which had been the predominant source of undergraduate admissions since the turn of the century, into a national and even international market; second, by reaching beyond the Jesuit and Catholic high schools that had been principal feeders; and third, by reaching out to women and minorities, especially African Americans. Eventually, to promote diversity, admissions established a point system for the evaluation of applications in which points were given for applicants from certain ethnic communities, from certain underrepresented areas of the country, certain Jesuit or traditional feeder schools, and other desirable characteristics.[82]

In 1971 the university decided to increase the number of transfer students by at least two hundred, to a total of nearly four hundred. Initially recruiting focused on local community colleges. By 1972 the university was receiving nearly one thousand applications to transfer to Georgetown, more than double what it had received six years earlier. The plan was to recruit transfer students for the schools and majors that were underpopulated. The result was far different—more than half the transfers went into the college, especially to majors that were already crowded, such as government and English.[83]

To recruit more effectively, the size of the admissions staff rose from four in 1971 to ten in 1975. By 1973 they were visiting more than eight hundred high schools in various regions of the country.[84] In 1969 a student-staffed high school recruiting committee was formed whose members returned to their high schools or invited high school seniors to spend a weekend on campus in an effort to promote Georgetown as a desirable college. The alumni interviewing program, which had begun in certain northeastern areas in 1965, began to spread nationally, so that by 1973 it was conducting more than 3,600 interviews across the nation. Applications soared. In 1971 the university set a goal of increasing undergraduate applications from four thousand to six thousand by 1975. They surpassed their goal by nearly two thousand. Within four years the number of applications had almost doubled. In 1972 they were up 12 percent from the previous year. The next year they topped that record by increasing by 23 percent. Only two universities had higher increases in their applications in the early seventies than did Georgetown—Dartmouth and Williams—and this at a time when the number of applicants nationally was beginning to decline.[85] The rate of acceptances declined even as the number of students admitted increased. Prior to 1971 the undergraduate schools had admitted 63 percent of those who applied. Four years later, that percentage had declined to 53 percent.

Part of the enormous jump in applications was the result of well-executed recruitment by admissions staff, students, and alumni. Part was the magnet that Georgetown itself had become as the most prestigious university in the nation's capital that made it increasingly attractive to students because of its cultural and political opportunities. More than one-quarter of the entering class in 1975 wanted a career in government or civil service, another quarter leaned toward a career in law, and Georgetown's Catholic and Jesuit tradition continued to draw one-third of those new students.[86]

"The Last Enclave Has Been Infiltrated"

No school changed more in its composition during the period than did the College of Arts and Sciences. It had the second largest growth of the undergraduate schools, surpassing 2,100 in enrollment by 1975. Catholics had dominated the college population in 1964 at nearly 95 percent. A decade later that majority had shrunk to 65 percent. International students went from 1.5 percent in 1964 to nearly 4 percent in 1975. But the greatest change was the admission of women to the college in 1969.

Coeducation at Georgetown had, in one sense, existed since the founding of the Nursing School in 1903. During World War II, the Graduate School and the School of Foreign Service opened their doors to women. The two offshoots of the latter, the Institute of Languages and Linguistics and the Business School, had counted women among their students from their beginnings; indeed, early on women had constituted a majority in the institute. Still, all of this influx of women had been, as it were, on the periphery of Georgetown's academic enterprise. The nursing students were isolated, first at the hospital on the east campus, then in the northeast corner of the medical center after 1956. Until the early sixties, most of the women in the School of Foreign Service took classes in the evenings, and they all lived off-campus. The institute itself was located off-campus until moving to the east campus in 1956. The main campus remained the cosmos of the college, geographically and ideologically the heart of the university. And the college remained a male world, true to the Society of Jesus's historic commitment of fostering male education.

By the late sixties, however, women were becoming increasingly integrated into the culture of the main campus. The facts on the ground increasingly belied the policy. Women were occupying Darnall Hall, as well as St. Mary's. Female Institute of Languages and Linguistics and School of Foreign Service students regularly took classes with men. Women became part of cocurricular organizations, such as Mask and Bauble, cheerleading, and the Reserve Officers' Training Corps (ROTC). "It didn't make any sense," President

Campbell later observed, "to have the college limited to men when most of the classes were in fact co-educational." By 1965 there were already nearly one thousand undergraduate women on campus.[87]

In the mid-1960s the dean of the college, Royden Davis, along with former dean Thomas Fitzgerald, now academic vice president, first considered extending coeducation formally to the college by admitting women. The college needed additional revenue to sustain its academic programs and operations. The tuition of two hundred or so new students over the next four years would represent a significant increase in their revenue. Beyond the financial factor was a demographic one, the shrinkage of the male applicant pool nationally.[88] The executive council of the college voted in the spring of 1969 to admit fifty to one hundred women per year. Faculty in general were very supportive of the idea. Not least among the reasons for their support was the prospect of their daughters enrolling in the college. The faculty had recently gained a tuition benefit for their children. Any daughter wanting a liberal arts education would be frustrated so long as the college was all male.[89]

"The last enclave has been infiltrated," Fitzgerald reported to incoming president Henle and the board of directors in the summer of 1969.[90] Indeed, some Georgetown Jesuits did regard the prospects of women in the college as a kind of desecration of sacred ground. One older Jesuit reportedly said, "They'll admit women to the college over my dead body!" When Harbin Hall, the high-rise that overlooks the Jesuit cemetery, became one of the coed dormitories in the early seventies, his statement proved prophetic. There was also some overt opposition from college students. One freshman, claiming to represent a "Committee of 100 Concerned College Students," in a letter to the *Hoya* contended that it would be "a disastrous mistake" to admit women to the college. Their presence on the east campus showed to him their deleterious impact upon the schools of which they were a part. "Apathy reigns supreme," he concluded. "Keep women out of the college!"[91] To one alumnus decrying the decision to admit women "in the face of mounting operating deficits . . . while hundreds of male applicants" were turned away, Henle replied that women who aspired to careers of leadership needed to go to a university rather than a women's college. Since the Society of Jesus had traditionally aimed their education at the preparation of leaders, it was fitting that they now open the doors to women, given women's changing status in society. He assured the alumnus that the decision to admit women was not made out of economic grasping but rather out of a sense of obligation to serve all of society, not just its males.[92]

Wanting to do it right, the college administration planned for the integration of women into the school for a year. Admissions hired its first female admissions officer in 1968 to recruit and interview prospective female college students. Little recruiting was necessary, as the deluge of female applications quickly showed—five hundred applicants for the fifty available slots. The admission of women unexpectedly led to an increase of male applicants as well.[93] On the whole, the academic qualifications of the admitted women, as in other formerly male institutions that went coed, were significantly higher than those of their male counterparts.[94]

Among the first women in the college were Susan Porreco Cardinale (1970, JD 1973; the daughter of Rocco Porreco), who, with her husband, started a law practice; Mary Anne Farrell (**C** 1972), who became a family physician for the Indian Health Service in North Carolina; Margaret Smith Crocco (1972), who earned a PhD at the University of Pennsylvania and taught at Teachers College, Columbia University; Christine Niedermeier (1973, JD 1977), the first woman to deliver the Cohongorotan Address, who practiced law in Connecticut and served in the state's general assembly before becoming a top administrator for the U.S. Securities and Exchange Commission and then the chief of staff to Senator Max Baucus; Joan M. Romano (1973), who became a clinical psychologist at the University of Washington; Patricia A. Mahoney (1974, JD 1979), who became an attorney specializing in communications law in Washington; Mary Beth Robb (1974, JD 1981), who made a career as an executive in human resource management; Nancy J. White (1973), who became a journalist; Nancy Arbree (**C** 1974, **D** 1977), who taught prosthodontics at the Tufts University School of Dentistry; Andrea L. Fishman (1974), who became a policy analyst for the World Bank; and Eileen Sweeney (**C** 1974), who was appointed as an administrative law judge for the state of Maryland.

Assimilation of the women into Georgetown's college life went fairly smoothly. There were occasional complaints about professors' discriminatory treatment, male students' regarding them as "dating anathemas," or conflicts between academic achievement and social desirability, but as women's overall numerical presence within the college rapidly grew, problems diminished and women began to alter significantly the educational experience and student culture at Georgetown.[95]

The quota for women in the college quickly broke down. The planning had been to add women gradually so that by the end of the decade they would constitute 22 percent of the college population.[96] As early as the college's second year of admitting women, admissions found itself "making enemies" of female applicants and their families by, in effect, imposing a higher standard for women applicants than for their male counterparts. Admissions personnel quickly became an advocate for increasing female enrollment in the college.[97] By 1971 there were already 362 women in the school. The following year the admissions office made it a policy for all undergraduate schools to admit the same percentage of women they constituted in the respective applicant pool.[98] In that year, for the first time in Georgetown's history, the entering undergraduate class had more females than males. In a span of four years, 1971–75, women undergraduates at Georgetown went from a small minority (30%) to a slight majority (51%). In only one school—business—did they constitute a minority (23%).

No Longer a Novelty

Another group that increased sharply during this same period were African Americans. "In 1968, black students were a novelty at Georgetown," a black Georgetown student, Frank Glascon (**C** 1972), remembered. Indeed, there were fewer than a score of African American undergraduates when Glascon entered the college that fall.[99] Four years earlier, Jesse Mann, then chair of the philosophy department, had made the suggestion that the university begin a summer program to prepare inner-city high school students to qualify for admission to college, particularly to Georgetown. Administration officials responded positively, and, beginning the summer of 1964, a college orientation program, initially directed by Professor Roger Slakey of the English department, ran for two months during the summer to abet the preparation of approximately one hundred disadvantaged students for college.[100] By 1968 more than sixty former participants in the program had begun college, but mostly at other institutions.[101] In that same year faculty and student subscriptions established a Community Scholars Program to provide scholarships for students in need from the District of Columbia. In addition, the main campus deans decided to commit 20 percent of their scholarship resources to support applicants from the inner city.[102]

When Robert Henle took over as president the following June, he expressed his concern about the very small number of African American students in the university—some 144 out of a student population of 7,730, only about 50 of whom were in the undergraduate schools. In February 1970, in a meeting with President Henle, black students urged him to step up the recruitment and admission of African Americans, to provide a support system for black undergraduate students, to hire some black professors, and to make available a place where they could gather. Later that year the president began to promote the targeted recruitment of African American students, and in March, precisely to assist black students in their academic and social life at Georgetown, he appointed Roy Cogdell as director of community programs, which eventually became the Office of Minority Affairs. The admissions office worked closely with the Black Student Alliance in recruiting potential applicants from the African American community in the District as well as from other cities. In 1970 Georgetown had 186 applications from African Americans. Of those, 57 (30.6%) were accepted and 30 enrolled, 10 in the college.[103]

During the tumultuous spring of 1970, the Black Student Alliance issued a call for the university to commit itself to a student population that would be 15 percent minority and poor students. The top two administrators in the admissions office, Joseph Chalmers and Charles Deacon, thought the university should consider this not a threat but a challenge. In September they submitted a proposal to increase the proportion of minority undergraduate students by extending the academic criteria used to admit children of alumni and benefactors (who typically made up 15% of a class) to black applicants and by enlarging financial aid to cover all qualified black applicants with need. They urged the administration to adopt the affirmative action policy of pursuing a goal of enrolling a minimum of 10 percent minority/poverty students by admitting all black/poor applicants who projected a 1.7 grade point average (the criterion used for legacy applicants) and by raising sufficient funds to support those with need.[104] The administration adopted the proposal and created the Community Scholars Program to implement it. The deans of the college and other schools committed 20 percent of their scholarship funds to supporting community scholars.[105] Visits were made to many public schools in the DC area, and the university reached out to black students nationally through such agencies as the Fund for Negro Students. The new policy brought instant results in the form of a sharp spike in black applications and enrollment, particularly in the college. By 1973 there were 170 African Americans among the undergraduates, 142 of them community scholars.[106] Ironically, the college, which had been the last school to integrate, became the school with the largest African American enrollment. By 1975 black students in the college made up 45 percent of Georgetown's African American undergraduates. Overall African Americans constituted 3.2 percent (172) of the 5,343 undergraduates. In 1975 they represented 4 percent of the entering class.

Charles Deacon, dean of admissions. (Georgetown University Archives)

Royden Davis, SJ, and the College in the 1960s

The dean who presided over the integration of the college was Royden Davis, SJ, who had succeeded Thomas Fitzgerald in that office in 1966. Under Davis's sure, gentle style of leadership, the college took great strides over the next two decades to raise the bar of academic excellence in undergraduate education at Georgetown. In the fall of 1966, Davis established the college academic council, an advisory group composed of elected student members. The next year he led a committee of faculty and students in a thoroughgoing review of the curriculum that took more than two and a half years to com-

Black Student Alliance, 1974.
(Ye Domesday Booke)

Royden B. Davis, SJ, dean of
the College of Arts and
Sciences, 1967–89.
(Georgetown University Archives)

plete. Out of this deliberative process came the recognition that students were coming to college much better prepared than they ever had before. In freshman year, under the existing curriculum, they repeated much of what they had done in high school and did not feel challenged by the general education courses then required. They also found that the current general education was too segmented, too much a "pyramid of separate building blocks."[107]

In the end the committee followed the national trend in curricular reform of favoring retention of some distribution in the humanities and the social and natural sciences and a reduction in the number of required courses, with an emphasis on the responsibility of the student to craft an appropriate core of general education courses. The revised curriculum reduced the number of required courses to ten: two in mathematics and science, two in literature, two in the social sciences (economics, government, history, psychology, and sociology), two in theology, and two in philosophy.[108] Neither history nor language courses were required any longer. For the freshman curriculum, the approved general education courses were intended, in different ways, to provide "an introduction to the way of man's thinking, knowing, and creating by exposure to the several fields of philosophy and theology, literature, science and mathematics, social sciences and the fine arts."[109] It set a maximum on the number of courses a department could require for its majors, thus preserving a large number of electives for the student to choose. It also proposed a new advisory program, with one faculty member and an upperclass student responsible for five or so freshmen, to enable the new student to get appropriate guidance in crafting his or her academic schedule.[110] The sciences developed special courses for nonscience majors to fulfill their math and science requirements.

The committee also proposed a four-four program (four courses per semester) for students in the college. That proposal ran into immediate opposition from many faculty, particularly those in the sciences. The outcome was a compromise that recommended that the dean use his influence with departments to develop four-credit options at the upper-division level to eventually allow juniors and seniors to carry a four-course load that allowed time for research and reflection.[111] "Our thinking," Dean Davis explained, "was that if only thirty-six courses were required, this would encourage department[s] to offer four-credit courses." What happened was that students did not take advantage of this option, but rather accumulated enough courses to graduate a semester or two early (thereby reducing revenues). Nor were enough departments interested in setting up such courses. After a trial period, the course and number of credits requirements were reset at 38 and 120, respectively.[112]

The college honors program had been, for a relatively few years in the late fifties and early sixties, an important part of the curriculum but had been discontinued after the 1963–64 school year. Whether the cause of its demise was student-faculty fatigue, as some suggested, or student discontent in a situation in which the quality of the students had outrun the quality of the program, as others suggested, or a fear of promoting elitism by academically segregating a certain group within the college, as still others thought, no one could afterward say with certainty. Thereafter, the honors program was decentralized as departments such as English and history began their own. This segmentation of the program survived the 1970 curriculum revision.

The multiplication of knowledge, the rise of many new fields and subfields, and the crosscutting of fields all led, as sociologist Daniel Bell observed, to a desire for courses that emphasized the broad relationships of knowledge rather than any single discipline.[113] In the college this segmentation and specialization yet interrelatedness of knowledge led to the creation of new interdisciplinary courses and majors. In the fall of 1968, sixty college freshmen began an experimental learning-living program. Housed separately in fourth-floor Healy, the selected freshmen took a special set of courses, at the center of which was an interdisciplinary seminar on nineteenth-century Europe that encompassed English, history, philosophy, and theology. The living part of the program was discontinued after the initial year, but the liberal arts seminar perdured as a highly successful model of the possibilities of interdisciplinary education and paved the way for the introduction of other interdisciplinary programs within the college.

In 1970 the college executive faculty approved a new major, American studies, which integrated the four disciplines of English, fine arts, history, and philosophy within an American studies program, with a director and core faculty from the participating departments. American studies majors

Thomas McTighe, professor of philosophy. (Photo by Bob Young. Georgetown University Archives)

would take a core of American studies courses team-taught by members of the American studies faculty, while enjoying the diversity of constructing their own concentration that focused on a coherent combination of courses from two disciplines. Significantly, many of the students in the program were graduates of the liberal arts seminar. At the same time, an interdisciplinary major was initiated that enabled a "limited number of qualified and responsible students" to craft their own major by combining, under the supervision of three faculty, a focused concentration of courses that cut across several disciplines. The group-focused American studies program quickly proved to be a popular major, soon bursting its cap of fifteen students per year. The individual-centered interdisciplinary major drew far fewer students, often but one or two a year.

The shifting popularity of majors reflected the changes in the morphology of knowledge. In 1964–65 biology was the leading major, followed by government, economics, English, history, mathematics, chemistry, philosophy, and physics. By 1975–76 biology and government were still the two largest majors, with English now the third largest, and a new major, psychology, in fifth place. Two other new majors—sociology and American studies—now occupied ninth and twelfth place, respectively.

Large portions of the graduates of the college continued to pursue law or medicine, while growing numbers immediately or eventually went on to graduate studies. In the class of 1970, one-quarter of the graduates chose law school, nearly one-fifth opted for medical studies, and 22 percent pursued graduate studies. Twelve percent went into business, 8 percent chose the military, and 4 percent went into government service.

Among those who made careers in academia were Frederick Snyder (1966) in legal studies at Harvard Law School; Leonard Cerullo (1966) in neurosurgery at the Rush Neuroscience Institute in Chicago; John R. Clarke (1967) in art history at the University of Texas–Austin; Michael Dorris (1967) in anthropology and Native American studies at Dartmouth College, where the indigenous American coauthored several novels with his wife on Native American life; J. D. McClatchy (1967) as a poet and teacher in Princeton's creative writing program as well as editor of the *Yale Review;* William V. Tamborlane (1968, **M** 1972) as a professor of pediatrics at the Yale University School of Medicine; Kenneth M. Casebeer (1968) as a faculty member of the School of Law at the University of Miami; James Gadek (1968) as a professor of medicine at Ohio State University School of Medicine; Leo Higdon Jr. (1968) as a professor of business administration at the University of Virginia's Darden Graduate School of Business Administration; Michael Perry (1968) as a professor of law at Northwestern University and then at Wake Forest, as well as the author of several books on law, human rights, and the U.S. Constitution.

Stewart Jay (1972) taught and eventually held a chair at the University of Washington Law School; Margaret Power (1975) became a professor of the humanities at the Illinois Institute of Technology; and Alice Babcock Monet (1976) became an astronomer at the Naval Observatory. Robert L. Barchi (1968) was provost at the University of Pennsylvania before becoming president of Thomas Jefferson University. His classmate Leo Higdon Jr. became president of Connecticut College. Garrett P. Kiely (1983) became director of the University of Chicago Press.

William J. Cassidy Jr. (1968, **L** 1974) became a partner in the law firm Hogan & Hartson in Washington; Dan Hurson (1969) became a civil and criminal trial lawyer in the District. Robert Hayes (1974) founded the New York Coalition for the Homeless as a legal advocate. Mary Janes Bowes (1976), after practicing law for an environmental management firm, was elected to the Pennsylvania Superior Court in 2001.

Kenneth J. Atchity (1965) taught comparative literature and creative writing at Occidental College before becoming a film producer, producing films including *Amadeus, Shades of Love,* and *Ballerina and the Blues.* Kevin O'Brien (1965) became a general manager in the television industry; Douglas R. Casey (1967) became a writer of business guides; Bill Danoff (1968), who worked at the music club the Cellar Door while he was a student, became a songwriter ("Country Roads," "Afternoon Delight") and performer; Brian Greenspun (1968) became a newspaper editor for the *Las Vegas Sun;* E. Paul Wilson (1968) became a novelist; Jack Hofsiss (1971) became a stage and film director; and Helaine Posner (1975) became the curator for the National Museum of Women in the Arts. Robert Baer (1976) became a writer; the film *Syriana* was based on two of his novels. Michael Dellaira (1971) became an opera and choral composer.

In the sphere of government, Robert Shrum (1965) became a Democratic political aide and consultant. Roger Altman (1969) became deputy treasury secretary. Frank Keating (1966), a president of the Yard, became governor of Oklahoma. Timothy A. Chorba (1968) became United States ambassador to Singapore during the Clinton administration. Thomas L. Siebert (1968, **L** 1972) served in the Clinton administration as ambassador to Sweden. Thomas Ambro (1972) and D. Michael Fisher (1966) were appointed by President George W. Bush to the U.S. Court of Appeals for the Third Circuit. John A. Barrasso (1974), an orthopedic surgeon in Wyoming, was elected to the U.S. Senate in 2008 after being appointed to fill out a term the previous year. Andrew Natsios (1971) headed the U.S. Agency for International Development during the George W. Bush administration. George Tenet (1976) became director of the Central Intelligence Agency under presidents Clinton and George W. Bush.

Among those to make the military their career, Christopher McNamara (1973) became a commander in the U.S. navy. George William Casey Jr. (1970) became chief of staff of the U.S. army in 2007.

In business, Robert J. Barrett III (1966) became an investment executive; Thomas Owens (1970) became a partner in the accounting firm Coopers &

Lybrand; Thomas Holzman (1972) became a top executive for NCR Corporation; Terrence McGovern (1973) became an investment banker; Philip Marineau (1968) became the CEO of several companies, including Levi Strauss & Co. and Pepsi North America. Morgan E. O'Brien (1966) was a cofounder and chairman of Nextel Communications, Inc. Stuart Bloomberg (1972) became chairman of ABC Entertainment. Frank McCourt (1975) became owner and chairman of the Los Angeles Dodgers.

Nursing: Struggling to Progress

As the college was deliberately taking steps to place itself within the top tier of colleges of arts and sciences in the nation, the School of Nursing was weighing similar ambitions. In November 1966, Ann Douglas, who had succeeded Sister Kathleen Mary as dean in 1963, wrote a "Statement of Definitions and Beliefs" in which she laid out the prospects and liabilities of the school. Georgetown nursing, she thought, "could be one of the outstanding schools in the country" given the facilities of the university, especially those of its medical center. The school faculty, she went on, contained a nucleus that was capable of revising the curriculum in a manner that would elevate it to the current state of the art for the academic education of nurses.

Unfortunately, Douglas found a lack of academic vision among the current faculty. "An academically oriented faculty with an appreciation of the meaning of higher education" she judged was "necessary for the growth of the school." Hospital service had to be better integrated into the academic program. There was a pressing need for nursing academics who could develop professionally in the realms of teaching and scholarship. There was a need for critical self-evaluation if they were to raise the quality of the education they were offering.[114] One can sense Douglas's frustration.

At the very time she was preparing the report, Douglas discovered that she would no longer report to the academic vice president but to the vice president for medical center affairs. Her meetings with Fathers Fitzgerald and Bauer failed to change the new structure. To Douglas, who saw the school as an integral part of the main campus, not an appendage to the medical center, this seemed to be the final straw that would ensure that her goals were not going to be realized anytime soon.[115] In February 1967, Douglas submitted her resignation.

For the next sixteen months, a faculty member, Rosemary McGarrity, served as acting dean. In the summer of 1968, a search that had taken over a year concluded with the selection of Sister Rita Marie Bergeron, OSB, the chair of nursing at the College of Saint Scholastica, Duluth, Minnesota, as the new dean of the school. During her second year in office, nursing became the last undergraduate school to establish an executive council. By 1970 the faculty numbered twenty-seven, with Bergeron being the only

senior faculty member to hold a senior rank—professor. All the rest were assistant professors (fifteen) or instructors (eleven). No member held a PhD, although four of the faculty were working toward their doctorates. By 1973 three held PhDs, but of these, two went elsewhere to become deans the following year. The faculty generally felt that it was unrealistic to regard the PhD as the prerequisite for tenure or research scholarship as the gateway to promotion. (Only 7% of the nursing faculty nationally held PhDs.) They saw their strengths as teaching and curriculum development, not research. It was unfair, they felt, to apply university norms regarding degrees and scholarship to nursing faculty. Dean Bergeron, however, took strong exception to this attitude and urged her faculty to adjust itself to the university's expectations about faculty, including those in nursing.[116]

Left: Rita Marie Bergeron, OSB, dean of the Nursing School, 1968–78. (Office of Public Relations)

Right: Rosemary McGarrity, faculty member of the Nursing School. (Photo by J. Russell Lawrence)

Few did. Loretta Nowakowski joined the faculty in 1967 after earning a master's degree in nursing at the Catholic University of America. She later earned a PhD in human development at the University of Maryland. Many years later she recalled the stress the faculty was under: "The pressure was on. They were all tenure track at the time. You had to publish and get a degree if you didn't have it . . . try to learn a new curriculum, teach your students, do your practicum, and have a life."[117] The result was a high turnover in faculty.

The school, like the college and the Business School, experienced considerable growth in enrollment during this period. Unlike the college and the Business School, however, the price of growth was a decline in the quality of nursing students. The school grew from fewer than 300 in 1964 to nearly 550 in 1975. But average SAT scores went down from 1130 in 1968 to 1101 by 1973. The percentage of those accepted rose from 59 percent to 72 percent. As in the college and Business School, the traditional dominance of Catholics weakened from 92 percent to 66 percent. To increase the number of applicants, faculty in 1970 began actively to recruit students in the Washington metropolitan area, with visits to high schools in the region. By 1975, DC-area students represented about one-quarter of the enrollment. The size of the entering class peaked at 152 in 1974. Thereafter enrollment began a slow decline.

In 1969, the same year that the college admitted females, the School of Nursing, anticipating a drop in female applicants as a result, voted to admit male as well as female applicants. Three years earlier the executive faculty had recommended that the school be allowed to admit males, but the administration did not honor the request. This time the university administration, although skeptical that the school would be able to attract a significant number of males, decided to approve the change on a trial basis. In fact, university officials were pessimistic about the ability of the school to enroll ninety students, male or female, a number they felt to be the absolute minimum to keep up with the rising costs of nursing education.[118] A high attrition rate that persisted at 30 percent or higher, owing to dropouts and transfers to other schools within the university, compounded the problem. In 1970, with only seventy-five students enrolled in the freshman year, there was some consideration of closing the school, but the new president, Robert Henle, opposed that and the school survived. As it happened, the first male student enrolled in 1973; there were very few thereafter.

By the middle sixties there was growing dissatisfaction in the profession with the disease-centered curriculum then in use. Ann Douglas, sharing this feeling, wanted a curriculum that would be more patient centered and less medical oriented. At her urging the school instigated a survey of innovative programs in other schools.[119] Out of that investigation the faculty formed a proposal to develop over a five-year period a new curriculum based on the concept of total care as an exemplar for other nursing programs. With a grant from the NIH, three faculty—Melba Anger, Loretta Nowakowski, and Marilyn Parker—were charged with shaping a curriculum in 1968. Dorothea Orem, who had developed the self-care theory of nursing, was brought in as their consultant. The curriculum that resulted prepared nurses for dealing with the total life culture of a patient—eating habits, hygiene, emotional state, and other areas relevant to health maintenance—that would assist the person in managing her or his own health. The entering class of 1971 was the first to utilize it.

Over the next several years the faculty continued to shape courses around the new philosophy of nursing education. The school became one of the first to design and implement a revolutionary curriculum geared toward the independent nurse practitioner.[120] As Dean Bergeron explained, "We want to prepare the nurse for her new roles so she can practice the discipline of nursing as an independent member of the health care team." The new curriculum was also intended to lay the groundwork for further specialties such as pediatric or family nurse practitioner and nurse midwife.[121]

Unfortunately, it proved difficult to provide clinical experience that accorded with the self-care concept. Physicians and nursing staffs were not really prepared to accommodate nursing students desiring to apply self-care theories. Finally, in 1975, the school established an experiment in collaborative primary health care by nursing students and medical students at the Georgetown health maintenance organization in Kensington, Maryland. It proved to be highly attractive to potential students. Within the first three years of the program the enrollment of the school nearly doubled, although the size of the faculty remained unchanged. Other schools began initiating new curricula using Georgetown's as a model.[122] Georgetown faculty presented papers at conferences and published papers on what became known as the Orem curriculum.

In 1973 the school became the first in the Washington area to offer a program in midwifery. With funding from the federal government, a postbaccalaureate certificate program in nurse midwifery was established. Students in the program received clinical training at DC General Hospital, where they attended patients with their instructors.[123] Additional grants from HEW and the March of Dimes enabled the program to continue to grow throughout the seventies.

That the school was the only undergraduate unit within the medical center troubled the faculty. Beginning in 1966 there was discussion in the executive council about aligning themselves with the main campus rather than with the medical center. In 1968 the faculty passed a resolution that they wished to be part of the main campus and report to the academic vice president. Acting dean McGarrity, after much lobbying, finally persuaded Academic Vice President Fitzgerald that the school should be part of his jurisdiction. But President Campbell, who had already submitted his resignation, indicated that he wished his successor to decide the matter. The new dean, Rita Marie Bergeron, who arrived shortly afterward, was of a different opinion. Influenced by current developments in professional nursing education, she eventually persuaded the executive council to reverse its resolution of 1968. The dean continued to report to the vice president for medical center affairs, with whom she quickly established good relations.[124]

Among graduates who did graduate study and eventually held academic positions were Colleen Conway (1965), who earned a doctorate at New York University and became dean of the School of Nursing at Vanderbilt University; Ellen Clarke (1966), who earned her doctorate in education from Harvard University and became a nurse researcher at Brown University; Joyce J. Fitzpatrick (1966), who became dean of the School of Nursing at Case Western Reserve University; Mary Bailey Pfeister (1967), who after a tour of duty in Vietnam as an army nurse became a professor at the School of Nursing of the University of Michigan; Pamela Kutsaftis Ferber (1976), who became a specialist in the pediatric division of the University of California at San Francisco; and Michelle Farquharson Beauchesne (1976), who earned a doctorate of science in nursing at Boston University and became a professor in the graduate school of nursing at Northeastern University. Richard Haas (1976), the first male admitted to the school, served in the U.S. Army Nurse Corps after graduation. He later earned a doctorate as an anesthetist and taught at the Medical College of Georgia.

Business: Mired at the Crossroads

James W. Culliton, head of the United States Tariff Commission, who had been an outside consultant in the search for a new dean of the School of Business Administration, wrote to President Campbell in January 1965 that he thought the school stood at a "crossroads that calls for bold decisions in this opportune moment." Culliton thought it was better to reduce it to the level of an institute rather than a school, but whatever course they took, there was important work to be done in charting the school's future.[125] The man chosen to be dean by Georgetown administrators was an insider, Harry P. Guenther, an associate professor at the school. He took office prepared to take bold measures to shape the school: replacing part-timers with full-time faculty and recasting the curriculum that had, in his mind, made the school "essentially a bookkeeping program," with its emphasis on accounting. A business curriculum, he explained, should prepare students for general management responsibilities, which meant that pedagogy should involve more analysis than description to adopt to changes that had occurred in the business world. He also intended to establish a graduate program in international business and business-government relations. He proposed to begin student and faculty exchange programs with foreign universities, particularly in the Middle East.[126] Guenther succeeded in replacing some part-timers with full-time faculty, much to the chagrin of some certified public accountants (CPAs) who had long taught part-time at the school. He accomplished far less in his other goals. Apparently frustrated by the opposition, among both the administration and the faculty, Guenther resigned in 1969.

A formal search committee found his successor in acting dean Gene Snyder, who taught business law. Once in office he encountered much the same opposition that Guenther had faced, and his aggressive management style probably exacerbated it. Appointed dean in the spring of 1970, Snyder set goals of increasing enrollment to a maximum of 1,200 and improving the faculty. President Henle, upon appointing him, had charged him with conducting a careful self-study and working up a plan to develop the school. Snyder failed to produce one.[127] He left the office and the school after two years. A new search brought in Edward Kaitz in April 1972. Kaitz did establish the first graduate program at the school, a master's degree in accounting, in 1975. But to many faculty and university administrators he was doing too little in providing leadership and effective management for a school that badly needed both. "The school began to fall apart," one faculty member commented. "Things were not getting done." A self-study committee charged with, among other things, evaluating the effective leadership of the school, returned a scathing evaluation of the dean, who resigned shortly afterward.[128] Joseph Pettit became acting dean of the school and, as several faculty remembered, finally "put it on its feet" by restructuring the curriculum to conform to the school's self-understanding as an academic, business-oriented enterprise with deep roots in the liberal arts tradition and by getting the faculty involved in decision making.[129]

Despite the Sturm und Drang of the school's administration, it experienced great growth in popularity during the period. Enrollment rose from 553 to 957, an increase of 84 percent. Like the college, its domination by Catholic students lessened, from 89 percent in 1964 to 70 percent in 1975. Women became a significant presence in the school, constituting nearly one-quarter of the enrollment by 1975. Conversely, international students were far fewer in 1975 than they had been in 1964, only 6 percent as compared with nearly 13 percent a decade earlier.

Accounting and management remained the most popular concentrations for students. Finance declined sharply in the number of majors from 1964 to 1974. Public administration more than doubled its majors in the same period. Economics was introduced as a major in 1972. Among graduates in 1970, one-third went into business employment, 13 percent went on to graduate school, 19 percent went to law school, and 6 percent went into government service.

Notable among graduates of the school were Jeffrey Gildenhorn (1965), who went on to found the American City Diners restaurant chain in the metropolitan Washington area; Stephen Rosenbloom (1967) became the chief executive of the Los Angeles Rams; Robert F. Hussey (1971) became the chief operating officer of several different companies; Ken Hakuta (1972) became a highly successful entrepreneur whose Tradex Corporation promoted various products, including the wall walkers that became a national craze in the 1980s; Robert Giaimo (1973), after managing a Blimpie's sub shop while he was a student, started the American Café in Washington two years after graduating, and he later developed a chain of Silver Diners in the metropolitan area; and Robert M. Bowlin (1975) became president of Sony Music International. Arlen Kantarian (1975) became chief executive of the United States Tennis Association.

Alfredo Cristiano (1968) in 1989 became president of El Salvador. Prince Turki al-Faisal (1968) became the chief of intelligence for Saudi Arabia before serving as ambassador to the United Kingdom and the United States. J. Richard Fredericks (1968) became U.S. ambassador to Switzerland in the Clinton administration.

Foreign Service: A School in Turmoil

Of the undergraduate schools, the School of Foreign Service experienced the smallest growth from 1964 to 1975. Indeed, enrollment in the school actually shrank from 1964 to 1971, despite a generous acceptance rate for applicants that reached nearly 74 percent by 1971. In that year the faculty decided to admit more women in order to increase enrollment. Women, who had constituted only 15.3 percent of the students in 1964, accounted for nearly 46 percent of the school's students by 1975.

The meager growth of the school was largely due to the internal turmoil that shook the school from 1967 to 1971; a struggle for the identity, mission, and curriculum of the school became acute. In November 1967, Professor Carroll Quigley issued in the *Hoya* a manifesto of how the school had lost the core faculty and curriculum that had defined it as the unique institution that Edmund Walsh had created. The campuswide integration of faculty according to disciplines in the fifties had eliminated the school faculty as a separate academic unit. With the structural separation of the faculty from the school, the distinctive curriculum that integrated economics, history, and political science at its core was essentially lost; no longer did students gain the comprehensive "understanding of international affairs as an area of decision-making and action."[130] Seven months earlier another faculty member long associated with the School of Foreign Service, Walter Giles, who had been Edmund Walsh's last secretary and saw himself as the guardian of Walsh's vision for the school, lamented in the *Hoya* how the school had declined over the past twenty years as the direct result of the centralization policies of presidents Guthrie and Bunn. Under Edmund Walsh, he wrote, the school had been "an independent and autonomous" part of the university. Now it was too often "the stepchild of the integrated departments."[131] Both articles subsequently appeared in the *Congressional Record*, submitted by senators concerned about the school that was the major provider of candidates for the foreign service.

In May 1968 the school's student academic council issued a thirty-two-page report on the state of the school that echoed Quigley's and Giles's critiques. The School of Foreign Service, they concluded, was in a state of drift and decline, and immediate steps needed to be taken to prevent its demise. Those steps were the restoration of a professionally oriented curriculum, in which there would be core courses that would restore the three disciplines of economics, government, and history to the center of the academic program, as well as the creation of a separate school faculty.[132] That same month,

Jesse Mann, professor of philosophy, and dean of the School of Foreign Service, 1968–70. (Georgetown University Archives)

Joseph Sebes, SJ, who opposed the creation of a core faculty, resigned as dean, a victim of the internal dissent.

The Middle States report of 1961 had questioned whether foreign service at Georgetown constituted a true school. Beginning in the fall of 1968, Jesse Mann, who had been appointed acting dean until a new dean could be found, began to seek ways to create a new faculty structure and curriculum changes that would "result in a definable and autonomous undergraduate school."[133] "I had . . . a very good year as dean," Mann recalled. "Suddenly, in my second year as dean, the whole house fell down."[134] At the beginning of the summer of 1968, an anonymous group called the Save Our School Emergency Committee sent a mailing to all alumni of the school that alerted them that the School of Foreign Service "is not the same school today" that they had known. Nothing distinctive of the school remained: not the curriculum, the faculty, the yearbook, the newspaper, the student council—all had been lost in the integration process that had swept the university over the past two decades. "Our hope," they wrote, "is to start a movement to revitalize our School . . . to its past pre-eminence."[135] Dean Mann thought he detected the work of Giles and Quigley behind the group.[136]

The school held a three-day conference in January 1969, in conjunction with its fiftieth anniversary, to examine and evaluate the curriculum and structure of the school. Various speakers discussed the history, reputation, purpose, student body, faculty, curriculum, and alumni of the school as well as the school's relation to the world. Earlier in that academic year Dean Mann had appointed an ad hoc curriculum committee to plan for a new curriculum. The committee, composed of faculty and students, did not include either Giles or Quigley. It quickly became bogged down over the question of

Open letter from
"Friends of the SFS,"
1969.

2·42-7   ·' 6U1   25 February 1969

An open letter to the
Students of the School of Foreign Service

    The SFS Executive Committee will continue it's discussion of
Dean Mann's Core Faculty proposals at 2:30 P.M. Thursday, 27 February 1969
in the Hall of Nations. A primary reason for the opposition which those
Core Faculty proposals will encounter is the question of control of the
purse strings. A Core Faculty implies SFS control of SFS finances.
SEIZURE OF THE SFS TREASURY WAS ONE OF THE FIRST STEPS IN THE UNIVERSITY'S
SYSTEMATIC EMASCULATION OF THE SCHOOL OF FOREIGN SERVICE.
    The Conference on the SFS, held here in October, produced the
following facts:
    Until 1950, the SFS had its own independent treasury, supported
by tuitions ($300/semester) and the genius of Fr. Walsh. Fr. Walsh had
accumulated a surplus in excess of expenses, with which he planned to build
an SFS building (the School at the time was housed in the Healy building).
A conservative estimate placed the size of that surplus at $2 million
(some said $4 million). Fr. Walsh also helped other divisions of the
University out of his School's funds.
    The University was a congeries of semi-autonomous Schools, with
the SFS probably the most successful. "Integration" was initiated to
correct that situation.
    On 22 February 1950 (Washington's Birthday, a school holiday),
Fr. Wilkinson, University Treasurer, sent people with wheelbarrows to the
SFS Office. Edgar L. Mitchell, School Treasurer, happened to be in the
Office on that day, but he only could watch Fr. Wilkinson's squad
unceremoniously clean out the SFS Treasury vaults. According to Harry
E.A. Zimmerman ("Records and Curriculum"), thousands of dollars in invoices
were lost in that act of legal piracy.
    Fr. Walsh, Founder and Regent of the School of Foreign Service,
Vice President of the University, was told nothing of the impending rape
of his School. J. Raymond Trainor, SFS Secretary from whom this account
comes, remembered that the SFS people were aware something was coming,
but had no idea what it was. Authorization for this seizure had to be
secured in Jesuit headquarters in Rome, because of the great power wielded
by Fr. Walsh in the U.S. and in the Vatican. An order from the head of the
Society of Jesus was needed to legalize the so-called "midnight raid."
    Fantastic as this story seems, it has been substantiated by
several persons associated with the SFS at the time. Although it may be a
most brazen example, it is but one of the outrages committed in the name
of integration. These and other related acts may not indicate a "conspiracy
to destroy the SFS," but they have helped immensely in the educational
sterilization of the Edmund A. Walsh School of Foreign Service. We are
witnessing merely the latter stages of that process.

Don Panzera
Friends of the
School of Foreign Service

whether the constitution of a core faculty should precede any curricular reform. One of the faculty members of the committee, Monika Hellwig, in a letter to the *Hoya,* voiced her suspicion that Giles and Quigley were exerting pressure on the student members to prevent the committee from doing anything before a core faculty was created, which, presumably, would subsequently control the committee.[137]

Meanwhile the "Friends of the SFS" had been issuing open letters to the community in which they argued that the unification of the schools was something that Edmund Walsh had fought, that the school's "independent treasury" of some $2 million to $4 million had been illegally seized by the university treasurer in a midnight raid in February 1950 as "ONE OF THE FIRST STEPS IN THE UNIVERSITY'S SYSTEMATIC EMASCULATION OF THE SCHOOL OF FOREIGN SERVICE," and that all the professors identified with the school "have been deliberately excluded from all influence."[138] In the *Hoya,* Gerard Yates, who had been dean of the graduate school at the time of the unification of finances, pointed out that, as a Jesuit with a vow of poverty, Edmund Walsh had no "legal authority over the 'independent treasury,'" that, in fact, Walsh had turned over to the university treasurer by check the funds he had held. There had been no "midnight raid" by the treasurer's "goons."[139]

During all of this, a search was going on for a permanent dean for the school. The committee, appointed by the president, was to be chaired by Richard Scammon, the director of the Elections Research Center. On the committee were five faculty members, including four with ties to the school (but not Giles or Quigley), two students, and an alumnus. School of Foreign Service students immediately protested the way in which the committee had been chosen and demanded that the executive committee of the school be allowed to nominate two-thirds of the committee. On February 20, as the executive committee was meeting in the president's office, some 250 students lined the steps leading to his office in protest of the search committee. At that meeting, the executive committee passed a resolution that, "pending a clarification of the structure of the School of Foreign Service," the search should be suspended.[140] Acting president Quain agreed to take the resolution to the board of directors. At a meeting of the board in March 1969, the interim dean of the school, Jesse Mann, presented another resolution from the executive faculty of the school that called for the creation of a core faculty and a separate budget, which he urged the board members to adopt in order to "assure the identity of the School." The resolution envisioned a process in which those professors wishing to be part of the school faculty might hold a secondary appointment with a particular department. Their salaries would depend primarily on the dean of the school. Tenure and promotion would come from the school. Finally the resolution affirmed the dean of the school as the "administrative head" directly responsible to the president. Despite Fitzgerald's opposition to the creation of a separate faculty, the board passed the resolution intact and agreed that the school should have its own budget but not its own fund.[141]

That resolution did not, as it turned out, resolve the matter. Although the committee appointed by the interim dean had devised a mechanism for the establishment of a core faculty and had begun the process of selecting, complaints began to accumulate by the start of the school year 1969–70 that the dean and the administration were simply sitting on the resolutions passed by the board of directors in March. The new president, Robert Henle, received a letter from more than 160 students demanding to know why nothing had been done about establishing a core faculty and why a new dean had not been appointed. A conference was organized in the Hall of Nations on October 10, 1969, at which Henle responded to the growing demands for action. He walked those assembled through the steps that had been taken thus far to create a core faculty and to find a new dean. The process of selecting a school faculty had proven to be a slow and complicated one; by that point he had finally been able to take the step of establishing a selection committee. He was being faithful to the precise recommendations that had come out of the executive faculty of the school itself. He could not undercut these by simply naming a school faculty to satisfy student demands. "What I can tell you," he promised, "[is that] there will be a core faculty." However, he assured them that, contrary to widely circulated rumor, he had not already chosen a dean. In closing he said, "There is no secret agenda with regard to this School, that it is the intent of everybody in the administration . . . to give this School a high priority in university development." He called upon everyone to put aside past suspicions and misunderstandings to work together to "bring an even greater future to this distinguished School of Foreign Service of Georgetown University."[142]

Organizing a search committee for a dean had proven to be as difficult as the selection of a core faculty. There was so much faculty disagreement about who should chair the committee that Henle had been forced to ask Edward Quain, the former acting president, to head it. As for the curriculum, he agreed that there was a need for serious revisions. Here too a school committee, including five students, had been working on a reform of the curriculum for nearly a year but had so far produced nothing. No matter what that committee recommended, Henle intended to initiate a comprehensive study, utilizing experts outside the university as well as persons within, to devise "an educational program for the school which will be unique and will put this school back . . . in the forefront of all schools" of international studies.[143]

In February, at an open meeting in the Hall of Nations attended by some 350 students (more than one-third of the school's enrollment), the executive committee of the school took up the question of student representation. An ad hoc committee claimed that more than two thousand faculty and students had signed a petition stating their conviction that, because "education is a cooperative venture of students and teachers," it was only proper that students should comprise half of the membership on all executive committees.[144] In the midst of the mass of students crowding the hall, the committee voted 8–7 to appoint a special committee to plan for the reconstitution of the executive committee.[145] To the crowd, confident that the special committee would follow the will of the community, it was a triumph for student parity in governance.[146]

A week after the executive committee meeting, Henle announced the new dean, Peter Krogh, and urged "everyone to put aside past differences and to work with our new Dean in order to restore unity of purpose, cooperation, and the academic excellence of this great school."[147] The thirty-three-year-old Harvard graduate had been the associate dean of the Fletcher School of Law and Diplomacy at Tufts, where he had earned a doctorate in international studies. He brought experience, tact, charm, immense energy, and a formidable presence to a position that had broken or severely drained his several predecessors. It quickly became apparent that the new dean was firmly in charge. Krogh took deliberate, small, but telling steps toward building community and ending factionalism, such as inviting faculty to his home for dinner, including the chairs of economics, government, and history, and holding weekly dean's seminar sessions with groups of thirty or so students gathered to hear foreign service personnel and foreign policy academics. He issued frequent reports on the school, initially quarterly, to communicate more efficiently with the School of Foreign Service community. He moved his office and staff from Nevils to the Walsh Building, adjacent to the lobby, to give the School of Foreign Service administration more visibility and a presence in the school's home. He created a distinguished board of visitors—Dean Rusk (for whom Krogh had interned), Paul Warneke, Senator Charles Mathias of Maryland, and future senator John Kerry, among others—to lend another stamp of legitimacy and prestige to his administration.

Peter Krogh, dean of the School of Foreign Service, 1970–95. (Georgetown University Archives)

With Krogh in place, the comprehensive evaluation of the school that Henle had promised did not take place. Instead, the president charged the new dean with completing a thorough revision of the curriculum, unifying the faculty, and "restor[ing] the morale and discipline within the school, both among the students and among the faculty."[148] Within two weeks of the announcement of Krogh's appointment, the president revealed the composition of a core faculty of eighteen professors, including eleven from the three root departments of economics, government, and history, four from the French and German divisions, and two from the English department. Half of the new faculty had long-standing ties to the school, including Jules Davids, Frank Fadner, SJ, Carroll Quigley, Walter Giles, Jan Karski, Gunther Ruff, Harold Heck, John Yoklavich, and Joseph Zrinyi, SJ. Several members were brought in by Krogh from the outside—Theodore Geiger, Leslie Gelb, and Jerome Kahan—as professorial lecturers in international relations.

In June, Krogh appointed a six-person committee to draw up a new constitution for the school. The new constitution that resulted established the dean as the primary authority in the school and an executive council that had

two administrators, ten faculty, and six students on it. All meetings would
henceforth be in executive session, unless two-thirds of the committee voted
otherwise. The curriculum committee finally produced a new curriculum in
the spring of 1972. All students now had to complete required courses within
the first two years. The curriculum itself aimed to be more interdisciplinary,
with equal weight being given to the three undergirding disciplines of economics, history, and government. Several courses that had previously been
required, such as Quigley's Development of Civilization and Giles's Government course, were now electives. For their junior and senior years' course of
studies, students would choose one of four international fields of concentration—diplomacy, economics, politics, or history and humanities. As Dean
Krogh reported to the board of directors in September 1970, the school was
"no longer primarily a preparatory school for the U.S. Foreign Service." Its
faculty and curriculum now marked it as a "school of international studies . . .
more a liberal arts school, but no less international in its orientation."[149]

In late November 1970, the president suspended Giles from the school
faculty because the professor had passed out a letter to his civil liberties seminar in which, it was alleged, he made a personal attack upon Dean Krogh.
Krogh had obtained a copy of the letter and forwarded it to Henle. Henle
charged a committee of senior school faculty and administrators to investigate the matter. They determined that the letter warranted the action that
Henle had taken, and the president rescinded Giles's appointment to the
school faculty. Giles admitted that his language had been "intemperate," sent
an apology to Krogh, and left the school faculty, which he had played a large
part in recreating. He returned to the government department, where he
continued to attract many foreign service students to his courses, particularly those in constitutional law, although they were no longer part of the
core curriculum.[150]

By the end of Krogh's second year as dean, President Henle reported that
"the School is on the move again."[151] By 1974 top administrators were com-
menting on "the dramatic improvements in [the] school in every area,"
ranging from enrollments to alumni relations, fund-raising, curricular reform, program initiation, faculty development, and reputation—all of which
were "due to [Krogh's] dynamic and indefatigable leadership."[152]

A 1970 survey showed nearly one-third of seniors going on to law school,
more than one-quarter to graduate studies, and nearly 28 percent into government service, either civil or military. Among those entering the foreign
service during these years were Kathleen Schloeder (1968), Daniel Fantozzi
(1971), Peter B. Alois (1972), Julia Moore (1972), and David Welch (1975).
Those who became ambassadors included Michael W. Cotter (1965) to Turk-
menistan, Gerald S. McGowan (1968, **L** 1974) to Portugal, Christopher C.
Ashby (1968) to Portugal, Brian D. Curran (1970) to Mozambique and Haiti,
Cynthia G. Efird (1971) to Angola, Mark R. Parris (1972) to Turkey, Clifford
Bond (1970) to Bosnia and Herzegovina, John E. Herbst (1974) to Uzbeki-

stan and Ukraine, Eileen A. Malloy (1975) to Kyrgyzstan, C. David Welch (1975) to Egypt, and Donald E. Booth (1976) to Liberia and Zambia. Alphonso Lopez-Caballero (1967) served as Columbia's ambassador to several nations, including Great Britain, France, and Canada. Kasit Piromya (1968) was Thailand's ambassador to several countries, including the United States and the Soviet Union, before becoming foreign minister in his country.

Among those making careers in the military were Douglas J. Murray (1965), who taught political science at the Air Force Academy; James L. Jones (1966), who became NATO's supreme Allied commander for Europe, after serving as commandant of the Marine Corps; Joseph Corcoran Jr. (1968) as a colonel in the air force; George Casey (1970) as a general in the army; and Kent Thomas (1974) as a colonel in the army. Those making careers in government and politics included Maureen Ryan Smith (1966) as an economist for the Department of Commerce; Gloria Macapagal-Arroyo (1968), also an economist, who in 2001 was inaugurated as the president of the Philippines; William Jefferson Clinton (1968), who served as governor of Arkansas before becoming the forty-second president of the United States; and Richard Durbin (1966, **L** 1969), who became a U.S. senator from Illinois in 1997.

Graduates of the school in academia included Michael H. Hunt (1965), who became a professor of history at the University of North Carolina at Chapel Hill; Martha Howell (1966), also a professor of history at Columbia University; Cheryl English Martin (1967), a professor of history at the University of Texas at El Paso; and Ralph Hattox (1976), a historian at Emory University; Mark von Hagen (1976), director of the School of Historical, Philosophical, and Religious Studies at Arizona State University; and B. Joseph White (1969), president of the University of Illinois from 2005 to 2009.

Susan Mooney Dodd (1968) became a short-fiction writer and a lecturer in the creative writing program at Harvard University; Gus Kaikkonen (1973), an alumnus of Mask and Bauble, became an actor and director on Broadway; Stephen Jimenez (1976) became a writer, producer, and director on television, and his documentary on Vietnam veterans won an Emmy Award in 1998; Patricia Orr Duff (1976) became a magazine editor, film producer, and television host. Bob Colacello (1969) became a biographer of celebrities. George Crile became a reporter for CBS and a writer; his bestseller *Charlie Wilson's War* was made into a film. Daniel Henninger (1971) became a columnist and editor for the *Wall Street Journal.* William Lawrence Rohter (1971) became the *New York Times* bureau chief in Rio de Janeiro.

In business, Michael P. Mortara (1971) became a bond trader for Salomon Brothers and later headed up a venture capital business for Goldman Sachs, before dying of a brain aneurysm at the age of fifty-one; Deborah Insley Dingell (1975) became president of the GM Foundation; and Jack Leslie (1975) became chair of BSMC Worldwide. Joseph R. Baczko (1967) was founder and president of Toys R Us International; later he was president and CEO of Blockbuster Entertainment. Elaine la Roche (1971) became the first female managing director for Morgan Stanley. Gary Perlin (1972) became the chief financial officer for Capital One Financial Corporation. James A. Firestone (1976) became the president of Xerox North America.

"Building Slowly—One Brick upon Another"

In Paul Dean the Georgetown law center had a dean with vision, yet one capable of taking the incremental steps to realize it. As one of his faculty put it, "Paul had a vision and a way of building slowly—one brick upon another. And he had the ability to gather about him others who shared the vision and were willing to build with him."[153] Developing a core of talented, dedicated faculty was fundamental to Georgetown's becoming a top-level law school. Initially he built mostly from within by selecting outstanding graduates from the school. In 1963 he brought in William Greenhalgh to direct the Criminal Justice Clinic and the Prettyman Fellowship Program. In 1964 Dean hired John Schmeertz and Bob Schoshinki and, in 1965, Dave McCarthy, Peter Weidenbruch, Jack Murphy, and Sherman Cohn. All those hired between 1963 and 1965, with the exception of Greenhalgh, were Georgetown law graduates. After that there were few in-house hires, as more and more outsiders began to apply for positions. In 1966, Sam Dash, Don Wallace, Don Schwartz, and Jonathan Sobeloff joined the faculty. These four brought more scholarly production than the school had ever seen. Schwartz became one of the top corporate law authors in the country. Dash did the same in the area of criminal law.

By the late sixties Georgetown was attracting top candidates for its openings. When, at the end of the 1966–67 year, several professors left the school to join either prestigious law firms or other law schools, there was some consternation among students about this brain drain. One recent hire and a former student, Sherman Cohn, told them that he remembered "when we did not have any faculty members worth stealing. Let us be thankful that we have gotten to the point where we do."[154] And the quality hires that the center continued to attract, such as Roy Shotland and James Oldham from Virginia and Stanford, respectively, in 1969, bore out Cohn's judgment. In 1972 four women joined the faculty: Judith Areen, Monica Gallagher, Anita Martin, and Patricia King. King became the first African American to receive tenure at the center.

For the faculty, Dean fostered a culture of scholarship by encouraging it, providing modest support in the form of secretaries and research assistants, and recognizing it as a requisite for tenure and promotion. The merit system that he introduced for determining salary increases also rewarded scholarship and effective teaching.[155]

One factor that persisted in hindering Georgetown's ability to attract top candidates was its salary scale, which ranked far behind the top-tier law schools. In 1966 Georgetown's average compensation was $15,000, com-

Patricia King, professor in the Law School. (Photo from Georgetown University Law School)

pared to Harvard's $24,000 and Yale's $20,500. In the late sixties, the dean made serious efforts to improve this situation with some success (the average salary approached $20,000 by 1970), but Georgetown still lagged significantly behind the leading law schools. By 1974 Georgetown had risen to twenty-ninth among law schools, but this was still far below where the school wanted to be.[156]

A new division at the center was the Institute of Criminal Law and Procedure, established in 1965 with a grant from the Ford Foundation to undertake research aimed at improving criminal justice. One of the first case studies was the Pre-Arraignment Project, to determine what impact the Miranda case had had upon local jurisdictions' prosecution of suspects. Its conclusion was that the case had little effect on police questioning procedures in the District of Columbia, and it received widespread attention in newspaper coverage. Later projects involved the evaluation of the rehabilitation of convicted felons and the utilization of technology developed for the exploration of space in solving crimes.[157] The latter was carried out in the forensics science laboratory, an offshoot of the institute based in both the law and medical centers, which attempted to apply advanced technology to solving problems of forensic science and to make their findings available to a larger public.[158]

The greatest weakness of the center was its antiquated, grossly inadequate facilities. In 1962, Paul Dean described the law center's complex of Victorian buildings on 5th and E streets as the "E Street Warehouse . . . unquestionably . . . the least adequate of any of the major law schools in the country."[159] Three years later he was able to announce that land had been purchased for $2,475,000 for a new building on New Jersey Avenue NW, four blocks from the Supreme Court building. Ironically, the tragic riots of 1968 proved to be a fortunate event for the law center because they devastated slumland to the east of the law school, which suddenly made it possible to purchase an entire city block at a better than reasonable price.[160] The purchased land was an area of 63,212 square feet bounded by F, 2nd, and G streets NW and New Jersey Avenue NW.[161] Edward Durell Stone, who was designing the Kennedy Center at the time, was chosen as the architect. Stone sought to design a building that would reflect its urban environment while projecting a college atmosphere.[162] The four-story square building positioned on a massive podium dotted by box-planted trees had a facade that alternated ground-to-roof columns of glass and glazed brick. At the center of the building was a two-story library overlooking a lower foyer surrounded by twenty-eight classrooms and fifty offices. The building also included a moot court auditorium with a capacity for 480 persons, a 290-seat amphitheater, a large conference center, and underground parking.

It was named for Bernard McDonough (**L** 1925), who had contributed $1 million to the university, the largest amount ever given by an alumnus. Ground was broken in the last week of April 1968 on the site on New Jersey

Bernard McDonough
Building at the Law School,
1971. (Georgetown University
Archives)

Avenue NW. Two and a half years later, the $11.3 million building was dedicated in September 1971. The building, as Wallace Mlyniec noted, symbolized the beginning of a new era for Georgetown Law. "McDonough Hall brought a permanence of place for academic excellence. . . . It did so with a modernist architectural statement of power and forthrightness that embodied Paul Dean's dream of a modern Law Center, built on a bedrock of excellence and justice."[163]

Dean's successor, Adrian Fisher, thought that the opening of the new building put the law center at a crossroads, providing it the opportunity to become a "truly great law school." Its library was seriously deficient, but its new housing made possible the great expansion in books and journals it badly needed; its faculty had made great strides in obtaining competitive salaries (in one year it had gone from fifty-third to thirty-third in national standings), but for a school with ambitions to crack the top ten law schools, it needed to raise them a good deal more, and the faculty-student ratio was still a serious concern.[164] The great leap in enrollment during this period without a corresponding increase in the size of the faculty meant that the student-faculty ratio got worse. By 1973 it was nearly 41:1 at the law center, almost quadruple the ratio at Yale.[165] Built to accommodate 1,800 students,

McDonough Hall by 1975 was already crowded by an enrollment that had soared far above the intended capacity of the building.

In the period from 1964 to 1975, enrollment more than doubled in the school (part of the university policy to increase enrollment to gain revenue), admission became a much more competitive process, and the student body became more diverse. Georgetown began to benefit from the growing popularity of the Law School as well as from the school's location. As Washington became a magnet for those seeking to study law and enter government service, no law school was closer to the judicial and legislative centers of the nation than Georgetown. In 1968 there was grave concern among center administrators that the draft would reduce enrollment in the school by as much as 20 percent and cause a deficit of more than $150,000.[166] Far from that attrition occurring, there was an explosion in the number of applications that Georgetown received at the end of the sixties and into the seventies. By 1970 Georgetown was receiving more applications than every other law school in the country, with the exception of Harvard. For the 1970–71 academic year, the entering class had 100 more students enroll than had been anticipated. For 1971 the school had more than 3,500 applications for 600 spots. Four years later the number of applicants soared to 7,100.

And the quality of the applicants improved sharply as well. Average LSAT scores improved from 597 in 1966 to 642 in 1970 and kept rising. In 1965 nearly 58 percent of the applicants were accepted. A decade later the acceptance rate had plummeted to 19 percent. The proportion of Catholics in the student body fell from 52.1 percent in 1964 to 42 percent in 1975. In 1964 women made up 3.2 percent of the school; in 1975 they made up 25 percent. By the seventies women were holding key positions. In 1969, Jo W. Gramling-Lopez (1972) became the first woman to be editor in chief of the *Law Weekly*. Sandra I. Rotherberg became the first female Prettyman Fellow the following year. Julianna J. Zekan (1977) became the first woman to head the Student Bar Association.[167] Minorities (African Americans, Native Americans, and Hispanics) who had composed less than 1 percent of the student body in 1965 now accounted for more than 11 percent in 1975.

The significant growth among minority students, particularly African Americans, was not an accident. The center first enrolled blacks in 1948, but by the late sixties only a handful were enrolled, one of whom, Curtis Smothers, was there as an army officer on a scholarship from the judge advocate general's corps. In 1967, Professor Jack Murphy proposed that the center begin actively recruiting black students from historically black colleges, that it eliminate application fees for minorities, and that it start a summer program to prepare black students for law school. The faculty adopted Murphy's proposal and broadened admission policies to accept students traditionally ineligible by normal aptitude testing.[168] They also set aside three scholarships for black students in the next entering class.[169] That winter of 1967–68, Murphy, together with some students and admissions staff, did a tour of predominantly black colleges in the South and of colleges in the Southwest with a substantial Hispanic presence. The number of African Americans and Hispanics in the following first-year class was proof of their success: twenty African Americans and five Hispanics. In 1972 the faculty voted to reserve 60 percent of its first-year scholarship funds for minorities. By 1974 blacks made up 6 percent of the school's student body.[170] A year later minorities comprised 15 percent of the first-year class. When a court in 1976 struck down the policy, the school continued to be liberal in awarding minority applicants with financial aid, although it no longer set strict quotas.[171]

The new minorities, including women, formed their own organizations to provide a base for their members and a recruiting instrument. Thus black law students formed the Black American Law Students Association (BALSA) in 1968, the same year that their undergraduate counterparts formed the Black Student Alliance on the main campus. Three years later a group of women formed the Women's Rights Collective, in part to recruit women students and faculty and lobby for courses relating to women and the law.

By the academic year 1966–67 students were very vocally, through the Student Bar Association (SBA), the new *Law Weekly,* or group action, expressing their discontent with many aspects of the school and demanding to have greater voice in shaping the school's policies and operations. One change that student protest did bring about during that year was a revamping of the curriculum so that most courses now became electives.[172] In February 1967 the dean met with student leaders as a step toward dealing with student complaints. He pointed out that the administration had been taking "great pains to open the channels of communication." He and his assistant deans were willing to meet with students on a weekly basis. He promised weekly meetings for the students with the librarian in order to improve the management of the library. For all their complaints about the shortcomings of the school, Dean maintained that the school really was among the top twelve law schools in the country. As a member of the executive committee of the Association of American Law Schools, he felt that he was in very good position to make such a claim.[173]

A major change in the curriculum occurred in 1967 when the faculty agreed to make all courses beyond the first-year offerings electives and to require eighty semester hours to qualify for a degree. Both these changes tended to ensure that more students would take clinical courses in their second and third years. In a period when clinical education was being scaled back at other law schools because of a lapse of outside support, Georgetown expanded its clinical programs. In 1971 a special dean, Bill Greenhalgh, was appointed for clinical programs. Greenhalgh took the initiative of combining the Prettyman Fellowship Program with the JD clinical program in order to provide more supervision of the latter by the fellows in the former.[174] Under Greenhalgh's direction Georgetown's clinical programs became the pacesetter for clinical legal education in the nation. Georgetown was also unique in making its clinical programs an integral part of the curriculum. And no other school had anything like the 20–30 fellows on a two-year program in which they earned an LLM in advocacy.[175]

There were a constellation of courses created in the sixties to deal with issues of urban justice and poverty, such as Law and the Urban Poor, Discrimination-Rights and Remedies, and seminars on law and the problems of poverty. Paul Dean thought that no other law school in the country had so progressive a curriculum in the areas of poverty and urban issues as did Georgetown.[176]

Mock trial in Street Law Program. (Photo courtesy of Ed O'Brien)

Among pioneer clinical programs were the Street Law Program, the Juvenile Justice Clinic, and the Appellate Litigation Seminar. Under the Street Law Program that began in 1971, Georgetown students taught a comprehensive course in everyday law to DC public high school students. By 1973 the program involved five hundred students in nine DC high schools and ninety youths in three correctional institutions. Two years later the Georgetown program had grown to include sixteen high schools and seven prisons. Early in its operation the program had secured the participation of law firms or legal organizations within the city to secure from each legal establishment a mentor to pair up with a particular school or prison. Eventually each participating school had a clinical fellow who directed and coordinated the operations of that clinic. The program by the middle seventies had been adopted by other law schools, school systems, and legal aid societies across the nation through the National Street Law Institute (later the National Institute of Citizens for Education in the Law) that was established in 1975 by Professor Jason I. Newman (**L** 1965) to provide textbooks and core curriculum to institutions utilizing the program.

The Juvenile Justice Clinic was founded in September 1973 by Judith Areen. The clinic provided student lawyers who defended children's rights in court. Under the supervision of two law professors and two practicing attorneys, the twenty students in the clinic represented children in four areas of juvenile law: neglect, persons in need of supervision, delinquency, and hearings by the school board administration on eligibility for special education programs. Besides preparing their individual cases for presentation in court, students met in a seminar twice a week to hear experts from various professions dealing with juvenile problems.[177]

In 1972–73, twenty-four law students, all members of the new Appellate Litigation Seminar, directed by Sherman Cohn, exercised their litigation skills by participating in the preparation of briefs and argument of cases before the United States Appeals Court.[178] The seminar was the first clinical program to utilize the three-tiered structure of operation: law students on the bottom, graduate fellows in supervisory roles above, and a faculty director on top. Eventually that structure was applied to all the clinical programs at the school.[179]

Moot court competition continued on the national level during the period. A high point occurred for Georgetown in 1973 when a team of three Georgetown law students won first place in the National Moot Court competition involving 130 law schools in New York City. Randy Mott, Sallie Helm, and Joel Kleinman were the winning team, coached by Frank Flegal. The judges voted Mott the best individual advocate. One of the judges, a justice of the New York Supreme Court, commented that the Georgetown team managed to do something he had never witnessed in all the moot court competitions he had judged: "superb oral arguments . . . first prize for the excellence of its brief and . . . first prize for the best oral presentation."[180]

A new "beyond the classroom" organized activity was the Law Center Players, faculty and students who in 1973 presented the first of what would become an annual tradition of Gilbert and Sullivan productions. The first production was fittingly enough "Trial by Jury." Professors David McCarthy, Richard Gordon, and James Oldham became perennial members of the players.

In 1964 the ABA's section on legal education and admissions to the Bar recommended that the normal degree awarded to graduates of law schools be the Juris Doctor rather than the LLB that had been traditionally given. The ABA argued that the academic rigor of the course of studies in law schools was comparable to or greater than that in other professional courses of study in which the doctorate was awarded.[181] Georgetown considered the matter that year but declined to make the change because the prestigious law schools continued to give the LLB. Three years later that had changed, with schools such as Chicago and the University of Michigan being among the sixty-five schools that had adopted the doctoral degree. The Georgetown faculty had also concluded in the interim that the profession had gained a greater importance within a society grappling with critical urban, social, and criminal issues and that the JD would more fittingly recognize the increased status of the profession. A student poll had also revealed overwhelming student support for such a change. The university subsequently determined to award the JD to law school graduates and to grant it retroactively to all school alumni. (As the dean pointed out to the president, conferring the JD on all law alumni, even those who had no college degree, would also benevolently dispose the alumni to the university's development campaign.)[182] At commencement of 1967 law graduates were awarded the JD for the first time.

When Paul Dean announced his resignation as dean in the summer of 1968, he backed the student request for seats on the search committee for his successor. Two students subsequently were appointed to the committee, along with faculty and alumni. The dean made known to the search committee that he favored David J. McCarthy Jr., his assistant dean who had proven so valuable in helping Dean move the center forward. (He wrote the committee that he was disturbed by the widespread talk that the new dean should not be "a Ghetto Catholic" like McCarthy, but rather an outsider, with a national image. He attributed this desire to an inferiority complex that instinctively undervalued its own. "It is notable," he chided, "that Harvard Law School does not suffer from this masochistic tendency.")[183] Despite Dean's support for McCarthy, the committee unanimously recommended Adrian S. Fisher to become the next dean. The fifty-five-year-old Fisher, a Harvard Law graduate, former clerk to Felix Frankfurter, past general counsel to the *Washington Post,* and current deputy director of the U.S. Arms Control and Disarmament Agency (he had played a key role in negotiating the limited test ban treaty with the Soviet Union in 1963), brought the glowing mainstream credentials that some thought Georgetown needed in a leader. Paul Dean welcomed his successor with the assurance that the committee could have made no better choice.[184]

In the late sixties the center began a concerted effort to assist graduates in securing judicial clerkships, positions Georgetown had traditionally seen few of its alumni secure. Within a short time the effort paid off, as the center was able to triple the number of clerkships held by its graduates. A survey in 1969 showed that Georgetown had more of its graduates—609— in the service of the federal government than any other law school (Harvard was a distant second with 480). More than one hundred Georgetown Law graduates worked in the Justice Department alone.[185]

Among graduates going into public and political service were Frank Wolff (1965) as Republican congressman from Northern Virginia; Steny H. Hoyer (1966), Maryland Democratic congressman and, since 2007, majority leader in the House of Representatives; Dan Lungren (1971), Republican congressman from California; Mickey Kantor (1968), who served as a lawyer with the Office of Economic Opportunity and later served as a political campaign director and official in the Clinton administration; Jacob Lew (1975), director of the Office of Management and Budget; Douglas Feith (1978), who was undersecretary of defense in the George W. Bush administration; Robert M. Kimmitt (1977), deputy secretary of the treasury, 2005–9; Richard Durbin (1969) as a member, first of the U.S. House of Representatives, then of the U.S. Senate from Illinois; Martin Frost (1970), who in 1979 became a Democratic representative from Texas and eventual chair of the Democratic Caucus; Mark Titenstein (1971), named U.S. ambassador to Romania by President Obama; Gary Bauer (1971), who was heavily involved in Republican politics and governance and served on the Republican National Committee, then as an assistant to President Reagan; Alan S. Frum (1971), who became the parliamentarian of the U.S. Senate in 2001; John Podesta (1976) as chief of staff to President Clinton and as director of the Central Intelligence Agency in the

Obama administration; James R. Hubbard (1971), who became the lieutenant governor of the U.S. Virgin Islands in 1987; David Jacobson (1976) as U.S. ambassador to Canada in the Obama administration; Steve Merrill (1972), who served as governor of New Hampshire from 1993 to 1997; Robert Kimmitt (1977) as U.S. ambassador to Germany in the George H. W. Bush administration; and James Webb Jr. (1975), who was wounded twice in action in Vietnam, where he won the Navy Cross, the Silver Star, and two Bronze Stars, was secretary of the navy in the Reagan administration and was elected to the U.S. Senate from Virginia in 2006 as a Democrat.

School graduates were prominent in judicial positions at both the state and federal levels: Fred I. Parker (1965) as judge of the U.S. Court of Appeals for the Second Circuit, Arthur J. Gajarsa (1967) as judge of the U.S. Court of Appeals for the Federal Circuit, Richard C. Bosson (1969) as chief justice of the New Mexico Supreme Court, Richard Linn (1969) as judge of the U.S. Court of Appeals for the Federal Circuit, Eugene R. Sullivan (1971) as chief judge of the U.S. Court of Appeals for the Armed Forces, Stephen P. Lamb (1975) as vice chancellor in the Delaware Court of Chancery, Margaret McKeown (1975) as judge of the U.S. Court of Appeals for the Ninth Circuit, and Vanessa Ruiz (1975) as judge of the District of Columbia Court of Appeals.

Curtis Smothers (1967) went on to serve in the judge advocate's corps of the U.S. army before becoming acting deputy assistant secretary of defense for equal opportunity in the military under the Nixon administration. Michael Millemann (1969) transferred to Georgetown Law in order to take advantage of its clinical programs and courses in rights and poverty law. Afterward he worked for the Legal Aid Society of Maryland and directed the University of Maryland's clinical law program. Joan Claybrook (1973) worked for nongovernmental agencies regarding consumer and public interest legislation before serving in the Carter and Clinton administrations; Robert M. McNamara (1973) served as a lawyer for the U.S. government for more than three decades, including as general counsel of the Peace Corps and the CIA; William Alberger (1973) served in the Carter administration as chair of the U.S. International Trade Commission.

Those who distinguished themselves in the legal academy included Edward T. Foote (1966), who became dean of the Washington University School of Law in St. Louis; Anthony J. Santoro (1967), who served as dean of the Delaware Law School; Mark A. Rothstein (1973), who became a professor at the University of West Virginia Law School (WVU) and later directed the University of Houston Law Center's Health and Law Policy Institute; and his wife, Laura (1974), who also was appointed a professor of law at WVU. Patricia A. McGuire (1977) was appointed president of Trinity College in Washington, DC, in 1989.

Faculty and alumni from the law center were prominently involved in the first political scandal to force a president from office. Georgetown-related people were key players in the Watergate drama from the very beginning, when the "plumbers" of the Nixon administration were apprehended following a botched break-in at the headquarters of the Democratic National Committee in the posh complex in Foggy Bottom in 1972 and subsequently brought before Judge John J. Sirica (1926) of the U.S. District Court and an adjunct faculty member at the center. Sirica's dogged pursuit of the full intent of the burglary and of the people behind the burglars led to the special investigation of the Senate Select Committee on Presidential Campaign Activities, whose chief counsel was Samuel Dash, who took a leave of absence from the center to direct the committee's investigation beginning in the summer of 1973. A number of Georgetown law students served as legal assistants to the committee under Dash. One of the senators on the committee was a Georgetown Law alumnus, Joseph M. Montoya (1939) of New Mexico. The witness who provided the breakthrough evidence of the White House cover-up of the truth behind the break-in was the White House counsel, another Georgetown alumnus, John Dean III (1965). When Archibald Cox was selected as the special prosecutor to examine the case, law center professor Charles Ruff became one of his chief assistants. In the summer of 1974, when the House Judiciary Committee took up the question of impeaching the president, two Georgetown Law alumni, Robert Drinan, SJ (1949) of Massachusetts and Lawrence J. Hogan Jr. (**C** 1949, **L** 1954) of Maryland were members of the committee. John E. Kennahan (F 1954, **L** 1956) served as committee counsel.

The scandal had a lasting impact on the school's curriculum. In the fall of 1973, with the scandal gripping the nation, the school was forced to add extra sections of its professional responsibility course. Three years later the faculty, in the wake of Watergate and the disgraced president, voted to make professional responsibility a required course.[186] Unlike most law schools, Georgetown had required ethics courses since 1920. After Watergate, the ABA required schools to introduce a Professional Responsibility course to their required curriculum in order to preserve their accreditation.[187] Georgetown already had a Professional Responsibility course for seniors, but in 1967 the faculty had changed the course from a requirement to an elective. The faculty instead adopted a pervasive approach to fulfilling the requirement by charging all the faculty with the duty of introducing the issue of the ethics of professional conduct into each of their courses.[188] This immersion of ethics and professional responsibility into the curriculum as a whole unfortunately had no enforcement mechanism built into it, and few, if any, faculty seemed to adapt their courses to meet this aim. Thus in 1977, after the ABA issued its new requirement for accreditation, the school reinstituted the requirement of a Professional Responsibility course for graduation. A number of courses, such as the Legal Profession and Professional Responsibility and the Administration of Justice, were made available to fulfill the requirement.[189]

In 1974, Dean Fisher's administrative limitations and personal problems forced him to announce that he was stepping down to return to teaching. A search committee subsequently recommended Associate Dean David McCarthy and Clinton Bamberger, dean of the Catholic University School of Law. Henle found both candidates "excellent," but chose McCarthy because he was "more familiar with the problems at the Law Center."[190] McCarthy, who had been a very effective associate dean under Paul Dean, brought extraordinary administrative skills to the position that he utilized to build a central structure and staff that enabled the law center to make its rise to the top tier of law schools. He also very actively promoted the expansion and growth of clinical education. He created the center's fund-raising office and was the force behind its alumni outreach. "He proved to be a perfect Executive Vice-President," one faculty member noted, to which level the dean's position had recently been elevated.[191]

Navigating the 1960s at Georgetown

Crisis, challenge, and conflict were central to the experience of American society in the ten years (1965–75) that became known as the sixties. Like that of the larger society, Georgetown's history from the middle of the 1960s to the middle of the 1970s was shaped in an atmosphere charged by those three elements. From the end of the 1960s through the first half of the 1970s, the university endured a financial crisis that only skilled financial management, an aggressive investment policy, enlarged enrollment, and increased tuition fees finally subdued. Frustration marked the efforts of the university to meet the challenge of acquiring vitally needed property contiguous to the main campus. An ambitious but undermanaged and underfunded construction campaign produced turmoil and a mortal threat to the financial health of the university that led to a radical reorganization that effectively divided responsibility for planning, management, and fund-raising in construction projects. A persistent inability to meet the goal of the university's first major financial development campaign—the Progress Fund—also raised critical questions about the institution's capacity to provide the financial resources it needed for its continued survival and advancement. That crisis was essentially defused by the combination of fortuitous legacies and federal funding that finally enabled the university to creatively claim success in completing the Progress Fund.

Financial concerns were partly responsible for the administration's perception of a tenure crisis that led to abortive attempts to impose a tenure quota on departments of the main campus and to regularize retirement at the age of sixty-five. The financial crisis also led the university to raise enrollment ceilings at both the undergraduate and professional levels in order to increase revenue. One consequence was the reorganization of the admissions office from a regional to a national operation that began to recruit for diversity not only geographically but also along gender and race lines. The decision to expand enrollment led indirectly to the admission of women to the college, which had a profound effect upon the educational experience and culture of the school and led to a change in admissions policy regarding women in the other undergraduate schools, which produced gender equity in enrollment by the middle of the 1970s. The administration also accepted the challenge raised by its minority students of adopting an effective affirmative action program of recruiting and offering support (both financial and academic) to black students that within a few years made them a significant minority among undergraduates.

This broadened recruitment as well as curricular reform, including the introduction of interdisciplinary programs, brought dramatic progress for the College of Arts and Sciences. The School of Nursing's efforts to become a full-fledged member of the academic community at Georgetown through administrative inclusion within the undergraduate schools of the main campus, faculty and student development, and curricular reform were largely losing ones, although the introduction of a self-care curriculum made the school a pacesetter among nursing schools. The Business School shared disproportionately in the university's success in attracting applicants, especially women, but the revolving-door leadership at the Business School produced stagnation in its academic life. Turmoil, occasioned by a crisis of identity, characterized the experience of the School of Foreign Service in the late 1960s. The appointment of a strong and decisive dean, under whose direction a core faculty was reinstituted and the curriculum reformed, set the school on a path of unprecedented progress by the middle of the 1970s.

At the law center, opposition to the transfer of school revenues to the general funds of the university resulted in the creation of three-campus budgeting that gave the school the financial autonomy to pursue the top tier in legal education. Student protest also brought about a liberalization of the curriculum. The urban crisis was a catalyst for the dramatic expansion of clinical programs at the school. The school, through members of its faculty and alumni, was caught up in the Watergate crisis, which impacted the curriculum by the growth of courses on ethical responsibility. The building of a distinguished faculty and the recruiting of a highly qualified, diverse student body helped put it within striking range of the goal of becoming a peer of the elite law schools. Nothing contributed more toward providing the school with the means to reach the top of legal education than opening its new home in 1970. By that year the law center was poised to enter a new era in its history.

All these developments were ways in which the university experienced the sixties. But it was in the areas of student life and the impact of the urban crisis and the Vietnam War that the tidal wave that was the sixties most affected the university. To that we now turn.

CHAPTER 3

The University in an Unraveling World
Georgetown in the 1960s (1965–75) II

Our students are growing away from us. The generation gap is widening, and all of us . . . should consider what there is he might do to bridge the abyss. . . . In many instances the problem was . . . that the two generations just do not understand each other.

THOMAS FITZGERALD, SJ, MAY 18, 1970

In the Eye of the Storm

If the sixties were a tidal wave that swept over America, as one critic has observed, the nation's campuses were the eye of the storm that produced the onslaught against the institutions and culture that defined the society.[1] The cultural revolution that engaged young America in the sixties touched Georgetown's students, though with some lag and less intensity. But the turning on to sex, drugs, and radical politics was part of Georgetown student life by the latter part of the decade.

In the sixties, students became increasingly conscious of their rights as students. President Campbell, in an address on academic freedom at the fall faculty convocation in 1967, noted that the question of student freedom was becoming an important aspect of the larger issue and that determining the boundaries of student freedom within the life of a university was a work in progress at Georgetown, as elsewhere.[2] In 1965 the college students drew up a bill of student rights, which they submitted to the administration for its acknowledgment. The twelve rights were all related to their academic life: the right of freedom of opinion in the classroom, the right to change courses, the right of having adequate time to prepare research papers, and so on. The faculty committee that was appointed to review the rights unanimously endorsed them, and they were subsequently promulgated by the administration.[3] By the end of the sixties, students were more concerned about student freedom as it related to liberation from the rules and discipline that had traditionally governed student life at Georgetown. In 1974 students put together a much more comprehensive undergraduate student bill of rights, which dealt with freedom of speech for students, freedom from censorship of their media, freedom from any infringement of their right to invite speakers of their own choosing, and freedom from denial of housing except through due process. The bill, with some modifications, became university policy in 1976.

In his inaugural address in 1970, President Henle made explicit the fundamental shift in perspective on the nature of an institution of higher education that his predecessor had adopted. Henle noted the familial character of the traditional American college, which in the Catholic landscape of higher education had been modeled on the religious community. "That model," Henle announced, "is dissipating and disappearing." He did not regret its passing but rather saw it as a liberating development that enabled Catholic educators to discover the unique character of university structure and function, one that could not be modeled on family or state, business or church. "The fundamental business of the university is learning. . . . It is the basic learning in which people seek to grow, to understand life, to understand the universe, to understand themselves in a very humanistic way, an artistic way, in relation to values and goals and goods of human life."[4]

In 1967, President Campbell raised the position of student personnel director to that of vice president to denote the importance of student life and welfare outside the classroom.[5] The new vice president of student development, Philip Tripp, explained that the relationship of the student affairs administration with students was no longer one characterized by in loco parentis or one that was contractual in nature. He preferred to see it as a collegial relationship, that is, a community of scholars both older and younger, in which the students are junior colleagues whose dignity, worth, motivation, and integrity are respected and appreciated as those of the faculty are. He saw his chief mission as the building of community in the dormitories.[6]

Barely a year later there was an overhaul of the student development office. Henle was clearly unsatisfied with Tripp's view of the direction student life administration should take. Indeed, he was unhappy with the performance of both Tripp and the dean of students, Charles Hartmann, particularly for their handling of, or failure to handle, the disrupting of San Francisco mayor Joseph Alioto's speech on campus in the spring of 1969. The president was prepared to sever Tripp's contract when the latter resigned in October to accept a teaching position at Ohio State University. Hartmann, whom Tripp had brought in, was given a terminal leave of absence. Henle appointed the dean of women, Patricia Rueckel, as head of student development. The president assured the board of directors that Rueckel's taking over would mean a basic change in the philosophy of student life at Georgetown.[7] Rueckel, as vice president of student development, brought counseling services to Georgetown's undergraduate community and professionalized the student health operation, which she broadened to include the treatment of mental health. Under Rueckel, student development began to stress counseling and community adjudication in its dealing with student problems and transgressions. In 1973, Rueckel created the Student Life Policy Committee (SLPC), which consisted of administrative, faculty, and student representatives. In that same year she created the position of dean of residence life, underscoring the importance, if not centrality, of residential living in student life.

Housing

The dormitories became the crucible of the cultural revolution occurring in student life in the late sixties. The university had since the 1950s set an informal goal of having 80 percent of undergraduates housed on campus. By the mid-sixties some officials began to question this goal; indeed, President Campbell had considered whether it might not be better to get "out of the hotel business" for students entirely. Upper-class students began opting in great numbers to enjoy the freedom that came with living off-campus. Those who remained on campus were pressing for more and more autonomy in their residential lifestyle as the hitherto prevailing in loco parentis began to crumble as a rationale for strict dormitory discipline.[8] If in loco parentis no longer applied, just what responsibility did the university have for housing students? Another factor was the projected national decline in the college student population. In 1969 the university made the decision that they would construct no additional dormitories. Indeed, by the end of the sixties plans had been made to phase out all student housing in the quadrangle area, as well as Loyola Hall on the East Campus—eliminating more than three hundred rooms.[9]

As it happened, neither a shrinking student body nor a continuing move off campus was a reality by the time Henle became president in 1969. In fact, there was growing pressure from undergraduates for the university to provide not less but more housing on campus. Against the national trend, Georgetown students were by a large majority choosing to live on campus now that a laissez-faire lifestyle dominated the dorms and many more women were being admitted to the university who overwhelmingly preferred on-campus housing. Indeed, having comfortable on-campus housing became a major attraction for prospective students. In 1970, President Henle commissioned the main campus planning and building committee to reevaluate the university's housing needs and determine how best to meet them. The committee's report recommitted the university to the ideal of a residential undergraduate community. The relationship of the university to its resident students, it acknowledged, was now more of landlord to tenant than it was in loco parentis. Nonetheless, there were special educational advantages to the university's being able to provide residential quarters for its students.[10] As the *Hoya* pointed out in an editorial in 1972, "When more than half of a student body lives off-campus, . . . any sense of community among students is effectively destroyed."[11] Henle sought ways to accommodate student preferences. He realized too that any future housing had to reflect the independence and autonomy of the new student lifestyle. As mostly a symbolic gesture of his concern to provide housing, he made available to students twenty-one townhouses that the university owned in the immediate neighborhood. In the meantime the housing shortage on campus became critical by 1972, when the university was able to house less than half the undergraduates, with more than five hundred upper-class students on waiting lists and a growing threat of transfers by students who were unable to live on campus. A much more effective step toward eliminating the housing shortage was the purchase for $6.2 million by the university in the late summer of 1973 of the Alban Towers Apartment Hotel on Wisconsin Avenue a mile north of the main campus, a structure of 275 units, half of which were vacant. The huge waiting list for rooms was immediately eliminated by the four hundred students who were accommodated in the available units at Alban Towers.[12] Still, by 1975, 2,258 students, fewer than half the undergraduates, were housed on campus.

The university had planned its first university village on the site of the O'Gara Building. Underground would allow parking for 450 cars, 30 classrooms, and 110 faculty offices. Above ground would be townhouses to accommodate more than 400 undergraduates in 6-person units comprising bedrooms, kitchen, dining room, living room, and baths. The pressing need for more student housing and the ability to finance that housing through the federal loan program within the year dictated that the townhouses be separated from the rest of the village plan and located elsewhere. The site of the former Annex II on 37th Street was chosen, but it failed to get zoning approval from the city for a housing complex of that size (the Board of Zoning and Adjustment set a maximum at 360 persons). Reluctantly, the university relocated the complex once again to the hillside between Reiss Science Building and Darnall Hall. Ground was broken in January 1975 and completed in the fall of 1976. The three-story, red-brick structure, named Henle Student Village, contained townhouses for 475 students. Total cost for the complex was $5.4 million. With its completion, more than half of undergraduates (54%) at last lived on campus.

Alban Towers, purchased by the university in 1973.

(Georgetown University Archives)

The admission of women to the college in 1969 was also the occasion for the beginning of coeducational housing on campus, initially on an experimental basis. Previously, women in nursing and the School of Languages and Linguistics had lived in separate dorms, the nurses in St. Mary's Hall, the female students of the School of Languages and Linguistics first at Meridien Hall on 16th Street, which the university rented, and then in Darnall. By the fall of 1974, a majority of the dormitories on campus housed both men and women, although segregation by corridor still prevailed.[13]

Jesuits remained in the dormitories, but no longer as prefects. Since the fifties, two lay prefects, mostly law or graduate students, were responsible for maintaining discipline on each corridor. The Jesuits were there as spiritual and academic counselors. They did not wish to be considered proxy parents. "Who has ever been the parent of 400 children?" asked Dean Royden Davis, SJ, who lived on a corridor in New South. "Concern yes," he went on, *"in loco parentis,* no!"[14] By the latter sixties, the lay prefects were seen more as counselors than enforcers of discipline, as the rigid rules governing study hours, drink, noise, and visitors of the opposite sex were either eliminated or greatly relaxed. The change in title from "lay prefect" to "resident assistant" that occurred at the end of the sixties reflected the

Henle Student Village, 1976.

(Ye Domesday Booke)

transformation of his role. The dorms, previously seen as primarily study halls, now became autonomous centers of a student life that was parallel to and independent of the classroom and laboratory. This bifurcation of student and academic life enhanced the status of the student as a free and unfettered person.

The issue of parietals, or periods in which members of one gender could visit dormitory rooms of the other, was a touchstone of the limits of student autonomy in the new culture of residential life. Parietals arose as a student demand in the fall of 1967. Under student pressure, the dean of men announced that there would be a trial for parietals in the men's dormitories during homecoming weekend in October. The students, however, refused to participate in the experiment because the dean had insisted that the doors of all students' rooms remain open during the parietal hours.[15] Two months later the college student council passed a resolution stating that it was their expectation that weekly parietal hours would be in effect across the campus by February 1.[16] The university did not meet the deadline implicitly set by the student council, but it did create the Student Affairs Policy Advisory Committee (SAPAC), comprising administrators, faculty, and students, to recommend policy on various student issues, including parietals. In March, SAPAC recommended restricted parietals on Fridays and Saturdays, which the board of directors approved as an experiment for the remainder of the semester, with the modification that doors in rooms in which females were present had to be open.[17]

The spring experiment became the custom; indeed, open parietals became the practice in many dorms over the course of the next year. When Patricia Rueckel replaced Tripp as head of the Office of Student Development at the beginning of 1970, one of her first actions was to scale back the parietals. Seeing the twenty-four-hour parietals as a violation of the rule prohibiting cohabitation, she ordered a moratorium on extended parietals.[18] The now unified student government passed a resolution of nonrecognition of the administration's right to establish parietal hours, but Rueckel managed to persuade the senate to repeal its own resolution.[19] An uneasy truce over the issue prevailed for the next year.

The issue rose again in the spring semester of 1971 when the SLPC, the successor to SAPAC, recommended that the university institute a trial period of twenty-four-hour parietals. Recognizing that their rejection of the proposal could well reignite a crisis over parietals, the board of directors delegated responsibility for setting regulations governing dormitory living to the vice president for student development. In July the board commissioned a task force on the quality of student life to investigate and evaluate student living at Georgetown, including the student conduct code, the disciplinary system, and the issue of parietals. That report, to the surprise of the administration, recommended twenty-four-hour parietals for upperclassmen for those corridors that approved of them. The board of directors, while noting that they would not tolerate any premarital sex, cohabitation, or violation of privacy, in July 1972 put into effect the recommended unrestricted parietals.[20] At the end of the following semester, the resident directors of the upper-class dormitories reported that the new arrangement had been a success; that the dorms were now cleaner, more civilized, and much less noisy; and that they had seen no signs of cohabitation. They recommended that the parietals be extended to freshmen, which the board failed to pursue. The following summer it authorized the president to modify or amend the intervisitation policy, where and when he saw fit.[21] That fall, students filed a complaint with the District of Columbia government that the university's parietal restrictions for freshmen were in violation of the city's Human Rights Act.[22] Whether or not that formal complaint played a role, by the middle seventies parietals were no longer in effect for any Georgetown student. One Jesuit who had been a resident in one of the dormitories at the time felt, like many of his brethren, that the administration never squarely faced the issue and ended by putting no limitation on situations in which "relationships among the sexes [could occur] which in normal situations would be considered compromising."[23] Another Jesuit, who had been the dean of men, rued that all too often, as in the case of parietals, student development administrators had yielded to student demands in allowing something without any guidelines or restrictions and, in the end, had eliminated any possibility that student life could serve as part of their moral and intellectual education.[24]

Sex

The quantum increase in women on campus that occurred as the sixties turned into the seventies affected the sexual atmosphere on campus. Coed dormitories and unlimited visitation practices created opportunities for sexual intimacy that would have shocked the community just a few years earlier. As *Ye Domesday Booke* observed in 1975, "There has been a phenomenal change in the residential arrangements that has made the opposite sex much more accessible. Every one of the six residence hall complexes are coeducational and Harbin has mixed community floors. In 1969, students were *asking* for parietals; today intervisitation restrictions have virtually been abolished. In 1969, men had to surrender their ID cards when women visited their rooms (on the few days it was permitted) and the door had to remain open. Today . . . anything goes and often does," although it hastened to say that the new environment created the milieu for platonic and intellectual relationships as well as physical ones.[25] It might have added that the former was still more likely to occur than the latter. Cohabitation there was, but it was not widespread. Still, if sexual intimacy was not yet the norm for gender relationships, it was present on a scale that was truly revolutionary in student culture. The article on sex in the yearbook was accompanied by a photo spread that included pictures of scattered clothing on a bedroom floor, of couples in bed, and of two students carrying signs, the male with "I am a bricklayer," and the female with "I am a brick," which testified not only to the change in sexual mores but also the disappearance of censorship of student media.

In 1972 a guide, *Human Sexual Response-Ability,* written by a group of Georgetown medical students and distributed to undergraduates by the student government, drew the condemnation of the cardinal archbishop of Washington, Patrick O'Boyle, who initially threatened to order by letter that the university repress the publication but was persuaded by President Henle not to publish the letter. The cardinal did make a statement in which he denounced the guide for its offense to the church's teachings on sexual morality and was critical of a Jesuit faculty member, Robert Baumiller, who had served as a consultant to the medical student authors. The university, taking its stand on the principle of academic freedom, responded that the pamphlet did not represent any official position of Georgetown University but that the university had to "respect freedom of expression within its campuses," including its students. "To perform its teaching and research functions effectively, the Catholic university must have a true autonomy and academic freedom in the face of authority of whatever kind—lay or clerical—external to the academic community itself. The right of students to publish material without censorship by the University is key to the issue of academic freedom."[26] The issue of academic freedom and church teachings on sexuality had first surfaced four years earlier when fifteen Jesuits at Georgetown had signed "A Statement on Conscience in the Church," in response to Cardinal O'Boyle's withdrawal of faculties from thirty-nine priests in the archdiocese for their opposition to the recent papal encyclical *Humanae vitae.* The signers argued that the dissenters were doing nothing more than bishops throughout the world who were interpreting the encyclical, according to their conscience, in different ways. Three weeks earlier, in September 1968, a lay professor of philosophy at Georgetown, Louis Dupré, maintained in a talk to a Catholic audience that the papal encyclical forbidding the use of artificial means of birth control was not infallible and that the individual conscience should remain the supreme arbiter in matters of individual morality.[27] Dupré apparently suffered no consequences from the archdiocese. Conversely, the fifteen Jesuits at Georgetown were ordered by their provincial superior, at the behest of the cardinal, to attend a meeting where the cardinal's two theological advisors, both Jesuits, lectured their Georgetown brethren about the necessity of obeying a papal encyclical "that was almost infallible."[28]

Drugs and Alcohol

"Those were . . . high drug use years," a Jesuit recalled. "I remember one night finding a student on the floor from drugs and booze. A good number of freshmen were on LSD and marijuana."[29] In the spring of 1968, the dean of men, Edward Klein, conducted drug investigations in order to identify student dealers. Klein's efforts drew criticism from students that he was conducting a heavy-handed inquisition. The results of the probe were the expulsion of three students and the suspension of another.[30] The lack of student cooperation in getting to dealers frustrated Klein.

A *Hoya* article in 1968 estimated that 30 percent to 40 percent of Georgetown male students had smoked marijuana at one time or another but that use in dorms was in decline because of the increase in enforcement of drug laws. Few students, it claimed, were regular users of drugs.[31] Two years later the president reported to the board of directors that drug use, especially that of marijuana, was growing on campus. Student development was attempting to deal with it through counseling, treating it as a psychological and medical problem rather than as a crime. By the early seventies, DC and campus police raids on dormitories began to occur, as police targeted dealers of drugs on campus. In 1973 the *Hoya* called for "the liberalization of the University's antiquated drug policy," on the grounds that its enforcement was inconsistent and hypocritical. "While some R.A.'s vigilantly hunt down offenders," it asserted, "others occasionally smoke with the students on their corridor."

"The marijuana phenomenon is too widespread," it concluded. "Even the most conservative scholars and athletes are not immune. . . . The University would be depopulated if all drug offenders were expelled."[32] By the mid-seventies drug use seemed to be in decline on campus. "Georgetown has had its fling with hard drugs," the yearbook noted in 1975. Marijuana was still very much present, but alcohol had returned as the clear drug of choice among students. In short, the keg culture was overwhelming the drug culture.[33] Or, perhaps more aptly, the Jim Beam culture. "The thing that really bothered me," a resident Jesuit noted, "was that hard liquor was the social thing to drink rather than beer. They used to have all-you-can-drink nights every Friday night in New South, with hard liquor at open bars. And they would come staggering out of there at three or four in the morning. . . . It was a very destructive culture."[34] Drinking was legal in the District for those eighteen years and older. Alcohol was openly available in the dorms. In 1970 the Pub opened in the basement of Healy and competed with the Tombs as a gathering site, where students could meet, socialize, and drink.

Work

By the late sixties a far greater number of students were either working off campus or holding government-funded work-study positions on campus. In 1972 it was estimated that at least 550 students were combining employment with their academic work. The number working was probably much higher, as the placement office had more than two thousand applications for jobs on and off campus.[35] A rapidly growing number of students were securing internships on Capitol Hill or for nongovernmental agencies throughout the region, as Bill Clinton had in 1966 with the foreign relations committee, which his senator, William Fulbright, chaired. As dress became more and more casual in the classroom and on campus, students in coat and tie or dresses were a near-certain sign that they were headed to work downtown. Indeed, students increasingly planned their classes on a Monday-Wednesday-Friday or Tuesday-Thursday timetable to accommodate their work schedules, a trend that was facilitated by the growing number of courses that met twice weekly for seventy-five-minute periods.

Religion

The religious composition among undergraduates changed sharply in the late sixties. Georgetown schools that had been, in the sixties, overwhelmingly Catholic—the college (91%), nursing (89%), the Business School (85%)—were, by the mid-seventies, still decidedly Catholic in affiliation but much less so than just a few years before—the college (65%), nursing (66%), and Business School (69%). Schools that were much less Catholic in 1967—the School of Foreign Service (72%) and the Institute of Languages and Linguistics (65%)—had a bare majority of Catholics (SFS, 50.1%) or a Catholic minority (SLL, 45.3%) by 1975. Overall, the Catholic proportion of undergraduates had fallen from 81.9 percent in 1967 (3,261 out of 3,980) to 59.3 percent in 1975 (3,363 out of 5,665). In less than a decade the undergraduate population had gone from being heavily Catholic to being marginally so, almost full circle to where the institution's proportion of Catholics among its undergraduates had been during much of the nineteenth century. In 1976 President Henle noted that religious pluralism was now characteristic not only among students at Georgetown but also among its faculty and administration. He viewed this development not "as a dilution of its Roman Catholic heritage and atmosphere . . . [but] as the very expression of its American Catholic tradition and of its positive ecumenism."[36]

Nonetheless, as the proportion of Catholics at Georgetown began to decline dramatically, questions arose about the distinctiveness of Georgetown as a Catholic and Jesuit institution and how to preserve this character. Maintaining a critical mass of Jesuits in the classroom and administration seemed the key to preserving its Jesuit character; maintaining a minimal majority of Catholics at the undergraduate level seemed a necessary prerequisite to retaining its claim to being Catholic. The development of a first-rate theology department was also considered crucial in the institution's claim of a distinct religious character. The creation of imaginative and effective campus religious programs that would involve students, faculty, and staff within the academic context, was still another need if Georgetown was to continue to be rightly called Catholic. To underscore the importance of religion at the university, Henle created the new position of director of campus ministries, with vice presidential rank. Lawrence Madden, SJ, became the first director in 1971. The creation of this new position was also an implicit recognition of the growing pluralism of religious affiliation among undergraduates.

Compulsory retreats for Catholic students at off-campus sites continued into the middle sixties. Changing demographics and the virtual consensus of those Jesuits involved with the retreats that they were "a disaster area" persuaded the administration to replace the tradition with one of voluntary retreats or days of recollection.[37] "It seems to me," Thomas Fitzgerald, the academic vice president, wrote to the university chaplain, "that we must try to practice at this point some of the arts of salesmanship."[38] That conviction was no doubt reinforced by the dismal student turnout the following week—on a Sunday—for the Mass of the Holy Spirit, the traditional rite for the opening of the school year. In fact all compulsory practice of religion ended in the sixties, including weekday attendance at mass. Many of those charged with enforcing the practice, that is, the Jesuits in the student personnel office, were convinced that mandatory mass and retreats were counterproductive in shaping religious character. They finally convinced President Bunn, who had always insisted that the traditional religious regimen was a sine qua non for a Jesuit college, to drop the requirement of mandatory mass attendance. Once Bunn stepped down, all enforcement of religious practices ceased. Along with the shifting cultural values in the larger society, Vatican II's stress on religious freedom and nurturing individual moral and religious accountability no doubt played some part in these changes.

That this dramatic change in discipline and rules affected the religious practice of students is clear; to what extent is not. The *Hoya* in September 1968 declared, "Plainly speaking, Georgetown is no longer a Catholic campus," but one in which there could be found "enclaves which strive to express Christianity in terms suitable to our time."[39] One Jesuit faculty member found it moving that in the new atmosphere of freedom, "without any nudging from rules, structures or authority figures, so many students—somewhere between 1500 and 2000, by one estimate—weekly join in the Eucharistic worship . . . of the Church."[40] That factored out to a top percentage of nearly 60 percent of undergraduate Catholics, a much higher figure than the percentage of national Catholics who were weekly worshipers by the latter seventies.

Student Government and Media

In the sixties there were three student councils: the east campus council, the college council, and the nursing council. Sentiment grew within the two campuses that students would have a stronger voice in dealing with the administration if their councils were unified. The first attempt to unify student government began in 1965, when Bill Clinton, sophomore class president of the School of Foreign Service, started a campaign with others to have one student council for the five undergraduate schools. The student councils of both the college and the School of Foreign Service supported the principle of unification, but in a referendum in March 1966 a majority of undergraduates, including 85 percent of the college students, voted against it. In March 1968 there was a second effort made, again with no success.[41] The third time proved the charm as a subsequent referendum and constitutional convention in the 1968–69 academic year resulted in the formation of the Undergraduate Student Government, which replaced the existing three-campus polity. Jim Clark (**C** 1970) became its first president in the spring of 1969. This body was also given control of the allocation of funds to student organizations and activities.

In the latter sixties the *Hoya* officially declared itself to be the newspaper for the university, not just the college, as it had been for its first four decades plus. Ironically, at the very time the paper was claiming this central place in the print media on campus, a competitor arose in reaction to the intramural focus of the *Hoya*. In 1969 a group of sophomores, led by Stephen Pisinski, himself a reporter for the *Hoya,* were very unhappy with the parochial nature of the paper and looking for a way to do something about it. Encouraged by the resident Jesuit on their corridor, Raymond Schroth, the students broached the idea of a second paper to Robert Dixon, the director of student activities. Dixon told them that if they wanted to start another campus paper, he could find the funding for it. Schroth suggested the name the *Voice*, after the *Village Voice*, whose tabloid size and penchant for going beyond orthodox journalism they adopted. What they wanted to do, Pisinski said, was "to provide an opportunity for students who were interested in issues beyond the campus a chance to investigate and write about those issues as they thought they affected the student body."[42]

In the beginning they had correspondents from other campuses in the United States and Canada. This was part of the ideal of the *Voice* as a student paper that "was breaking out to the larger world."[43] The appearance of the *Voice* clearly had its impact on the editorial policies of the *Hoya*. By 1970 the older paper had broadened its news coverage to match the *Voice*'s extramural focus, and the *Hoya*'s editors in the fall of that year called for a merger of the two papers, as they now differed only in style, not content.[44] The *Voice* editors, however, suspected that the *Hoya*'s offer was a thinly disguised effort to take over the upstart journal and rejected the proposal.[45] One merger of campus publications did occur in this period. The School of Foreign Service's *Protocol* and the college's counterpart, *Ye Domesday Booke*, combined in 1967 to form one undergraduate yearbook under the older title of *Ye Domesday Booke*.

Choral Groups

The size of the glee club shrank in this period. By 1975 there were only twenty members, all males. In 1973 the club, accompanied by members of the National Symphony Orchestra, performed its fifty-third Mi-Careme (mid-Lenten) concert at the Kennedy Center. The highlight of the following year was the glee club's performance tour of Italy, including a concert for Pope Paul VI, in March 1974. At the end of that academic year, Paul Hume retired as conductor of the glee club, a position he had held since 1950. Paul Hill took over as director. The following year, 1974–75, marked the end of the Mi-Careme concerts, a tradition at Georgetown that dated to 1921.

Part of the reason for the smaller numbers in the glee club was the rise of other choral groups on campus. In the early 1970s students formed the Georgetown University Chorus under the direction of Paul Hill. In 1975 it had more than seventy members. The chorus presented a variety of programs ranging from classical oratorios such as Handel's *Messiah* to concert performances of musicals such as Gershwin's *Porgy and Bess*. In 1973 two sophomores, Gerald Elston and Joseph H. Coleman, founded the Georgetown Gospel Choir. Elston and Coleman started the group to promote cultural and social exchange among various ethnic groups. By 1974 it had twenty-nine members.

Debating

Debating reached a new plateau of success in the seventies. Between 1970 and 1974, the Philodemic Society won the annual national round-robin tournament three times, making it the number one debating team in the country. During that stretch Georgetown defeated teams from Northwestern, Harvard, the University of Southern California, the University of North Carolina, Dartmouth, Boston College, and the Massachusetts Institute of Technology. James Unger, Georgetown's coach, attributed the team's remarkable record to its depth. "Unlike most schools, our success is not oriented around one two-man team. We have several that could win in top competition."[46] Typically there would be twenty to thirty members that constituted the pool for selecting the two-person teams for the thirty or so tournaments that the Society participated in during an academic year. Building depth in debating teams was a Georgetown tradition that Unger's predecessor, William Reynolds, had established before his retirement in 1967.

By that time the character of debate was rapidly changing from a competition that combined eloquence with information to one in which the need to convey as much knowledge as possible in a short period of time defined the style of presentation. "The pace of the game is fast," one writer noted, "often so fast and furious that a debater sometimes sounds more like an auctioneer than an advocate." But selection of facts and logical development of them also were crucial to success. "It's really a public speaking chess match," one debater observed. Another thought of it as "a very technical art—a coldly analytical game in logic. To win you have to be able to develop strategies." Among the outstanding debaters for the Society in those years were Howard Beale (**C** 1972), Dallas Perkins (**C** 1972), Stewart Jay (**C** 1973), Tom Devine (**C** 1974), and Michael Bott (**C** 1975).[47]

WGTB

No student organization was more affected by the cultural revolution of the sixties than the radio station WGTB-FM. Since 1960 the station had been operating on the lower part of the FM band, the area set aside by the Federal Communications Commission (FCC) for educational/public broadcasting, and offered a breadth of programs, ranging from news, student and faculty discussions, music, and coverage of Georgetown athletic events. As programs expanded (by 1972 the station operated around the clock), the personnel did as well. By 1964 the staff numbered 150. In 1969 the board of directors authorized Frank Heyden to enlarge the power of the university's FM radio station from several hundred watts to three thousand watts. Heyden erected a new tower on the roof of Copley Hall for the FM transmitter antenna, and the station began reaching a much larger portion of the metropolitan community at its 90.1 frequency. In that same year radical students, a number of whom were already on the staff of WGTB, announced the goal of converting the station into an all-rock music format. Recruiting posters for WGTB now identified the station not as the "Voice of Georgetown," but as "Radio Free Georgetown." When Peter Chowka (**C** 1971) became the station manager in 1970, he implemented the rock-oriented programming. Nearly half the students on the staff left, either forced out or having resigned in protest of the radical change in the format of the station. To fill the void, Chowka brought in many nonstudents as disc jockeys. Father Heyden, frustrated that station management no longer controlled its programming, shortly thereafter resigned from his position as moderator of the station. When the newly installed antenna tower fell from the roof of Copley (either blown off by high winds, as the administration announced, or sabotaged by former staffers, as some suspected) in 1971, Henle closed the station, but only temporarily in order to find a way to reform it. He appointed a committee of faculty and student representatives as well as outside experts to make a thorough evaluation of WGTB and to provide recommendations regarding its future. That committee subsequently recommended that the station be continued as a student extracurricular activity and that, in order to ensure proper management, a full-time professional executive director be appointed and a board of review be created. After being off the air for a year and a half, WGTB returned with a full-time general manager, a five-person review board to oversee programming, and a stipulation that students make up at least 60 percent of the staff.[48]

Over the next several years the station acquired a reputation that transcended its regional market as a leader in alternative programming. The rock group Yes named it the best rock station in the nation. Several of its programs, such as the "Royal Stokes Jazz Show," became syndicated nationally. But the station became increasingly removed from university life, both in its focus and in the number of students involved with it. "WGTB stopped actively recruiting new student members," one former staffer recalled, "and seemed to constrict itself into a drug oriented clique. . . . Drug deals and station business were of equal importance."[49] It also ran afoul of the FCC for alleged obscenity in program matter and language. In December 1975 the administration removed the general manager and in his place put a student development administrator. Henle charged the review board with restructuring the station's management and operation. When the board found this charge impossible to accomplish while the station was continuing to operate, the university stepped in and closed the station a second time within six years, a move that a majority of Georgetown students supported.[50]

One of the members of the review board, James Walsh, SJ, told the faculty senate that "we have a marvelous resource in WGTB; it is an important resource of both the University and the Community. It is too important to be a mere student activity." The challenge, Walsh asserted, was for the university through WGTB to utilize the rich academic resources of the university to serve the cultural, social, and political needs of the larger community by creative selection of public affairs topics and music.[51]

In May 1976, President Henle appointed Robert Uttenweiler of Temple University as the new general manager. In announcing the appointment to the board of directors, the president, responding to a board member's question as to whether there was a real need for a radio station at Georgetown, pointed to the great potential the station had as the voice of a private, Catholic, Jesuit university. Should the university lose WGTB for whatever reason, Henle thought, it was extremely unlikely that it would ever get another FM station.[52] Uttenweiler proceeded to reorganize the staff and programming. In June 1976, WGTB returned to the air with twenty-four-hour programming.

Black Student Alliance and Other Minority Centers

When Wendell Robinson (1970) arrived at Georgetown, he found that there were fewer than twenty other African American undergraduates at the university. He felt isolated and unwanted; he could not lose the feeling that "the Georgetown student body was unsympathetic to the cause of blacks." That feeling of rejection was all too pervasive for the early black students on campus. Patricia Harris, the first black member of the board of directors, reporting on a meeting she had with African American students in the spring of 1971, had found them "alienated, not so much angry as hurt and rejected. They appear to have retreated into a shell."[53] Even in moments of success African Americans could still feel they were treated as less than equal. Sandy Chamblee (SLL 1972) was elected homecoming queen in 1969 but discovered that those running the weekend activities were apparently less than thrilled about her selection. Unlike past queens, she was not introduced at halftime during the football game and, at the homecoming dance, only at a late hour. The experience left her angry.[54] Looking to gain solidarity and fellowship, Robinson became one of the founders of the Black Student Alliance in 1968, for which the university provided a house at 3619 O Street. One of the first accomplishments of the Alliance was the organization of the first Black Awareness Week at Georgetown, to which they were able to attract Congresswoman Shirley Chisholm and film star Jane Fonda as speakers.[55]

In the late sixties other ethnic groups that organized included Cubans and Jews. The Cuban Student Association included a score or so of undergraduates, most of whom were émigrés from Cuba in the early 1960s.[56] In

Opposite: WGTB Studios.

(Georgetown University Archives)

1967 a Hillel chapter under the auspices of B'nai Brith was established. Chavurah House on N Street became the center for various social, intellectual, and religious activities for the two hundred or so undergraduate Jewish students in the university. A year before Chavurah House opened, an incident at a basketball game on campus brought a charge of blatant anti-Semitism upon the university. At the New York University (NYU)-Georgetown game in February 1966, several Georgetown students seeking television exposure (the game was televised nationally), donned costumes, including a pair who dressed as an Arab and the other wearing a German helmet. The pair came out before the game shouting "Sieg Heil!" and similar slogans, a routine they had performed at several earlier games without reaction. This time it provoked sensational accounts in Washington and New York papers that had the one Georgetown student in full storm trooper regalia, complete with swastika armbands. Angry letters from NYU's predominantly Jewish students and others, including the Anti-Defamation League, followed. Father Anthony Zeits, then the director of student development, apologized for any offense that the costumed pair had given, but insisted that no anti-Semitism had been intended. Georgetown sent a delegation, including Zeits and student government leaders, to explain the incident in person to their counterparts at NYU. At the end of their meeting they issued a joint statement that concluded, "In retrospect it seems clear that the incident can be most accurately described as innocent in origin, but which had possibly offensive implications. Clearly no malice was intended, nor was any question of Anti-Semitism Involved."[57]

Athletics

Athletics seemed to be the area of student life most insulated from the revolutionary changes and culture of dissent that infested campuses in the late sixties. In a student world that was questioning, if not outright rejecting, traditional authority, athletes continued to follow their coaches and to respect discipline and rules. Even in this bubble-like atmosphere, however, the culture of the student movement occasionally gained entrance. Ironically it was Georgetown's most successful sport of the era—track—that was one of two Georgetown sports to experience a revolt against authority in the year that the student revolution became a critical issue, 1968.

An era ended in 1969 with the retirements of the athletic director, Jack Hagerty, and the director of intramurals, George Murtagh. Hagerty had been with Georgetown as football coach and then director of athletics since 1932, with the exception of his three years in the navy during World War II. Murtagh and Maurice Dubofsky, who died suddenly in January 1970, had been with Hagerty nearly as long. Col. Robert Sigholz, who had come to the university in 1967 as director of the ROTC, became athletic director upon Hager-

Francis X. Rienzo, *left*,
director of athletics, 1972–99.
(Photo by J. Russell Lawrence.
Georgetown University Archives)

ty's retirement, despite vocal opposition from many students, including the captains of seven varsity teams. His strong personality proved to be his undoing in the office. The long-running feud between Sigholz and basketball coach Jack McGee, which became newspaper fodder in 1971–72, ended in the late winter of 1972, when both resigned, McGee voluntarily and Sigholz constrained to.[58] Frank Rienzo took over the duties of athletic director while remaining coach of track.

A notable development of the period was the establishment of Hoyas Unlimited. In the spring of 1970 a group of undergraduates initiated the formation of a boosters' club comprising students, alumni, faculty, and athletic staff, not only to promote the various athletic teams, but also to raise funds to support them, particularly the minor sports at Georgetown. The club's initial project provided permanent lights for the lower athletic field. Eventually, through the leadership of Patrick McArdle (**C** 1972) and others, Hoyas Unlimited became an umbrella organization under which nineteen support groups, ranging from the Hoya Hoop Club to the Hoya Crease Club, effectively raised funds for Georgetown athletic teams in various intercollegiate sports.

From its return to Georgetown for a single-game season in 1964, intercollegiate football grew slowly in the sixties as a club sport, with the administration exercising close control over its schedule. In 1966 the board of directors sanctioned a four-game schedule against other club teams, with Mike Agee as coach. In 1967 the board approved a five-game season, which the faculty assembly had recommended with the understanding that no scholarships or grants-in-aid would be given. In 1968 Maurice "Mush" Dubofsky, an assistant under Jack Hagerty from 1933 to 1948, returned to Georgetown to become head coach. In his first year he went 3-2 with wins over Iona, Seton Hall, and Saint Peter's and losses to Fordham and Catholic. In 1970, Scotty Glacken, who had played for Dubofsky at Saint John's and been his assistant at Georgetown, succeeded him upon Dubofsky's sudden death in January. That year football again became a varsity sport and the schedule expanded to eight games. Under Glacken the Hoyas had winning seasons for three straight years. Quarterback Jeff Gray, running backs John Burke and Ralph Edwards, and defensive back Bill Sherry were standouts.

After a rebuilding year, the Hoyas, with nineteen starters returning in 1973, went 6-2, winning handily against Duquesne, Manhattan, Saint Peter's, Fordham, Hofstra, and Catholic University. The 35–10 victory in New York over Fordham, who had become Georgetown's chief rival in the new era of football, was to Coach Glacken "the finest thing that has ever happened to me either as a player or a coach."[59] John Burke, senior running back, set six school records during his final season, including most yards rushing (858), most touchdowns (15) in a season, and most touchdowns in a game (4). The 6-2 record was good enough to rank the Hoyas tenth among Division III teams in the East. That same year Pierce O'Donnell and other alumni formed the Gridiron Club to support and aid in the development of Georgetown football.

Jack McGee, who replaced Tommy O'Keefe in 1966 as basketball coach, had over six years a record slightly below .500—sixty-seven wins and seventy-one defeats. The high-water mark during his tenure came in 1970 when the team's eighteen wins earned a spot in the sixteen-team National Invitational Tournament (NIT). Despite the fact that the NIT by then was no longer the premier tournament in basketball, but a consolation competition for those not quite good enough to be among the thirty-two teams that qualified for the NCAA tournament, making any tournament for the first time since 1953 was a very big thing for Georgetown. "NIT! 'THE PROMISED LAND'" screamed the *Hoya*'s headline. This achievement, said Georgetown observers, could be the breakthrough that the team had long sought. The exposure and recognition that the NIT tournament would give them might well open the basketball-rich markets, particularly in New York, to the recruitment of top-flight players by Georgetown and move basketball from the middle-of-the-pack status it had occupied for the past quarter century to the elite level.

Georgetown met Louisiana State University (LSU) in the first round of the tournament at Madison Square Garden. LSU, with All-American Pete Maravich, was heavily favored. Georgetown had a solid starting five, led by

Charlie Adrian. In the game Georgetown's tough defense, anchored by Mike Laughna and captain Mike Laska, proved surprisingly effective at containing LSU's high-powered offense. Laska held Maravich to 20 points, much below his average. Sophomore Arthur White had a breakout game in leading Hoya scorers with 22 points. But LSU managed to hold on by the slimmest of margins, 83–82. Even so, Georgetown, with the great press it had received from its razor-thin loss, and with three starters returning, thought that the team had taken a big step toward turning the corner into a new era. Unfortunately, the next season proved a very disappointing one, and the big-time recruits from New York or elsewhere failed to materialize. Things got disastrously worse the following year when the team managed to win only three games. Jack Magee resigned, and the search for a new coach commenced.

Charles Deacon, the director of admissions, thought that hiring a black basketball coach would be a giant step in the university's outreach to its surrounding community "and [would] establish a better identity for Georgetown within the community." Deacon knew of an ideal prospect for the position—John Thompson, who had been a star at Carroll High School when

John Thompson, Jr., basketball coach, 1972–99. (Mitchell Layton Photography)

Deacon had been at Gonzaga and had gone on to further success at Providence College and with the Boston Celtics. He broached the idea with President Henle and his assistant, Dan Altobello, who both thought it was a fine idea. Henle asked Deacon to chair the search committee and attempt to get Thompson selected as a candidate. Through Maurice Lancaster, who was assistant director of admissions and a friend of Thompson, Deacon convinced Thompson to apply for the vacant position. Deacon had little difficulty persuading a majority of the committee (two faculty, two alumni, and two students) of Thompson's qualifications as well as the benefits to the university of having a black head coach. "Most of us," Deacon commented much later, "were very aware of what an impact a successful basketball team, with a black coach, would have on the image of Georgetown with blacks, both locally and nationally."[60]

The committee recommended 5 to 2 that the president appoint Thompson. In announcing Thompson's appointment, Frank Rienzo, now the athletic director, told the *Washington Post* in March, "We don't expect John Thompson to work a miracle, but we'll be happy if he does."

Little did Rienzo realize just how much happiness Thompson would bring him over the next twenty-three seasons.[61]

Utilizing the new National Collegiate Athletic Association (NCAA) rule that made freshmen eligible for varsity competition, Thompson often started three or four freshmen, including three he had brought with him from Saint Anthony's: Merlin Wilson, Greg Brooks, and Jonathan Smith. The team found itself overmatched against such powers as Maryland, Saint John's, Saint Joseph's, and Virginia but scored upsets against Saint Bonaventure, Fordham, Seton Hall, and Boston College. They finished 12-14. Smith was the leading scorer. Wilson set a school single-season record of 366 rebounds. During Thompson's second season, the Hoyas were clearly an improved club and by mid-February, with a 13-9 record, seemed headed to the NIT for the second time in five years. But four straight losses at the end of the year cost them an invitation and a winning season.

The 1974–75 season promised to be a breakthrough for Thompson's team, with virtually all starters returning and two promising freshman guards, Derrick Jackson and Craig Esherick, as well as a center, Ed Hopkins, now joining them. The start of the season did not disappoint, as the team's record stood at 7-2 by January. At the end of that month, however, their win total still stood at seven, but the losses had climbed to eight. Six consecutive losses left many in Hoya Nation with little patience and set some to grumbling about this black coach and his by now predominantly black team. Despite a win on the road against a ranked Penn State team, as spectators at McDonough rose for the national anthem at the next home game, someone on the roof of McDonough unfurled a banner through an open window that read, "Thompson, Nigger Flop Must Go." The banner was quickly removed, and few in the gymnasium had actually seen it, but the racial slur hung over the place like a lethal cloud. The next day at a press conference, President Henle condemned the incident as "the work of a couple of bigots." In a statement the team said that they had all come to Georgetown specifically to play for Coach Thompson and that this shameful act only made them more committed to playing for him.[62] The players proceeded to back up their commitment by winning their next five games, eighteen games in all that season, including victories over George Washington and West Virginia in the Eastern Collegiate Athletic Conference Southern Division playoff. What Georgetown coaches had failed to do for thirty-two years, Thompson had achieved in his third season. For the first time since 1943, Georgetown was in the NCAA tournament.

The Hoyas met Central Michigan in the first round of the NCAA tournament at Tuscaloosa, Alabama. In a game that prefigured later ones that would earn the team the sobriquet "Heart Attack Hoyas," Georgetown had the ball in the waning moments of the game with the score tied. Jonathan Smith took a jump shot at the top of the key that caromed high off the rim toward the foul line, where Smith and a Michigan player collided as they

both went for the ball. Smith was charged with the foul, although the game film showed that his opponent, not Smith, had initiated the contact. Central Michigan won 77–75.[63]

Georgetown versus West Virginia, 1975. (Georgetown University Archives)

The crew, coached by Tony Johnson, dominated small-college rowing in the latter sixties, as it won the Dad Vail championships three straight years from 1966 to 1968. Previously the Hoyas had won the Dad Vails in 1962 and 1964. The 1968 team, led by Mike Vespoli (**B** 1968), finished the season undefeated. Jay Forster (**B** 1971) and Erik Meyers (**F** 1971) were also prominent members of the team during this period.

Lacrosse, coming off its most successful season (4-4) in 1964, expanded and upgraded its schedule in 1965. In 1968 the team achieved its first winning season. Led by Bill Guilfoyle, Phil Porter, and Charles Blazek, the team went 6-2. After a second winning season in 1969 (8-5) against tougher competition, the sport gained varsity status, and Georgetown joined the Southern Lacrosse Association, a division of the United States Intercollegiate Lacrosse Association. Unfortunately, recognition as a varsity sport brought no scholarships, equipment, or budget. Players attempted with limited success to raise money themselves by various means. Varsity competition proved to be a rough transition for the team. "We lost a lot of games," Jim Feeley, the coach from 1971 to 1973, recalled. "We were essentially still a club team."

By the spring of 1975, the *Hoya* was referring to the team as "the laughing stock of the Athletic Department."[64]

Since its inception in 1952 as a nonscholarship varsity sport, playing a limited regional schedule that included national powers Maryland, Howard, and Navy, soccer had enjoyed only two winning seasons (1959 and 1960). At the end of another losing season in the fall of 1965, the team demanded that the athletic department find a coach for them who was committed to winning and could instill discipline. In Ricardo Mendoza, an air force sergeant, they found their man. Mendoza brought ambition, discipline, and infectious enthusiasm to Georgetown soccer. Relying increasingly on Latin Americans with extensive soccer experience, Mendoza in his first year led the team to a school record by winning seven matches against four losses, including a bitter 3–2 defeat by Maryland. The team's success brought excitement about the sport for the first time on the Hilltop. The *Hoya* began running a weekly column by Mendoza on the intricacies of the sport ("Get a Kick Out of Soccer"). The coach was confident that Georgetown was capable of gaining national recognition in the sport and strengthened the team's schedule as a means to achieve it. The team, led by fullback Dick Callahan, goalie Dick Gregorie, and two talented juniors, Alfredo Montero and Emilé Sicré, started the season by defeating George Washington, American, and Catholic University and tying Morgan State. Entering the Maryland game undefeated, the team battled the perennial power evenly for most of the contest before giving up two late goals. The last month of the season proved a disaster as Georgetown lost six of its last seven games and finished the year 4-6-1.

With Montero and Sicré returning as cocaptains—and an array of underclass talent in forward Jacques Gelardin, halfback Ignacio Gil-Czares, goalie Luis Martinez, and Roger Epee, a freshman halfback from Cameroon—the *Hoya* judged the team "a possible powerhouse" in 1968.[65] After two dominating opening victories against Towson State and Gallaudet, the team lost badly to Howard 5–0, then played a scoreless contest against Maryland before losing 1–0 on a goal in the final two minutes to the eventual NCAA champion. It finished the year 6-4, its four losses coming to top-ranked teams (Howard, Maryland, Morgan State, and Navy). Roger Epee, a freshman, made the All-South team. The following season, with most of its top players back and with the notable addition of fullback Roberto Hoguin, the team again had a strong start with three wins (Towson, American, Gallaudet), an impressive tie against Howard, and a frustrating loss (2–1) to an excellent Loyola squad. As with the 1967 season, the team collapsed in the second half, with only one win (George Washington) and four losses (Morgan State, Maryland, Baltimore, and Navy).

When the air force transferred Mendoza out of the region in 1970, an alumnus, Paul Kennedy (**C** 1967), who had cocaptained the team in 1965 and 1966, succeeded him as coach. With Mendoza's departure, the Latin

American players disappeared as well. The result was a squad that lacked depth. The season was a woeful one, with only three victories in twelve contests. Over the next several years, despite a much weaker schedule, Georgetown enjoyed only one winning season, going 6-3-5 in 1972. The team's nadir came two years later when it won just four games out of fourteen. A sport that had seemed in the mid-sixties to hold such promise for Georgetown athletics once again fell far short of success, much less of attaining national prominence.

The mid-seventies marked the rise of women's sports at Georgetown, the result of the transforming effect of Title IX of the Education Act of 1972, which prohibited any discrimination against women in educational programs and activities, including sports. Georgetown liberally interpreted this sports clause to mean that the university had to provide an equal number of major sports and an equal number of scholarships for men and women. Basketball and track were designated as the major sports for men. Track and either basketball or volleyball were designated as the major sports for women. Scholarships equal in number to those given for men's track and basketball were awarded to women in track, basketball, and volleyball, with the determination to be made in the future whether basketball or volleyball would be the second major sport for women. At the time, volleyball, although only established in 1972, had proven to be more successful than women's basketball. In 1975 the university also established women's teams in lacrosse, swimming, and crew. In that same year the field hockey team went undefeated in nine matches against regional competition and placed third in the Maryland state tournament. Leading the Hoya defense were Jane Milliken, Jane Burke, Eleanor Meredith, Carroll Bull, and goalie Lisa Fronc. Aileen Ruch and Carrie Vibert powered the offense.

Track continued in the mid-sixties to be the most nationally prominent sport at Georgetown, and cross-country was the strength of Georgetown track. In the fall of 1964 the cross-country team finished its regular season 8-0 in dual meets. They capped their season by winning the Intercollegiate Association of Amateur Athletes in America (IC4A) championship by the overwhelming margin of 20 points over their chief rivals Notre Dame and Villanova. Georgetown had six finishers among the top eighteen. Joe Lynch finished first in a meet-record time of 24:41.3 for the five-mile course. A week later at a snow-packed, four-mile course in Michigan, the team finished sixth at the NCAA championships. Lynch was again the top Hoya runner, finishing eighth. All in all, the team completed the most successful season in the history of Georgetown's harriers.

In the indoor season of 1965, Joe Lynch won the mile in 4:06 at the Boston Knights of Columbus games. Eamon O'Reilly won the two-mile event at the later Knights of Columbus meet in New York with a time of 8:56.6. At that meet Georgetown also won the two-mile relay with Lynch, Jeff Moreland, Rick Urbina, and Ed Duchini. In the late winter of 1965, Duchini won

Rick Urbina winning the
1000-meter event in record
time at Madison Square
Garden, 1966. *(Ye Domesday
Booke)*

the IC4A championship in the six hundred. Georgetown as a team finished
seventh at the IC4As.

The following fall Captain O'Reilly, Urbina, Jim McDermott, and Bob Zieminski ran away with the IC4As, winning by an even greater margin than in
1964—28 points. O'Reilly's winning time of 24:24.1 eclipsed the record set by
Lynch the previous year. In the indoor season of 1966, Urbina won the
1,000-meter event at the New York Track and Field Federation Meet in the
record time of 2:08.8. Urbina was also on the winning two-mile relay team,
together with O'Reilly, Robert Zieminski, and Paul Perry. O'Reilly was victori-
ous in the two mile. At the IC4As that winter, Urbina prevailed in the 880,
and O'Reilly won the two-mile race in 8:57.8. The Hoyas were fourth in the
overall standings. Later, at the NCAA indoor championships in Detroit, Urbina
took top honors in the 880-yard run by sprinting into the lead in the final
stretch to win in 1:51.9. The team finished sixth.

Over the following three fall seasons, the team failed to repeat its IC4A
cross-country triumph of 1965. The 1968 season was particularly disappointing, as the team finished the regular season 6-1, including a dual-meet besting of Villanova, the current IC4A champion, only to finish second to the
Wildcats in the IC4As, despite Georgetown's Steve Stageberg's winning top
individual honors.

That deflating finish to the cross-country season seemed to bring to the
surface the discontent that many team members had about Coach Benedek's
training methods and treatment of the team. At a meeting in early December

to plan for the coming indoor season, a dispute broke out between Benedek and some members of the team about the level of preparation they would need to maintain over the Christmas break. Unvoiced was the conviction of a majority of the team that Benedek was prone to overtraining them, by insisting on two-a-day training sessions and cramming in long runs up to fourteen miles, which some thought was responsible for the frequent injuries and cases of mononucleosis that struck the team. Many also resented the negative approach that Benedek used as an instrument of motivation but that many thought backfired by eroding their confidence. At a second meeting that day, the team voted to boycott Benedek and train under captain Steve Stageberg. The coach, they declared, was too authoritarian, incapable of communicating with them, and wrong-headed in his methods. As one of the leaders of the revolt put it, Benedek was committed to the European system of training that stressed quantity: "We favor the American system, which stresses quality [of workouts]."[66] Another top runner charged that Benedek's reputation for body-breaking training methods and his authoritarian attitude was badly hurting their recruiting efforts, especially in the New York area, which was a premier source for distance runners.[67] Benedek's response was that, far from being overworked, the disappointing results of the IC4As and the NCAAs showed that they had failed because they had not trained hard enough. "The boys had the potential to be champions," he asserted, "but they just didn't work hard enough."[68]

The athletic board set up a special committee to investigate the matter. On December 14 the chair of the committee, Royden Davis, SJ, announced that the team would train and run under Benedek or not at all. The board did promise a further review of the issue at the end of the school year. The athletic department thought the matter resolved. When practice resumed in the beginning of January, however, only four runners showed up to work under Benedek. This led to the cancellation of track for the rest of the academic year and the decision not to renew Benedek's contract. Rumors swelled about the impending discontinuation of track as a major sport at Georgetown. Captain Stageberg thought, "The program's gone."[69] It was not.

A search committee was set up to find a successor to Benedek. In the spring of 1969 Frank Rienzo, who had had great success as a coach at Archbishop Molloy High in New York City, was named head coach of Georgetown track. One of Rienzo's goals was to make the program more comprehensive, to expand it beyond the relay and distance events on which track at Georgetown had traditionally concentrated. He began to recruit hurdlers, pole vaulters, shot putters, and sprinters as well as the traditional middle- and long-distance runners. He also restored dual meets to both the indoor and outdoor seasons of the team. His first great success came in a traditional area of competition for the Hoyas, the steeplechase, when Joseph Lucas (**C** 1972) won that event at the Penn Relays in the spring of 1972 and later in June won the NCCA championship in the steeplechase. For his achievements

Joseph Lucas, NCAA steeplechase champion, 1972. (Georgetown University Archives)

Lucas was given the Outstanding Track and Field Competitor Award and named an All-American for the second year.

Lucas's triumph was one of the few bright spots in the sport at Georgetown over the next few years. Cross-country in particular suffered a precipitous drop in competitiveness at the regional and national levels. Whether Georgetown recruiting suffered from the residue of the dispute between coach and team in 1968–69, or whether the wider net Georgetown was now casting brought in fewer top-flight, middle-distance runners, the cross-country team's performance at the IC4As plummeted: eighth in 1969, twenty-second in 1970, sixteenth in 1971, and fourteenth in 1972.

At the end of the 1974 outdoor track season, Rienzo stepped aside as coach to devote all his time to being athletic director. His assistant of two years, Joe Lang, became head coach. Lang's particular coaching strength was in cross-country, where the Hoyas had won seven dual meets (a school record) in 1973. Under head coach Lang, the team handily surpassed that success the following fall. Behind cocaptain Jack Fultz, the Hoyas sent out a very young but very talented group: sophomores Gordon Oliver, Ken Moliski, and Tim Conheeny and freshmen Jim Peterson and Mark Ogden. They went undefeated in thirteen dual-meet competitions, including victories over perennial powers Villanova, Penn State, and William and Mary. Led by Peterson, they finished fourth and seventh at the IC4As and NCAA championships, respectively. Peterson became the first freshman in Georgetown history to be named an All-American. The following fall the team, minus Fultz but with freshman David Dobrzynski, completed Georgetown's best back-to-back, cross-country seasons. The following April, on a freakishly warm day in Massachusetts, Fultz shocked the road-running world when he won the Boston Marathon, taking the lead at the six-mile mark and never losing it.

Student Activism and the District of Columbia

Title I of the Higher Education Act of 1965 authorized partial funding for community service and continuing education programs that universities and colleges undertook. Georgetown officially committed itself to provide community service when it cosponsored, together with Howard University, a conference called "The University and the Community: An Urban Affairs Conference toward Improving Local Community Leadership" held at Howard in December 1966. In 1967 the law center, with a grant through Title I, established an Institute for Urban Service Aides that provided courses in sociology, political science, psychology, and the history of cities to employees of the city's human service agencies. At the same time, the Institute of Languages and Linguistics, with a grant from the Office of Education, developed a master's program in theoretical and applied linguistics to prepare inner-city teachers to offer special English courses for their students. The departments of English, government, and history developed master of arts in teaching programs that were especially aimed at those who taught in urban schools.

But it was at the student level that the university contributed the most in its involvement with the city. In the late spring of 1965, the *Hoya* noted the emergence of the "new breed" at Georgetown, students intent on "social engagement."[70] A social consciousness stirred by the civil rights movement and the progressive ideals and policies of the Kennedy-Johnson administration led students at Georgetown, as elsewhere, to commit themselves to a Peace Corps–like mission of assisting and raising up the poor and disadvantaged in their midst. In the middle of the sixties, that commitment was epitomized by the Georgetown University Community Action Program (GUCAP), which had its beginning in 1964 as an outreach instrument created by John Haughey, SJ, and the Main Campus Sodality. GUCAP was an umbrella or coordinating force for various student urban projects. "Our purpose," the group stated in its initial report, "is to find the projects, tell you what they are, and serve you in their execution in any way necessary." Initially it coordinated twenty-two projects, ranging from tutorial programs to volunteer work at community hospitals to organizations promoting civil rights.[71] A veteran faculty member, Riley Hughes, remarked that GUCAP's ultimate

Members of GUCAP in action tutoring. (Georgetown University Archives)

purpose was "to make the idea of service a part of the University's blood-stream."[72]

Within a year eight hundred students were involved with GUCAP. The *Hoya* observed in the fall of 1964 that from a handful of volunteers eighteen months earlier, GUCAP "has mushroomed into the largest student group on campus."[73] By 1966 Georgetown students were taking part in fifty-four social action projects in the District. Through outreach efforts such as those GUCAP promoted, the image of Georgetown as an ivory tower for upper-class Catholics began to change.[74] Helping to change that image as well was the ending of segregation as a policy at Georgetown hospital in 1966, when the board of directors instructed the hospital administration to assign rooms to patients on the basis of age and sex only, although it left open the possibility of a patient securing a roommate of the same race at the patient's request.[75]

Georgetown and the Civil Rights Movement

In March 1965 a dozen Georgetown students led by Richard McSorley, SJ, drove to Selma, Alabama, to participate in a memorial service for a Washington clergyman who had just been murdered there. One of the participants, Phil Verveer, returned to campus to report to the east campus student council. In an emergency meeting, the council passed three resolutions expressing their solidarity with the civil rights movement, establishing an emergency fund to provide support, and starting a petition campaign to secure federal protection for civil rights workers.[76] On St. Patrick's Day, Verveer led several hundred Georgetown students and faculty in a march to the White House to deliver a letter of praise for the Voting Rights Bill, which President Johnson had proposed to Congress two nights earlier. Later that week, twenty-five faculty and students joined Martin Luther King Jr. for the Selma-to-Montgomery march, following the violence at the Pettis Bridge on Bloody Sunday.[77]

GUCAP sponsored two trips to Mississippi in the academic year 1966–67. Four students went to Grenada in December to support a local boycott of white merchants aimed at ending violence against blacks in the newly integrated schools. A larger group of ten traveled to Sunflower County in April to assist in the drive to register black voters in the wake of the Voting Rights Act of 1965.[78]

In the following school year, GUCAP turned its attention to the civil rights of the university's own workers, specifically to attempts to unionize them. The organization pressed the university to take a stand on the issue, but the director of nonacademic personnel replied that there was no "great need for a union at Georgetown."[79] A year later, in the spring of 1969, GUCAP members, joined by the newly formed Black Student Alliance, assisted a Teamsters local in a union-organizing drive by persuading workers, through pamphlets and personal contacts, to register for a vote on union recognition. Despite student optimism that the drive had been successful, the workers rejected by a nearly two-to-one margin unionization under the Teamsters.[80]

At GUCAP's initiative, students in March 1968 formed the Georgetown University Committee to Support the Poor People's Campaign (GUPPC), the effort of Martin Luther King and the Southern Christian Leadership Conference (SCLC) to repeat in the coming summer the march on Washington of five years earlier, this time to protest economic discrimination. Then came King's shocking assassination on April 3. The next day, after a noon memorial service in the quadrangle, the cochairs of GUPPC led a delegation of hundreds of Georgetown students in another march to the White House, this time delivering a petition for the declaration of a national day of mourning for King.[81] They had just delivered the petition and had positioned themselves in Lafayette Park to sing some civil rights songs when the police ordered Father Haughey and other leaders of the group to "get these kids the hell out of here and get them out fast." Immediately north of the square, buildings on Fourteenth Street had begun to burn, as rioting began. Haughey got the Georgetown group back to campus as quickly as possible. There, with many others, they watched the eastern sky fill with smoke. "Then it got dark and . . . you could really see [the flames]," Haughey remembered. "Kids were crying because there was a sense that something had died."[82]

It would be three days before the fires and looting and rioting ceased, with nine hundred businesses in ruins, property damage of nearly $25 million, and eight people dead.[83] At the law center on Friday, just blocks from the spreading disorder, school administrators dismissed classes. Deans McCarthy and Molleur, as well as faculty and some two hundred students, made their way to the nearby Criminal Courts of the District in response to a frantic call from court officials for legal assistance in processing suspects. McCarthy and Molleur helped coordinate the legal representation that many attorneys voluntarily offered for those arrested by stationing students in each of the District courts to determine where there was need of legal assistance. The center's faculty and legal interns provided guidance for the lawyers on such recent legal developments as the Bail Reform Act by holding briefing sessions every hour for three days. Faculty and students organized an information center where they provided news, by phone and in person, to families inquiring about relatives, and they issued updates on the situation to quell rumors. Over that long weekend, more than 1,800 hearings of felony cases took place. It was, as one faculty member observed later, a kind of baptism by fire into the field of community service.[84]

Students on the main campus staffed a collection center at Holy Trinity School for food, clothing, and bedding for those made homeless in the violence that had engulfed central and northeastern Washington. Other students, such as Bill Clinton, made deliveries to those in the affected areas along the 14th Street corridor that horrific weekend. On campus several hundred National Guardsmen had taken over McDonough Gymnasium as a base. That Monday a student group issued a call for a three-day fast and sponsored a teach-in at the Hall of Nations on the problem of poverty in urban America.[85]

Professor Jesse Mann, who had earlier been designated as the coordinator for the university's involvement with the upcoming Poor People's Campaign, persuaded the university to establish a Planning Committee for Southern Christian Leadership Conference Affairs to prepare the university for the impending campaign as well as for aftershocks of the recent riots. The committee recommended in late May that the university "offer full cooperation to Resurrection City," the name given to the encampment that SCLC planned to erect on the Mall, including having certain representatives of Georgetown visit the site and meet with SCLC officials as well as allowing SCLC people to conduct teach-ins on the lawns and classrooms of the school. The administrator of the Jesuit Community at Georgetown, Paul Rock, who had previously served as the pastor of a black parish in Southern Maryland, sent several truckloads of goods and provisions to the Resurrection City encampment.[86]

University officials feared that protesters might attempt to disrupt the upcoming commencement in early June. As it turned out, there were some efforts to do just that. A group of radical students staged a sit-in outside the president's office in Second Healy. A student group petitioned Mayor Walter Washington, the commencement speaker, not to participate in the event. Other dissidents sought to bring in support from other universities as well as from Resurrection City in creating disturbances at graduation. The Tuesday before graduation, there was another shock to the nation's psyche. Robert Kennedy, the presidential candidate who had assumed the antiwar and anti-injustice mantles of Gene McCarthy and Martin Luther King, was gunned down in California, just two months after King's assassination. As the nation mourned anew, most of the senior week activities, including the prom, were canceled. Despite a strong sentiment among many students that commencement not take place, the administration decided to go through with it.

With ROTC cadets posted at the steps of the stage to repel any stage stormers, the commencement came off without incident. In his homily at the Baccalaureate Mass, Father Dexter Hanley observed how "the sharp crack of an assassin's gun has blasted the ears of all America. . . . But this graduation will be a fitting tribute to him whom we mourn today in proportion as we rededicate ourselves to the ideals for which we stand and which he pursued. . . . [T]he demand grows ever louder for action and for action *now*. If you do not pledge an all-out assault against racial and economic injustice, you betray your ideals, deny your dreams, and crush the hopes of mankind."[87] Looking back on the spring, the academic vice president concluded that the university had to continue to take meaningful steps "to relate [itself] to the urban crisis."[88]

Vietnam and the New Left Come to Georgetown

The other major source of the cultural and social maelstrom that was engulfing the nation's campuses by the late sixties was Vietnam. Widespread opposition to the war at Georgetown developed later than at many other
prestigious universities, but when it did, it became a powerful force. In the
fall of 1965, Georgetown students were involved in the formation of a pro-
war group, the student ad hoc committee for freedom in Vietnam. A daylong
symposium at a Washington hotel, sponsored by the group, served as a
counter teach-in to support the U.S. effort in Vietnam as part of the "war
against Communism." Frank Keating, the president of the Yard and one of
the organizers of the event, announced that the symposium was "an answer
to the demonstrations, picket lines and civil disobedience of those who
would have us withdraw from Viet Nam." At its conclusion the several hundred students, chanting slogans such as "Win the War in Vietnam! Beat the
Vietcong!" marched to the nearby Vietnamese embassy.[89] Student opinion in
the mid-sixties strongly supported the war. In a poll conducted by the *Hoya*
in February 1966, 62 percent of the two thousand students polled approved
of the Johnson administration's Vietnam policy.[90]

By the end of 1966, student concern about the war, if not outright opposition to it, was clearly growing. Before the close of the year a few students,
including Jamie McCormick, began a Student Peace Union chapter on campus, which by the following spring claimed more than seventy members.[91]
The *Hoya* reported that, in a peace demonstration at the Pentagon in October
1967, at least 130 of the marchers were from Georgetown. Fifty Georgetown
students participated in a counterdemonstration led by the Young Americans
for Freedom, which had just established a chapter at Georgetown.[92] In the
spring of 1968, Academic Vice President Thomas Fitzgerald wrote that the
uncertainty about the reach of the military draft was increasingly leading
students to believe that they likely would be conscripted for the war. "During
the next few weeks," he went on, "their frustrations will probably be intensified. The campus may well be a restless and angry one."[93] This proved not to
be, as the draft touched few Georgetown students. As a new academic year
began in September 1968, Fitzgerald again warned that students would reflect the "unrest and frustration" of the nation. The coming year, he thought,
"will not be an easy one. . . . It is clear that we now have on campus a small,
antagonistic group of the New Left."[94]

The new group was the Georgetown chapter of the Students for a Democratic Society (SDS), which had evolved from its founding in 1960 as a reform movement to an anarchistic, revolutionary group by the decade's last
years. The SDS surfaced at Georgetown during registration in September
when they set up a table under a banner that read "Department of Liberation" and passed out copies of a thirty-page booklet that they identified as a

radical handbook for the Georgetown students.[95] The following month Fitzgerald reported that, at a regional meeting of the organization in Washington, SDS members had agreed that each university chapter in the city should sponsor demonstrations and teach-ins and work to effect a student strike in early November.[96] The SDS did attempt to organize a boycott of classes on election eve and election day in November, but the attempt fell flat. SDS had too few members, less than a score, and too little support on campus to accomplish such a mass protest.

By the beginning of 1969 it was palpably clear that life on campus had changed in a fundamental way. Perhaps as never before, it had become part of larger society; indeed, it seemed it had become a cauldron for all those forces raging in the larger world. As Royden Davis observed during the Tropaia exercises in 1969,

There was a time perhaps when campuses were serene, havens of quiet dialogue. The athlete was king and ritual was always relevant. There was a time perhaps when change came into our lives with grace and gentleness, so that the unknown was romantic and fear was little felt. Today the world is very much with us on college campuses. Upon graduation no one really goes out there—for the world with strife and war, with murder and hunger, with revolt and passion, with fear untempered by hope stalks the groves of academe or seizes her halls with angry power. Change is rapid, fearsome, intrusive. Old men fear the chaos they think they see while young men fear—not chaos—but established placidity which bottles up change.[97]

In the late winter of 1969 the freshman class staged a public, Guy Fawkes–style revolt against the Georgetown establishment, specifically student government and the *Hoya*. Organized by their class officers, hundreds of freshmen poured out of their dorms onto the quadrangle where over the blaring sounds of a rock band and kegs of beer they proceeded to burn copies of the *Hoya* and an effigy of "Joe Hoya." They also stated their intention to withdraw from the Yard, the college student council. For the remainder of the semester, freshman representatives boycotted the council's meetings.[98]

A few days after the freshman revolt, there was a more traumatic protest on the main campus. The editor of the *Hoya*, Donald Casper, had invited the mayor of San Francisco, Joseph Alioto, who was a friend of the Casper family, to give a talk at Georgetown. When the SDS learned that the mayor, who had recently gained notoriety by ordering police onto the campus of San Francisco State to break up a strike organized by radical groups on campus, was to be a speaker at Georgetown, they made plans to disrupt his talk. The FBI, learning of the plans, warned Georgetown officials. A group of approximately eighty protestors, most from other universities in the region, confronted Alioto as he was escorted by student ushers from Third Healy into Gaston Hall. Alioto and his entourage managed to force their way into the hall. As soon as the party made their way to the stage, an SDS member at the hall's control panel turned off the lights. In the darkness, the doors were opened to allow in those protestors still outside. A few persons in the audience stormed the stage in an attempt to control the microphone at the podium. In the ensuing struggle the podium was overturned and the microphone temporarily cut off. When the lights were finally turned back on, Alioto got to the podium and attempted to address the crowd. One of the demonstrators still on the stage began shouting obscenities into the microphone, and other protestors in the hall echoed them. Giving up on the effort to have the mayor address the audience, the dean of student activities and some students then led him out of Gaston by a rear exit and escorted him down through Old North to the Jesuit residence, where he gave his talk in a small parlor.[99]

The Georgetown community, including its students, reacted to the aborted lecture with outrage. A student message of apology to the mayor quickly amassed several thousands of signatures, and any sympathy that SDS had built among the students seemed to dissipate after the incident. The administration instituted disciplinary procedures against the Georgetown students known to have been part of the disruption. One student pleaded guilty to overturning the lectern in Gaston Hall and was suspended for a year. Two others either had their charges dropped or were acquitted of complicity.[100] The Alioto affair proved to be the last stand of SDS at Georgetown. That June the Congressional House Internal Security Committee, in its investigation of SDS nationally, made the Georgetown chapter its first target, and several Georgetown administrators, faculty, and students testified before the committee, but by that time SDS was virtually history on the Hilltop.

That spring a new radical group emerged on campus—the Georgetown University Radical Union (GURU). Their first public action was a condemnation of the university as part of the "military-industrial complex" because of its relationship with the International Policy Academy, a CIA-connected institution; its sanctioning of classified research on campus; and its sponsorship of the Center for Strategic and International Studies (CSIS). In a letter to the *Hoya*, Thomas Fitzgerald explained that the university's involvement with the academy was nothing more than the English language classes that the American Language Institute, as part of its contract with the Agency for International Development (AID) provided for some students of the academy.[101] A review of government-sponsored research at the university revealed no program as being classified. The government sponsors of most of the research were NIH and NSF. Only three contracts of university personnel were with the Department of Defense. As for the CSIS, another object of student protest, Henle pointed out that the center did no contract research for the government; indeed, on principle it received no government money.[102]

ROTC

The ROTC, with its four hundred student cadets, became a central target of antiwar sentiment on campus. In October 1967, Father Richard McSorley announced that the Student Peace Union was launching a campaign against the presence of ROTC on campus.[103] The following May Day protestors attempted to disrupt the traditional military exercises. As cadets carried out a counterinsurgency maneuver on the lower field, protestors planted crosses on the hill above to simulate a cemetery and posted a large sign reading "WHY?" with a bagpiper playing nearby.[104] The changing attitude toward ROTC on the part of such student institutions as the *Hoya* and student academic committees showed how far mainstream sentiment at Georgetown had shifted toward a radical posture by 1969. The *Hoya* expressed its frustration with the status of ROTC by remarking that it enjoyed "the dubious distinction of being a non-academic discipline with all the rights and privileges of an academic department."[105] In 1968–69 the student academic committees of the college and the School of Foreign Service called for drastic reform of the program. Neither committee called for an abolition of ROTC on campus. Instead the recommendation from the college group was that ROTC at Georgetown be reformed in a way that could serve as a model for what it should be on other campuses. In a student referendum on ROTC in May 1969, fewer than one-fifth of the voters wanted ROTC removed from Georgetown. More than half wanted it relegated to an extracurricular activity. Another 13 percent wanted its academic status reduced to a pass-fail basis.[106] In the spring of 1970, the president appointed a special committee to study the matter. The committee concluded that the university should seek new contracts with the army and air force that would remove academic credit from courses given by ROTC personnel.[107]

In the summer of 1969, Vice President Fitzgerald wrote the faculty, "Something has been going on within our undergraduate student body; my impression is that large sectors of it are becoming radicalized. By October we could have some serious trouble."[108] By the fall, antiwar sentiment clearly prevailed on campus. The *Hoya* came out in favor of the October 15 moratorium as a suitable reflection of the unprecedented opposition of the American people to the government's policy in Vietnam.[109] The student senate followed suit in endorsing the upcoming moratorium and called on President Henle to cancel classes and arrange a special mass for the occasion. Henle announced that a mass would be scheduled on that day for the twelve Georgetown alumni who had died in Vietnam. Classes would go on, but students would not be penalized for attending other activities, including teach-ins, which the president encouraged.[110] That month Henle established a neutrality policy for the university on any controversial issue. "When there is a wide and honest difference of opinion on complicated issues, the University, while actively concerned about the common good, must not by identifying with a partisan view appear to bind its faculty, students, administration or others associated with it to that view." This would apply to the war, the Three Sisters Bridge, and any other controversial issue that arose.[111] Fifty students of the Vietnam Moratorium Radical Caucus, wearing red armbands, walked out of Henle's inauguration at McDonough Gymnasium in protest of the university's "neutrality" about the war and its sufferance of ROTC and CSIS on campus.[112]

With the administration's approval, some 1,600 students who had come to Washington for the moratorium march were housed in McDonough and in the dormitories. On the eve of the moratorium, about 400 students gathered on Copley lawn to share a symbolic meal of bread and water. After Father McSorley addressed the crowd, they lit candles and followed him silently through the streets of Georgetown. Once under way, many others, including neighbors recruited by students going door-to-door in the previous days, doubled the number of marchers, accompanied by 30 policemen and nearly as many newspeople.[113] On the day of the moratorium, teach-ins and other related activities drew large numbers of students as many professors, despite the administration's decision, canceled classes or conducted their own sessions on Vietnam. At the Law Center, the leftist writer I. F. Stone addressed a gathering on "Why Vietnam"; later a group of students marched to the Justice Department to protest the war.[114]

By the time of the moratorium, a new issue had arisen on campus that drove students to protest and engage in civil disobedience. At the start of the academic year, construction had begun on the Three Sisters Bridge, named for the three prominent rocks in the Potomac River just west of Key Bridge.

Candlelight procession on Copley Lawn for Vietnam Moratorium, October 1969. (Georgetown University Archives)

The new bridge was to be a key link of a major realignment of traffic patterns into the city from the west, as part of a general highway development within the city under the auspices of urban renewal. The six-lane bridge was to funnel traffic from Virginia into an enlarged Canal Road of eight lanes at the south end of Glover Archbold Park, adjacent to campus. The road would enter a tunnel across the southern portion of campus and proceed underground to link up with the Whitehurst Freeway. The university expected to lose at least two acres of its precious land to the project, and the main campus planning and building committee recommended that the university become a party to the suit that the Georgetown Citizens Association had filed to prevent construction of the bridge and expanded highway. President Henle, however, decided that the university would remain neutral in the matter.

A large number of Georgetown's students disagreed, concerned about the dislocation, particularly of the poor and black citizens, that the highway expansion would create, and they took to the construction site in protest. In October 1969, a graduate student, Matt Andrea, and a few of his friends occupied the three "islands" without incident. Their action drew hundreds of supporters to the shoreline close to the construction site. Three days later, when protesters attempted to block further construction activity, the police moved in and dispersed them. The same scenario played out the following day. On the third day, which happened to be Moratorium Day, some two hundred demonstrators rushed the site once more. One hundred and forty-one persons were arrested, mostly students, including ninety-seven from Georgetown. Another attempt in the afternoon to suppress construction resulted in further arrests.[115] Construction was halted soon after to allow for public hearings to take place, which the court suit was successful in proving was necessary for due process to be fulfilled. The hearings were never held, as support for the project collapsed and the construction site below the C&O Canal at the south entrance to campus remained for years a reminder of the ill-fated bridge that would have diminished Georgetown's campus.[116]

By the beginning of 1970, membership in GURU had grown to perhaps one hundred. GURU's first public action in 1970 was a sit-in by thirty members at Professor Quigley's Development of Civilization class in Gaston Hall. Quigley was known to be a consultant of the Department of Defense and active in giving talks to military personnel. In this particular class the GURU members occupied the rear seats in Gaston and stomped their feet, shouted obscenities, and attacked his cozy relationship with the military.[117] The following month GURU demanded that President Henle cancel on-campus interviews scheduled with fifteen corporations whom the radical group identified with rapacious international capitalism. Henle refused to do so.[118]

In the late winter of 1970, sit-ins began to occur in military science classes taught by ROTC staff. On the third occasion, campus police were called in but, despite their threat to arrest those conducting the sit-in, class went on and the protesters remained. The president ordered undergraduate deans to take disciplinary action against those who sat in on classes without permission. At least two students were eventually put on probation for disrupting classes. The *Hoya*, reversing its opinion about the place of ROTC at Georgetown, urged that the "infiltrations" continue until ROTC was removed from campus.[119] The academic vice president feared that this might prove a "moment of grave crisis for the University. . . . This is not a question of war or peace, or whether one believes that ROTC should be on campus. It is a question of academic freedom, and I think we should be prepared to suffer boycotts or even the suspension of all classes rather than submit to such interference."[120] He likely did not realize how quickly events would lead to just such a choice.

A May to Remember

On Thursday evening, April 30, 1970, President Nixon told the nation in a televised speech that American and South Vietnamese forces were moving into Cambodia to attack sanctuaries that the Vietcong and North Vietnamese had established there. Within an hour after Nixon's announcement of the invasion, students across the country began to demonstrate and call for strikes. During the following week hundreds of campuses went on strike, including Georgetown.

At Georgetown, like so many campuses struck by protest in the decade, the strike was over a mix of university and national issues, brought to a boil by the spread of the war into Cambodia. The student senate met in a packed Gaston Hall on Sunday night to consider sanctioning a strike for several issues, ranging from the war in Southeast Asia to university reform. One student who was there recalled the atmosphere as being "crazy." The crowd was hell-bent on the senate's taking action. A graduate student thought that this must have been what the French Revolution, in its sansculotte stage, had been like.[121] Surprisingly, nine senators voted against the strike, but twenty prostrike votes satisfied the crowd, and the strike was set to begin the following Wednesday.[122] The university's response was that it would not negotiate demands under the pressure of a strike.

The next afternoon, word came of the shocking killing of four students at Kent State by national guardsmen. The following night, Tuesday, the quadrangle was the site of a mass rally. From student windows in the surrounding buildings hung banners with the symbol of the strike, a red fist.[123] Meanwhile the Graduate Student Organization and students of the law center voted to strike. In a paraphrase of the Declaration of Independence, citing the grievances that the Nixon administration had brought upon the nation, the Graduate Student Organization voted to suspend all university activities and to free students to "extend the strike at the University to the whole

country" with the goal of bringing the troops home from Southeast Asia and of bringing about the release of all political prisoners.[124] That same evening the student senate voted to suspend academic activities for the remainder of the school year. The law center faculty, meeting on Wednesday in a hall packed with students who spilled out into the hallways, issued a resolution to give students the option of delaying or, for seniors, taking an administrative pass on their final exams, in order to allow members of the law center community "to act upon their individual consciences in this crisis."[125]

On Wednesday the strike began, with pickets around some classroom buildings and teach-ins on Copley lawn. Many observers felt that student anguish was mounting. "The news from Kent State and from Cambodia," one later wrote, "suggested to many students that the charges they had often heard were indeed true, and that they found themselves victims of a corrupt and heartless society."[126] That night the undergraduate student senate met again and, in the deepening crisis, discarded the local issues that had been the main focus of the strike and called upon the faculty and administration to join with them in showing their deep concern about the issues engulfing the country and, specifically, to terminate immediately academic activities on the main campus so that students could be free to participate in demonstrating on Capitol Hill and in their home communities their intense opposition to the war and the Nixon administration.

Thursday morning found the campus calm, but some felt chaos and violence lurking beneath the peace. Silent pickets ringed the classroom buildings. One class that morning was disrupted by strikers; threats of violent actions surfaced. Many faculty wanted to have a meeting and discuss the situation. When the president of the faculty senate refused to call one, an English professor, Keith Fort, took the initiative to do so. Meanwhile President Henle and his academic vice president, Thomas Fitzgerald, realized that the situation on campus had drastically changed from the day before. They knew that the law center faculty had stated that being in the center of a national crisis made it impossible for many students to carry on academic life as usual. They knew too that many undergraduate students were deeply troubled by the turn of events. They sensed the growing threat of violence in the city and on campus. Academic Vice President Fitzgerald assembled all the deans, including the dean of the law center and the chancellor of the medical center, in his office Thursday morning. There was a lengthy discussion of the student strike as well as the impact of the invasion of Cambodia and the tragedy at Kent State. They agreed that the university should honor the students' request for administration and faculty to join them in a forceful expression of concern about the national crisis. But they also thought that the administration should not act unilaterally but with full faculty involvement. They decided to encourage as many of their faculty as possible to attend the informal meeting in Copley formal lounge scheduled for that afternoon and hoped to use that as a forum for getting an appropriate resolution.

At noon hundreds attended a mass celebrated in the quadrangle by Father Henle. Nearly 175 faculty showed up at Copley for the hastily arranged assembly. Faculty passed through a walkway to Copley lined on both sides by students. At the meeting impassioned speeches were given for and against support of the strike. At one point Fitzgerald rose and, claiming to speak only as a professor of classics but for what he took to be the sentiment of an overwhelming majority of the faculty, insisted that those "who were right on the doorstep of the national government, just could not conduct 'business as usual.'" He maintained that they had to admit the troubled atmosphere of the campus made it virtually impossible for students to prepare for and take examinations; that somehow they had to make it possible for those desiring to do so to engage in political activity. It was a turning point. The faculty voted 156 to 13 to suspend, really to end, the school year. Faculty members would make their own arrangements for determining grades and post them on their office boards.[127] Upon hearing the results of the faculty vote, President Henle formally announced at 4:30 to the students waiting outside that, "in recognition of the deep concern of our students and faculty," he was suspending classes for the remainder of the semester.[128] Fitzgerald met with student leaders and dissuaded them from pursuing other issues that had been on their agenda earlier.[129] The students, having gained the faculty and administration's endorsement of their concern about the national situation, had, as the president's commission put it, "succeeded in making their universities strike against national policy."[130]

The president of the undergraduate student government reported to the executive committee of the board of directors meeting the next day that the combined actions of the president, faculty, and students had "done much to make Georgetown become a real community." That cooperation was continuing, he said, in preparing to house and support the antiwar protestors who were pouring into town for the demonstration the next day. The university provided housing and food for more than two thousand demonstrators. There was no violence or incidents of any kind on campus, although a radical threat to firebomb Lauinger Library because it bore the name of an alumnus, Joseph Lauinger, who had been killed in Vietnam, prompted student government to assign students to patrol its perimeter during the weekend.[131] Others read a very different message from that tumultuous Thursday: that what had happened that day had served not to unite but to divide the community, particularly its faculty. Many faculty thought that suspending classes in the spring of 1970 had been at the cost of academic integrity; they felt they had been "shanghaied" by the students and the administration.[132]

The bitterness in the faculty senate was quite severe. "People like [Valerie Earle and Jeane Kirkpatrick] moved rightward," one faculty member judged. "The determination [was] that such a thing would never happen again. . . . The scars went deep for real long."[133] At the orientation conference for the new faculty the following September, faculty senate president Earle told them that Georgetown, like many institutions of higher education in the United States, was in a crisis of identity and purpose. "Some would have the university abandon its long tradition of detachment and objectivity and would convert it to a role of social and political activism. Others—I stand with them—believe that every quality and value that makes a university great, unique among institutions indispensable to a free society, is menaced by the drive for involvement."[134]

In July, Professor Cyril Zebot of the economics department wrote a letter to the *New York Times* in which he warned, "If our universities are to be preserved for their only objective, they must be freed from recurring interruptions, shouting demonstrations, rump meetings and all forms of intimidation. . . . Our universities need administrators who will not keep caving in until it is too late to salvage their battered institutions."[135] Zebot also prepared a resolution for faculty endorsement: "Any future interruption of the regular academic calendar at Georgetown University must be approved by a two-thirds majority vote of currently teaching fulltime faculty members in referendum by secret ballot."[136] By September more than seventy faculty had signed the resolution. That month he issued the first number of the "Agenda for Georgetown," in which he called for campus reforms to meet the crisis. "Some of our particular difficulties at Georgetown, in this time of widespread university crisis, are due to an unviable coexistence of elements of old-fashioned paternalism (especially in administration-faculty relations) and an almost total permissiveness (especially in administration-student relations)." Any reforms had to be based on the recognition of the proper boundaries of "the *areas of autonomy* (self-rule, self-government, self-management) of each of the three elements in a university"—administration, faculty, and students—according to their respective levels of interest and competence. There needed to be a clear set of rules constituting acceptable campus behavior, rules that would prohibit "direct action" for political ends on campus as well as regulate student living in the dormitories.[137]

By the end of October, Zebot had 123 sponsors for his resolution, which the faculty senate supported by a vote of 21 to 14.[138] In November a group of seventeen faculty signed a statement in which they voiced their concern that the resolution amounted to "a kind of loyalty test." They pointed out that nearly 80 percent of the full-time faculty on the three campuses had chosen not to sign it. They also noted that the resolution required only a simple majority for passage but would require a two-thirds majority to close the university; they also were bothered by the resolution's establishment of the faculty as the sole determining voice of authority in cases of emergency.[139]

The resolution went to a referendum of the full-time faculty in November. Before the results could be known, President Henle vetoed the resolution that the senate had passed, and the issue became moot. "Agenda," now listing an editorial board of fifteen faculty, mostly from the sciences and social sciences, and an advisory panel of fifteen other faculty, claimed that the senate vote of October and the faculty referendum in November on the resolution (303 in support, 128 opposed, they claimed) had set a new stage for the "continuing renewal of Georgetown, spearheaded by its Academic Faculty." "Agenda" was ready to lead the way.[140] The editorial board now included the chairs of the science departments—Louis Baker, George Chapman, and William Thaler—plus political scientists Karl Cerny, Valerie Earle, and William O'Brien; historians Frank Fadner, SJ, Donald Penn, and Walter Wilkerson; economists Joseph Tryon and Zebot; Richard Gordon of the law faculty; and Thomas Macnamara of the Medical School. Later that month the group issued its "State of Georgetown," in which it decried the "creeping or even contrived internal erosion" of due authority and order within the university. "Campus rules are all but gone. Students have gained full membership on the Executive Committees of undergrad schools. . . . In the higher echelons of the University government there is no effective faculty influence. The University Faculty Senate is merely an advisory body." As a needed reform they called for the autonomous governance of departments and of schools. At the departmental level, faculty would elect its own chairs and set its own policy; at the school level, executive councils would be the ultimate policymaking bodies.[141]

At a meeting of the board of directors in March, the president reported that the group was adamantly opposed to any progressive reform "that would give Georgetown a distinctive character and quality." Unfortunately, he went on, the group dominated most of the departments, as well as the faculty senate, meaning that "any significant change must be made from the top down by vigorous leadership from the Administration."[142] The president clearly overestimated the influence and reach of the group. Nevertheless, it marked a polarization of the administration and a portion of the faculty in matters of governance, planning, and the limits of education.

The events of May left Thomas Fitzgerald with the deepened conviction that "our students are growing away from us. The generation gap is widening."[143] The administration feared a resumption of May madness when school resumed in the fall. GURU had sent a mass mailing to freshmen and had threatened to disrupt registration. "This year gives every promise of being equally as challenging and harrowing as the last," Fitzgerald warned the faculty just before the beginning of classes.[144] But nothing happened. "The start of school has been a peaceful one," Henle reported to the board in October.[145] That "eerie tranquility" that Kingman Brewster had unexpectedly encountered at Yale in the fall of 1970 settled too on Georgetown, as well as on schools across the country. "Things settled down in the fall of 1970. . . . Increasingly it was back to the books. And there was an economic downturn. And the change in the draft laws made a big impact on protests and involvement."[146] By mid-October the *Hoya* was remarking about "a mood of lethargy" and "cloud of ennui" that had descended upon the campus. Students seemed to be "both weary and fearful of future political activity." This attitude was attributed partly to a predictable reaction to the trauma of the previous semester's experience and partly to the academic pressure that the new fall calendar had imposed by cramming a semester into the three and a half months between Labor Day and Christmas.[147] This new calendar was also a major factor in the lack of any student pressure for Georgetown to adopt the Princeton plan of suspending classes in mid-October so that students could be free to participate in preelection campaigns.

May 1971

The following May there was another major student demonstration against the war in Washington, but this time Georgetown students were more witnesses than participants. Requests to provide housing for protesters in the residence halls and McDonough Gymnasium were turned down by the administration.[148] The *Hoya*'s plea that opponents of the war had no choice but to take their part in the "massive civil disobedience" in the planned demonstration got little response on campus.[149] At the beginning of May, thousands of demonstrators converged on the city with the announced goal of shutting it down on Monday, May 3. On Sunday morning they were driven by police from West Potomac Park where they had been camped. About 2,500 of them

Scene from campus with police firing teargas at protesters, May 3, 1971. (Georgetown University Archives)

sought refuge on Georgetown's campus, two miles to the west of the park, much to the surprise of Georgetown officials. At first the refugees occupied the playing fields on the west side of campus, but rain in the afternoon forced them to seek shelter in the corridors of many of the university's dormitories and other buildings. President Henle, who was in Rome at the time, had delegated chief authority to James Kelly, the vice president for administrative affairs, to deal with any emergency that might arise during the planned demonstration. Final examinations were scheduled to begin that Monday. Kelly, after weighing the logistically impractical option of removing the intruders forcibly, decided to let them be, as their occupation of the hallways was a peaceful, if noisy, one, and to make food available to them.

Very early the next morning, the demonstrators, crying, "Shut down the city," departed from campus, but many left belongings behind, an indication of their intent to return. On their way off campus, some, leaving by the rear exit, overturned a dumpster on the hill overlooking Canal Road. The dumpster went crashing onto the road surface. Miraculously, despite it being morning rush hour, the rolling projectile hit no vehicle when it landed. When the demonstrators attempted to block Key Bridge and other arteries into the city, police used tear gas to disrupt them. This forced many of them back onto campus. Without permission, District police on motor scooters periodically entered the front gates and broke up clusters of demonstrators by releasing tear gas. Police helicopters circling overhead also poured tear gas on those below. Soon a heavy cloud of gas hung over the campus. Students heading for their first exams found themselves with burning eyes and choking on the fumes. They returned to their dorms. Kelly had to postpone the scheduled examinations. Campus police, augmented by eighty or so District police, formed a cordon around the campus to prevent any return to campus by the demonstrators.[150]

At the law center, protesters were in the streets attempting to block the intersections leading to the Capitol. Tear gas drifted over and around the building as police tried to disperse the human blockades. The school itself quickly became a legal defense center as the Prettyman interns and others represented many of the thousands of youth who were arrested. The Pretty-man offices, functioning as a bail office, received monies from parents and others for the release of the protesters.[151]

By the following October the president could report with confidence that "there is a distinct shift by students away from radicalism and the radical movement. There is an increasing awareness of and interest in study, career, and conservatism. Confrontation as a methodology is out."[152] The new president of student government, John B. Kennedy, told the board of directors in March 1972 that student government had abandoned the politics of confrontation in favor of a politics of community and that their chief focus now was not on national or international issues but on academic ones.[153] A month later the student senate voted its support of the upcoming observance of the moratorium but refused to cancel or postpone the spring festival, planned for that same day in late April. It did provide a moratorium booth at the festival where students could sign petitions to end the war.[154] That same April the *Hoya* endorsed the Democratic and antiwar candidate, George McGovern, for president and urged students to get involved in his campaign, but few apparently did.[155] The following fall, two months before the election, the editors again urged their fellow students "to accept the McGovern challenge." "It is the unique responsibility of the young to help create the future" that McGovern was committed to bringing about. The plea fell on deaf ears.[156]

That student government now saw itself more as a service provider than as an issue advocate was evident in its creation in March 1972 of Students of Georgetown, Incorporated (the Corp), a company that served as an umbrella for the provision of several student enterprises. Organized by Roger Cochetti, its first business was a short-lived sandwich shop in Healy basement. More permanent ventures followed, including a shuttle bus system (Georgetown University Transportation System—taken over by the university in 1974), a record co-op, a furniture co-op, a travel agency, a food mart (Vital Vittles), and various rental programs.[157] The *Hoya*, in evaluating a particular administration within student government in 1974, caught the change nicely: "[Doug] Kellner and [Neil] Shankman brought with them 'services' and it has become the watchword of Healy Basement. The best talent in Student Government is not running for office but quietly working in the Corporation or the S[tudent] E[ntertainment] C[ommission]. The Food Coop and the Shuttlebus have replaced self-determination and tripartite planning mechanisms."[158]

The following October found student protestors again chanting radical slogans and carrying antiwar placards in Healy Circle, but this time it was art imitating life. The protestors were students working as extras in the filming of *The Exorcist,* the horror tale set at Georgetown that William Blatty (**C** 1950) had spun into a bestseller. The film crew virtually took over the campus for two months that fall of 1972, and many faculty and students had walk-on parts in the various campus scenes of the movie. Two months later, in January 1973, a real army of demonstrators converged on the city to disrupt Nixon's second inauguration, but they found no welcome at Georgetown. The house councils voted to close their lounges to out-of-town visitors. Student president Kennedy's proposal to open McDonough Gymnasium and the New South faculty dining room to the demonstrators was rejected by a university committee set up to deal with the contingencies of the inaugural weekend. When five hundred or so protesters showed up at Healy gate and other entrances seeking accommodation, they were turned away by university security, although sympathetic students led some onto campus through unguarded routes. ROTC cadets and guards patrolled the campus and made random checks of student IDs.[159]

It was significant that when students did hold a demonstration in February 1973, it was to protest academic-related issues. On what was designated as the First Annual Memorial Lemon Day, students marched into the Healy building at high noon to deposit lemons outside Father Henle's office, where the board of directors were meeting, to protest the increase in tuition, the overcrowding of classes, the underfunding of academics in general, and other related issues. Among those placing lemons outside the president's door was the executive vice president for academic affairs, Edmund Ryan, SJ. The chair of the board, Father Albert R. Jonsen, observed that "the 'lemonstration' . . . was imaginative and amusing, [but] its point was not lost on the Directors. We do appreciate the concern for cost and quality of education at Georgetown."[160]

As spring returned to DC, the *Hoya* lamented that, unlike in the past, it would not likely bring with it any new migration of student protesters to the nation's capital. All the old causes—the war, poverty, civil rights—no longer stirred the conscience of the nation, including its young, even though they were all three still vital issues. Still, despite the quiet spring, the editors thought they detected "a sense of uneasiness in the air that portends the calm before a storm. It may be a long, hot summer."[161] It was not, nor was the fall that followed particularly tempestuous. When the board of directors, at the behest of some students, restored credit for ROTC courses in the summer of 1973, there was little student reaction to this overturning, barely three years later, of one of the significant achievements of the protest movement at Georgetown. In 1974 "streaking" became a rite of spring at college campuses across the nation, including Georgetown, where nude students, mostly males, made their shock appearances in unlikely settings such as the rooftops of townhouses, New South dining hall, Healy Circle, and the library (one particularly imaginative Hoya, clad only in tie, rode a motorcycle into Lauinger Library during a peak late evening study hour, to the applause of fellow students). Campus culture in the mid-seventies seemed far closer to the goldfish eating, telephone-booth-stuffing high jinks of the twenties than to the radical politics and protest of the sixties.

The Sacking of an Alter Ego

Within weeks of the appearance of the first streaker, however, the campus seemed to be back in the cauldron of the late sixties, with candlelit rallies, call-to-arms editorials, and sit-ins outside the president's office. As in 1970, students and faculty joined their voices in protest against the administration, only this time they were raising their voices in support of a highly popular administrator who had just been ousted by the president of the university.

Edmund Ryan, SJ, had come to Georgetown in 1972 to occupy a new position that made him in effect the chief academic officer of the university. As vice president for educational affairs, Ryan, the board declared, would be "the alter ego of the President," so one with the president's "philosophy, policy and practice that he will serve as an extension of the President into [academic] areas."[162] The new position was apparently created to neutralize the authority of the academic vice president, Thomas Fitzgerald, who had fallen out of favor with the president after the spring of 1970.[163] Henle, who had gotten a very positive impression of Ryan from the latter's work on the university board of directors, had selected Ryan without going through the process of a formal search.

Despite their unhappiness with the manner in which Ryan had been appointed, both faculty and students quickly came to think highly of him. The new vice president was in many ways a striking contrast to the president, an "alter ego" indeed. Whereas the barrel-chested, intense-looking Henle was an introvert with little bent for the social world, the lean, ever-smiling Ryan had an engaging, outgoing personality with a soft-spoken, deferential style that instantly attracted people to him. The always accessible Ryan made the president seem more removed than he was. From the time he arrived on Second Healy, Ryan seemed to be the face and voice of the university, appearing in television interviews or on panels or other public fora to comment on subjects from the sacred to the silly. When *The Exorcist* was being filmed on campus in the fall of 1972, Ryan was sought out by reporters and television news anchors for the church's and university's positions on the subject of demons and the rituals of exorcising them. When streaking became a phenomenon on campuses across the country, Martin Agronsky interviewed Ryan on his show about the fad.

He received much publicity in the fall and winter of 1973–74 when his negotiations with a German Federal Republic official led to the establishment of the student exchange program through which the German Federal Republic, which could not accommodate all students seeking higher education, committed itself to sending fifteen thousand students over the next five years to study in colleges and universities in the United States that had vacancies due to the shrinking college-age cohort in the population.[164] That same winter, appearing on NBC's "Today Show" to discuss the financial hardship that soaring college costs were imposing on middle-class families, Ryan's proposal to nationalize the voucher system for college students that he had successfully lobbied for at the state level in New Jersey drew considerable attention, even reportedly from the Nixon administration. Under his proposal the federal government funded two years of a student's undergraduate, or one year of his postgraduate, education for every year that the student pledged to devote to some form of national service.[165]

In February 1974 the *Hoya* ran an interview with Robert Henle in which the reporter raised the question of whether the mandatory retirement age for faculty would apply to the president. Henle replied that administrators were exempt from the mandatory retirement policy and that he had no intention of walking away from the presidency in the middle of a capital development campaign. The reporter commented that there was speculation that the board of directors was going to take up this matter at its next meeting in March and that Ryan, who was seen as the most likely successor to Henle, might move on if the board renewed the president for another three years. The piece quoted the vice president of the board as agreeing that Ryan's leaving would be a "great loss to the University."[166] Four years earlier the board had in fact decided that the same retirement schedule that was in effect for faculty should apply to administrators as well: sixty-five being the normal retirement age, with continuation on a year-to-year basis, with the consent of the appropriate body, until the age of seventy.[167]

Three weeks after the article in the *Hoya,* at the end of their private weekly meeting, Henle informed Ryan that he was very displeased with his performance as executive vice president—that he was spending too little time

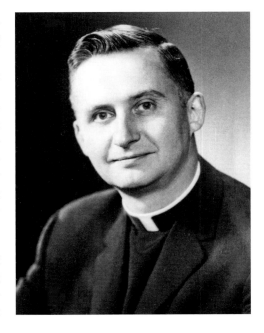

Edmund Ryan, SJ, vice president for educational affairs. (Georgetown University Archives)

in his office and not keeping up with his correspondence, that he was appearing on television and radio too much, that he was spending an inordinate amount of time on STEP, that he was undermining the loyalty to the president of the persons who reported to Ryan, and that he was using students to put articles unfavorable to the president in the student newspapers. "I'm really embarrassed and don't want to bring this up," the president concluded, "but many people think you're conducting a campaign to get me to retire and to get yourself put in as president. You are attempting to upstage the President."[168] Ryan, in a nine-page, single-spaced reply, attempted to refute all the charges that the president had raised against him in the meeting.[169] Ten days later at a board meeting, Henle brought up the "rather severe personnel problem" he was experiencing. After apparently recounting the particulars of Ryan's recent behavior, the president indicated that he thought some form of counseling might be the best course to take with the vice president. The board concurred but assured Henle that they were prepared to take "more radical action" should Henle ask them to do so. In light of this situation, Henle explained, he could not leave Ryan in charge of the university while the president was taking his planned leave during the summer, and he asked the board to authorize a five-person cabinet to function as the chief executive during his absence rather than the executive vice president for educational affairs, whose contract called for him to act as president in that individual's absence. The board approved his proposal.[170]

Three days after the board meeting, Ryan, at the conclusion of his weekly meeting with Henle, brought up the rumors that were flying about campus that he "had been ousted" from his position of provost (i.e., chief executive in the absence of the president). A stunned and angry Henle informed Ryan that this was confidential information, but that the truth was he no longer had confidence in Ryan's ability to administer the university in his absence and that the top administrators under him no longer wanted to report to him.[171] Henle remembered that Ryan's reaction was one of "extreme outrage," claiming that such a move was a direct violation of his contract and was grounds for legal action.[172]

When Ryan began questioning those vice presidents and other administrators who reported to him about their satisfaction with being his subordinates, Henle suspected that he was trying to get them in his camp. Ryan, for his part, became increasingly convinced that there was a cabal, led by Daniel Altobello and George Houston, that was determined to force him out of Georgetown. When he discovered files missing from his office, he suspected that they had been lifted by the secretary of the university or someone working for him. He dismissed a secretary in his office in late March whom he thought was a plant of the cabal. He feared his office was being bugged. He wrote the president on April 1 informing him of his suspicions that his office had been stealthily entered and records removed. He had had the lock to his office changed and did not wish anyone, including security, to have a master for it.[173] He also began requesting that he meet with the president only in the latter's room in the Jesuit Community, not the president's office. Finally, on April 4, Henle told Ryan that he had two options: submit his resignation within a week, to take effect at the end of the school year, or be dismissed.

Ryan had been in contact with Jesuit officials outside of Georgetown, who counseled him to attempt to work out his problems with Henle. When Ryan pleaded that the president invite people he trusted to hear Ryan's explanation for what had transpired and get their judgment before firing him, Henle, according to Ryan, replied, "It would do no good. You've gotten to them."[174] A letter from the Maryland provincial, Aloysius Panuska, to the president in which he begged Henle to allow Ryan a hearing before taking any summary action that might have grave consequences for the university and the Jesuits failed to budge him.[175] A week later, on Holy Thursday, Ryan returned with a letter stating why he could not resign. Henle glanced at it, then handed Ryan a letter that informed him he was being terminated, effective immediately.

"He was in open revolt," Dan Altobello remarked a dozen years later. "Henle refused to do the one thing he needed to do: to let the world know that Ed Ryan was crazy."[176] One top administrator, with as much inside information as anyone, thought that Altobello had prodded Henle to fire Ryan. "Ryan thought he should be the 'alter ego.' Dan felt this was usurping the position he held. Henle had to terminate Ryan because of his erratic behavior, but the timing was horrendous."[177] Another administrator thought that it was a case of two people "badly misunderstanding each other. I don't think Ryan understood the feelings of an aging president trying to hold on to the job; Henle did not understand this bright young man who was terribly insecure." Insecurity fed off insecurity.[178]

The reaction of the university community to news of Ryan's termination was shock and anger. Few outside of a narrow band of administrators had any inkling that there was trouble between the two officials. That a Jesuit president would fire his fellow Jesuit top assistant on one of the church's most sacred days, Holy Thursday, only compounded the sense of outrage. It seemed not only capricious but also a clear violation of the university's grievance code, which had only recently been adopted. The code, its principal author declared, was deliberately written to provide administrators such as Ryan the same protection and rights that faculty were given.[179] Twenty-six members of the Jesuit Community, including the director of campus ministries and the director of international programs, in a letter to Henle expressed their grave concern about the apparent arbitrariness of his action, the irreparable harm this was doing to Ryan's reputation, and the damage it would very likely have in recruiting Jesuits to Georgetown. They pleaded for an explanation and a full hearing for Ryan. The faculty senate passed a resolution asking the board of directors to apply the university code governing academic freedom and conduct of the faculty and academic administrators of the university to Ryan's appeal. On Tuesday evening, April 16, a rally was held in the quadrangle with close to one thousand students holding candles. Before the rally student body president Jack Leslie accused Father Henle of a "series of Machiavellian political moves, disgracing to an institution of higher learning." At the rally, several Jesuits, including Lawrence Madden, the director of campus ministry, made speeches in support of Ryan, as did two students. The rally ended at midnight, with the crowd chanting, "We want Ryan! We want Ryan!"[180]

A student writer of the *Hoya,* in an article titled "Is Henle Through at G.U.?" saw the firing as "the symbolic struggle between Jesuit academicians and the Altobello clique over control of Henle and thus, the University." He did not expect that Ryan would be returned to office by the board. "Georgetown has lost an outstanding opportunity because a couple of pikers wanted more power, it seems. . . . The only consolation we may get is that the Board may recognize what has happened. If that is true, something will be gained. . . . It's too damn bad [Ryan] was pressed into service as a kamikaze pilot."[181]

Meanwhile Ryan had engaged a lawyer who attempted, through the university counsel, to arrange a meeting between the two principals, but the president refused to consider it. That Friday, April 19, the executive committee of the board met for its regularly scheduled meeting. Henle gave a brief report on the events leading to his termination of Ryan and asked the committee to review his decision. The committee subsequently invited Ryan, who had asked for a hearing, to present his side of the matter to them. Ryan recounted his version of the events of the past five months and pleaded for them to restore him to office until he could have a hearing before the full board.[182] The committee refused to restore Ryan to his position but did agree to have the full board review Ryan's termination at their May meeting. At Henle's motion, the committee unanimously affirmed that the university code governing academic freedom of the faculty and academic administrators did not apply to the executive vice presidents of the university in their relationship to the president and board of directors of the university.[183]

In the month that led up to the meeting of the board, students gathered close to four thousand signatures on a letter to the board in which they pledged not to donate anything as alumni to the university unless a sufficient explanation for Father Ryan's dismissal was given to the community. Student government hired a lawyer from the firm of Arnold and Porter to represent their attempt to get Ryan reinstated. Outside the president's office, students began holding silent vigil from nine o'clock to six o'clock each day with a sign on which was the question "Why?" A larger group of Jesuits, now numbering thirty-three, including the rector of the community, wrote a letter to the board in which they pleaded that, for the sake of Ryan's reputation and the university's, the reasons for his dismissal be made public "to restore the confidence of the University community, the Society of Jesus, and the general public in the fairness and devotion to truth of Georgetown."[184]

On Sunday, May 20, graduation day, Ryan gave the homily at the Bacca-laureate Mass in McDonough Gym. Immediately after he finished, most of the students broke into a steady, appreciative burst of applause. The board met the following day to take up the review of Ryan's termination. In an ini-tial discussion, members of the board raised the possibility of a reconciliation between Ryan and Henle. Edward Bennett Williams, the university counsel, replied that he and others "more skilled than he" had attempted to bring about reconciliation but without success. He had concluded that the dispute was one "pertaining to the fundamental management and operating proce-dures of Georgetown University." The board went into executive session to hear testimony from both Henle and Ryan.[185] Among the points that Ryan made in his presentation was that the chief administrators who reported to him had all denied that they had requested they be freed from being under Ryan. Three other top administrators—Matthew McNulty, Malcolm McCor-mack, and Aloysius Kelley, SJ—had all expressed confidence in Ryan.[186]

The board deliberated until 6:30 PM, at which time Edward Bennett Wil-liams delivered an offer from the board to Ryan that they were ready to re-instate him if he agreed to resign immediately. Ryan countered with the offer that he be reinstated with the directive to work out his differences with Henle through the mediation of the Maryland provincial. More than two hours later, Williams returned to deliver a statement of the board that regret-ted the precipitate manner in which Henle had fired Ryan, declared that the deposed vice president was an excellent administrator, but that differences about approaches toward governance had gotten beyond the point at which both men could effectively continue to work together, hence the board was terminating Ryan's appointment while continuing to pay his salary. Finally, the board charged the chair with appointing a five-man committee to inves-tigate the whole governmental structure of the university and to determine the effectiveness of its functioning.[187]

The board moved quickly, through its special committee, to evaluate the university's organizational structure. In the early summer the committee in-terviewed deans, department chairs, Jesuits, members of the faculty senate, and student government officials. At the board's July meeting, they made their report. Subsequently the board made its recommendations to the pres-ident regarding a reorganization of the university's governing structure. It also made clear that it would maintain an ongoing evaluation of the imple-mentation of its recommendations. For its own future, the board resolved to meet more frequently and to have one member of the faculty senate and one of the student government present at its meetings. Under the new organiza-tion, the three chief academic officers—the executive vice president for aca-demic affairs, the chancellor of the medical center, and the executive vice president for law center affairs—became the top executives in the university below the president. The academic vice president became the first vice pres-ident and provost. Daniel Altobello was replaced by Virginia Keeler as secretary of the university and appointed to the new position of vice president for administrative services.[188] Ryan had to have been pleased. As the new executive vice president for academic affairs, Aloysius Kelley told the faculty senate the following November, "Although the university has never departed from its primary commitment to education, an illusion might have been allowed to grow over the past several years that Georgetown had become a business."[189] The new structure was meant to underscore the preeminent position of education.

Aftermath

For the first time in university history the board became a force in its own right, independent of the president. The creation of the new structure was but the first manifestation of this new reality. In May 1975 the board formed a nominating committee to choose candidates for the board of directors. Previously the president had submitted names to the corporation who then elected those named. At that same meeting they named Father Malcolm Carron, who had headed the special committee the previous summer, to be the new chair. They also changed the policy on the retirement of administrators: retirement was now to be normally at sixty-five; administrators could continue to serve, with explicit board approval, until sixty-seven, when retirement became mandatory.[190]

Edmund Ryan was a man under great stress during the controversy. This became obvious to one board member who, along with the other members of the board, received a twelve-page letter from Ryan a day after their meeting in which he rehashed all of the charges and his responses. It had, she said, the tone of someone coming unhinged.[191] Two months after his termination was upheld by the board he was admitted to the psychiatric ward of Saint Vincent's Hospital in New York City after his breakdown became all too apparent. He recovered quickly and within six months was elected president of Seattle University, a position he held for a little more than a year when recurring health problems forced his resignation. The following year he found a congenial niche as an academic administrator at Lemoyne College in Syracuse, where he served productively for several decades.

Robert Henle never recovered from the affair. He was clearly on a short leash with the board. His drinking, which had very likely affected his behavior during the spring of 1974, grew worse in the following year. He began to let things slip in the office. Dan Altobello had to confront him with the fact that his drinking was becoming a public problem.[192] The confrontation had no apparent effect. Finally the rector of the Georgetown Jesuit Community virtually ordered him to seek treatment. In mid-September 1975 the president announced that "with the advice of my friends and my physician, I have decided to take a fall vacation from the University at an undisclosed location."[193]

He returned to campus and his office a month later. Four days later at a board meeting, Henle asked the board for a clear understanding of when they expected him to retire and what his postretirement relationship with the university would be. He suggested that the end of the 1976–77 academic year would be an appropriate retirement date. He would then be sixty-seven and would have had an opportunity to complete Mandate 81. The board had already instructed the Committee on Board Personnel and Nominations to recommend the composition of a search committee for a new president. In effect Henle was pleading that they postpone the search for a year.

In executive session the board determined not to extend his term to June 1977 but to proceed with the search for a new president. Two Jesuit members of the board were delegated to inform the president of their decision over lunch. Henle graciously agreed to offer his resignation, as of June 1976. When the board reconvened, Henle returned to a standing tribute. There would be no continuing presence at Georgetown for him as chancellor or president emeritus, as Henle had obviously hoped. He returned to Saint Louis University, where he was appointed to the McDonnell Chair in Justice in American Society and renewed his prodigious scholarly activity for another two decades.

At the board's last meeting with Henle, it commended him for his achievements during his seven years as president: the "greatly increased financial stability of the university," the creation of an excellent administrative structure, and the imparting "to all segments" of the institution a renewed sense of their mission and goals, a strong stress on academic goals, and an emphasis on the moral and religious development of its students.[194] Henle's own appraisal of where the university stood as he departed took a longer perspective. "In the last thirty years," he found, "Georgetown from an almost independent group of small schools has come to be a highly integrated and richly complex university. It has grown in size and at the same time has moved from 'good' to 'great,' . . . in[to] the front rank of American universities." Yet, as if recognizing that that evaluation was too generous, he immediately noted that the university had "now reached a mature stature," a higher plateau upon which one might be tempted to rest but could not. Maturity could become stagnation if the institution failed to improve its physical and human resources, and all of that would require a much larger infusion of financial resources than Georgetown had ever been able to muster. He was optimistic that his successor would find them.

In retrospect, the Henle-Ryan controversy served as a last hurrah for the decade of protest and conflict that historically became known as "the sixties." If the sixties could be said to have ended in America with Richard Nixon's resignation in 1974, they ended at Georgetown a year later with the resignation of Robert Henle. If few at the university realized at the end of 1975 that an era was ending, they would soon realize that a new one had begun.

PART TWO

INTO THE CENTER FRONT OF
AMERICAN HIGHER EDUCATION

CHAPTER 4

The Second Healy
Georgetown and the Prestigious Circle, 1976–89

The most important qualities in any university president are leadership and vision. Father Healy . . . brought a vision of remarkable clarity and force. Georgetown was to be a leader among American universities. In 1989 we are . . . and it happened on his watch.

DOROTHY M. BROWN

"Le Grand Tim"

Because of the personal and administrative failings that had led to the forced resignation of his predecessor, Timothy Stafford Healy inherited a weakened presidency and a faculty whose support for Jesuit leadership had seriously eroded. When the board was conducting its presidential search in the spring of 1976, there was a serious attempt within the faculty senate, more pointed than its prior effort in 1969, to open the search beyond members of the Society of Jesus. The motion to do so was tabled, but it was clear that faculty confidence in Jesuit leadership had weakened seriously in light of recent events. The board itself, as discussed in the previous chapter, had taken unprecedented steps to assert its authority over the president. In its last action before electing a new president, it recommended to the corporation, the five-member entity that was the legal owner of the university, that it change its bylaws to eliminate the president from ex officio membership in that body.

Timothy Healy had been the search committee's unanimous choice over the other two Jesuit finalists and was elected by a majority of the board to the presidency.[1] Of the three finalists, he was probably the least known to the university community. For the past six years, he had been outside the Jesuit network of higher education, serving as vice chancellor of the City University of New York. As one of the members of the search committee mentioned privately to a fellow Jesuit, Healy had imagination, intelligence, a great background in education, and a deep commitment to its Jesuit tradition. He would, this member predicted, create a lot of enthusiasm both inside and outside the university.[2]

There is no doubt that he was a shaker and a mover—he made people take notice. The profile of the ideal president for Georgetown that the search committee developed in 1976 probably seemed wildly overreaching when it called for a person with a broad vision, committed to long-range planning, who could clearly appraise its critical needs, both physical and human, and simultaneously clearly articulate those needs and radically enlarge the university's endowment to realize them. A top priority for him would be "amicable and effective relationships between the faculty and the administration." He ought to be, they went on, a person who would become a national spokesman for private institutions of higher education, a person who could establish rapport with a wide spectrum of communities ranging from the federal government to the local community to foundations and other major potential benefactors. He needed to change Georgetown's image as an isolated island on the fringe of Washington into one that was an integral, involved element of the city. He needed to build up the role of the university in public research and international outreach. He had to take advantage of Georgetown's unique location—its Washington connection.[3] Quite a list. Yet what is most remarkable is how much of that profile Tim Healy fulfilled.

"A National Spokesman"

Despite his sailor's tongue, his volcanic temper, and his type-A personality, Tim Healy was innately a shy man. He was nonetheless a kind of academic Irish politician who made Georgetown the ward from which he cast his larger-than-life presence upon the larger political, academic, and social worlds. "Le Grande Tim," indeed, as his classmates at Louvain in Belgium had long ago dubbed him. Georgetown gave him a platform that he used as no one before him had. As one faculty member later reflected, Healy brought a vision of Georgetown's identity and potential and articulated that sense of self with remarkable clarity and force.[4] He brought Georgetown to national prominence with his words alone. Certainly no one in Georgetown's history had better reflected on the relationship of university to church and republic. No one better exploited the "weight to our establishment" that the location of the federal government in Washington gave to Georgetown. He brought the university, as one administrator judged at the end of Healy's tenure, into the center front of American higher education.[5]

Tim Healy was a master networker, and he cast his net widely and deeply. During his first month at Georgetown, Katherine Graham hosted a luncheon for him with the editorial staff of the *Washington Post*. The following week he was the subject of a feature story in the *Washington Star*. It was the beginning of a close relationship between Healy and the two Washington papers, particularly the *Post,* whose editorial head, Meg Greenfield, became a close friend of the new president and regularly gave him a forum for an op-ed piece on various matters, from the liturgical season to the connection between sports and education. He was appointed to presidential commissions beginning in 1978. That same year he was elected to the board of directors of the National Association of Independent Colleges and Universities, which included seven hundred institutions of higher learning. In 1980 he served as chair of the board of the American Council of Education, the first Catholic to do so. The following year the Consortium on the Financing of Higher Education (COFHE), a group of thirty top universities, visited Georgetown and invited the university to become its first Catholic member. COFHE would become a reference point for Healy in appraising Georgetown's progress over the rest of the decade. In 1986 a poll among leaders of higher education named him one of the five most effective university presidents in the country. It also might have added "most influential." He was at home, a *Time* columnist later noted, with several layers of the establishment.[6]

He made effective use of Georgetown's own media to promote the institution. Not without turmoil, he remade the Office of Development and Public Relations during his first years in office. By 1983 the Council for the Advancement and Support of Education (CASE) ranked that office third best among major universities (behind Brown and Michigan) for the general excellence of its programs. Georgetown won the Grand Award for its publications as a whole: *Georgetown Magazine,* the *Mid/Week Report,* and others. By 1980, with support from Healy, Georgetown University Press grew into a genuine university press, with revenues of nearly $300,000, and a growing reputation. In 1982 the press moved beyond the volumes on language and linguistics that had been its nearly exclusive concentration to

Timothy S. Healy, SJ, president of Georgetown, 1976–89. (Photo by Fabian Bachrach. Georgetown University Archives)

begin a Studies in Ethics series. This marked the beginning of the diversification of the press from language-related producer to publisher of books in certain selected areas, such as linguistics, ethics, and education.

Tim Healy's utilization of the university's most potential source of outreach, Georgetown's FM station, WGTB, was another story. When Healy became president, the station had just returned to the air after being shut down for some months by his predecessor in order to reclaim the station that had essentially been taken over by outside operators whose programs, featuring scabrous language and offensive content, were threatening the FCC's renewal of its license. A board of review had concluded that the station needed to be under the direct control of the president and that its programming should reflect the nature of Georgetown as a Catholic and academic institution. Healy set up a four-person board of administrators to oversee the station. In the spring of 1977, the station held a fund-raising marathon that brought in more than $35,000. It introduced news and public service programs, such as the half-hour "American News Forum" and "Closed Mondays," an interview program that focused on the fine and performing arts in Washington. Hard rock no longer dominated its music; among its fifty-six music shows were a wide variety that ranged from classical to jazz to folk to electronic rock. Station manager Robert Uttenweiler announced in January 1977 that WGTB had over the past year doubled its number of listeners in the region.[7]

Then, without warning in the spring of 1978, the president announced that Georgetown was transferring its license to the University of the District of Columbia. He claimed that it was costing too much to operate and did not serve the academic interests of Georgetown. As he put it, "WGTB is a great animal that doesn't belong in this zoo."[8] Students and faculty both faulted the president for making the decision without consulting the Georgetown community. Supporters of the station argued that Healy's claim that it would cost $100,000 annually to properly operate WGTB was more than double what an appropriate budget would be.[9] And given what the station could deliver for the university in public service, influence, and recognition, even $100,000 was a very economical investment. James Walsh, who had been on the original review board, contended in a report to the faculty senate that "the educational mission of Georgetown University properly extends beyond our gates, and a radio station that truly reflects this institution can be a precious resource." It could be, he went on, an important means of fulfilling Georgetown's commitment to be of service to the people of this [Washington] community, as well as "a valuable means to influence public thinking on matters of civic, national, and international concern."[10]

The faculty senate in a resolution (unanimously passed with only the four administrators present opposing it) urged that all possible efforts be made to retain the license for the university.[11] Stan Wasowski, then president of the senate, made a plea to the board of directors at its May meeting to resist the president's intention of transferring the license. The Archdiocese of Washington, Wasowski reported, was willing to contribute $30,000, if money was needed to operate the station at Georgetown.[12] The board, however, had almost a year earlier authorized the president to transfer the license and now had no intention of reversing itself. In April the president offered the station and most of its operating equipment to Duke Ellington High School for the Performing Arts for the sum of one dollar. When Ellington officials declined the offer, it was made to the University of the District of Columbia, which accepted it. A group calling itself the Alliance to Preserve Radio at Georgetown formed during the summer with the goal of persuading the FCC to deny Georgetown's request to transfer its license. By the end of July it had gathered more than twelve thousand signatures to submit as part of its brief to the FCC.[13] The FCC continued to delay its decision. Healy informed the board that the station would be closed when its budget for the year ran out. So at the end of January 1979 the chief engineer for the station announced, "This is WGTB-FM, owned and operated by the President and Directors of Georgetown College for Georgetown University in Washington, DC, going off the air forever." Within twenty minutes four hundred students gathered in Healy Circle and chanted "Bring Back GTB."[14] The Georgetown FM station, alas, was history.

Stanislaus Wasowski, professor of economics, and president of the faculty senate.

(Georgetown University Archives)

The University and the District

"A developing city on Georgetown's doorstep," Timothy Healy wrote in one of his early annual reports, "conditions whatever the University does. There is no way in which the University can thrive by pretending that the District of Columbia is not there, or that it is not important."[15] The District, a city mostly inhabited by African Americans, was a reality that helped shape Healy's priorities. Over the next decade the university created so many partnerships and working relationships with the DC public school system and with community organizations that Healy in 1988 created the position of vice president for urban affairs to oversee and coordinate the various projects and programs.

Under Healy's initiative, the university began cooperative programs with several of the District's high schools. It provided faculty assistance to Vincent Reed, the superintendent of schools, in developing a competency-based curriculum for elementary school students. By the mid-eighties the community focus program, under the Center for Minority Student Affairs, was started to provide resources for various elementary and secondary schools within the District of Columbia, which by now were educating not only African Americans and Hispanics but also Vietnamese and other Asians. Later the center sponsored a mentor program in which African American, Asian American, and Hispanic students from the university tutored minority children in public elementary schools. The Dental School opened a clinic on North Capitol Street. The law center directly provided for the legal

Student tutor at Sursum Corda.
(Georgetown University Archives)

needs of the community through its street law program and other clinical education programs. In 1976, heeding Healy's call to reach out to the city, Daniel Burke (**C** 1978) and other students organized the Community Action Coalition, a successor to GUCAP, that, like its predecessor, served as an umbrella organization for the many social outreach programs that undergraduates had begun, including tutoring inner-city children, securing legal services and housing, providing home care for cancer patients, and working with immigrants and the elderly. In 1979, to create a living-learning-service center focused on the city, the first floor of Copley Hall was reserved for forty undergraduates involved in social action programs within the District. By the mid-eighties about one-quarter of male undergraduates and one-third of female undergraduates were involved in some sort of social service. All told, more than one thousand Georgetown students were engaged in work that intrinsically acknowledged the city on their doorstep and the needs of its polyglot population.

Appraising the University's Critical Needs

Healy very quickly realized that he needed better resources to analyze and plan for the needs of the university. One of his first steps was to move the Office of Institutional Research directly under the president's office, where it could function as the major informational source for the president. At the same time, he appointed an assistant to the president for planning; three years later he upgraded the position to the level of vice president, in which post Burton Sonenstein, and later Joseph Pettit, were able to coordinate the various areas of planning within the university. "Once I got a look at the whole spectrum of the university," Healy later recalled, "the section most overmatched by its competition was the main campus, and that sort of set the agenda for the first decade" of his administration.[16] He found the university's main campus badly lacking in two things: the academic, residential, and recreational facilities that would attract the best and brightest students to Georgetown and the endowment to make those facilities possible.

Over the course of his thirteen years as president, Tim Healy oversaw the construction of a dozen buildings, more than any previous president had built during his tenure. The first was the recreational complex that was already being planned but not yet funded. Georgetown's McDonough Gymnasium was barely twenty-five years old but was badly outdated and limited to housing the university's intercollegiate teams of basketball and volleyball. There was virtually no indoor recreational space for the nonvarsity athlete, that is to say, almost all of the undergraduate population. Recreational facilities were becoming a major feature that prospective students expected universities to provide. The planned facility was primarily for the use of the general student population: undergraduates, graduates, and professionals.

Pool in Yates Fieldhouse,
1980. (Georgetown
University Archives)

Healy committed the development office to raising $2 million to comple-
ment the fees (that students in a referendum had voted to tax themselves
over the next thirty years) that would provide the bulk of the $7.5 million
to construct it. In the summer of 1977, construction began on excavated
land beneath Kehoe Field (to best utilize the extremely limited space that
the university had for its growth and expansion). Two summers later Yates
Field House, named for Gerard Yates, SJ, the former graduate dean and
government professor, opened. It contained a twenty-five-meter pool,
dance and exercise studio, eight courts for racquetball and squash, and an
enormous cathedral-like main area, with its hyperbolic paraboloid arches,
below which twelve courts could be variously configured for basketball,
volleyball, tennis, and track.

Academic facilities—classrooms, offices, auditorium—were another critical need. In March 1978 the board of directors authorized the construction
of an intercultural center to house several schools of the university, including the School of Foreign Service, the School of Languages and Linguistics,
the School for Summer and Continuing Education, and the graduate school,
as well as the departments of economics, government, history, and sociology. This project had been part of Mandate 81 but was one of the shortfalls of
that disappointing campaign. Now the money for the center came primarily

Bunn Intercultural Center, 1982. (Georgetown University Archives)

from the federal government, supplemented by funds raised by the university. The Office of Federal Relations at Georgetown, under Byron Collins, continued during the Healy years to be the major fund-raiser for the university, as it successfully garnered grants of scores of millions of dollars from the federal government, often in the form of national demonstration models. The intercultural center was the result of legislation that generated funding for the first such model designed by university architect Dean Price. It authorized the construction of "facilities for model intercultural programs designed to integrate the academic requirements of substantive knowledge and language facility."[17]

The passage of Public Law 95-240 eventually provided $17 million in grant money and $4.1 million in loans. The university raised $2 million on its own. The 215,000-square-foot center, named for former president Edward Bunn, provided 270 faculty offices, 49 classrooms, a 325-seat auditorium, language laboratories, and a central computer facility when it opened for the fall semester of 1982. The roof consisted of 35,000 square feet of solar panels, steeply sloped to become maximal receptors of solar energy, which was intended to provide the main heating and cooling for the building (an intention that faulty technology prevented from being fully realized). The $12 million roof on the intercultural center came as the result of the Solar

❦

DEDICATION OF ALUMNI SQUARE

In honor of
Joseph E. Beh (F'41)
Wallace Groves (C'23, L'23, GL'24, G'25, H'81)
J. Nevins McBride (C'29, H'78)
Eugene P. McCahill (C'21, G'22, H'55)

MAY 31, 1986 — GEORGETOWN UNIVERSITY

Program for dedication of Alumni Square in Alumni Village, 1986. (Georgetown University Archives)

Photovoltaic Energy Research Development and Demonstration Act of 1978, which Georgetown was responsible for introducing. In addition to the previously mentioned schools and departments housed in the new facility, the Bunn Intercultural Center also became the home of the Office of International Programs. As School of Foreign Service dean Peter Krogh noted at the cornerstone laying in 1980, "Georgetown's growth in the international field has been so substantial that today, across the board, Georgetown rivals any university in the world in the resources it can address to international education. The Intercultural Center, as the major educational building in the nation's capital with a focus on the world, will symbolize and synthesize these substantial resources."[18]

In 1976 another Georgetown demonstration project secured some $14 million from Congress to build an energy plant that would utilize a fluidized bed combustion system that would burn without pollution high sulfur coal, the cheapest and most abundant energy source. This was to serve as a model for universities, colleges, and hospitals nationwide. Eventually more than two score institutions around the country adopted similar systems. In 1980 the plant won Power magazine's Environmental Protection Award "for its pacemaker's role in protecting the nation's air and water."[19]

There were no demonstration projects for housing, another major need of the university in the late seventies. With the completion of Henle Student Village in the fall of 1976, barely half the undergraduates were now housed on campus. Fortuitously in the following year, the U.S. Congress approved the College Housing Loan Program, which provided the funding for the erection of three student villages, from 1977 to 1985, that housed more than 1,500 students. The three buildings were labeled alphabetically A, B, and C, in the hope that donors would emerge who would like to have a building bear their names. Sadly, only Village B escaped its anonymity when four alumni—Joseph E. Beh (**B** 1941), Wallace Groves (**C** 1923, **L** 1923), J. Nevins McBride (**C** 1929), and Eugene P. McCahill (**C** 1921)—made major benefactions in the 1980s. The complex was renamed Alumni Village, with the four constituent buildings bearing the names of the four donors, respectively. Alumni Village, designed by Hugh Newell Jacobsen, artfully disguised its apartment units as Victorian brick row houses that in front blended well with the surrounding neighborhood while providing for a communal atmosphere in the courtyard in the rear of the structures, a skilled accommodation, as Benjamin Forgey, the architectural critic for the Washington Post, noted, of both town and gown.[20] When the Nevils Complex became vacant with the opening of the intercultural center in 1982, that series of buildings was creatively renovated to provide multilevel apartments for 260 additional students. By 1986, with the opening of Village C, a complex of three

Topside exterior view of
Leavey Center, 1989.
(Georgetown University Archives)

traditional dormitories with seven hundred beds, nearly three-quarters of
the undergraduates were living on campus.

The creation of such a highly concentrated residential campus underscored the need for a university center, something Georgetown had been
seeking to add for almost two decades. In 1985 it became possible, thanks to
a combination $7 million grant from the Urban Mass Transportation Admin-
istration (another demonstration project), loans from the Department of Education, and private funding, including a $7 million donation from the Leavey
Foundation, for which family the facility was named. The four Victorian-
styled towers that echoed the rear side of the Healy Building fronted a multistoried complex with elevated wings on the ends. Above a buried aquatic-
storage tank and chiller system to produce and store energy (the model
demonstration), there was a three-level, one-thousand-car parking garage.
Atop that was a floor that housed restaurants and eateries, lounges, faculty
club, game and music rooms, a bookstore, and shops. At the western end was
a four-story convention/hotel wing; at the eastern end was a seven-story
wing containing offices for student development staff and student organizations. On top, between the two elevated wings of the complex, was an
esplanade. The building represented the first stage of the podium-based university urban academic village, running north–south in cascading drops
from the medical center to the bank overlooking the Chesapeake and Ohio
Canal that Dean Price had designed in the early seventies.

The Leavey Center, like the other planned academic and residential
buildings, featured energy-producing and storage facilities at bottom, underground parking, academic or residential facilities, topped by green space
for sport or recreation. "It's an urban vision of Jefferson's plan," the university architect commented.[21] The allusion was to the Jefferson-designed academic village at the University of Virginia, where a lawn, running between

resident classroom buildings, presented a stunning vista of the Blue Ridge Mountains. At Georgetown, athletic and recreational green space would provide a similarly arresting view of the Potomac and the Virginia palisades beyond. Benjamin Forgey was impressed. "It is a daring plan and in ways a brilliant one. By focusing future construction on the interior of the campus it simultaneously reduces town-gown tensions, clears the way for greatly enhanced energy efficiency, foresees the elimination of disfiguring surface parking lots and provides an exciting opportunity" to create a special academic community, although Forgey had his doubts concerning scale, texture, and visual connection as the future podia multiplied in their advance toward the river.[22]

A Land-Locked Institution

That Georgetown had adopted such a plan focusing on the interior of the campus was partially the result of its failure to acquire more land. In the late 1970s there had been two distinct opportunities to acquire significant portions of land toward the north and east. In April 1977, John Archbold finally offered his estate of thirty-nine acres to the university for $14 million. The university found the price too steep, especially considering the tax liability of $467,000 that would accompany the sale, and rejected the offer but indicated its possible future interest in the property.[23] Apparently the university never pursued the possibility of acquiring a smaller piece of the property.

At the time of the Archbold offer, it was already in negotiations with the Sisters of the Visitation to acquire a little more than eight acres of their property on the southwest corner of Reservoir Road and Thirty-Fifth Street. President Healy initially saw the purchase as a protective measure that would provide the university with the means of expanding, as it no doubt soon would have the need to do.[24] In June 1977 the university offered the convent $3,606,000 for the property, the approximate figure that the Sisters had been asking, based on an appraisal of the value of the land.[25] The Sisters, however, had learned that the land had increased in value since the 1975 appraisal. A new one in the summer of 1977 put the value of the property at $4.5 million.[26] In May 1978 the chair of the board's medical center affairs urged that the university acquire the property. They would need to acquire a loan of $5 million and amortize it over the next ten years.[27] At the same time, Chancellor McNulty, who had assumed the position of representing the university in its discussions with the Sisters about the land, informed them that the university was willing to pay $4.5 million for the property, with a down payment of $500,000. The lawyer for the Sisters informed McNulty that, although the Sisters had wanted a down payment of $750,000, they were open to the university's smaller offer, but they needed a decision by February 1, 1979.[28] In January the medical center committee of the board recommended that the university purchase the land, with the stipulation that it would resell it within the next three to five years should it not be able to finance the purchase. The committee admitted that the medical center had no pressing need for the property but warned that, should the university not take advantage of this precious opportunity to acquire such a scarce resource, it would have serious regrets in the future. But the board's Committee on Finance reported that it had concluded that the university had no immediate need of the property, that the asking price was too high, and that it would not be a good investment for the university.[29] The committee recommended against the acquisition, and the board ratified that recommendation.[30] Several days later an investment group purchased the land for $4.8 million.

Some members of the university community, particularly in the medical center, strongly suspected that there were conflicts of interest among some members of the board and the administration. No evidence has surfaced to bear out that suspicion. A more likely explanation is that President Healy did not at heart want to acquire the land for the medical center. He did not favor any expansion of the medical center beyond that already authorized, and he assured the board in April 1977 that he intended to limit any further expansion of the center. Denying them the Visitation property was one fundamental means of accomplishing that goal.[31] Whatever the reality, the land was developed and the avenues of expansion to the north and east lost. All too soon it seemed obvious that the university could have used the land and somehow found the financial wherewithal to obtain it. President Healy later admitted that the decision not to acquire the property was the one he most regretted having made.[32]

The university still possessed a large swath of land—some 641 acres of it—in distant Loudoun County near Dulles Airport. This was the land that Marcus Bles had given to the university in 1969. By the late 1970s the administration had determined that the Bles land was too remote to have any practical use for the university. Ironically a buyer emerged in 1983 who offered $6.4 million for the tract.[33] That would have more than paid for the Visitation property.

Building an Endowment

Robert Henle had often described Georgetown as a "living miracle" for being able to accomplish so much on such little capital. Tim Healy realized from the start that only by building an endowment could Georgetown hope to become what it had so long aspired to be—a first-class institution of national and, indeed, international prominence. A former administrator under Healy noted that "Tim was afraid of Georgetown's finances."[34] But he quickly learned to turn to those who had the knowledge and acumen to fathom Georgetown's financial state and needs. At a board meeting in the summer of 1977 he formed a development committee to evaluate the university's economic needs and to begin plans for a major fund drive that would raise $200 million by the end of the next decade.[35] As for fund-raising, he willed himself to overcome his own nature and became quite proficient in cultivating and capturing major donors, both corporate and individual. Healy was attempting to complete the drive that had frustrated his predecessor, and by the end of the year he was able to announce that Georgetown had successfully completed phase 1 of Mandate 81 by raising more than $55.2 million in gifts and pledges.[36] In two years about $16 million dollars had been raised to put this campaign to bed.

Georgetown's endowment, totaling $37.3 million when Timothy Healy took office, was virtually of no account in supporting the university's operations. Income from the endowment made up but 1 percent of the university's annual revenue.[37] The finance committee, which oversaw the endowment, reported in the spring of 1979 that the major manager of the endowment had not, over the past eight years, been keeping the endowment up with the rate of inflation. The endowment was actually shrinking. The committee recommended that the treasurer investigate the addition of another investment manager who would concentrate the endowment in small, specialized, high-growth companies.[38] Other managers were found who followed the recommendation of the finance committee. By the end of the fiscal year in June 1980, the new managers had appreciated Georgetown's endowment by more than 42.1 percent, which was the best performance of any university in the country.[39] By June 1981 the endowment stood at $71.6 million, an increase of 91.67 percent since 1976.[40] Within two years, thanks to aggressive management of the fund and new additions from fund-raising, it increased by $60 million, almost tripling in size in two years. The endowment per student had doubled from 1975, from $3,582 to $7,015. Even so, this was but half of what the average per student endowment was among COFHE schools.[41]

Adele Wells, vice president for development. (Photo by Harvey Ferdschneider. Georgetown University Archives)

The development committee, headed by George Sharffenberger, had studied the development office and concluded that reorganization and a new method of operation was badly needed. In 1979, Adele Wells, who was brought in as the new vice president for development, overhauled and expanded the development office staff. Annual gift income skyrocketed from $6.5 million in 1978–79 to $22.5 million in 1980–81.[42] Meanwhile, the committee had reached the obvious conclusion that Georgetown's endowment was pitifully small compared with the institutions with which it saw itself in competition. If Georgetown hoped to maintain—and what's more, to improve upon—the academic excellence it was achieving, it had to dramatically increase its endowment. It proposed a major new campaign, focused heavily on increasing Georgetown's endowment, to begin officially in 1982, by which time it hoped to have raised privately about one-third of the goal of the campaign. The Georgetown University Campaign, as it was officially known, had a goal of $115 million, of which $71 million would go to the endowment. "This campaign," Adele Wells explained, "is the first in Georgetown's history to focus on endowment rather than 'bricks and mortar.'"[43] The university needed to build the endowment for two principle reasons, Healy wrote in announcing the start of the campaign. It needed to maintain and increase an excellent faculty. It needed to ensure that it could continue to attract outstanding students of diverse backgrounds—"rich and poor, black and white, near and far."[44]

To provide fund-raising leadership, Healy looked to the board of directors as well as the board of regents; he had significantly expanded the membership of both to fifty members precisely for the purpose of creating a nationwide base upon which to build the fund-raising network. A consulting firm had warned that Georgetown's past failures at securing effective alumni leadership at regional levels in conducting capital campaigns made it a dicey proposition for the university to attempt a major national fund-raising campaign.[45] Healy, Wells, and Scharffenberger proved the warning to be groundless. A National Council for the Georgetown University Campaign was formed. Regional councils operated from New York to Southern California, each made up of more than one hundred alumni. For the first time, a Georgetown fund-raising campaign was organized at a national level and promoted through effective publicity at that level. There was also a centralization of fund-raising with the integration of the alumni association, which had been an independent organization with its own fund-raising mechanism, into the new Office of University and Alumni Relations.

Just after Christmas 1982, Timothy Healy had to undergo quintuple bypass surgery for his heart. But he was back in the office quickly and soon heavily involved in the new campaign. By the fall of 1983, thanks to the new leadership and organization of fund-raising, the university had reached nearly $70 million of its goal. Georgetown's endowment now stood at more than $100 million. The campaign itself passed the $100 million mark a year later. That represented more money than Georgetown had raised in its entire history prior to the Georgetown University Campaign. A study by the Council for Financial Aid to Education showed that Georgetown had outperformed every other institution of higher education in its increase in funds raised between 1978 and 1983. Alumni giving was up 158 percent, corporate giving was up 141 percent, and support by nonalumni individuals was up 140 percent.[46] Because of the swelling of income, the university in 1985 raised the goal of the campaign from $115 million to $145 million.

The mid-eighties proved to be a boom period for fund-raising by American higher education in general. From 1984 to 1986, universities on average experienced an annual rise in total gifts of 15 percent.[47] Georgetown continued to be one of the pacesetters. Each year the fund-raising dwarfed that of the previous year, peaking in 1985–86 at $31.5 million. The alumni annual fund, which had surpassed $1 million for the first time in 1978, reached nearly $6 million by the end of the eighties, with more than twenty thousand alumni and parents contributing. By 1989 the campaign had raised $178 million, $63 million over goal. Among the gains for the university were ten endowed chairs and $20.5 million for financial aid. Endowment per student now surpassed $20,000. In 1987 the university privately launched the Bicentennial Celebration Fund, with a goal of $110.1 million, for increasing the endowment ($34.25 million), financial aid ($14 million), facilities ($36.25 million), and other needs, by soliciting large gifts from directors, regents, corporations, and foundations. By the spring of 1989 nearly $70 million had been quietly raised.[48] All this was accomplished barely a decade after the university had struggled to complete the Mandate 81 goal of $52.3 million. There was no bolder indicator of how far the university had come in the course of the eighties.

The management of the endowment continued to be impressive. From 1983 to 1988, Georgetown had an annual return of 15.3 percent, which put it in the top quarter of the performance of portfolios. This was one of the factors that Healy cited for the remarkable growth of the endowment in the 1980s. The other two were a strengthening economy and the Georgetown University Campaign itself. At the close of the 1980s the endowment stood at nearly $230 million. Healy had wanted the endowment to reach the $200 million mark by its bicentennial. He had more than met his goal.

Two Financial Patterns: One Old, One New

The university continued to maintain a balanced budget during the latter seventies and through the eighties, despite continuing sharp increases in energy, health insurance, and administrative costs. A great growth in the endowment and in general gifts, along with a continuing increase in student enrollment and the institution of a faculty practice plan among the departments at the medical center, were major reasons that the budgets remained in the black. By 1985 the faculty practice plans were producing more than $50 million in revenue for the university. Tuition no longer constituted the majority of university income, but two campuses, the main campus and the law center, were still heavily dependent on tuition.[49] The budget itself grew from $140 million in 1977 to $472.3 million in 1989. Tuition for undergraduates rose from $3,500 in 1977 to more than $11,000 by 1988, as annual increases of 10 percent or more became standard. At the same time, federal support of tuition declined as the bulk of that financial aid changed from grants to loans. Georgetown increased its financial aid annually to keep pace with its increase in tuition and to offset the decrease in federal aid. But the rising percentage of working students during the academic year—34 percent of seniors in 1985—and the increasing percentage of students who owed more than $5,000 upon graduation (over 50% by 1983) were two strong indicators that student financial needs were not being adequately met.

The eighties brought a new mechanism for financing capital projects and a new ability to utilize debt capacity as a resource. A federal law allowed the District of Columbia to issue tax-exempt municipal bonds for the first time, and Georgetown University was able to avail itself, through these bonds, of long-term financing for the Leavey Center, the law center expansion; the telecommunications renovation and installation; and other major projects that did not have federal funding. Georgetown's rapidly improving financial condition, with balanced budgets and a soaring endowment, produced high credit ratings (AA from Moody's in 1988) that allowed the university low interest rates for the bonds it floated as well as a high debt capacity. An expanding student base with tuition increasing at a double-digit rate annually provided a major means for retiring the debt on schedule. In 1985 the university secured $70 million in tax-exempt bonds from the District and applied for $132 million more.[50] The university was privy to information that the federal government would soon move to put a cap on the amount of money any private institution could raise through tax-exempt bonds and wanted to maximize its utilization of this avenue for fund-raising before it was sealed off. In December 1987 the board authorized the president to borrow through tax-exempt bonds or commercial loans an additional $160 million to finance new capital projects that the university was undertaking.[51] Less than a decade before, the board had felt that the university could not take on a debt of $4.5 million that would accrue from the purchase of the Visitation property. Now it was approving the assumption of a debt in excess of $360 million. In June 1988 the university, failing to get authorization from the District of Columbia for tax-exempt bonds, put on the market $80 million of taxable exchangeable bonds through the First Boston Corporation. It marked the initial offering of Georgetown bonds on the commercial market.[52]

Faculty Development in a Time of Stagnation

By the late seventies the academy was experiencing a period of consolidation and contraction that would extend through most of the eighties. An economy in recession and declining funding from state and federal governments produced either policies of no new hiring or faculty reductions on most campuses across the nation. Georgetown was one of the few that escaped this pattern. During the eighties faculty expanded on the main campus. By the latter eighties, the faculty-undergraduate ratio had improved to 1:15, still below COFHE averages but much better than a decade earlier, despite the sharp rise in enrollment. Two new departments were created: demography within the Kennedy Institute/Graduate School and computer science within the college, both precipitating the creation of new faculty positions. Much of the expansion was the result of the decision to concentrate the university's resources on certain selected disciplines and programs to raise them to a position of excellence on the academic landscape. Thus in just two years, from 1984 to 1986, the main campus created twenty-three new faculty positions, most of those at the senior level.[53] In a buyer's market, Georgetown was reaping the first fruits as departments and programs were consistently hiring the best people available from the premier schools in the nation.

Over the course of the Healy years these selected departments were greatly strengthened, if not transformed, by the influx of faculty. Biology added Edward Barrows, Ellen Henderson, Joseph Neale, David Nishioka, and Diane Taylor. Economics gave appointments to James Albrecht, Laurie Bassie, Stuart Brown, Matthew Canzoneri, John Cuddington, Gary Hufbauer, Paul McNelis, SJ, Susan Vroman, and Daniel Westbrook. Anthony Arend, Harley Balzer, James Lengel, Robert Lieber, Eusabio Mujal-Leon, James Schall, SJ, Angela Stent, Arturo Valenzuela, and Clyde Wilcox joined the government department. Fine arts added Alison Hilton, Carra O'Meara, Elizabeth Prelinger, and Cynthia P. Schneider. History became a much stronger department through the advent of Tommaso Astarita, James Collins, Jo Ann Moran Cruz, Andrzej Kaminski, John McNeill, Kathryn Olesko, David Painter, James Shedel, Richard Stites, Judith Tucker, Nancy Tucker, and Jeffrey von Arx, SJ. Linguistics brought in Peter Lowenberg, Deborah Schiffrin, John Staczek, and Deborah Tannen. Wayne Davis, Alfonso Gomez-Lobo, John P. Langan, SJ, Edmund Pellegrino, Terry Pinkard, and Robert Veatch received appointments to the philosophy department. Spanish added Thomas Walsh and Hector Campos. With scholarship and/or scholarly promise the major criterion (in practice if not by stated preference) in the hiring process, faculty hires who were Catholic became far fewer than they had been two decades earlier.

The accelerated pace and scope of publications was one indicator of a far more scholarly faculty. In the history department, for instance, in the latter eighties (1986–90) twenty-three faculty had published or edited eighteen books and seventy-nine articles or chapters in books, compared with fourteen who had authored or edited nine books and thirty-one articles or chapters in the seventies (1973–78). In philosophy ten faculty had written or edited four books and published thirty-four articles or chapters in books from 1973 to 1978; in the latter eighties the corresponding numbers were eighteen faculty, twenty-three books, and 146 articles or chapters. That increase in production continued into the nineties. In one ranking of research universities in the nineties, Georgetown stood just below the top tier, or twenty-fourth overall in its publications output.[54] In the expansion of academic research and funding and its dispersion among a greater number of universities that marked the 1980s, Georgetown was clearly one of the beneficiaries in commanding a larger portion of the research and development shares.[55]

A smaller part of the expansion came from the raising of monies for chairs and the unilateral creation of university professorships. The first chair created under Healy was the Konrad Adenauer Chair established by the Federal Republic of Germany in 1976. By 1986 ten additional chairs had been created. Then there were the university professorships that Healy initiated unilaterally in the late seventies when Henry Kissinger was given a joint appointment to the School of Foreign Service and the Georgetown CSIS. By 1985 at least seven university professorships had been put in place, despite complaints of ordinary faculty that these professors had not gone through the normal appointment and tenuring process. To attract—and keep—such academic stars as Kissinger, Anthony Hecht, and others, Healy apparently worked out complex financial arrangements, including deferred compensation, which the board of directors approved in October 1981 as part of a policy to recruit and retain outstanding faculty.[56]

A sign of the growing prominence of Georgetown faculty was the unprecedented recruitment of eleven members for posts in the Reagan administration in 1980–81. The most conspicuous was government professor Jeane Kirkpatrick, selected by Reagan to be the United States ambassador to the United Nations. Among the others were William Steerman from the Russian Area Studies Program (RASP) program to the National Security Council and Chester Crocker from CSIS to assistant secretary of state for African affairs. At the same time, no fewer than fourteen members of the former Carter administration accepted positions at Georgetown to form what one writer dubbed "a veritable miniature government-in-exile."[57] Most of the Carter alumni found appointments at the law center, including Eleanor Holmes Norton, Judith Areen, and Adrian Fisher. Undersecretary of state for political affairs, David Newsom, and Donald McHenry, Kirkpatrick's predecessor at the United Nations, both joined the School of Foreign Service faculty.

Despite the president's persistent efforts, Georgetown's schools, with one exception, made little headway in adding minority faculty, particularly African Americans, to its ranks. In 1980, Healy set up an Office of Affirmative Action and brought in Rosemary Kilkenny Sabai to head it. In 1985, with Healy's encouragement, the provost announced a five-year plan for affirmative action in hiring faculty. Three new positions would be set aside each year for minorities, a third of whom were to be African Americans.[58] A few new African American faculty were the result, far short of the plan's goal. Part of the reason for the paltry results was the intense competition among prestigious institutions of higher learning for black candidates to fill their academic positions. But Georgetown, outside of the law center, did not exercise the aggressive measures in recruiting potential black faculty that it had taken to increase its minority student enrollment. Meanwhile, the law center had put together not only the most diverse student community, with nearly 20 percent of its students comprising African Americans, but the most diverse faculty as well, with the largest number of tenured black members on the faculty. In 1988, Healy urged the faculty senate to take the initiative in goading each department on the main campus and medical center to hire at least one black faculty member within the next three to five years. "If we are training young people for citizenship in an integrated society, the body of the faculty who do the preparation must itself be integrated," he told the senate."[59] A year later he committed the university to home-grow some black faculty by supporting three African American Georgetown graduates through graduate school in the hope that they might return to Georgetown after completing their doctorates.[60] But as of 1989 there were still only two tenured African American faculty on the main campus.

At the same time, salaries for faculty were steadily improving, as annual raises were consistently above the cost of living increase. The benchmark for faculty salaries had been set during the early seventies by the Henle administration at the 80th percentile of the AAUP ranking of the salaries of professors in research institutions. In the seventies, salaries for Georgetown professors of all ranks fell considerably short of that mark. During Timothy Healy's first year, the main campus planning committee made the improvement of faculty salaries its top priority. A decade later all ranks were substantially above that 80 percent level, with assistant professors standing the lowest at 89 percent. These, of course, were campuswide averages that did not distinguish between the salaries of professors in English or theology from those in marketing or economics. A mid-eighties survey of the main campus faculty found that more than half of them found their salaries still to be insufficient.[61] No doubt the extremely high cost of living in the Washington metropolitan area influenced this opinion. Even for those who felt underpaid, there were compensating factors: one was the improvement of retirement benefits that took place in the eighties, when the university increased its contribution to the faculty investment funds. Another was the reduction of teaching loads as nonlanguage departments went from three courses each semester to 3-2 or 2-2, and language departments went from 4-4 to 3-3. In 1984 junior faculty fellowships were set up to allow untenured faculty to receive a sabbatical to complete some major scholarship (often the revision of a dissertation) that would establish the person as a solid contributor in his or her field (as well as help them prepare for the application for tenure). Summer research grants were also tripled at this time from five to fifteen.

The growing stature of Georgetown's faculty was reflected in the increasing number of prestigious awards that main campus faculty won: Guggenheim, MacArthur, Rockefeller Foundation, and Woodrow Wilson Center fellowships, as well as awards from the National Endowment for the Humanities and the NSF. James Devereux, SJ, a former English professor at the university who had become the superior of the Maryland Province, said in 1987 that he would stake "his sacred honor," if not his life, on the assertion that Georgetown now enjoyed the most learned lay and Jesuit faculty that it had ever had in its two-hundred-year history.[62]

Georgetown's Libraries

In the fall of 1977 the main campus planning committee had made the library its second top priority. By the late seventies inflation and a lack of campus funding had severely hampered the library's growth. Beginning with the 1978 fiscal year, the library received increases of 10 percent or more in its budget. In the 1982–83 academic year, with a 17 percent increase in its budget, the library added more than forty-one thousand books and bound journals to its collection. In November of that year it celebrated the acquisition of its one-millionth volume for the Lauinger Library Collection, a first edition of John Milton's *Paradise Lost*. In 1989 the university and the Maryland Province of the Jesuits reached an agreement whereby Georgetown would permanently house the Woodstock Library, one of the best theological collections in the country. During these years the library's special collections also took giant steps forward as it acquired several important collections, especially in Jesuit, Catholic, and political history. Its head, Martin Barringer, could say with confidence in 1986 that "we have the best collection in North America on the early history of the American Catholic Church," after that division had become the depository of the archives of the Maryland Province of the Society of Jesus, including those of Woodstock College, and acquired the papers of Father John LaFarge and *America* magazine. The papers of Graham Greene, Evelyn Waugh, G. K. Chesterton, Hilaire Belloc, and Douglas Woodruff, all members of the Catholic Renaissance in Great Britain, also greatly strengthened its Catholic holdings. Other major acquisitions were the papers of Harry L. Hopkins, Senator Brian McMahon, and Lady Barbara Ward. As Barringer observed, the strength of Georgetown's special collections was its comprehensiveness.[63] The whole greatly outweighed the sum of its parts.

The Heart of Georgetown

For Tim Healy the heart of Georgetown was its undergraduate programs, especially its College of Arts and Sciences. In his 1978 report to the university community, he noted the utmost importance of making undergraduate education at Georgetown something that attracted the very best students in the country and offered them the financial assistance to make that education affordable. In 1978, under Healy's prodding, the board of directors voted to provide financial aid that would meet the need of all admitted undergraduate students. This allowed the university to attract the most gifted students, regardless of their socioeconomic status. In 1975 only 10 percent of the undergraduate students at Georgetown received financial aid; by 1989 more than half did. A major boost toward the broadening of financial aid came in the early eighties with the establishment, by the alumni admissions program, of the John Carroll Scholarship program. Through individual gifts and foundation grants, by the nineties the program was supporting nearly one hundred John Carroll scholars, independent of financial need.

A National and Diverse Student Population

Along with the university's commitment to provide much greater financial assistance to students, it made the decision to become more national. "We were looking to become national at a time when everything supported it," explained Charles Deacon, the director of admissions. "The 70s became an era when we developed interviewing committees around the nation and the world."[64] A critical instrument in achieving a truly continental pool of applicants lay in the broadening of the alumni interviewing network that Dan Altobello had established in 1964. By 1989 that network comprised more than 3,600 interviewers working in places throughout the nation and beyond, from Maine to Hong Kong, and interviewing more than 96 percent of those applying to Georgetown. This recruiting drive began in the early eighties, when the national cohort of eighteen-year-olds declined by more than 10 percent. Nonetheless, Georgetown succeeded spectacularly in increasing both the number of its applicants and the quality of those admitted, as well as diversifying their demographics. Smart, comprehensive recruiting was one factor, Georgetown's growing visibility under Healy another. Washington itself was becoming an increasingly attractive area in which to study, particularly to the growing numbers of young men and women who wanted to be politically involved while in college. (By the late eighties, about 45% of Georgetown's undergraduates were involved in internships of one sort or other.) With a strong reputation for its political science and international relations programs, Georgetown had a leg up in securing applications from those wishing to pursue those interests in the nation's capital.

Gradually Georgetown crafted a public identity that combined four characteristics: a Catholic institution, academic renown, a location in Washington, and an international composition and focus. From 1973 to 1986, the number of undergraduate applicants skyrocketed—from about 5,500 in 1973 to nearly 12,400 by 1986. In the same period the number of those accepted to Georgetown actually declined from 2,750 to 2,531. In 1975, Georgetown had accepted about 44 percent of its applicants. By 1986 it had fallen by more than half to 20 percent. For the college and the School of Foreign Service, the change was even more impressive. In 1975 the college accepted 35.4 percent of its applicants. In 1986 that amount had shrunk to 17 percent. In the School of Foreign Service it went from nearly 50 percent in 1975 to 20.8 percent in 1986. The Business School went from 45 percent to 20 percent; the School of Languages and Linguistics from a whopping 74 percent in 1975 to 36 percent in 1986. Only nursing remained stagnant at about 69 percent, a phenomenon that had more to do with a declining profession than the quality of the school. As one would expect, higher selectivity meant higher quality, at least as measured by standard tests. In 1975 all Georgetown schools were below 1200 in combined SAT scores. By 1986 the college and the School of Foreign Service were approaching or surpassing the 1300 mark.

As early as 1979 Barron's Education Services was rating Georgetown as one of the toughest colleges to get into, putting it in the top 40. By the end of the next decade Georgetown stood in the top 20 according to selectivity. And the geographical distribution of Georgetown had changed as well. In the early eighties, 72 percent of Georgetown's undergraduate applicants came from the Mid-Atlantic region; by the late eighties it was 37 percent and dropping. Among the other regions of the country (New England, South, Midwest, West, and Southwest), there was near equality in distribution, with every region but the Southwest accounting for between 12 percent and 14.5 percent of Georgetown's undergraduate enrollment (the Southwest accounted for 4 percent).

In religious demographics, Georgetown's undergraduates became more diverse, although the Catholic proportion of undergraduates stabilized at 60 percent in the eighties after dropping sharply in the latter sixties and less so during the seventies. The college and the Business School, which had been the most Catholic of the schools in the 1960s, experienced the greatest change. In 1960 the college had been 96 percent Catholic, the Business School 90 percent; by 1982 Catholics in the college constituted 68 percent of enrollment, in the Business School 63 percent. The drastic shift in the types of schools from which Georgetown entering students were coming was one measure, albeit a limited one, of the change in the religious identity of the undergraduate student body. In 1969 students from Catholic high and preparatory schools had made up a majority of the applicants and constituted 57 percent of those accepted. By 1990 they constituted but 20 percent of applicants and 24 percent of those accepted.[65]

The minority population grew as well, particularly among African Americans in the late seventies and eighties, and Asian Americans in the late eighties. Twice in his recent past Timothy Healy had attempted to establish community colleges for black students, once in Bedford-Stuyvesant, and again in Westchester County, New York. As one administrator and former assistant to Healy remembered, "He thought the great fault line in our republic was racism. He was convinced that our universities must provide leadership in breaking down the barriers to education for our nation's African Americans."[66] Healy fostered an aggressive recruiting of African Americans at the undergraduate, graduate, and professional levels, especially from the District itself. Georgetown, Healy once said, had much to learn from a large presence of blacks within its community, with their own unique experience that they could bring to Georgetown.[67] It was no accident that the percentage of African Americans in the university rose from 3 percent in 1976 to 10 percent by 1989, significantly better than the percentage at selective colleges and universities.[68] At the law center, that percentage was more than double. In the undergraduate schools, there were, in 1977, 82 black males and 135 black females. By 1987 there were 322 black males and 455 black females. Despite a shrinking pool of black applicants nationally, their number of applicants to Georgetown continued to rise.[69]

The sharp increase in black applications and acceptances resulted in part, no doubt, from the success that John Thompson and his teams began to enjoy in the eighties; a larger part stemmed from the decision of Healy and Charles Deacon to aggressively recruit black applicants and provide them with the financial and academic means to succeed at Georgetown. One of

Samuel Harvey Jr. (far left), and the staff of the Center for Minority Student Affairs, 1970s–80s. (Georgetown University Archives)

Healy's first acts during the summer of 1976 was the creation of the Center for Academic Supportive Services (later the Center for Minority Student Affairs) under the directorship of Samuel Harvey Jr. The center's purpose was to support and promote minority programs for students within the university and the Washington metropolitan area. It supervised the community scholars program that prepared African Americans (and other minorities) for Georgetown during a six-week summer session. The center's staff grew to twenty members, plus many student tutors, by the mid-eighties. In 1977 the center was responsible for the creation of the writing center, led by James Slevin of the English department, to provide assistance primarily to minority students in improving their writing skills. Three years later it helped set up the math assistance workshop.

In 1981 the liberal studies program, a full academic year replacement for the summer-long community scholars program, started under the direction of Paul Cardacci, in which faculty and teaching assistants conducted a year-long program for selected first-year minority students. By 1989 minorities constituted one-quarter of the incoming undergraduate freshman class, and the largest group was African Americans. And the retention rate of minorities was remarkably high—more than 91 percent graduated, better than the graduation rate of 87 percent for all undergraduates.[70] By the end of the eighties, Georgetown had gained a national reputation for its ability to attract and graduate minority students; other universities and colleges began to look to Georgetown as a model and to adopt its strategies and programs for reaching out to minorities.[71]

Rhodes, Marshalls, and Mellons

As with the faculty, the dramatic improvement in the quality of undergraduates manifested itself in the prestigious awards that Georgetown students began to win in increasing numbers in the eighties. This was not a simple development of excellence attracting recognition. Tim Healy set out in the late 1970s to secure Rhodes scholarships for Georgetown students, an effort he later widened to include Marshalls, Mellons, and Fulbrights as well. He brought in Edgar Puryear in 1983 to be the university's fellowship secretary, who was to coordinate and prepare Georgetown's applicants for the awards. In reality, Puryear concentrated heavily on the Rhodes competition. John Hirsh became, in effect, the secretary for Marshall scholarships. In 1982, Elaine Hadley became the first Georgetown student to win a Marshall Scholarship. Beginning in the eighties, Georgetown, which had not won a Rhodes scholarship since Bill Clinton received one in 1968, became a regular recipient of Rhodes scholarships, peaking in 1986 when Georgetown students or alumni won three. Between 1984 and 1996, Georgetown won fourteen Rhodes scholarships, better than one a year. Only four schools in the country had better records. Marshalls and Mellons came to Georgetown students in noticeable numbers as well.

Curricular Patterns

Among majors within the college, biology, government, and English continued to dominate the field, with nearly half the college students majoring in one of these three disciplines in 1976, and 53 percent doing so in 1989. However, by 1989, government, unsurprisingly, was the most popular major, surpassing biology, which dropped to third place behind English. More than one in five students were now majoring in government. The natural sciences (biology, chemistry, computer science, mathematics, physics), which had accounted for 35 percent of majors in 1976, by 1989 composed only 24 percent of majors. The humanities (American studies, classics, interdisciplinary studies, English, fine arts, history, languages, philosophy, and theology) made up 28.5 percent of all majors in 1976; thirteen years later they composed 39 percent of majors, very likely reflecting the greater proportion of women in the college. Apparently benefitting from its restoration to the general education requirements, history made the largest gain in the period, more than doubling its majors to occupy fourth place. Computer science, which became a major in 1985, had twenty-one majors, good for fourteenth place, by 1989. The social sciences (economics, government, psychology, and sociology) comprised virtually the same percentage of majors in 1976 (36.4%) as in 1989 (36.8%). Psychology also showed an increase in majors, moving from sixth to fifth place in the fourteen-year span. Both mathematics and sociology suffered severe declines of 50 percent. Economics and chemistry experienced significant fall-offs as well. In the School of Foreign Service, more than half of students majored in international affairs throughout the period. By 1989, nearly 57 percent of all School of Foreign Service students were international affairs majors. Another 20 percent majored in international politics, up from 14 percent in 1976. International economics, which had accounted for 14 percent in 1976, fell to 8 percent by 1989. Humanities and international affairs was a modest gainer in the period, going from 5 percent in 1976 to 8 percent in 1989. History and diplomacy as well as regulation both lost majors during that span of years, together accounting for only 6.5 percent of majors by 1989.

In the Business School, the biggest shift in majors occurred in accounting, where the percentage of students concentrating in this field plunged from nearly half (48.8%) to 14.6 percent. Finance and marketing, which had accounted for 31 percent of majors in 1976, made up 73.2 percent in 1989, with finance majors alone composing 46.5 percent of the total. This increase reflected the rapid growth of the financial industry within the economy in the 1980s. In the School of Languages and Linguistics, there was great consistency in the choice of majors. French, Spanish, and English as a foreign language remained the three most popular fields, constituting 54.3 percent of all majors in 1976 and 44.5 percent in 1989. Russian accounted for 8 percent in 1976 and 9.8 percent in 1989, with German slightly behind at 7.4 percent (1976) and 7.6 percent (1989). Japanese made the greatest gain in majors during the period, from twenty (2.3%) in 1976 to fifty-two (6.8%) in 1989, no doubt a reflection of that nation's rise as an economic power. Linguistics majors, at 6 percent, remained unchanged. Only interpretation (1976, 6.7%; 1989, 1.5%) and Portuguese (1976, 3.6%; 1989, 1.1%) experienced steep declines in the number of students majoring in them.

Double majoring, a new possibility in the eighties, became a way for students to extend their concentrations to more than one discipline. Most double majors were initially in the college, but by the latter eighties the business school had by far the most, with about one-quarter of their students double majoring. Finance and management was the most frequent combination. In the college, English, economics, government, and history led the way as constituents of a double major; in the School of Languages and Linguistics, it was language and linguistics. A less intense form of this bifurcated specialization, which proved even more popular, was the coupling of a major in one discipline with a minor in another (usually requiring six courses rather than the eight required for a standard major).

Evaluations and Academic Development

Self- and peer-examination became a regular instrument utilized to promote and assess academic development, part of the quest for excellence. In the latter seventies the provost ordered all departments and programs to undertake periodic reviews, which consisted of two processes: a self-study of the department's programs, including enrollments and curriculum, as well as of the faculty's teaching, scholarship, and service, and an evaluation of the department by a visiting team of experts through their examination of self-study and interviews with students, faculty, and administrators. In 1980 the provost appointed a three-team task force to carry out this evaluation on a campuswide scale that included personnel, programs, and structure of the main campus schools. The yearlong investigation resulted in many proposed changes, such as the adoption of a four-course load per semester for undergraduates; the appointment of a dean of the faculty to represent the faculty and to oversee its performance; the establishment of a committee on appointments to serve as a vetting advisory body on all departmental and school appointments; the elimination of the conflict of interest inherent in the dean of the School of Foreign Service's (a de facto department head) having jurisdiction over the departments of economics, government, and history by relocating them under the dean of the college; a main campus committee on curriculum that would ensure the coherence and compatibility of programs across school lines; the dissolution of the School of Languages and Linguistics, with the language departments becoming part of the College of Arts and Sciences and linguistics becoming a program only within the graduate school; the selection of a core of disciplines in which the university would invest its resources in graduate education so that those selected fields could have the distinct possibility of

J. Donald Freeze, SJ, provost, 1979–91. (Georgetown University Archives)

becoming distinguished; and making two courses per semester the normal teaching load for those faculty actively engaged and productive in scholarship.[72] Most of these recommendations eventually were put into effect by the middle of the next decade.

The Quest for a Core

A move to develop a single core curriculum across schools emerged in the mid-eighties. Three major national reports on curriculum in 1984–85 all sounded the alarm that the undergraduate curriculum needed sweeping reform in its general education requirements and that these needed to have a coherence and interrelatedness that they currently lacked.[73] At Georgetown the newest five-year plan called for a main campus review of the core curriculum within the several undergraduate schools. In 1985 the provost called on all departments, executive councils, and the faculty senate to deliberate about the nature of liberal education and the place of a core curriculum within it. Specifically he charged the main campus faculty to come up with recommendations that responded to the questions, "What skills, knowledge, and wisdom should every Georgetown graduate have?" and "How are such skills, knowledge, and wisdom to be imparted through the curriculum?" The ensuing mandated discussions produced a very lackluster response to the questions posed. The recommendations that emerged from the campuswide dialogue related much more to the process than to the content of a core curriculum. The working paper that came out of the faculty senate's educational affairs committee on the topic, for instance, pointed to the need for reform of the academic calendar (to increase the span of the semester to allow for greater time for reflection), smaller classes for general education courses, a reeducation of the faculty that would result in the acquisition of a common fund of knowledge to undergird core courses, and the implementation of a semester schedule of four courses of four credits (4-4) each that would allow for more intellectual development of the students.[74]

Undeterred by the tepid response of these main campus academic groups, the provost, in the fall of 1985, brought in several academics to address the faculty on their experience in developing a core curriculum on their campuses. In the following semester, the provost, in conjunction with the faculty senate, appointed an eleven-person committee to consider what should constitute a core curriculum at Georgetown and how it could be made part of every undergraduate's education. A year later the committee made its report. It had identified certain areas of knowledge and attendant skills that were necessary constituents of any core curriculum appropriate for Georgetown's unique liberal arts tradition, the sine qua non elements for providing a foundation for attaining a "purchase on a future of responsible intellectual growth." Comprising the core areas were (a) foundational questions (involving critical reflection on "issues of God, being, knowing, and moral/religious consciousness"), the answering of which would promote the acquisition of wisdom; (b) natural sciences (involving the formation of an adequate understanding of the nature of scientific inquiry and of its methods, limitations, and results); (c) literatures and the arts (involving the exposure to aesthetic texts and monuments that form part of our cultural heritage or that of others); (d) historical studies, particularly the study of Western civilization (involving the attainment of an indispensable context for the various forms of knowledge and culture); and (e) social sciences (involving the bridging of the intellectual concerns of both the humanities and the natural sciences).[75]

As Dorothy Brown, a member of the committee, later noted, the committee had attempted to craft the broad dimensions of an undergraduate core while respecting the separate identities of the several undergraduate schools. "The actual crafting of guidelines for core courses and actual development of core courses" was left to the next stage of building a core, the creation of core area subcommittees. That stage never occurred. The executive councils of the undergraduate schools took up the report, which was also the subject of three general faculty meetings in the spring of 1987, but nothing really came out of it. There was "a brief flurry of declamations followed by an immense silence."[76] In the final analysis, Georgetown lacked all three of the elements needed for the successful creation of a core curriculum: administrative leadership, a faculty open to change, and financial resources. With the main campus still more than 80 percent tuition-dependent for its revenue, what little money existed for academic development had already been committed to those departments chosen to achieve excellence in graduate education.[77] The establishment of a core continued to elude the main campus academy.

One recommendation of the core committee that was acted upon was its call to consider the feasibility of shifting to a semester schedule of 4-4. In September 1989 the provost announced the formation of a new committee, comprised of the dean of the college, two students, and eight faculty, to study the question. Five months later the committee recommended in its report that the university not adopt a 4-4 curriculum. On the one hand, a large majority of the committee members felt that the imposition of a 4-4 schedule would seriously reduce the breadth of a Georgetown education; on the other hand, there was a lack of conviction among committee members that a 4-4 curriculum would mean a deeper educational experience for students in the particular courses taken.[78] That report effectively ended a perennial discussion, going back to the sixties, on the desirability of reducing the standard number of courses per semester. Georgetown would not follow the curricular path that most COFHE schools had chosen to take.

The College: Growing in Stature and Breadth

The Healy years were a period of remarkable stability in the deanships of most of the undergraduate schools: Royden Davis, SJ, at the college, Peter Krogh at the School of Foreign Service, James Alaitis at the School for Languages and Linguistics, and Ronald Smith at the Business School. Continuity at the top provided the leadership that enabled the schools to flourish in the eighties. The steadily rising graduation rates of the schools (from 85.7% in 1981 to 91.1% in 1988) was one measure of their improving academic health. The very high percentage of graduating seniors (over 95%), who would then encourage others to attend Georgetown, was another.[79] Under the serene and unobtrusive guidance of Royden Davis, the College of Arts and Sciences continued to grow in stature and breadth. The college fostered a women's studies program. Minors were established in that field as well as in medieval studies and peace studies. Dean Davis was particularly responsible for the growth of the fine arts department. During his deanship, the department grew from two persons to a full-time faculty of twelve: four in the history of art, four in studio art, one in speech, one in music, and two in theater. And the department, within its new home, the Walsh Building, had its own Black Box Theater in the converted Hall of Nations. In 1980, Davis oversaw the creation of the Ward Law Hamilton Lectureship in American Folklore, through which a leading scholar of folklore and/or folk music would offer a course or seminar during a semester of the academic year. Two years later this lectureship was complemented by another, the Ralph K. Davies Lectureship in Theatre Arts.

Royden Davis was emblematic of the personal and humane character that marked relations between faculty and students at Georgetown. Timothy Healy once wrote that "there is better faculty-student rapport here than in any of the five universities in which I have taught or studied [the other four were Louvain, Oxford, City University of New York, and Fordham]. . . . On the whole the daily working of the University gives off an aura of happiness and contentment which is quite extraordinary."[80] In no small way Davis set the tone for the college community. Indeed, by the time he retired in 1989 after a quarter century in the office, Royden Davis had accomplished more in shaping and developing the college than all of his predecessors combined.

By the early eighties a growing number of graduates were choosing the law as their profession, 31 percent of men and 15 percent of women. Another 20 percent, of both men and women, were making careers in business. Health care was the third leading career choice of 13 percent of the men and 16 percent of the women.[81] Among those becoming attorneys were Dan Burke (1978), who continued his commitment to community service begun at Georgetown by heading up the Community Development Corporation in Chicago; Thomas F. English (1980), general counsel for New York Life; John Farmer (1979), who became the attorney general of New Jersey in 1999 after serving as assistant U.S. attorney; Lisa Murkowski (1980), who was elected U.S. senator from Alaska in 2003; Lisa Madigan (1988), attorney general of Illinois; Robert Spolzino (1980), who was appointed a justice of the Supreme Court of New York State in 2001; Ronald Klain (1983), chief of staff to the vice president in both the Clinton and Obama administrations; Anne Slaughter Andrew (1977), United States ambassador to Costa Rica in 2009; Joseph P. Lockhart (1982), press secretary for President Clinton; and Luke O'Neill (1981, **L** 1984), who left an international law firm to work with inner-city kids, eventually founding a school for them in Massachusetts that incorporated the Outward Bound program's principles of service-based learning and rising to challenges.

Graduates of the college to make careers in business included Theodore Leonsis (1977), who became a top executive of America Online as well as the principal owner of the Washington Capitals of the National Hockey League and of the Washington Wizards of the NBA; Stacy H. Davis (1985), who in 2000 became president and CEO of the Fannie Mae Foundation; Emily Chen (1988), who became a vice president of Goldman, Sachs & Company; Elizabeth Tsehai (1989), who founded and became president of E. T. Communications, a company that promoted African products and services; and Mary Callahan Erdoes (1989), who became CEO of JP Morgan Bank.

Dorothy M. Brown, professor of history and academic planner for the main campus in the 1980s. Executive vice president of the university, 1998–2002. (Georgetown University Archives)

Among those making careers in health care were James J. Chun (1982, **M** 1986), who was appointed director of adolescent medicine at the Naval Medical Center in San Diego; Robert Joseph Doherty (1983, **M** 1987), the founder of the Georgetown Emergency Medical Service, who became a professor at the University of Maryland Medical School before his death at thirty-five in 1997; Patricia Conrad Rizzo (1986, **M** 1990), who headed Georgetown's oncology unit in northern Virginia; and Dominique Gooby Toedt (1989), who became a major in the Army Medical Corps.

Among those making careers in the academy and related areas were John DeGioia (1979; **G** 1995), who became Georgetown's first lay president in 2001; Paul Croce (1979), who chaired American studies at Stetson University; Kelley Wickham-Crowley (1979), who became a professor of medieval literature at Georgetown; Anne Derwinski McCarthy (1980), who became dean of the University of Baltimore Merrick School of Business; Joseph Donohue (1981), who was appointed professor of English at the University of Massachusetts-Amherst; Kevin Delaney (1982), who became a professor of sociology at Temple University; William Ferraro (1982), who became a professor of history at the University of Virginia; Maria Cristina Garcia (1982), who became a professor of history at Cornell University; Daniel Porterfield (1983), a Rhodes Fellow who returned to Georgetown to hold several administrative positions; Mark S. Humayun (1984), who was professor of ophthalmology and associate director of research at the Doheny Eye Institute at the University of Southern California; and Scott R. Pilarz (1981), who in 2003 became president of the University of Scranton.

A significant minority of college graduates made careers in communications and the mass media, including Maria Shriver (1977) as a reporter and news anchor for major networks NBC and CBS; Mary Jordan (1983) as a bureau chief for the *Washington Post,* who in 2003 won a Pulitzer Prize for a series of articles about corruption in Mexico's criminal justice system; Quinn Hillyer (1986) as an editorial writer and syndicated columnist with the *Mobile Register* in Alabama, then the *Washington Examiner;* Mary A. Kelly (1986) as a reporter with the *International Herald Tribune;* Crystal Wright (1989) as a reporter and producer for ABC News; Kelly Flynn (1988) as an executive producer for the Cable News Network (CNN); and Miles O'Brien (1981) as a correspondent for CNN. Tara McKelvey became an editor for the liberal journal of opinion, the *American Prospect.*

Graduates who made careers in the arts included Sara Huger Noone (1978), whose work as a painter was cut short by Parkinson's disease; Pearl Bailey Bellson (1985), who received an honorary degree from Georgetown in 1977 that inspired her to return to school to earn the degree she had sought as a schoolgirl before embarking on her renowned career on the stage and screen; Richard Thompson (1986), an alumnus of Mask and Bauble, who became a highly successful actor on Broadway; Mary Fortuna

(1989), who became an actress on the stage and television; and Hilary Bir-
mingham (1989), who established a career as a film producer.

The Flowering of the School of Foreign Service

Under Dean Peter Krogh, the School of Foreign Service by the latter seventies had regained its prestige within the world of international studies. Applications continued to increase at a dramatic rate. By 1977 there were
1,372 applicants; by 1984 there were more than 2,000. From 1974 to 1986,
applications had increased by 186 percent, with scarcely more than 20 percent of applicants being admitted.

Dean Krogh gave particular visibility to the school when he inaugurated
a television series on the local PBS station, WETA, in 1981. The hour-long
weekly show, "American Interests," hosted by Krogh, was the first news
hour on television to focus exclusively on foreign affairs. In the first half,
the dean provided a background report on a topic that served as the introduction to an interview with an expert on the topic, either from academic
or government circles. By 1983 the show was being carried by 130 PBS
stations, as well as on the Learning Channel and on the Catholic Telecommunications Network of America. In 1988, "American Interests" was succeeded by another Krogh creation, "World Beat: Great Decisions in
American Foreign Policy," which featured reports from around the world,
together with interviews and studio discussions, all anchored by Krogh. In
its first year, the show won an Emmy award for a program it aired on the
Middle East.[82]

Krogh not only provided visibility for the school but became a prodigious
fund-raiser to support programs and to create new programs as well as faculty positions. By the eighties he was raising several millions of dollars annually. Endowed chairs, regional programs in African and Asian studies, an
institute for the study of diplomacy, and a program in international business
diplomacy were the major results of the benefactions. In March 1978, Krogh
inaugurated the Institute for the Study of Diplomacy. Bringing together former as well as active diplomats, the institute had as its mission the engagement of studies on a range of historic and contemporary diplomatic issues
and topics. It also enabled on-site diplomats to serve as mentors for students
doing internships. The institute sponsored publications of the case studies,
symposia, lectures, and seminars held under its auspices. Under the direction of retired ambassadors Martin Hertz and David Newsom, the institute
proved to be an important addition to the school over the next decade.

Among the chairs established at the school were the chair in Arab studies, held by the historian Hisham Sharabi; the Sun Yat-sen Chair in China
Studies in 1980; the Seif Ghobash Chair of Arab Studies, with a grant from
the United Arab Emirates, in the same year (Michael Hudson, director of

the Center for Contemporary Arab Studies, became the first holder); the Kuwait Chair in 1981, with Professor Hanna Batatu receiving the first appointment; and the Marcus Wallenberg Chair in International Finance Diplomacy.

In 1978 the Landegger Program in International Business Diplomacy was established. The program, under the direction of Theodore Moran, integrated courses in economics, languages, business, and public policy that allowed undergraduates to earn a certificate in international business diplomacy, as well as opening the field to students seeking a master of science in foreign service as a choice for an honors concentration.

Beyond the revisions in the general education requirements noted earlier, the school made other changes in the undergraduate curriculum. A review of the curriculum in 1976 pointed to a flaw in the core curriculum: During the first two years of a student's program, all of the required courses were composed of large lecture classes, none of which had any direct application to international affairs. The upshot was a failure to build any bonds between school faculty and students or to establish any strong identity with the school itself. A remedy for this failing was the creation of sophomore seminars taught by members of the core faculty, including the dean, on topics related to world affairs.[83]

The master of science in foreign service program reached elite status by the eighties. Under the leadership of Allen Goodman, the curriculum was reformed, new faculty added, energetic recruitment of applicants begun, and fellowships significantly increased to attract outstanding candidates. By the end of the eighties, the program was receiving one thousand applications, had become one of the three top graduate programs in international relations, and was placing more graduates in the presidential management internship program than any other institution.[84]

Although only a small minority of the school's graduates chose the foreign service as their career, School of Foreign Service alumni continued to constitute the largest bloc within the field, annually accounting for about 10 percent of those being accepted as foreign service officers. By 1990 entering foreign service officers from Georgetown outnumbered the combined numbers of the next two highest institutions—Harvard and Yale.[85] Among graduates in the foreign service were Michael Dodman (1981), Paul Sutphin (1982), Michael Zak (1982), Carolyn Gorman (1984), and Sharon Hudson-Dean (1990). Karl Hofmann served as executive secretary of state during the George W. Bush administration; Maura Harty (1981) was U.S. ambassador to Paraguay in the Clinton administration; Hugo Llorens (1977), Richard B. Norland (1977), Frank Lavin (1979), Stephen D. Mull (1980), Eric G. John (1982), and David Hale (1983) served as U.S. ambassadors to Honduras, Uzbekistan, Singapore, Lithuania, Thailand, and Jordan, respectively, in the George W. Bush administration; during the same administration Jackson McDonald (1978) served as ambassador to the Republics of

Gambia and Guinea; Tatiana C. Gfoeller (1982) and Judith G. Garber (1983) were named by President Obama as ambassadors to Kyrgyzstan and Latvia, respectively. Henry Cuellar (1978), the son of migrant parents, practiced law in his native Texas before being elected as a Democrat to the U.S. House of Representatives in 2004. Those in other areas of government service included Paul Clement (1987), who became solicitor general of the United States during the George W. Bush administration, and David Addington (1978), who was chief of staff to Vice President Richard Cheney.

Relatively few sought a profession within the academy. An exception was Debora L. Spar (1984), who, in 2008, became president of Barnard College. An increasing number of school graduates made careers in business, including Amy Kuhner (1979), until a life-changing experience led her to establish "Sunshine House," an end-of-life care center for children in Connecticut. Megan Smolenyak (1982) made a career in industrial management before becoming an author and producer of television programs dealing with immigration and ethnic history and then cofounding an online television network, Roots Television; Joseph Kelliher (1983) was named chair of the federal Energy Regulatory Commission in 2005; and Yunho Song (1986) became the managing director of the Global House of Trading for Fuji Capital Markets. In communications, Marianne Connor (1982) became a film producer, and Linda Gradstein (F 1985) became a familiar voice on National Public Radio as a correspondent in Jerusalem. Mark Landler (1987) became a correspondent for the New York Times. Timothy Sullivan (1988) served as an AP bureau chief. Charles Arian (1981) became a rabbi and director of Hillel Foundations in Charlottesville and Washington, respectively, before joining the Institute for Christian and Jewish Studies in Baltimore; and Brian Poulson (1981) joined the Jesuits and became president of Saint Ignatius College Preparatory School in Chicago.

The Business School: Center Front

The resignation in the summer of 1976 of Edward Kaitz as dean of the Business School ignited the fire of transformation that swept away the debris of years of academic turpitude. Joseph Pettit, then dean of the School for Summer and Continuing Education, was brought in as acting dean, while a search was commenced for a successor to Kaitz. "Joe Pettit really came into the school for one year and put it on its feet," a faculty member recalled. Pettit oversaw the completion of the self-study that the school had embarked on during the spring of 1976 and strongly supported its conclusions, including its delineation of "the nature of an undergrad school of business in a Jesuit liberal arts setting," what its educational philosophy and objectives should be, and how to strengthen the uniqueness of its identity as a Jesuit business school. "He got the faculty et al. involved in the decision making process," something previous deans had not done.[86] He appointed an academic personnel committee to formulate standards for the faculty in the school, to be used in making faculty appointments and in annually evaluating the performance of faculty. A research and library committee was also put in place to examine ways in which to foster research that was particularly congruent with the school's educational mission.[87] The report and the structural changes in effect pointed out the path and provided the means for upgrading the quality of the school.

After a year's search, Ronald Smith, dean of the College of Business Administration at the University of Nebraska, was appointed dean. He proved to be a constructive and effective dean over the next decade. During his first year as dean he appointed as assistant dean William Droms, a member of the faculty since 1974, whose expertise included managerial economics and administrative theory. Under Smith, faculty from strong academic backgrounds were brought in, including Harvey Iglarsh in international business and Douglas McCabe (PhD, Cornell) in industrial relations in 1976; Annette Shelby (PhD, Louisiana State University) in business communications in 1979; Ilkka A. Ronkainen (PhD, South Carolina) in marketing in 1981; Horton Sorkin (PhD, Minnesota) for accounting in 1982; Robert Thomas (PhD, Wharton School, University of Pennsylvania) for marketing in the same year; Pietra Rivoli (PhD, Florida) in marketing in 1983; Karen Gaertner Newman (PhD, University of Chicago) for management in 1984; William B. Gartner, from the University of Virginia; Ricardo Ernest (PhD, Wharton School, University of Pennsylvania); and Dennis Quinn (PhD, Columbia) for management and business policy in 1987. Smith was responsible for the establishment of the Bolton Sullivan/Thomas A. Dean Chair in International Business. To foster and assist faculty research, he introduced summer research grants.

With the necessary faculty either in place or scheduled to be so, particularly in marketing and management, in 1981 the school inaugurated a master in business administration program. The program was unique in that it was designed for liberal arts graduates, with special emphasis on business ethics, international business, and business-government relations. At the same time, a joint juris doctor/master of business administration program was begun with the law center. Thirty-seven students, a majority of them women, were selected from 351 applicants for the initial MBA class in the fall of 1981. Twenty-nine completed the two-year program in 1983 and took positions with major firms throughout the country. As the reputation of the program spread, applications correspondingly increased.[88] In 1988 the American Association of Collegiate Schools of Business fully accredited the program as well as that of the master of science in taxation.[89]

In the spring of 1982, the school established the National Center for Export-Import Studies (NCEIS) as a medium for consolidating and disseminating information and research on international trade and as a resource for the development of a national trade policy. In conjunction with other elements of the university—the School of Foreign Service, the CSIS, and the International Law Institute—the center was committed to utilizing the expertise of producers, consumer advocates, federal and regional officials, and representatives of trade and business associations to reexamine America's trade policies, mechanisms, and regulations, with the goal of forging a productive export-import policy.[90] The Center sponsored conferences to investigate and evaluate U.S. trade policies and regulations and published books on the results.

In 1983 the school, with funds derived from a major gift, launched the Government Financial Management Institute, whose main purpose was the pursuit of methods to improve financial analysis, planning, and management at all levels of the public sector, from local to federal. Like the NCEIS, it sponsored conferences and seminars on various topics of public financial management.[91]

Among the notable graduates from the undergraduate program were Thomas J. Bryan (1977), who became vice president of Coldwell Banker Residential Brokerage; Frank Comerford (1977), who made a career in television management, becoming president and general manager of New York's WNBC in 2002; Cheryl R. Cooper (1978), who became chief of staff at the Association for the Advancement of Retired People (AARP) before becoming executive director of the National Council of Negro Women in 2002; Warren Olsen (1978), who was elected president of IBJ Whitehall Asset Management Group in 1999; Eileen O'Connor (1981), who raised five daughters, then worked as a correspondent for CNN, before becoming president of the International Center for Journalism in Washington; Jennifer Sullivan (1984), who left a career in investment banking to raise four sons as well as to manage successfully the congressional and gubernatorial campaigns of her husband, Mark Sanford; and Maureen Brekka (1987), who became global marketing director for Jack Daniels' international product development. Michale A. Todman (1979) became president of Whirlpool North America. Roberto R. Herencia (1981) became president of the Banco Popular North America, Chicago. Gail Giblin MacKinnon (1985) served as executive vice president and chief government relations officer for Time Warner Cable. Christopher M. O'Meara (1983) became executive vice president and chief financial officer for Lehman Brothers. Daniel K. Lahart (1983) entered the Jesuits and became president of Strake Jesuit College Preparatory School in Houston, Texas.

When the university decided to convert the Nevils Complex from academics to housing in the late seventies, Dean Smith secured Old North, the university's oldest building, as the new home for the Business School. The relocation of the school was made part of the university's intercultural education program that the federal government funded, with $5 million in federal loans going for the renovation of Old North. The twin-towered 1795

Interior of the restored
Old North, new home of
the School for Business
Administration, 1983.
(Georgetown University
Archives)

structure was restored by Mariani & Associates of Washington, with the interior adapted to reflect federal-style architecture, including a central winding staircase and galleries on the first and second floors. On a sun-drenched day in early November 1983, former president Gerald R. Ford participated in the rededication ceremony for the building. At the conclusion of the ceremony, to the strains of "Stars and Stripes Forever," hundreds of red, white, and blue balloons were released from the fourth-floor windows of Old North, fitting notice, as it were, that the Business School had, as Dean Smith remarked, "moved from the periphery to the heart of the campus," a confirmation in brick that the university had finally accepted business education as a legitimate partner in the academy.[92]

The previous May the school had achieved a goal of long standing: accreditation of its undergraduate program by the American Association of Collegiate Schools of Business. That program had, since the latter seventies, been drawing great increases in applications, as the school benefited from the rapidly rising reputation of the university and from the growing status of business education generally within society. As the number of applications increased by 25 percent a year, there was an accompanying increase in the quality of the students admitted. Those students in turn brought higher expectations about the level of education that affected the teaching a progressively improving faculty was challenged to provide.

That spring Dean Smith resigned, the apparent victim of the imminent threat of a revolt among the younger faculty whom he had succeeded in bringing in but with whom he evidently had increasing difficulty dealing. He left an enviable legacy upon which his successor, Robert Parker, could and did build. Parker brought a rich experience in international business management and planning. Even before he took office, he showed his administrative skills in securing resources for the school. As part of his agreeing to take the deanship, Parker had secured five additional faculty positions for the school, a move that gave school faculty and administrators considerable confidence that the new dean would effectively lead the school to the next level. "It is not beyond our reach," a veteran faculty member noted.[93]

Nursing: Surviving the 1980s

If the Business School reaped the benefits of a growing demand for business education among college applicants by the eighties, the Nursing School experienced the consequences of a declining profession that motivated fewer and fewer to seek a nursing degree for a profession that held little appeal for female students, who by the last quarter of the twentieth century had far more (and more attractive) career choices than the traditional women's work in hospital nursing. In the fall of 1977 enrollment in the school reached an all-time high of 570. Thirteen years later it had shrunk to 201, barely one-third of the size it had been when Timothy Healy had become president. Running counter to the dominant trend among Georgetown's undergraduate schools, nursing's applications fell steadily through the eighties, as did the quality of the applicants, at least judged by SAT scores. Drastically smaller enrollment, of course, meant a severe drop in revenue (the school was 98% dependent on tuition) as well as a suddenly overstaffed faculty. The end of federal capitation grants to schools of nursing in the early eighties put additional financial pressure upon the school. Questions began to surface about the wisdom of sustaining a school in a market in which there was an oversupply of nurses. Given the low opinion that top administrators at Georgetown had of the school and its profession, the school administration and faculty became very concerned about their future within the university.

In July 1980, Elizabeth Hughes became dean of the school. She brought a rich background in nursing, in the clinical, teaching, and administrative ar-

Elizabeth Hughes, dean of the Nursing School, 1980–86. (Georgetown University Archives)

eas, and held a doctorate in human development from the University of Maryland. Her most recent position had been as associate dean for undergraduate studies at the School of Nursing at the University of Maryland. Equally impressive to the Georgetown search committee was her experience in the field of gerontology. Hughes had developed a model geriatric screening program for the Baltimore County Health Department. As the university bulletin, the *Georgetown Record,* commented in announcing Hughes's appointment, her "first challenge will be in graduate studies. Her clinical experience and interest in gerontology . . . sustained through continued research and publication," put her in an excellent position to oversee the new graduate program that was beginning in the fall of 1980.[94]

Graduate education was one area in which the school saw the opportunity to bolster its academic stature and to increase enrollment. Planning for a master's program had begun under Dean Bergeron in the late seventies. Two major fields of concentration—gerontological nursing and midwifery—were chosen, and three holders of doctoral degrees, including Virginia Mermel, who became the director of graduate education, were added to the faculty to assume primary responsibility for teaching in the program. Midwifery, which had been a certificate program, proved very attractive as a graduate major, and in no time there were more qualified applicants than the program could accommodate. The other major, gerontology, engendered far fewer applications. Federal nurse traineeships as well as foundation grants were secured to provide financial assistance for students in both majors.[95]

In 1982 the school was awarded a grant of $500,000 from the Robert Wood Johnson Foundation to design and put into operation a "teaching nursing home" where, in conjunction with other demonstration projects around the country, a model for the high-quality nursing care of the elderly could be established. Graduate students in the gerontology field under the guidance of faculty secured clinical experience in the home. The experiment, under the direction of Norma R. Small, a retired Army Nurse Corps colonel who had been on the faculty at Walter Reed Army Institute of Nursing, continued for five years, with limited success due to financial restraints and a shortage of nurses to supply both example and oversight.[96]

The graduate track in midwifery continued to prosper, despite the fact that faculty and students were unable to secure privileges to practice in Georgetown University Hospital. Most of their clinical experience was gained at DC General until the opposition of doctors and administrators at the university's hospital subsided enough for the midwifery personnel to be given privileges there in 1985. Meanwhile, a third track, in nursing administration, had been added to the graduate program in 1982. Ada Davis became director of that track as well as the graduate program in general. Seeking students who were nurses already in executive positions, Davis employed as her faculty mostly adjuncts who were administrators or those involved in the policymaking of health care in the Washington area.[97] Thirty-two nurses enrolled in the program for its initial year of operation in 1982.[98] In time, the track proved most attractive to those aspiring to executive positions, particularly staff nurses at Georgetown Hospital, rather than to those already holding them.

In the same month that Elizabeth Hughes took over the deanship in the summer of 1980, almost one-quarter of the graduates of that year failed their state board examinations. To prepare students better, changes were made in the curriculum, including making the chemistry courses more rigorous, adding to the clinical training for seniors, and providing nurse mentors for those in clinical practice. Finally, a review course was made available to those preparing for the state boards. By 1985 the success rate for school graduates taking the boards reached 93 percent.[99]

The last semester of the undergraduate program involved a practicum, consisting of six hours of seminar and eighteen hours of clinical experience each week in a specific field of nursing, depending on the senior's choice. In the latter seventies, the faculty decided to give seniors the opportunity to experience the practice of nursing in other countries. So, in 1978, a group of seniors began to do the practicum abroad, first in Guatemala, then, beginning in 1981, at the Manchester Royal Infirmary in England. The Manchester practicum continued for several years, as did one in Dublin, where Janet Donahue was the faculty member accompanying the dozen or so seniors for their spring clinical work.[100]

To realize fiscal stability for the school, Hughes pursued a triple track: reducing the number of faculty; building an endowment; and stanching, if not reversing, the decline in enrollment. In 1983 she eliminated several faculty positions and increased the workloads of those remaining, all the while exhorting the undergraduate faculty to pursue doctoral studies and/or appropriate research and scholarship to enable them to secure academic ranks beyond that of assistant professor.[101] Dean Hughes then became the first dean of the school to make fund-raising a major part of her responsibilities, as she took to the road to solicit foundations, corporations, and individuals for grants or donations. By 1982 she had raised nearly $1 million to support programs and scholarships—an impressive start—but her overall efforts were curtailed by the limits that the university and medical center development offices set on her scope of solicitations.[102]

Finally, she brought the recruiting of applicants within the school by appointing a full-time recruiter to seek students and promote Georgetown as an ideal place to prepare for a career in nursing by visiting the places that had been traditional suppliers for the school.[103] Recruiters and multimedia presentations, taking their lead from Dean Hughes, began to underscore the value of nursing education as an excellent preparation for other professions, ranging from law to business. To provide a means to realize this alternative use of a nursing degree, Hughes secured an agreement with the medical and dental schools at Georgetown to admit nursing graduates to their schools who had fulfilled certain special requirements.[104] Another attempt at increasing enrollment resulted in an agreement with some women's colleges to have interested students transfer to the school for their final two years of study. The joint endeavors, alas, produced few students for the school.[105] Indeed, for all the efforts put into recruitment, enrollment continued to fall during the eighties, but, perhaps because of Hughes's aggressive recruiting, the drop-off was modest at first, a decline of sixty students from 1980 to 1985. The upshot of the reductions, fund-raising, and recruiting was a surplus in the budget by the time Elizabeth Hughes resigned in 1985 to pursue opportunities as a consultant in the health industry.

In February 1986, Alma Woolley succeeded Hughes as dean. A mother of four, after raising her children she went back to school to earn a master's degree in nursing education and a PhD in higher education administration from the University of Pennsylvania. Woolley came to Georgetown from being director of the School of Nursing at Illinois Wesleyan, which had a curriculum based on the same Orem model of self-care as Georgetown. She inherited a school that was again facing a budget deficit, a faculty surplus, and a curriculum that had abandoned the Orem philosophy in virtually every way except course titles. Even before she arrived, she learned that

Alma Wooley, dean of the Nursing School, 1986–92.

(*Ye Domesday Booke,* 1988)

Chancellor Matthew McNulty, a staunch supporter of the school, was retiring. His successor, she feared, had little respect for nursing education. "Rumors," she wrote, "that the school was slated for closing were rife among students, parents, and faculties throughout the campus." McNulty assured her that there was no substance to the rumors.[106]

Woolley's immediate concern was to prepare for the accreditation visit of the National League of Nursing scheduled for the fall of 1987. As part of the self-study, there was a revision of the undergraduate curriculum to integrate the Orem philosophy more fully into individual courses, workshops were held for faculty to update themselves on self-care concepts and methodology, and the graduate program was refined to accommodate more appropriate specialty practice. The result was a successful reaccreditation of the undergraduate program and accreditation of the graduate tracks, with the team recommending that physical facilities be improved and that faculty increase their scholarship.[107]

The medical center essentially put on hold the school's attempt to build an endowment. It also prohibited the formation of a national advisory council for the school that Woolley hoped would both advise about and contribute to fund-raising.[108] The school found itself on a much curtailed budget. When the university announced in the spring of 1987 that the Dental School would close (see chapter 5), reports circulated that the Nursing School would be the next. Some of those admitted to the class of 1991 withdrew their acceptances; some sophomores and juniors made preparations to transfer. Despite assurances from the president and the executive vice president that the university had no intention of closing the Nursing School, total enrollment plummeted to 266 by the time the fall semester commenced, with just 58 in the entering class.[109] The school administration and faculty, having little confidence in their future within the medical center, explored the possibility of making nursing a department within the College of Arts and Sciences. Problems with integrating the undergraduate nursing program within a liberal arts curriculum and having the nursing faculty meet the standards necessary for tenure and promotion on the main campus proved too formidable for this restructuring to get beyond the initial stage of discussion with the provost and the dean of the college.[110]

To increase enrollment, the recruitment efforts that Dean Hughes had initiated were expanded under Dean Woolley. Campus visits for prospective students were begun. New videotapes were prepared for those too distant to visit Georgetown personally. Enrollment continued to drop but not at the parlous rate it had from 1985 to 1988. As Dean Woolley notes, "It never fell to the point where it could have been used as a strong reason for closing the school as it did in many other institutions."[111]

In reality, by the latter eighties the opportunities for nursing were increasing outside of the acute-care milieu and interest in nursing correspondingly rose, although at some lag behind the improving circumstances.[112] Enrollment finally began to rise again at the school by 1991. For the entering class of the fall of 1992, there were 207 applications, out of which 85 enrolled, the largest first-year class since the early eighties. By the early nineties, it seemed clear that the School of Nursing would remain part of the university as it entered its third century.

Student Life in the Post-1960s

With the completion of Henle Student Village in the fall of 1976, a majority of Georgetown undergraduates were again living on campus. Residence life by the latter seventies was a major division of the bureaucracy that student development had become since the early 1960s. Valerie Yokie, dean of residence life, headed an ever-growing staff that included associate and assistant deans, resident directors, resident assistants, clerical personnel, and housekeeping.

The professionalization of residence life, with its several layers of progressively detached authority, led to what one faculty member described as a suburbanization of the residence halls, by which the campus residences were regarded as separate worlds where students socialized and academic culture had no place. Keeping students happy and maintaining the peace in living quarters became the overriding policy of residence life. Residence directors were expected to devise, and resident assistants to assist them in implementing, a very active social program for those in their buildings. Psychological counseling was seen by administrators as the primary remedy for individual student problems and for conflicts between students. Enforcement of official policy tended in practice to be ignored, if not discouraged, by administrators.

In March 1977 residence life officials informed five resident assistants, three males and two females, that their positions would not be renewed for the next academic year. No reasons were given to the assistants for the decision. The associate dean of residence life told a reporter for the *Hoya* that two of the five had been fired because they failed to support the programming that the residence directors in their buildings had put together.[113] Students delivered a petition to the vice president for student development, Patricia Rueckel, in which they demanded an explanation for the dismissals. At about the same time, two senior faculty had gone to the academic vice president, Aloysius Kelley, SJ, about a problem their daughters were having with roommates who persisted in bringing boyfriends in for overnight stays. When the daughters complained to a resident life administrator, they were told to get counseling to better cope with the situation. Kelley promised to take action.[114] Shortly afterward Edward Glynn, SJ, head of the student life policy committee, announced that his committee would conduct an open forum at which students, faculty, and administrators would be invited to speak about residence life policies and procedures.

The forum proved to be the catalyst for an eruption of complaints and criticisms. Scheduled for one night, the hearings in a packed Copley formal lounge had to be extended two additional nights to accommodate all who wanted to speak. A group of students from Second Copley wore T-shirts on the front of which was printed, "Students and Jesuits for a better Residence Life." In all, fifty-nine persons, including administrators, Jesuits, lay faculty, and students, testified about their experience with residence life and offered recommendations for its improvement. One Jesuit told the story of a female student who had complained to residence life about her roommate's cohabitation with her boyfriend in their room on weekends, only to be advised to move elsewhere or get counseling. She had had to appeal to the Student Judicial Board (composed of students and faculty), which ordered the roommate to get a room elsewhere. Others complained about the top-heavy, financially draining bureaucracy and suggested a paring down of personnel, including the elimination of resident directors, whom they depicted as useless, and replacing them with faculty housemasters. Others spoke about the failure of residence life to enforce its own policies, including its failure to support resident assistants who were trying to enforce them. Still others contended that the basic problem was the failure of residence life to adjust its approach to governance to the new climate that prevailed in student culture in the late 1970s.

The day after the hearings ended, Rueckel submitted her resignation. Yokie followed within forty-eight hours. Both cited personal reasons for leaving. The student life policy committee issued a report on its findings the following June. The committee discerned a consensus within the testimony on "the absence of what might be called a commonly agreed upon 'ethos pattern,'" a culture or set of social pathways that defined student living and behavior. That loss, the committee judged, was a price the university had paid as part of the sectarian community of higher education "moving from an age of restraints, authority, and respect for the past into an era of self-expression, secularization [and] dependence on federal funding," in which it "assumed an increasingly lower religious profile." "If we are to remain anything more," they continued, "than a loose association of buyers and sellers driven together by our mutual self-interests, we must turn to the religious and intellectual roots of the institution to find the sources of a more ennobling understanding of ourselves." Ironically, students in the seventies were condemning student development administration for its reluctance to assert principles grounded in Georgetown's identity and tradition. The committee called on student development authorities "to seize the initiative in positively shaping the residence hall environment" by strongly asserting and supporting policies rooted in Georgetown's character and taking steps to make residence life an integral part of the educational experience, such as the development of social action programs for members of a house or the involvement of faculty in resident hall life through house seminars or lectures.[115]

In the wake of Rueckel's and Yokie's resignations, President Healy reorganized student development to underscore its involvement in the academic mission of the university. Rueckel's replacement, William Stott, was appointed dean of student affairs rather than vice president for student development, and now reported to the academic vice president rather than directly to the president. The head of residence life became an associate dean.

One of Stott's first concerns was to find ways to decrease the compartmentalization of classroom and residence hall that had become such a focus of complaint during the spring hearings. One obvious way was to make the faculty more a part of the dorm experience, either by having some lay faculty living in the halls and involving them (as well as the resident Jesuit faculty—some twenty-five in the late seventies—on corridors and in villages) in activities within the halls or by inviting faculty to give a seminar or talk on a particular corridor or house lounge. Several halls in the late seventies initiated programs of faculty seminars or talks. The following year a faculty speakers bureau for undergraduates was formed, with eighty faculty agreeing to participate. Brochures listing the faculty members and their topics were prepared for the resident assistants on campus.[116]

A more ambitious avenue for ending the suburbanization of the dorms, at least as a demonstration project, was the creation of a residential college, like the ones at Oxford or Yale that integrated room and board as well as the learning tools of the academy (classrooms, library, faculty offices, etc.) within in a separate space shared by students and faculty in a distinct community. During his first year at Georgetown, Timothy Healy, no doubt influenced by his own experience at Saint Margaret's College at Oxford, had asked Patricia Rueckel to examine the residential college concept and its possible adaptation by Georgetown.[117] A seventeen-person study group of faculty, administrators, and students was subsequently formed and, over the course of several months in the winter and early spring of 1977, made plans for the establishment of a residential college at Georgetown. St. Mary's Hall, because of its diverse facilities for learning, dining, and living, was chosen as the site for the college. The college community was to be composed of 220 students divided equally between freshmen and upperclassmen and faculty, who would teach the philosophy, theology, and English courses that all the students would, in time, take. Three of the participating faculty would live in apartments within St. Mary's. Others would have their offices there and take meals with the students. The college was scheduled to become functional for the fall semester of 1978.[118]

Rueckel's sudden resignation in late April 1977 effectively halted the move to inaugurate a residential college within the next year and a half. Under Dean Stott a new group, now called the Living/Learning Program Planning Committee, resumed its deliberations, in the course of which it reconsidered the feasibility of the concept for Georgetown. They concluded that the best way to begin to address the problem of "the relationship between formal classroom education and the residential experience" was not through the creation of a residential college but through a more modest experiment that would cluster one group of "representative freshmen" and another of upperclassmen within a residence hall. The freshmen would all be enrolled in the same philosophy, theology, and English courses, but not on-site. The upperclassmen would pursue their majors in their respective schools but would participate in a house seminar on some special topic.[119] In the fall of 1981, Project Quill, with a grant from the Association of American Colleges, got under way in Copley Hall with fifty-five students, both freshmen and upperclassmen, and seven faculty members, including the directors of the project, Dean Stott and assistant dean of the college, Hubert Cloke.

The legalization of abortion by the Supreme Court in 1973 occasioned the rise of a counterforce in the largely Catholic Right-to-Life movement. In 1976 Georgetown students formed a Georgetown University Right-to-Life Committee (GURLC), which by 1980 was one of the largest collegiate chapters of the movement. GURLC sponsored dorm seminar series to promote discussion and examination of various right-to-life issues and hosted a student convention in January before the annual March for Life in the capital. GURLC members staffed the Pregnancy Crisis Center a few blocks from campus, where alternatives to abortion were counseled. In 1980 the committee began the G.U. *Right-to-Life Journal*, which featured articles by Georgetown students, faculty, and alumni.[120]

In cocurricular activities the Healy era saw the continuance of Georgetown's dominance in debate, even as the format for the activity changed radically, with the focus on the quantity of informed argument presented rather than on the eloquent delivery of one's case. From early October to the national championship in March, Georgetown typically had two or three teams on the road, participating in more than a score of tournaments. By the eighties the gender barrier had fallen, and the Philodemic Debating Society had female members as well as males. In 1983, John Barrett won best speaker award at the national debate championships, the latest in a long list of Georgetown recipients of this highest forensic honor. Indeed, the Philodemic, by the end of the eighties, had produced more champion individual speakers than any other institution over the previous forty years. It also was in the top tier of schools qualifying teams for the national debate tournament. During the seventies and the eighties, teams from the Philodemic won every major college debate tournament several times.[121]

In theater, Mask and Bauble, despite the retirement in 1976 of Donn Murphy, who had directed Mask and Bauble productions since 1955, maintained an ambitious schedule of staging several plays and musicals each semester. Its home moved from Stage I in Poulton Hall to Stage II, a black box created out of a classroom in Poulton, which Mask and Bauble members in the spring of 1975 took over and transformed, in protest of Stage I's cramped and inadequate facilities, to Stage III, a larger Poulton classroom that members converted into another black box, after an agreement was reached with the administration. Finally, in the early 1980s, they moved their productions to the Hall of Nations, which they converted into a larger black box when that space became available, with the departure of the School of Foreign Service to the intercultural center.

In student publications the main campus continued to be the beneficiary of two excellent newspapers: the *Hoya* and the *Voice*. In the eighties the older paper began to produce two issues a week, which enabled it to increase its coverage of student activities, including sports, as well as to expand its attention to featured stories, something the *Voice* had been doing for some time. The era saw the brief emergence of several journals: *Three Sisters*, a literary magazine that had a brief life in the late seventies; the *New Press*, a women's journal begun in the spring of 1988; and two journals of opinion, the *Guardian* and the *Blue and Gray*. The *Guardian*, founded by Kurt Edward Sticher (**F** 1985) and Scott Walter (**C** 1987), prided itself on being an avowedly conservative periodical (its subtitle was "Georgetown's Journal of Ideals and Tradition"). Its monthly issues began with the droll manifesto, "to bear rhetorical arms for traditional American sanity, for years under attack by the unrelieved dreariness of the intolerant and puritanical Left. . . . We claim as our motto . . . take the long view and tell better jokes." The *Blue and Gray,* which succeeded the *Guardian* in 1987 (the *Guardian's* last editor, Jon Bacall [**C** 1988], was cofounder, along with Mark Johnson [**C** 1989], of the *Blue and Gray*), attempted to be less ideological than its predecessor by offering diverse viewpoints in its articles and occasional pieces. The poetry journal, *Saxifrage,* founded in the early seventies, continued to publish through the eighties. In the spring of 1988, a senior in the college, Soraya Chemaly, founded the *New Press,* a periodical devoted to women's issues.

Georgetown's Chimes remained one of the top men's a cappella groups among the nation's colleges and universities. Besides appearing Thursdays at the Tombs, the group annually sponsored and anchored the Cherry Tree Massacre, a contest of college a cappella groups that the Chimes first staged in 1975 and by the eighties had expanded to three performances, with a changing lineup of groups from men's and women's colleges. In 1980 a female counterpart, the Grace Notes, founded by Sue Vrana (**N** 1983), first performed as a quartet in Arts Hall before appearing in the Cherry Tree Massacre in February 1981. "We want to bring nostalgic music to this campus," announced Vrana. Kathy Ursic (**N** 1983), Jeannine Belmonte (**C** 1984), and Vera Vuchick (**F** 1981) were the other original members. To magnify their close harmony on standards such as their signature song, "Java," the Notes expanded to a sextet in 1981.

A sign that the main campus was becoming a community unto itself was the creation of the intramural, student-run Georgetown Emergency Re-

Grace Notes. (*Ye Domesday Booke,* 1985)

sponse Medical Service (GERMS). Organized in the spring of 1984 by Robert Doherty (**C** 1983, **M** 1987), GERMS provided medical assistance, including ambulance service, to people on campus with medical emergencies. Nearly fifty student members, all certified emergency medical technicians, staffed the three-person teams that responded to calls from their headquarters in the university hospital. When not on duty, members wore beepers to be alerted to campus medical emergencies. The university provided minimal funding for the service, although it purchased a used ambulance for GERMS' use at its beginning. The hospital donated most of GERMS' equipment and supplies.[122]

The Society of Stewards

The student organization that drew the most attention in the eighties was ironically one founded to escape attention: the Society of Stewards. Founded in 1982 when females were on the verge of composing 50 percent of the undergraduate student body and when minorities were becoming a significant presence within that body, the secret society that was outed in the late eighties could be seen as a deliberate attempt to counter the increasing heterogeneity of Georgetown's undergraduate society by forming an inner core of white, largely Catholic males who held leadership positions or were influential in some way on campus. The Stewards, initially formed from members of the coed service fraternity Alpha Phi Omega, claimed that their principal goals were to serve the university and preserve its traditions. Ignored among these traditions was the university's opposition to secret societies such as the Stewards because of their incompatibility with the open communities Jesuit liberal education rested upon.

The Stewards would identify persons who were either leading organizations or were potential leaders. By 1988 the members of the Stewards included, among others, the vice president of student government and the speaker of its assembly; several editors, past and present, of the *Hoya;* cofounders of the *Blue and Gray;* the captain of the golf team; the president of APO; the executive producer of Mask and Bauble; the head of the District Action Project; and the student who performed as the school mascot, Jack the Bulldog, at athletic contests.[123] During orientation each new freshman would receive an unsigned letter about campus traditions. Each spring the group would petition the dean of student affairs for the university's official recognition, only to be told that Georgetown would neither recognize a secret society nor allow any of its activities on campus.[124]

None of this was public knowledge as 1988 began. In February of that year, the chair of the Georgetown University Student Association Assembly and the head of the District Action Project organized a conference on leadership and service at Georgetown. Two female students, Rosie Hidalgo

(**C** 1988) and Margaret Dowley (**C** 1989), looking over the list of speakers, became suspicious about the absence of any women or minorities on the program. When the conference on leadership and service began the next morning, one of the speakers, R. J. Cellini, condemned the established student organizations at Georgetown for providing such ineffective leadership and pointed to secret societies, such as the Skull and Bones at Yale, as much preferred alternatives for promoting leadership. In the course of his remarks, Cellini twice accidentally mentioned "Stewards" in referring to student leaders, then quickly corrected himself. At the open forum in the afternoon, various leaders of mainstream student organizations on campus expressed their outrage at Cellini's presentation. Hidalgo made a plea for openness and transparency among all campus organizations. "I stand before you all today and say that I am vehemently opposed to the Stewards. It's like a cancer. Unless we stop it now, it will penetrate deeper into every organization on campus."[125]

The revelation of a secret society that evidently had its tentacles in many places of power produced shock waves across campus that weekend. The *Voice* ran a special edition that Monday to cover the developing story. Twelve students admitted to being Stewards or were identified as such by midweek. Three editors of the *Hoya* were forced to resign when they were identified as Stewards members. On Monday night three members called a press conference during which they announced to a standing-room-only crowd in the Village C formal lounge that the society was disbanding but refused to release a list of members.[126]

The next day the *Hoya* wrote in an editorial,

These [secret] organizations are in direct opposition to the definition of a university: free and open association among diverse individuals in an academic and social setting. . . .

By acting together, these men could create the appearance of strong campus consensus on issues ranging from student government to curriculum changes. This danger is only enhanced by the possibility of Stewards controlling the campus media [and other organizations].[127]

The following month Dean John DeGioia, in a letter to undergraduate students, informed them that "Georgetown University does not tolerate the activities of a secret club or organization. Such clubs or organizations are contradictory to the moral commitments upon which this community is built."[128] Despite this formal announcement of the administration and the Stewards' own public statement about dissolving their group, some were skeptical that the university had seen the last of the Stewards. "I truly do not believe that the Stewards have disbanded," Joe Rand wrote in the *Voice*. He quoted one steward who told him, before the group became publicly known, "Nothing is going to end this, not you, not the *Voice*, not Tim Healy. . . . [W]e'll just hunker down and wait it out." Rand expected the group to "go underground for a few years, wait for its opponents to graduate, and then reestablish the society."[129]

Rand, as it turned out, had underestimated the tenacity of the Stewards, at least their alumni members. That spring alumni Stewards announced their intention of recruiting undergraduate replacements for those who had quit the society in February.[130] A year later, Brian Jones (**B** 1990), an African American who had just been elected president of the College Democrats, announced that he was the new undergraduate leader of the Stewards.[131] The following fall, the College Democrats, in a close vote, stripped Jones of his office due to his being a Steward. The *Voice* warned, "Until the campus knows who the Stewards are, all clubs must remain vigilant, in order to ensure that club decisions are made by club members, and not by some clique of men meeting in secret."[132] The Stewards clearly had survived on campus and would continue to be a troublesome presence into the nineties.

Alcohol and Drugs in the 1980s

Student use of alcohol and drugs became matters of varying concern on campus in the eighties. As Timothy Healy wrote in 1986, "Most of us realize that alcohol is a greater problem on campus than any drug."[133] That sentiment was one shared by Georgetown students. In a May 1986 poll, 56 percent of those responding thought that the use of alcohol at Georgetown was excessive, 43 percent thought it moderate.[134] Alcohol abuse, chiefly in the form of binge drinking, was becoming an increasingly prominent issue on campuses across the country. Surveys showed that more than 40 percent of college students admitted to binge drinking (more than five drinks at a sitting) at least once a week. To many observers of the Georgetown campus, that figure seemed low for the undergraduate population there. One of the inducements to drink at Georgetown was that the legal age for drinking, unlike most of the rest of the country, was eighteen in the District of Columbia. That changed in 1986 when the city council of the District of Columbia, in order to conform to federal law, passed legislation raising the minimum drinking age from eighteen to twenty-one. Those who had turned eighteen before the law went into effect were grandfathered from its application, but in the future most Georgetown students would no longer be able to drink legally. In the spring of 1987 the administration formed an alcohol and drug task force, in part because of the new restrictive age limit on drinking and in part because of the growing awareness of alcohol abuse by students.

The new policy that emerged from the task force's study restricted drinking in dorm rooms to all who met the minimum age standard set by the District, in apartments only where "all occupants and guests are in compliance with . . . the laws of the District of Columbia." How this would be enforced was not stated. At dormitory parties and other public gatherings, a maximum of two half-kegs of beer was permitted for a minimum of 80 persons. Alternative beverages—a minimum of three cases for each keg—also had to be available. There was no attempt to exclude underage students from the parties, only the provision of nonalcoholic drinks for affording them a compliance with the law. Another consequence of the task force was the introduction of alcohol awareness programs to educate students on the dangers of excessive drinking and the need for a responsible attitude about alcohol.[135]

Excessive drinking became a very public issue at Georgetown's graduations beginning in the late 1970s. For a decade, undergraduates at the main campus commencement brought champagne bottles under their robes to the ceremony, during which they would begin opening the bottles, spraying those in the immediate vicinity and sending corks like heat-seeking missiles in all directions, including the stage. In an attempt to dry up the event, the Baccalaureate Mass was celebrated immediately before the commencement ceremony (it had previously been celebrated on the morning of graduation, which was held in the late afternoon), in the same site used for the graduation rites. This only resulted in an earlier start for student imbibing and a serious disruption of the sacred ambiance of the mass. The final indignity came at the commencement of 1988, when, well into the second hour of rowdiness and drunken behavior, the commencement speaker, a symphony conductor, attempted to enter into the spirit of the goings-on by asking for a bottle of champagne, which a couple of students happily supplied and which she proceeded to chug to the loud applause of the assembled students, if not their parents and other guests. The president, never one to suffer quietly either fools or foolish behavior, had to be dissuaded from terminating the commencement on the spot. It proved to be the last general main campus commencement. The following January the provost announced that, because of the bacchanalian behavior of the previous May, in the future each school would hold its separate graduation ceremony. The Baccalaureate Mass, now moved to the morning after commencement, became the sole remaining common graduation event for students on the main campus.

Drug use occasioned much less concern among administration officials. Students themselves saw it as a much smaller problem. In a 1986 poll, 9 percent thought that the use of "illegal substances" on campus was excessive, 60 percent thought usage was moderate, and 31 percent found it minimal. Those figures alone, of course, strongly suggest that drugs were still very much a part of student culture more than a decade removed from the sixties. The drug policy the university adopted in the summer of 1987 basically adopted federal law in "strictly [forbidding] the use, transfer, possession and/or sale of illegal drugs on campus. Individuals involved in the sale or transfer of illegal drugs are subject to suspension or dismissal from the University."[136]

The Georgetown University Protective Services (GUPS) actively enforced the drug policy. It regularly cooperated with the DC police in apprehending suspected dealers and users, including the use of undercover agents posing as students. By 1988, GUPS was making one to two drug-related arrests a month. In one case campus security carried out a three-month investigation of a freshman suspected of dealing drugs from his New South room. It culminated in the discovery of marijuana and packets of white powder, thought to be Ecstasy, along with balance scales for weighing drugs. "We had some suspicions that he was allegedly selling drugs," said the student's resident assistant. "There's a lot of marijuana around. I believe it's extensive at Georgetown. The administration doesn't know how big the drug problem is, but more and more they're finding out."[137] That week the *Hoya* asserted in an editorial that "the New South drug incident should set off early warning signals. Non-alcoholic abuse is a very real and dangerous possibility on this campus."[138]

The next month, *Community Matters,* the student affairs newsletter, published a warning about Ecstasy: "a drug that has recently become popular on many college campuses. It produces a high similar to one evoked by a combination of LSD and amphetamines. It also causes brain damage, permanent 'Parkinson-like' symptoms and death. . . . Someone who has taken 'ecstacy' [sic] should not be left alone."[139]

Champaign bath at Commencement, 1980.
(*Ye Domesday Booke*)

A New Conference and an Unprecedented Decade of Athletic Success

The Healy era saw the return of Georgetown as a sports power in three sports (basketball, track, and crew), the emergence of women scholarship sports, and the creation of a new sports conference of which Georgetown was a principal founder. The Big East was the result of a new NCAA requirement that, in order to be eligible for an NCAA championship, one had to be in a league that competed in at least six sports. Frank Rienzo and Dave Gavitt, then the athletic director at Providence College, began conversations about a multisport league in 1976 that eventually included Jake Crouthamel, the athletic director at Syracuse University, and Lou Carnesecca, the basketball coach and athletic director at St. John's University.[140] The original four were looking for an additional four teams that would be compatible, in both their academic and athletic programs, as well as located in major media areas along a corridor running from Massachusetts to the District of Columbia. Boston College, Connecticut, and Seton Hall accepted. Villanova agreed to come in as the eighth team but wanted to give the Atlantic Ten a year's notice before joining. All eight schools agreed to play their basketball home games in major arenas.[141] The new league sponsored competition in several sports, including track (cross-country, indoor, and outdoor), golf, tennis, and swimming (eventually it covered baseball, soccer, volleyball, football, and lacrosse), but was initially at its core a basketball league that, led by the four founding schools, quickly became a major force in intercollegiate circles.

The basketball team under John Thompson Jr. had gotten to the NCAA tournament in 1975 for the first time since 1943. Thompson had been named to the coaching staff of the gold-medal-winning U.S. Olympic team in 1976 as an assistant to Dean Smith. The following year President Healy renegotiated Thompson's contract and made him an advisor on urban affairs. That marked the beginning of a radically new scale of salary for the basketball coach, one that by the end of his tenure in the 1990s would exceed $600,000 annually, far more than any other person in the university, faculty or administrator, was realizing, with a deferred salary of $400,000 per year that would continue well into the next century.[142] President Healy was also instrumental in establishing a special committee for the admission of basketball players, which enabled Thompson to enroll more blue-chippers in his program. In 1977 as well, the Hoya Hoop Club was formed to provide the kind of financial support for basketball that boosters at other institutions with big-time basketball programs did. It all represented a commitment by the university to the prolegiate sports culture that it had not exhibited since the 1920s, one that would eventually affect its relationship to other sports as well. By the latter eighties, the Hoops Club was raising more than one-quarter of a million dollars a year, which was more than the entire basketball budget had been in 1976. Georgetown merchandise had become the biggest seller in the country among nonmajor football institutions, producing more than $4 million a year.

For the 1977–78 season, a man-sized Jack the Bulldog made his first appearance. Under that costume Pat Sheehan (**C** 1981) worked the crowds at Hoya games for the next four years. In 1982, his successor was joined by a real bulldog, Rocky. Thereafter the human and animal bulldogs would be a constant pair at major Georgetown sporting events. The team itself, after a 19-9 season in 1976–77 in which they qualified for the NIT, was expected to have unprecedented success the following season. Thompson's two best recruits to date, John Duren and Craig Shelton, were now sophomores, teaming with guards Derrick Jackson, Mike Riley, and Craig Esherick and forwards Al Dutch and Steve Martin. That season did become the most successful season in Georgetown's history as the team won twenty-three games, one more than the 1942–43 squad that reached the NCAA final, and gained national recognition. In the NIT for a second straight year, the Hoyas went to the semifinals before losing in double overtime at Madison Square Garden to North Carolina State on a thirty-five-foot shot at the buzzer.

Looking for a shooting guard to complement Duren and Shelton, Thompson recruited Eric Floyd in the western North Carolina town of Gastonia, named for Georgetown's first student. Floyd, despite his 23 points per game, had remained under the radar of the major college programs and came to Georgetown with no fanfare. In the opening game of the season, Maryland discovered just how good Floyd was when he led Georgetown with 28 points in defeating the Terrapins at the Capital Centre, 68–65, for the first time since 1970. Georgetown racked up 22 wins in the regular season, defeated Syracuse 66–56 to win the ECAC Upstate New York/Southern Division championship, and was ranked twelfth in the nation in one poll. In the NCAA tournament it lost to Rutgers in the second round of the East regionals.

In the 1979–80 season, Georgetown won twenty-six games, the most any Georgetown basketball team had ever won. That included ending the regular season with a ten-game winning streak and winning the Big East tournament by defeating St. John's and Syracuse, the eighth- and second-ranked teams in the country, respectively. Seeded third in the East Region of the NCAA tournament, Georgetown won the first two rounds of the tournament by close scores as it got by Iona and Rutgers to reach the Sweet Sixteen. In Philadelphia, Georgetown utilized its depth and signature court-long pressure defense to stifle Maryland for a second time that season and won more decisively than the final score (74–68) indicated. In the regional championship game against Iowa, Georgetown ran up a 14-point lead early in the second half, only to see the Hawkeyes catch fire, shooting 71 percent and making all fifteen foul shots to catch Georgetown, although the Hoyas themselves shot 68 percent in the final half. The game was decided by an Iowa layup at the buzzer, when Craig Shelton's hand was caught in the net as he went up to block the shot as he had done several times earlier. The

81–80 loss left the Hoyas deeply frustrated at coming so close to making the Final Four, but the season marked the arrival of Georgetown as a national basketball power.

That year both the University of Florida and the University of Oklahoma tried to woo Thompson from Georgetown. He stayed, in part, perhaps, because of the athletic department's commitment to move the team's home games to Capital Centre. The purchase by a group of alumni of a $350,000 house for Thompson might also have been a factor in persuading him to remain at Georgetown. And it is likely that Thompson's deferred compensation package originated at this time. A year and a half later, Patrick Ewing, the top high school prospect in the nation, arrived. He joined a very talented group of athletes, including Eric Floyd, Gene Smith, and Fred Brown, and provided the final piece for the relentless, in-your-face pressure defense that was becoming the Hoyas' trademark by providing a final line of resistance to any break in the press. Over the next four years, Georgetown, led by Ewing, reached the NCAA finals three times. In the 1981–82 season, the team raced to a 26-6 record, including winning the Big East Conference tournament for the second time in three years, which earned them the title "Beast of the East." Eric Floyd was named first team All-American. John Thompson was voted coach of the year. Seeded number one in the West, Georgetown easily defeated Wyoming, Fresno State, and Oregon State to make the Final Four. In New Orleans they bested Louisville 50–46.

Then, in a classic NCAA final against North Carolina, the Tar Heels, leading 61–60, went into a four-corners stall with less than three minutes to play. Finally, with less than a minute on the clock, Georgetown fouled Matt Doherty. The strategy worked when Doherty failed to make the one and one. Georgetown took the lead on a Sleepy Floyd jump shot with thirty-two seconds left. Against a 1-3-1 Georgetown zone, a Tarheels freshman, Michael Jordan, hit a shot from the corner to retake the lead at the fifteen-second mark. Georgetown brought the ball down for a final shot, only to have Fred Brown inadvertently pass the ball to North Carolina's James Worthy, who was fortuitously (for the Tar Heels) far out of position. At game's end, the television cameras recorded for posterity Thompson's bear hug around the disconsolate Brown. Thompson's McArthur-like response to those at the ensuing press conference was, "You may remember I first used this quote two years ago in Philadelphia [following the Iowa loss] . . . and I say it again now: I shall return."[143]

Two years later, he did. Ewing, now a junior, was surrounded by an even more talented supporting cast of players, including Fred Brown, Gene Smith, Bill Martin, David Wingate, Reggie Williams, Michael Jackson, Horace Broadnax, Ralph Dalton, and Michael Graham. The team captured the Big East title. Ewing, named first team All-American, led the team in scoring, averaging 17 points a game, and anchored the defense that kept opponents below 40 percent in shots made, an NCAA record low. Georgetown

won its third Big East tournament and was again sent west for the NCAA tournament. Georgetown went on to win the West regional and advanced to the Final Four for the second time in three years.

NCAA championship game against University of North Carolina, 1982. (Georgetown University Archives)

Georgetown's semifinal opponent was Kentucky, with its twin towers, Sam Bowie and Mel Turpin. Although Georgetown was a slight favorite, many shared the sentiment of Thompson's good friend George Raveling: "My heart is with Georgetown, but logic dictates Kentucky." Logic prevailed in the first half as Raveling's worst fears became reality. Ewing went to the bench with three fouls midway through the first twenty minutes. Kentucky led by ten at half time. The second half was one for the ages. Thompson inserted Gene Smith as the catalyst for an aggressive defense that kept switching between man-to-man and zone, thoroughly confusing the Wildcats. Kentucky, with a basketball history only UCLA could match and with three NBA first-round locks on its roster, went 16 of the final twenty minutes in which it put 2 points on the board. Georgetown won going away, 53–40. In the final against Houston, the Hoyas led handily for most of the game, as the Houston star, Akeem Olajuwon, plagued with early fouls, played little. Georgetown won 84–75. As now senior Brown came off the court at the end of the game, Thompson again wrapped him in his arms, and said, "We've got it now, baby."[144] The Hoyas were finally the NCAA champions in basketball.

The following year Georgetown was considered by many observers to be one of the truly great teams in college basketball history. Losing but twice in the regular season and seeded number one in the NCAA tournament, the

Hoyas easily advanced to the finals in Lexington. Rollie Massimino, coach of Villanova, the Hoyas' opponent in the final, remarked that his team would have to shoot in the 50 percent range to have a chance. Little did he know. The Wildcats shot a seemingly impossible 78.6 percent, many of them long jumpers from the corners and beyond the top of the key. The only shot the Wildcats missed in the second half was one blocked by Ewing. They won by two, 66–64. It had taken a miraculous game by Villanova to prevent the Hoyas from repeating as champions. Georgetown had won thirty-five games. The three it had lost had been by a total of 5 points. Patrick Ewing was named the national player of the year.

Georgetown remained in the basketball spotlight for the remainder of the decade, reaching the Elite Eight three times. Reggie Williams led the Hoyas to a 24-8 record in 1985–86. The following year, Williams, backed by Perry McDonald, Mark Tillmon, Jaren Jackson, Dwayne Bryant, and Charles Smith, led Georgetown to a fifth title in the Big East tournament. Seeded first in the Southeast regional, Georgetown made it to the regional final, where it was upset by Providence. In 1987–88, Charles Smith had an outstanding season, but the team itself was disappointing, finishing the regular season at 20-9. In the NCAAs, the Hoyas defeated Louisiana State on a Charles Smith twenty-five-foot bank shot in the final minute, but lost its second-round game to top-ranked Temple. The next year the Hoyas had a new dominant presence at center in the person of Alonzo Mourning. Smith, who was named the Big East player of the year, and Mourning, with his stifling defense (his 169 blocks for the year set a school record), led the Hoyas to a sixth Big East tournament championship and a fifteenth consecutive appearance in the NCAA tournament, where they made it to the Elite Eight. Thompson completed his seventeenth season just one victory shy of four hundred. His .747 winning percentage was among the ten best of active coaches.

Frank Gagliano, most successful track coach in Georgetown's rich history. (Georgetown University Archives)

Georgetown Sports: More Than Basketball

In track, Georgetown under Joe Lang, and then from 1983 on, Frank Gagliano, produced champions among men and women in the eighties. Gagliano would match in track the sustained success that John Thompson had in basketball from the eighties well into the nineties. In 1979 the two-mile relay team of Ron Stafford, Phil Reilly, Aubrey McKithen, and Kevin Byrne finished fourth in the NCAA indoor championships, the highest relay finish in the nationals in Georgetown history. That same year Chris Catherine Shea (1982) broke the world record in the one-mile walk by finishing in 6:58.9. In 1980, John Gregorek (**C** 1982) placed third in the 3,000-meter steeplechase at the U.S. Olympic trials. He had set the best time

(8:21.4) ever recorded by a collegiate runner in the event. Unfortunately, when the United States boycotted the Olympic games at Moscow because of the Soviet invasion of Afghanistan, Gregorek lost his chance to participate in the steeplechase there. He earned All-American honors in cross-country, indoor track, and outdoor track. *Sport* magazine picked him as the "Top Track and Field Prospect of the 1980s."[145] James DeRienzo (**B** 1980) was an outstanding performer in the distance medley relay, 1,000 meter, and 800 meter. In 1980 he won the 1,000 meter at the indoor championships and earned All-American honors. Christine Mullen (1981) won the indoor national collegiate championships in both the 600 meters and the 1,000 meters in 1979, the sole person to win in two events, and set an American collegiate record in the 600. A year later she repeated as the champion in both events.

In the fall of 1981 the men's cross-country team finished second in the Big East championship meet, with John Gregorek capturing the Big East individual title. The team then placed fourth at the IC4A championships. Pia Palladino (**C** 1983) led the women's team and earned All-American honors. In the winter Gregorek anchored the Hoyas' distance medley team (with Patrick McCabe, John Pedati, and Kevin King) that left their competition far behind in the NCAA Indoor Championship with a time of 9:45.97. It was the first NCAA relay championship since 1963. That spring Gregorek, Aubrey McKithen, Rich Caton, and Brian McNelis broke Villanova's sixteen-year hold on the distance

Left: John Gregorek, middle distance and steeplechase All-America. (Georgetown University Archives)

Right: Chris Mullen, middle distance All-America. (Georgetown University Archives)

medley at the Penn Relays by winning that event and setting an American collegiate record with their winning time. Gregorek capped his outstanding career by winning both the 1500-meter run, and, ninety minutes later, the 5,000-meter run at the IC4A outdoor championships. "His confidence, determination, and desire have made him great," his coach, Joe Lang, observed. "He has the ability to focus in on a specific goal, . . . he can keep his mind on that goal over a long period of time."[146] A month later he finished second in the 1500-meter NCAA championships.

Suzanne Girard was named All-American in cross-country, indoor, and outdoor track in the 1983–84 seasons. In Big East competition she shattered the record in the 1500 meters. In 1985, Kevin King became Georgetown's first men's individual track champion since 1966 when he won the 3,000-meter run at the indoor championships. Georgetown placed fifth overall in the NCAA indoor track championships that year. A year later, at the NCAA indoors, the team bettered their standing in 1985 by finishing third.

Coach Gagliano recruited athletes not only for middle distance racing but also for sprints, hurdles, and field events, making the Hoyas more competitive in indoor and outdoor meets. Raymond Humphrey proved to be a consistent winner at the long and triple jumps. At the outdoor NCAA championships in 1985, Humphrey finished second in the long jump by leaping 26 feet, 4¼ inches. A year later he led Georgetown to a second place finish at the Big East indoor championships as he won both the long jump (25' 1") and the triple jump (53' 3"). For the latter achievement he was named the meet's outstanding performance. At the NC4A indoor championships that same season, Georgetown placed third. Humphrey again captured both the long jump (25' 10") and the triple jump (54' 5¼"), the latter a meet record. It marked his second straight IC4A sweep of the two jumps, the first time this had ever happened in the sixty-four-year history of the event.

At the NCAA indoor championships, the 3,200-meter relay team, composed of Miles Irish, Dennis Dee, Phil Franshaw, and Mike Huber, failed by .06 second to best Arkansas for the championship. The Hoyas' time (7:20.78) was still an American record (three of the four Arkansas runners were foreign nationals). In the winter of 1987, Michael Stahr won the NCAA indoor championship in the mile. In the outdoor season, the distance medley relay team (John Trautmann, Darron Outler, Irish, and Stahr) set a world record (9:20.96) at the Penn Relays in April in a near photo finish with Villanova and Mount Saint Mary's. Stahr's final mile leg of 3:54.9 proved the difference. In the spring at the Penn Relays, the 4 × 800 or 3,200-meter relay team (Mike Stahr, Patric Mann, Darron Outler, and Bob Leonardo) won the Championship of America Award by besting Arkansas. The team culminated its ascension during the decade by becoming the first team in Big East history to capture the triple crown of track and field competition: cross-country, indoor, and outdoor track. That success enabled Georgetown to secure for the first time the Commissioner's Trophy, given to the school that accumulates the most points in the league's nine championship events.

When Frank Gagliano retired at the end of the 1990s after coaching track and field for sixteen seasons, he had a magnificent record of accomplishment unmatched in Georgetown's proud history in the sport: twenty-three Big East championships, eight indoor and two outdoor titles in IC4A competition, and firsts in eight Penn Relay Championship of America meets. An incredible 140 of his runners had earned All-American honors. Seven of his charges had won individual NCAA championships. Five had become Olympians. Gagliano was named NCAA coach of the year in 1991.

By the early eighties, crew was the largest collegiate sport on campus, with about one hundred men and women participating. It was a sport in which President Healy, with his Oxford background, took particular interest, and in the summer of 1982 he sent a shell to the prestigious Henley royal regatta in England (the Hoya's heavyweight eight made it to the quarterfinals). The team itself, the men coached by Jay Forster (**C** 1970) and the women by John Devlin, won the championship event for small college crews, the Dad Vails, three times between 1982 and 1989. At the 1983 Dad Vails, the women's crew played a vital part in securing the title, as its varsity and junior varsity eights both won gold medals in their events. The women's crew earned seven trips to the U.S. collegiate championship, winning the gold medal in 1988. In 1989 the university raised crew to the status of a major sport. Don Johnson, who had been very successful in coaching crew at Georgetown earlier, returned to be head coach in that same year.

Georgetown football, under Coach Scotty Glacken and playing a nine-game schedule, continued its rise in Division III play in the late seventies. The 1978 team compiled the best record (7-1) that any Hoya team had compiled in the sport since 1939. Georgetown finished seventh that year in voting for the Lambert Trophy, awarded to the best small-college team in the East. Kicker Ed Delgado and safety Jim Corcoran were two of the standouts for the Hoyas during the period.

For the soccer team, also a nonscholarship sport, victories were hard to come by for most of the seventies and eighties. In the 1984 season, under Coach Keith Talbatznik, the Hoya booters, with a very inexperienced squad, still managed to win six games, the most victories in a season since 1968. Four years later, led by Andy Hoffman, John Janenda, David Barron, and goalkeeper Bryan Gowdy, the Hoyas won an unprecedented twelve games to qualify for the Big East championship tournament. Janenda and Hoffman were named to the All Big East tournament team. Barron led the team in scoring with ten goals and four assists. At the end of the 1988–89 year the athletic department announced that soccer was becoming a scholarship sport at Georgetown.

Lacrosse struggled to break a cycle of losing seasons that went back to the sixties. But throughout the eighties they failed to do so. The 1989 season was all too typical, with a record of five wins over weak teams (Radford, Guilford, Stony Brook, Kutztown, and Notre Dame) against eight losses.

Baseball remained a minor sport but enjoyed a brief period of success in the early eighties under Ken Kelly, who succeeded Tommy Nolan as head coach in 1978. The team, which had had only three winning seasons in the past twenty-seven years, won no fewer than twenty games each season. In the 1981–82 season (there were both fall and spring schedules), the team went 22-19-1, competing in the East Coast Athletic Conference. Joe Niciforo, Dwight Madison, Steve Iannini, and Tom Bass were standouts. In 1983, Georgetown qualified for the college World Series tournament for the first time in its history but lost in the opening round. In the following season, despite half the team being freshmen, the Hoyas improved to 31-17, their best record since 1951. With Kelly stressing aggressive base running and situational hitting, Steve Iannini led the team in both hitting and stealing bases. Iannini, together with Bill O'Malley and Scott Elliott, were the main persons responsible for Georgetown's leading the nation in stolen bases per game. Again they earned an invitation to the NCAA tournament. The following year, 1984–85, the team competed in the Big East for the first time and won more than twenty games and secured a Big East playoff berth. Iannini was one of the nation's leaders in hitting (thirteenth) and stolen bases (eighth). His teammate Joe Gervais was third in the nation in steals. During Kelly's tenure (1978–85), despite the fact that baseball was a nonscholarship sport at Georgetown, four of his players signed professional contracts.

No women's sport in the period had more success than volleyball. Under Coach Joe McClure, the team became a regional power. During a six-year stretch in the late seventies and early eighties, the team, led by captains Mary Jean Ryan (**C** 1980) and Molly Murphy (**C** 1982), had a gaudy record of 180 and 74. In 1979–80 the team lost twelve times in fifty-two matches and made it to the American Intercollegiate Association of Women (AIAW) regional finals in Pittsburgh, where the Hoyas played the heavily favored defending champions, the Panthers, to a virtual deadlock before finally yielding in four games to Pittsburgh. Two years later the Hoyas compiled an impressive 31-7 record and again qualified for the eastern regionals of the AIAW.

Women's basketball, with Francis Carr as coach, enjoyed winning seasons in the late seventies and early eighties before experiencing a drought of successful seasons in the rest of the decade. In 1977–78 the team, in its fourth season and first with scholarships, went 11-9 led by cocaptains Mary Margaret Dolan and Ria Meagher. The following year they improved to 15-9. In 1979–80, with a much more demanding schedule, the team surprised everyone in reeling off thirteen straight victories and ended the year with only three losses in twenty-four games. Erin Reid was voted the most valuable player of the team. Abbie Dillon became Georgetown's all-time leading scorer, with 1,116 career points. K. C. Comerford, a freshman, averaged more than 20 points a game. After 1981, the team found competition in the

Volleyball team in action, 1980. (Georgetown University Archives)

Big East a formidable challenge. By 1988–89, now under Coach Patrick Knapp, they came closest to reaching .500 with a 13-16 record. During the regular season, they registered wins over Notre Dame, Providence, St. John's, Villanova, and Boston College. In the Big East tournament, they realized their first victory by defeating Pittsburgh in the first round.

In tennis, the Kuhlman sisters, Julie and Suzanne, held the number one singles spot for eight years, from 1975 to 1983. Suzanne Kuhlman (1979–83) dominated Division II competition. A four-time All-American, she ended her career with a perfect 60-0 mark in dual meet competition. In 1979–80, led by Kuhlman, the team captured the eastern championship of Division II. Two years later, the team, headed by Kuhlman and Valentina Garcia, compiled a 17-3 record. The pair won the Eastern AIAW doubles championship. In the Division II national championships in Colorado, Kuhlman placed second among top singles players, Garcia fifth among second singles. In Kuhlman's senior year the team finished 13-5 with Kuhlman winning the 1983 Division II NCAA tournament. In 1983–84 a freshman, Kathy Federici, took Kuhlman's spot as the top singles position and made it to the finals of the Big East tournament. She also won the singles title at the Mid-Atlantic collegiate tennis championships. The following year she advanced to the quarterfinals of the NCAA Division II tennis championship.

Field hockey's fortunes at Georgetown dramatically improved in the early 1980s as the team recorded several winning seasons, culminating with a 14-2-3 mark in 1984 under Coach Sandie Inglis. In 1977 lacrosse became a varsity sport for women at Georgetown. Like their male counterparts, the women's lacrosse team struggled in posting victories their first several seasons. In 1985, however, with Inglis coaching lacrosse as well as field hockey, they did have a breakout year by going 8-1-1.

In 1985 full-time coaches were established for volleyball, field hockey, men's and women's lacrosse, soccer, and baseball. At the same time, partly occasioned by the revenue acquired from the success of the men's basketball team, Frank Rienzo began a movement to build endowments for certain sports, both major and minor, at Georgetown. A National Committee for Fund-Raising for Athletics was created. Golf received the first endowed scholarship. These moves probably had more than a little to do with Georgetown's winning the Big East Commissioner's Trophy for excellence in men's athletics for the first time in 1988. The following year, the last one of Tim Healy's tenure, the school made the decision to upgrade crew and lacrosse to major sports at Georgetown. Crew, though not lacrosse, had a history of success at Georgetown to build upon, but both sports, particularly lacrosse, had a very loyal core of alumni and parents committed to fund-raising. Scholarships were established, and Rienzo recruited two highly successful coaches to take the reins of the now major programs: Don Johnson for crew and Dave Urick for lacrosse. It represented the university's ambitious attempt to double the number of its teams prominent in intercollegiate athletics. The investment paid substantial dividends, particularly in lacrosse. By the end of the 1990s both the men's and the women's lacrosse teams had become national powers, consistently ranking in the top ten in the nation; the women made the NCAA championship finals two years in a row (2001–2).

Into the Circle of the Elite

Edward Bunn had begun Georgetown's movement into the modern world of higher education. Gerard Campbell, in his short term as president, had restructured the institution to enable it to complete that journey, including the establishment of the mechanism for development that would secure the financial foundation needed for Georgetown to become an eminent university. Robert Henle provided financial stability to an institution teetering on fiscal catastrophe and established a decentralized system of budgeting that gave at least one of the university's three campuses—the law center—the economic autonomy to take giant strides in reaching the top tier of schools in the nation.

In Timothy Stafford Healy the university had a president who brought the confidence, imagination, and voice to a promising situation that finally enabled Georgetown to enter the ranks of the elite universities in the world. He inherited a strong set of deans in the undergraduate schools who continued to provide effective leadership through the late seventies and the eighties. He harnessed the admissions process to attract to Georgetown from pools that transcended national boundaries a diverse undergraduate and professional student body that was among the most selective in the nation and provided the financial aid to a majority of those accepted to make that possible. By taking opportunistic advantage of a buyer's market and by creating a large number of chairs and university professorships, he moved the institution a long way toward developing a distinguished faculty. He set the university on a path of construction of unprecedented magnitude to supply the academic, residential, and recreational facilities that the university desperately needed to establish itself as a top-deck institution.

To finance all this, he fully utilized the fund-securing capabilities of the Office of Federal Relations as well as the newer instruments for attaining capital ($400 million plus, in Georgetown's case): tax-exempt bonds as well as taxable ones. Under Timothy Healy the university enjoyed extraordinary success in fund-raising, a field in which Georgetown had known mostly frustration and failure through most of its history, to raise money on a scale hitherto thought impossible for Georgetown. In one major campaign during Healy's presidency, the university raised more money than it had done previously in its entire history. Such fund-raising and astute management allowed the endowment to grow more than sixfold to provide the financial undergirding that made possible Georgetown's aspirations to become a first-class university.

Under Healy's commitment and prodding, the university reached out to the population of its city through service and clinical programs that involved thousands of Georgetown students at both the undergraduate and professional levels. He gave the university a presence in national and international circles that it had never before known. He took full advantage of Georgetown's location in Washington to advance its unique character and to articulate the relationships among church, state, and university. At the same time, he became a national spokesman for higher education. The admission in 1981 of Georgetown as the first Catholic member of the Consortium on the Financing of Higher Education was a sign of the university's emergence as the preeminent Catholic institution of higher education.

By many measures—the scale of construction across three campuses, the quality and diversity of its undergraduates, faculty achievement, the scope of its fund-raising and the enormous growth of its endowment, the prominence that Healy's national image personified—one could conclude that by the time Tim Healy stepped down as president in 1989 he had indeed brought Georgetown into the center front of American higher education. But in completely assessing its status as a university, one, of course, must consider Georgetown's experience in graduate and professional education during Healy's era. And if "Catholic" was an essential part of its self-understanding as a university, then that bears examination as well. Those matters will be more fully explored in chapter 5.

CHAPTER 5

End of a Second Century
Not with a Whimper, 1976–89

As we close our second century, strengthening doctoral studies leaps out as the first imperative for our third. Past and present success in collegiate, legal and medical training and research provide the model to make Georgetown complete its being—to add the doctoral research faculties that will make us what the nation's capital much needs, a great University.

TIMOTHY S. HEALY, SJ

A New Importance

Graduate education at Georgetown had always been, if not in structure or allocation of resources, at least in understanding, at the periphery of the university's mission. Indeed, when the university framed its first mission statement in 1981, it was framed within the context of the main campus and its undergraduate schools. Timothy Healy many times referred to undergraduate education as the "heart and center of Georgetown." In fact, the president tended to be wary of, if not scornful toward, any form of educational endeavor beyond the traditional arts and sciences. (He once said that Georgetown "should be slightly embarrassed to have a business school; and confounded at the thought of a[n] engineering school.")[1] Ironically, graduate and professional education at Georgetown became, during Healy's tenure, more important in the goals that the university laid out for itself and consequently more integral to the university's sense of self and of its well-being. Research and service, particularly through the growing number of centers and institutes within the university, reached new levels of accomplishment and influence. Yet if graduate and professional education had a dynamic presence at Georgetown, it exhibited a certain oscillation as well, as important elements were discarded or separated off and others brought on or given new resources.

Graduate Education: "In Dramatic Transition"

Graduate education at Georgetown in the late seventies was arguably the weakest link in the university's academic divisions. Despite a bleak academic market in most fields and the termination of federal fellowship support that tended to depress the quantity and quality of graduate applicants nationally in the seventies, enrollment at Georgetown, after an initial drop, rebounded strongly, reaching a high of 2,216 students by the fall of 1980. The enrollment was overwhelmingly part-time.[2] The Georgetown graduate school was fundamentally a sundown school—most classes were held in the evening. There were a plethora of master's and doctoral programs, with an emphasis on professional master's programs, particularly in international relations (national security studies, MS in foreign service) and in area studies (Arab, Latin American, Russian). A master of business administration and a master in public policy were established in 1981–82, both of which proved to be solid programs. But for most of the graduate school programs, admission standards were lax; there were few fellowships, and those that existed carried low stipends.

The position of the dean, as the 1981 Middle States self-study delicately put it, was more of a hortatory than administrative position.[3] He had little or no power, despite the organizational restructuring of the early seventies that involved the dean in the budget process and in faculty development and that empowered him to establish periodic reviews of departmental programs. In 1977, Dean Herzberg had taken the initiative, following a review, of suspending the graduate program of the mathematics department. The faculty senate protested that the dean had not followed appropriate procedures in the suspension and established guidelines for the future that would have the dean work with the executive council of the Graduate School and the particular department whose program was in question in a very cumbersome process designed, not to facilitate the abolition or suspension of a program, but to resolve the problems that were making the dean consider its elimination.[4]

At this time, the board of directors put in motion a comprehensive review designed to sidestep the faculty bureaucracy that had hitherto made any comprehensive change in graduate programming virtually impossible. A year later Dean Herzberg reported to the board that he was encountering resistance from department heads and others in attempting to carry out the comprehensive review.[5] In response the board requested the administration to develop a mechanism for evaluating and making decisions about graduate programs.[6] For that reason the administration chose to focus on graduate education in its self-study for the 1981 Middle States Association evaluation. That study concluded, as the dean and other administrators had clearly hoped it would, that Georgetown needed to concentrate its finite resources on a relatively few graduate programs and strive to make those first rate in quality, whether PhD programs or professional master's programs. The Middle States team agreed. "Both . . . concluded," the graduate dean later wrote, "that given our traditions, our history, our size, and the size of our endowment, we . . . should do what we can do best and exploit all of our comparative advantages."[7]

In 1982 the main campus five-year plan made "the development of recognized national leadership in selected graduate programs" a top priority. This commitment finally put in motion a reform that deans and other officials had been pleading for since the early fifties, that Georgetown had to winnow its graduate programs and focus on a small number of them that gave promise of being highly competitive in their respective graduate fields. With a new dean in place (Herzberg had died suddenly in the summer of 1980, and Richard Schwartz succeeded him in the following year), the provost and the council of deans, including Schwartz, worked closely with five professors on the main campus to implement the recommendation of the Middle States Association and the charge of the main campus five-year plan. Departments across the main campus were asked to submit proposals for achieving excellence in their particular graduate programs. The provost and his group weighed the proposals and announced in the spring of 1983 that they had selected five doctoral programs—Arabic, chemistry, history, Spanish, and linguistics—to be given the necessary resources to achieve excellence: additional faculty, graduate fellowships, and other assistance. Master's programs in Arab studies, foreign service, business administration, and English were also singled out for development. Programs in mathematics, physics, and several languages were suspended. Other major programs—in biology, economics, government, and philosophy—were found to be integral to the university's commitment to graduate education, but in need of further planning.

Much of the faculty was in shock at this development. The administration had radically reshaped graduate education by bypassing the ordinary channels of departments, the executive committee of the graduate school, and the faculty senate. "No first-class university does this kind of stuff," Valerie Earle, faculty senate president, remarked. In a May meeting, the senate, by a vote of 36 to 0 with four abstentions, urged the board of directors to rescind the plan to restructure the Graduate School programs. The board stood by its decision but did call for the establishment of a new governance structure in the Graduate School. Eventually the doctoral programs in government, economics, and philosophy were added to the elite five, and the master in Latin American studies and Russian studies put in the select company as well. Looking back, Dean Schwartz pointed out that the review clearly revealed that the school's strength lay in the social sciences, chemistry, and linguistics. The school's reputation in and commitment to international studies was a compelling factor in the choice of the MS in foreign service and area studies programs. Philosophy, with an emphasis on ethics, was selected, in part, because of the university's Catholic/Jesuit character.[8]

The positive consequences were immediate. Over the next several years, twenty-three faculty positions were added to the selected departments. Doctoral programs reduced their numbers in general, became much more selective in their admissions, and became day operations with full-time students. Most master's programs within the social sciences were terminated. Given the shift to full-time doctoral programs that severely reduced, if not eliminated, the traditional pool of applicants from the federal agencies and services, the Graduate School administration began a serious recruitment process in which representatives of the school toured campuses and took part in graduate fairs across the country. Across the departments the quality of doctoral candidates clearly improved. The Graduate School increased the number of its fellowships and made their stipends more competitive. Students in the dissertation stage of their studies could now secure travel grants to enable them to do research in distant archives and depositories. An associate dean for research was appointed to apprize faculty of grant and fellowship opportunities as well as to assist in the preparation of applications for the same. This dean also was in charge of the summer grants for research and curriculum development that were greatly increased. Dean Schwartz introduced a quarterly report, *Research at Georgetown*, which publicized the research by Georgetown faculty to provide a forum for sharing their scholarly endeavors with other members of the academy.

At the end of the eighties, 80 percent of the applicants for graduate programs were now outside the Washington metropolitan area. Four-fifths of graduate students were enrolled in master's programs, largely professional rather than academic. The revenue from those programs supported the pared-down doctoral programs, which now saw a larger portion of its PhDs go into the academy. Those from history, for example, included Douglas Egerton (1985, LeMoyne), Lawrence McAndrews (1985, St. Norbert's), Alan Gallay (1986, Ohio State), Douglas Brinkley (1989, Rice), Martha Hanna (1989, Colorado), Susan Poulson (1989, Scranton), Michael Fischbach (1992, Randolph-Macon College), June Hopkins (1997, Armstrong Atlantic), Loretta Long (1998, Pepperdine), Richard Wiggers (2000, Ottawa), and Catherine Sampsell (2002, Georgetown).

In 1984 the establishment of a new committee on graduate school governance, with its members nominated by the faculty senate, as well as the addition of several other departments and programs to the list of those "targeted for excellence" and the appointment of senior faculty to strengthen those graduate programs, did much to win broad faculty support for the reforms. By 1989, Dean Schwartz wrote, in assessing Georgetown's place within the marketplace of graduate education, "We do very well in Ethics, in International Relations, in Sociolinguistics, in Neuropharmacology, in Russian and Eastern European history, and other areas [such as Middle Eastern studies] where we have carved out and built a specialty. . . . We must, in short, be unique and that means special programs and special emphases within traditional programs. . . . In those fields where we have not just [the advantage of reputation but location as well, for example, public policy,] we can compete with anyone."[9] By 1989, if Georgetown still lacked a truly distinguished graduate program, the school had probably made the most progress of any main campus school during the period.

Centers: Additions and Partings

Within higher education there was a proliferation of centers and institutes throughout the seventies and eighties. Georgetown shared in this growth industry. On the main campus it had four major centers when Tim Healy came into office in 1976: the Center for Strategic and International Studies, the Kennedy Institute, the Woodstock Center, and the Center for Contemporary Arab Studies. During the Healy years a number of others were added. Some proved to be very transitory, tied to one or two individuals; others perdured, such as the Institute for the Study of Diplomacy, established in the School of Foreign Service in 1978, that brought together former and active diplomats to study contemporary issues around the world.

The Center for Immigration Policy and Refugee Assistance was another long-term creation. This was the dream child of Donald Herzberg, who for three years had planned the center but died before it could be begun. Healy, who on becoming president had singled out immigration policy as one of the areas that the university should give its attention to, honored Herzberg's intentions by beginning the center in 1981. It incorporated the refugee assistance programs in which Georgetown medical and other students had already been engaged in Cambodia, Thailand, the Philippines, and elsewhere. The main goal of the Center, its first director, Harold Bradley, SJ, pointed out, was to organize an international and national network of policymakers who would be given the fora to exchange ideas and research and in this process influence the shaping of national and international immigration policy.[10]

During the early eighties the center sponsored public meetings and lectures on immigration policy involving federal and state legislators, refugee policymakers, academics, and refugees. It carried out pilot studies for the State Department on migration trends throughout the Americas. It coordinated six-month internships for graduate and undergraduate students to work with international refugee agencies. It oversaw the clerkships for medical, dental, and nursing students in refugee camps. It operated a reception house—Abraham Welcome House—for newly arrived refugees. It administered the DC Schools' Project, a Department of State program begun in 1984 in which Georgetown undergraduates tutored Central American students in the DC school system. By 1986 more than two thousand Washington immigrants, including Asians, Africans, and South Americans, had participated in the program. The project itself had become a model for other universities to adopt in responding to the needs of their local immigrant groups. The center had also established the small business management training program for Vietnamese American entrepreneurs in 1985. In 1987 it created the Herzberg Chair in International Migration; the sociologist Charles Keely became the first holder.

The Center for Contemporary Arab Studies was established in 1975 and quickly gained recognition for its unique academic program devoted solely to the study of the modern Arab world and for the annual symposia it hosted on Arab affairs. From the beginning, Peter Krogh, the dean of the School of Foreign Service under which the center operated, and President Henle had solicited funding from various Arab countries. "I went to all of them," Krogh later remarked, "whether they had diplomatic relations with the US or not, whether they were moderate or radical, whatever their stripe."[11] Jordan, Qatar, Iraq, and Libya were among the first countries to support the center. Libya had pledged three-quarters of a million dollars to establish a chair in Arab studies.

In 1978, Father Healy, without advising the center of his intentions, returned the Iraqi money. As Peter Krogh pointed out, this was the first time in university history that a donation had been returned to its giver. Three years after returning the Iraqi money, Healy returned the Libyan money as well (at least the $600,000 already paid), with an additional $42,000 for the interest earned. The president claimed that Libya's adoption of terror as a normal method of international policy made the acceptance of its money a contradiction of everything that Georgetown stood for.[12] Hisham Sharabi, Georgetown's distinguished historian and holder of the chair, along with others connected with the center, thought that Healy was under Jewish pressure, both in and outside the university, to return the money to the two Arab governments. There undoubtedly was much Jewish anger toward Georgetown for having taken the Libyan gift. Healy himself had seemed to recognize this by certain gestures he had made to show his goodwill toward Israel, including a trip to that country and the bestowal of an honorary degree to the Israeli ambassador to the United States. But his renunciation of the money seems to have been done, at least in part, on its own merits. Georgetown, just two years after the Iraqi affair, accepted two large grants of $1 million each from Kuwait and Oman. Two years after infuriating those connected with the center by rescinding the Libyan money, the university made the center's academic program, the master of arts in Arab studies, one of the graduate programs it targeted for excellence.

The center continued to grow during Healy's tenure; indeed, it was a major recipient of benefactions and chairs over the course of the eighties. An important addition to its faculty was Ibrahim Iskandar Ibrahim, a scholar of Middle Eastern history and public policy who, as a member of the center for twenty-five years and its director in the early nineties, played a key role in the center's development as a pacesetter in its field.

The Georgetown Center for Strategic and International Studies (CSIS) was highly appreciated by Healy as an important asset of the university during his early years at Georgetown. He played an important role in the recruitment of Henry Kissinger for a joint appointment to the center and the School of Foreign Service. The president noted the tremendous contributions the CSIS was making to the university through its cutting-edge research on energy, food resources, and human rights.[13] An article on the center in the summer 1980 issue of *Georgetown Magazine* noted that "the Center has given Georgetown increased prestige and a wide window on the world." Its joint appointments, the article went on, had significantly enhanced the university faculty.[14] It also played an important role in administering federal commissions on the reconstruction of Lebanon, on United States security, and on United States–Japanese relations. David Abshire, the director of the center, saw it having a unique role in making Georgetown a preeminent university.[15]

But in the early eighties some faculty members and alumni worried about the image of Georgetown projected by CSIS through its conservative pundits who were seemingly everywhere in the media. Abshire admitted that CSIS members "swamped television, and there is no question that it riled many of the Georgetown faculty."[16] Three top officials in the Reagan administration had come from the center. Healy felt building pressure to sever connections with an institution that a growing number of people saw as a think tank for the Reagan administration. Healy created a distinguished committee of external evaluators to determine whether the operations and mission of the center were consistent with the university's identity and mission. At the same time, the center, under new direction (Abshire having become the ambassador to NATO under Reagan), sought to cut loose from the university, mainly for fund-raising advantages. When the external evaluators reported that the missions of the center and the university were, in their judgment, fundamentally incompatible and that the continued alliance was a threat to Georgetown's own fund-raising capability, the two parties were ready to part amicably. In June 1987 the Georgetown Center for Strategic and International Affairs became simply the Center for

Strategic and International Affairs.[17] Tim Healy joined the board at CSIS. The separation was probably inevitable, but it still represented a loss of an important intellectual asset for the university in international affairs.

The Law Center: Crossing the Threshold

By the 1980s the Georgetown University Law Center (GULC), in terms of its students, its faculty, and its reputation, had clearly moved from being a regional law school to a national one. Not only was it one of the largest law schools in the country (in 1980 it received more applications than any other U.S. law school), but also its students were increasingly diverse in their ethnic and geographic backgrounds, and their quality continued to rise. Its faculty also continued to expand (by 1980 it was the largest in the country) and to attract members from the top legal institutions and legal firms in the nation. It boasted having one of the most, if not the most, extensive legal curriculum, at both the undergraduate and graduate levels, of any law school. In its curriculum, clinical legal education was particularly emphasized: 10 percent of the law center's budget went to the operation of the clinical programs, and nearly two-thirds of its students participated in some form of clinical experience during their JD program. It housed four legal research institutes and published four legal journals. When the accreditation team of the American Bar Association (ABA) and the American Association of Law Schools (AALS) visited the law center in the spring of 1978, they found a very strong school, with an exceptionally able dean and highly capable faculty, a very selective student body rich in diversity, and clinical programs that it judged to be the best in the country. It was, they reported, "on the threshold of greatness." Its overcrowded facilities and poor faculty-student ratio (39:1) were holding it back from taking that next step. But the team left with the encouraging word that, if the administration was successful in carrying out its long-range plan, it had an excellent prospect of "gaining a place in the select handful of premier law schools."[18]

When David McCarthy became executive vice president for law center affairs, one of his earliest moves was to begin a broad-based planning process that would set up priorities for the center to address. In 1978 the resulting long-range plan set out the goals of the center for the next decade.

A primary underpinning for a top-tier law school was a complex administrative structure dealing with admissions, records, library and information services, financial aid, graduate and undergraduate programs, development, and placement. Much, if not most of this work had previously fallen to faculty. McCarthy now created the administrative positions needed to do it professionally and staffed them with talented administrators, such as Everett Bellamy, Anne Collins, Kevin Conry, Andrew Cornblatt, Martha Hoff, Barbara King, and Abbie Willard.

David McCarthy, executive vice president for law center affairs, 1976–83. (Georgetown University Archives)

Increasing the size of the faculty was an obvious need to facilitate the reduction of the teacher-student ratio. The long-range plan envisioned not only a larger faculty (at least ten new positions) but also a distinguished and diverse one. In 1977 there were fifty-four full-time faculty. In the course of the next five years, under McCarthy's leadership, intense recruiting of targeted professors and new graduates led to an array of outstanding appointments. In 1978 Stephen Goldberg and Stanley Metzger, a nationally known figure in international law, joined the center. The following year Linda F. Donaldson came to the center from the Office of the General Counsel in the Department of Health, Education, and Welfare, and Warren F. Schwartz gave up a chair at the University of Virginia School of Law to move to Georgetown. In 1980 Robert Drinan, SJ, who had represented Massachusetts in Congress for the previous decade, moved down the street to join the center's faculty. Also in that year, Stephen B. Cohen of the faculty of the University of Wisconsin School of Law accepted an appointment, Patricia White joined the faculty as a professor of tax law, and the well-known sociologist Norman Birnbaum joined the center from Amherst College. The following year, when Ruth Bader Ginsburg was named to the Supreme Court by President Clinton, her husband, Martin Ginsburg, one of the most distinguished legal professors in the country, accepted an appointment from Georgetown. "Georgetown had gotten good enough," Sherman Cohn noted, "for a man of his stature to be willing to be with us."[19]

Others joining the faculty in 1981 were Daniel I. Halperin, formerly a professor at the University of Pennsylvania School of Law; Elizabeth Hayes Patterson, who had been chair of the DC Public Service Commission; Eleanor Holmes Norton, who had chaired the Equal Employment Opportunity Commission; Philip Schrag, former deputy general counsel of the U.S. Arms Control and Disarmament Agency; and Silas Wasserstrom, former chief of the Appellate Section of the District of Columbia Public Defender Service. In 1982 the school added Susan Low Bloch, the top graduate in her class at the University of Michigan Law School and a former law clerk to Justice Thurgood Marshall, as it did Alexander Capron, who left a position at the University of Pennsylvania; Peter B. Edelman, former clerk to Justice Arthur Goldberg; and Wendy Collins Perdue, former law clerk to Judge Anthony Kennedy and an associate at the Washington firm of Hogan and Hartson. By the end of McCarthy's term in 1983, the faculty had grown by one-fifth. Three-quarters of the faculty were now extramural in their legal training, and included sixteen from Harvard, thirteen from Yale, and three each from Chicago, Columbia, and Michigan. They brought with them a wide diversity in specialization, including some with interdisciplinary backgrounds.[20]

In 1983, Robert Pitofsky succeeded David McCarthy as executive vice president and dean of the law center. Pitofsky, an expert on trade regulation, had first taught at Georgetown from 1973 to 1978, during which time he was named by *Time* magazine one of the ten outstanding law professors in America. In 1978 he took a leave of absence to serve as a commissioner of the U.S. Federal Trade Commission under the Carter administration. He had returned to the Georgetown University Law Center in 1981. Pitofsky stepped up McCarthy's recruitment of outstanding scholars, particularly those with interdisciplinary credentials. Among those added over the next several years were Anita Allen, a lawyer and philosopher; Gregg Bloche, a lawyer-physician; and Daniel R. Ernst, a lawyer and historian.[21] The enlarged faculty greatly increased the scholarly output. In 1988–89 more than 90 percent of the faculty published: They produced nine monographs, fifteen texts or casebooks, and forty-eight articles in refereed journals or chapters in books.

The expanded Office of Admissions, working under Dean David Wilmot, systematically built a network of feeder schools across the nation that it regularly visited in search of the most qualified applicants, particularly focusing on schools in the Sunbelt regions and on minorities. That widespread outreach probably softened the impact of a nationally declining applicants' pool by the middle eighties. Georgetown applications did drop from more than 8,100 in 1982–83 to 6,751 in 1986–87, but the law center continued to lead the nation's law schools in the number of applicants, and the quality of the applicants remained very high with a median LSAT of 42. The staff regarded the entering class of 1987 to be "the strongest . . . class that GULC has ever had," in both its quality and its diversity.[22] Minorities now accounted for 25 percent of the class; women were nearly as numerous as men at 48.2 percent. Part of the

Robert Drinan, SJ, professor in the Law School.
(Georgetown University Archives)

recruiting success no doubt lay in the student ambassadors program that the center had instituted, wherein a college student who had been admitted to Georgetown would be contacted by a current Georgetown law student, often from the same school or region as the applicant, who would tell him or her all the reasons for studying law at Georgetown.[23] That same year (1987) GULC was ranked thirteenth, immediately behind Duke and ahead of UCLA and Cornell, among law schools by *U.S. News and World Report*.[24]

The curriculum, Dean McCarthy commented in 1981, "has exploded in the last twenty years. The number of seminars and the opportunity for students to do research and to write . . . are exponentially greater than in the classic . . . law school." A major aim of the curriculum, particularly through its seminars and clinics, was, as McCarthy put it, "to ensure that [every Georgetown student confronted] the social questions of this society and the role of the lawyer in those questions."[25] By the 1980s the curriculum contained many interdisciplinary courses that interrelated the law with the physical and social sciences, the humanities, medical ethics, and psychiatry. Several joint-degree programs were begun to better enable students to combine disciplines. Thus the center and the history department initiated a JD-MA history program; a JD-MBA program was started in 1985 with the Business School. Three years later, in conjunction with the Johns Hopkins School of Hygiene and Public Health, the center began to offer a joint JD-MS in public health. The undergraduate curriculum became more internationally oriented as well. By the 1980s, students had the opportunity to focus their studies on international law, as the center offered the most courses and seminars in international law, comparative law, and foreign law of any law school in the country. At the graduate level, the center was increasingly attracting foreign lawyers to enroll in its programs, particularly its master of laws (common law studies).[26]

The long-range plan had underscored the importance of continuing clinical education as a prominent feature of the undergraduate program. One of the new clinics, established in 1978, was the Harrison Institute for Public Law, an outgrowth of the DC Project. It provided legal assistance and education for groups of citizens and community organizations in fighting tenant eviction, placing children in special education programs, and representing neighborhood organizations before DC agencies. In 1981 the sex discrimination clinic began as a result of women students' pressure for a clinic dealing with women's issues. The Center for Applied Legal Studies (formerly the Administrative Advocacy Clinic) trained students to represent area residents in Social Security disability and military discharge hearings, as well as in small claims court. At McCarthy's initiative, clinical instructors in 1983 were given faculty status in order to better integrate the clinics within the general curriculum of the school.[27] With the changed status of clinical instructors, the full-time faculty reached seventy-two, and the number of students participating in clinics grew as well. By one estimate, nearly half of those earning JDs each year had participated in one or another clinic.[28] By the end of the eighties, Georgetown continued to be recognized as having one of the finest clinical programs in the nation.

The center's library had traditionally been one of its weakest elements. During the late seventies and the eighties, the center's administration made a concerted effort to change that. With a larger portion of the budget dedicated to the library's development, it had more than doubled its volumes, from 175,000 in 1976 to 450,000 a decade later. In 1983, McCarthy brought in Robert L. Oakley from the Boston University School of Law to become director of the library. Oakley set the ambitious goal of bringing the library into the top ten in the United States within the next decade.[29] Oakley proceeded to put together a highly competent staff and to accelerate acquisitions for the library. By 1987, the year the center broke ground for a new facility, the library ranked fifteenth in size among law libraries. When the new library was dedicated in 1988, providing the housing for one million volumes and the facilities needed in the digital age of information services, Georgetown had acquired all the makings of a world-class law library in the immediate future.

The institutes of the school served as the major loci of research within GULC. The Institute for Criminal Law and Procedure conducted studies on various topics of criminal law; the International Law Institute, which Donald Wallace Jr. directed, focused its research on the legal aspects of international trade and investment. The institute also continued to sponsor conferences, both national and international, and, through its Investment Negotiation Center, trained private industry officials and bureaucrats of developing nations in fiscal investment and procurement. Moreover, it had responsibility for the joint JD-MSFS program. It had affiliations with similar institutes in Germany, Belgium, Japan, and Argentina. The Institute for Public Interest Representation (INSPIRE), created in 1978, utilized staff and students to represent handicapped people, racial minorities, consumer groups, and others in the courts and government agencies on issues ranging from corporate responsibility, civil rights, and immigration policy to deregulation.

In 1986, Robert Drinan, SJ, with benefactions from the ABA and several law firms, established the *Georgetown Journal of Legal Ethics,* a quarterly that was the first of its kind in the English-speaking world, devoted exclusively to legal ethics and professional responsibility. Its first issue appeared in June 1987, with articles that had been solicited by Drinan from distinguished law professors across the country.

The Law Center Players, formed in 1973 as the Gilbert and Sullivan Society, continued to offer productions of Gilbert and Sullivan musicals but expanded its repertory in the eighties to include musicals beyond those of the D'Oyly Carte company. In 1987–88, the society, billing itself as "America's Only Theater Company with Its Own Law School," restaged its original offering, *Trial by Jury,* as well as *Guys and Dolls* and *The Pirates of Penzance.*

The period saw a definite shift in the choice of law practice by graduates. In 1979 one-quarter of the graduates started their careers in federal, state, and local government or some other form of public interest. A decade later the proportion of graduates committing themselves to public service had declined to 7 percent.[30] During the same time, the proportion of those going into private practice kept rising, from about 50 percent in the late seventies to 61 percent by 1988. Among the declining minority going into public service were Mitch Daniels (1979) and John Lynch (1978), who in 2005 became governors of Indiana and New Hampshire, respectively; James McGreevey (1981), now former governor of New Jersey; Robert Barr (1977), who became a Republican representative from Georgia; Frank Howard (1977), who became a staff attorney for the Legal Aid Society of Washington; Albert R. Wynn (1977), who became a Democratic representative from Maryland and deputy whip for his party in the House of Representatives; Lane Allen Evans (1978), Democrat, who represented the 17th District of Illinois from 1983 to 2007; Mazie Hirono (1978) was Hawaii's lieutenant governor from 1994 to 2002, and four years later was elected to the U.S. House of Representatives; James McGovern (1978), who served as staff director of the Senate Armed Services Committee before becoming undersecretary of the air force in the Reagan administration; Marc Morial (1983), mayor of New Orleans from 1994 to 2002, after which he was president and CEO of the National Urban League; Janet E. Garvey (1979), who was U.S. ambassador to the Republic of Cameroon; Mazie Hirono (1978), who practiced in Honolulu before being elected lieutenant governor in 1996; David M. Satterfield (1978), who was U.S. ambassador to Lebanon in the Clinton administration; Isaias Torres (1978), who as an immigration lawyer in Houston was the lawyer for the plaintiffs in *Plyler v. Doe* in 1982, in which the Supreme Court affirmed the right of children of undocumented immigrants to education; Elaine Kaplan (1979), who became head of the U.S. Office of Special Counsel during the Clinton administration, which has responsibility for protecting the rights of federal workers; Alan Eastham (1982), who was U.S. ambassador to Malawi and the Republic of the Congo under the George W. Bush administration; Elizabeth Frawley Bagley (1987), who was U.S. ambassador to Portugal; Terry McAuliffe (1984), who became chairman of the Democratic National Committee; and Laurie S. Fulton (1989), who served as U.S. ambassador to Denmark during the Obama administration.

Center graduates who rose to important judicial positions included John O. Colvin (1978), chief judge of the U.S. Tax Court; Laura Denvir Stith (1978), chief justice, Missouri Supreme Court; Helen E. Hoens (1979), associate justice, New Jersey Supreme Court; Jeffrey R. Howard (1981), judge, U.S. Court of Appeals for the First Circuit; Rives Kistler (1981), associate justice, Oregon Supreme Court; Kent A. Jordan (1984), judge, U.S. Court of Appeals for the Third Circuit; and Lorie Skjerven Gildea (1986), associate justice, Minnesota Supreme Court.

When the ABA-AALS inspection team revisited GULC in the fall of 1985, it rated it as "one of the country's fine law schools." It found a larger and stronger faculty, a greatly improved student-faculty ratio, and a dramatically expanded library collection that had moved it from "a second-rate one at best to a leading law library."[31] All that the school now needed was an appropriate building to house it, and that was on the immediate horizon.

Physical expansion and renovation were the most pressing needs for the center by the mid-eighties. Because of the great increase in enrollment, the school had already outgrown McDonough Hall by the time it opened in 1971. With the addition of a fourth day section, total enrollment increased by nearly 30 percent more to reach more than 2,500 by 1977. The increase in faculty, programs, and library collections had only aggravated the overcrowding. There was virtually no space for any student social life or interaction. Faculty, students, and administration all decried the lack of space. As Chairman Peter Mullen warned the board in 1985, the Georgetown Law School was in grave danger of undermining the enviable status and reputation it had slowly acquired over recent years if it did not take steps to improve its physical facilities in the near future.[32] The board committed to building a new library and to renovating the McDonough building at an estimated cost of $47 million.[33] The center had already been preparing for the badly needed expansion. Dean McCarthy had appointed a new building committee in 1979 and continued the acquisition of property adjacent to the McDonough building. By 1981 the university owned that entire city square.

When Robert Pitofsky became dean in 1983, he established a development office at the law center, with Patricia McGuire (**L** 1977) as director. Her first mission was to raise $15 million toward the funding of the new building, estimated to cost $32 million. The family of Edward Bennett Williams, together with the law firm that he founded, contributed one-third of the $15 million, and the library was accordingly named for the alumnus and former adjunct professor.

The building committee of the center chose the local architectural firm of Hartman and Cox to design a building to house the library. Hartman and Cox specialized in the postmodernist-contextual style that had emerged in American architecture in the 1970s. The Edward Bennett Williams library was a splendid example of their work, with its neoclassical allusions in its rotunda and curved east end and the way it blended into its environment, most immediately with the adjoining McDonough Hall, which it echoes through its podium setting, similar height, and repetitive facades, while making its own architectural statement.[34] The five-story, 100,000-square-foot building contained, besides stack space and service

Robert Pitofsky, executive vice president for law center affairs, 1983–89. (Susie Fitzhugh. Georgetown University Archives)

areas, several student lounges, a computer lab, a special collections exhibit area, group study rooms, a two-story main reading room, a media collections area, study carrels, and offices for the *American Criminal Law Review* and the *Georgetown Law Journal.* Computerized catalogs and online research services brought GULC into the digital age of legal information technology. The building opened for the spring semester of 1989. Simultaneously McDonough Hall was thoroughly renovated to provide additional classrooms as well as offices for faculty, clinics, and student organizations. G Street was closed between the two buildings and landscaped to provide, for the first time, a true campus for the center.

Medicine at Georgetown in the 1980s

Research to the Fore

In 1979 the medical center, like the rest of the university, began to develop a five-year plan of goals and the means for achieving them. One goal was to establish the medical center as "one of the nation's premier institutions for research in carefully selected aspects of the health sciences to the limits its resources will allow."[35] Those areas would certainly include cardiovascular research as well as gastrointestinal oncology. Later, other areas would receive the resources that would allow them to be truly distinguished and nationally recognized: specifically, in biomedical information technology, AIDs and human virology, the neurosciences, and perinatal medicine. The plan also set as a priority the securing of additional clinical facilities for research, teaching, and patient care. For the present, the planners, all too aware of the escalating costs of both medical care and medical education, pledged to achieve "the management effectiveness and administrative responsiveness necessary to retain program viability and financial stability during the 1980s."[36] On the whole, they did.

Appointing noted or promising faculty researchers was obviously crucial to the progress of the medical center as a research institution. Beginning in the latter seventies there were a bloc of such appointments. The Lombardi Cancer Center was the beneficiary of several. In 1977, Lucius F. Sinks was named professor of pediatrics and chief of the new Division of Pediatric and Adolescent Oncology at the center. Sinks had an international reputation for his research on the biochemistry of malignant disease and his treatment of childhood malignancies. In 1978, Stuart Holden was named chief of the division of urologic oncology. A decade later Marc Estes Lippman, a leading expert on the treatment of breast cancer at the National Cancer Institute, was named director of the center. Lippmann in turn brought with him a number of his former colleagues at the institute.

In September 1979, John B. Henry, an internationally known authority in the field of pathology at the Medical Center of the State University of New

York, was appointed dean of the Georgetown Medical School. When he resigned as dean in 1984, he became director of the clinical laboratories at Georgetown. Other significant appointments included Robert B. Wallace, longtime chair of the Department of Surgery at the Mayo Clinic, who was appointed professor and chair of the Department of Surgery at Georgetown in 1980; John Thomas Queenan, a well-known authority in the field of perinatal medicine, who was appointed professor and chair of the Department of Obstetrics and Gynecology; and Martin Dym, who joined the Department of Anatomy in 1981 as professor and chair. That same year Martin G. Lewis joined the Department of Pathology as chair, and Gary Brooker was brought in to chair the Department of Biochemistry. In 1982, Charles Edward Rackley, a renowned authority in the field of cardiology, was named professor and chair of the Department of Medicine. The addition of Rackley greatly strengthened the center's ability to deal with cardiovascular disease, as Rackley's expertise nicely complemented that of Robert B. Wallace in cardiovascular surgery and that of Larry Elliott in cardiovascular radiology. Three other notable additions to the center in 1981–82 were Kenneth Kent, a pathbreaking researcher in coronary angioplasty, who came to Georgetown from the National Heart, Lung, and Blood Institute; Klemens H. Barth, a specialist in vascular and interventional radiology from the Johns Hopkins University; and Albert B. Sabin, the inventor of the oral polio virus vaccine, who joined the Department of Microbiology at the age of seventy-five. Gary R. Pearson, an internationally known microbiologist, came in 1984 from the Mayo Clinic to chair the Department of Microbiology.

The 1980s represented an unprecedented expansion of national academic research, from less than $7 billion to nearly $12 billion.[37] Medical centers continued to be the main engine driving the expansion. During the eighties Georgetown's medical center kept breaking records in the amount of grants received for research. In 1980–81 private and federal research grants exceeded $20 million.[38] By the end of the decade they had topped $50 million.

A major locus of Georgetown's medical research was the Lombardi Cancer Center. For several years the physicians' offices, research laboratories, and outpatient clinics of the Lombardi Center were scattered throughout the medical center, with no place of its own. In 1979 the board approved the construction of a facility, long in the planning, for the center. The estimated cost for the facility was $10.5 million (later raised to $11.5 million), of which the National Cancer Institute had provided $4.1 million.[39] Construction began in March 1980 on the 92,421-square-foot structure and was completed a little more than two years later, in July 1982. By then the staff had grown from an initial 3 oncologists in 1970 to more than 60 physicians and scientists. The number of patients treated had grown from the 375 in 1970 to 1,200 a year by the early eighties. Grants for research were now averaging $5 million annually.[40]

Early on, the decision was made to concentrate on gastrointestinal cancer. By 1982 the chemotherapy regimen, FAM (Fluorouracil, Adriamycin, and Mitomycin C), designed at the cancer center, had become the standard treatment for certain gastrointestinal cancers, especially stomach and pancreatic tumors. The center also conducted extensive testing of interferon, a substance produced by human cells in response to viral infection, as a natural defense against cancer. Much of the testing was funded by Hoffman-Laroche, a drug company that was one of the chief producers of concentrated interferon. Other trials were in conjunction with the National Cancer Institute.[41] Despite its designation as a national comprehensive cancer center with the new facility, abundant grants, distinguished leadership, and strengthening staff, the Lombardi Center still had a distance to go to reach prominence by the end of the eighties.

John B. Henry, dean of the Medical School, 1979–84.

(*Grand Rounds*, 1982)

In 1985 the Department of Obstetrics and Gynecology received a $15 million grant from the Agency for International Development (AID) to undertake a comprehensive program, including research, information, education, communication, training, and technical assistance to developing countries in the area of natural family planning.[42] Two years later the Department of Radiology, in collaboration with George Washington University, was awarded a $5 million contract by the U.S. Army as one of two sites to develop, implement, and evaluate a radiology digital picture archiving communications system.[43]

Georgetown's strength in the neurosciences, and particularly its neurosurgical staff, enabled it to establish a Center for Intractable Epilepsy in 1988. The center offered an in-house monitoring of epileptic patients that recorded brain wave patterns to allow physicians to locate the site of the neurological disorder. Once the epileptic area was identified, surgery removed the damaged part of the brain in order to greatly reduce the seizures patients had previously experienced. During its first year, the center conducted five successful operations.[44] In 1988, Georgetown's neurology department also set up an Alzheimer's Disease and Memory Disorders Clinic under the direction of Robert Friedland to provide a broad range of diagnostic, management, and treatment services.[45]

As part of the new emphasis on research, departments such as anatomy, biochemistry, and pharmacology undertook joint research projects and held weekly research seminars for medical faculty, students, and others in the metropolitan area. By the middle of the eighties, there was still a yearning among faculty for stronger leadership focused on creative research that would take advantage of the talented faculty at Georgetown.[46] When the university appointed a new executive vice president for the health sciences in 1986, it chose John Griffith, who came with a strong resume in research and publishing.

John Griffith was convinced that the medical center's chief research focus should be in the field of biomedicine, which he saw at the heart of the ongoing revolution of the understanding of health and disease. By the eighties the profile of medical research, indeed of all academic research, was undergoing a profound change, not only in its areas of research, but also in the sources of its funding. At the center of the sea change in research was the revolution in biotechnology. As Griffith explained in 1988, "*[E]ither* we become, more and more, a catalyst in our own right to the ongoing explosion of biomedical knowledge or we risk being left behind in the forward advance of medicine and health care." To choose the former would enhance their status not only as researchers but as educators and caregivers as well.[47]

Most of the funding for this revolution came from NIH, particularly the National Cancer Institute. In all, nearly half the funding for academic research derived from NIH during the eighties.[48] Georgetown medical research received strong support from NIH; it ranked forty-first in per capita funding from NIH.[49] Its biggest grant was the $36.8 million given in 1987 to microbiologist John Gerin (**C** 1959) and his team from the National Institute of Allergy and Infectious Diseases to study AIDs, viral hepatitis, and other viruses.[50] Gerin, director of the Division of Molecular Virology and Immunology, and his associates made an important contribution toward the controlling of hepatitis B through research into the virus that causes it and the development of a vaccine to prevent it and the liver cancer that often followed it. The seven-year grant from NIH enabled them to develop effective antiviral drugs to disrupt and foil HIV in those already infected and to develop vaccines to prevent infection.[51]

A new major source of support for medical research was private industry. Industrial investment in research increased dramatically in the early eighties, and a large portion of this new investment went to university medical research.[52] Within industry, support came especially from the large, multinational pharmaceutical firms.[53] Between 1981 and 1984, at least eleven multiyear, multimillion-dollar contracts for research in biotechnology between universities and chemical or pharmaceutical firms

Lombardi Cancer Center, 1982. (Georgetown University Archives)

were entered into, the largest being the ten-year, $70 million deal concluded between the German firm Hoechst and the Harvard affiliate, Massachusetts General Hospital.[54] In 1985, Georgetown and the Italian pharmaceutical company Fidia entered into a partnership on a slightly lower scale, with the company pledging to pay the university more than $60 million over the next two decades to house the Fidia-Georgetown Institute for the Neurosciences.

The university was especially sensitive that the joint endeavor would raise charges of commercialization against Georgetown. As John Rose, the vice chancellor of the medical center pointed out at the institute's opening in November 1985, "This will be an institute devoted to basic research, to the discovery of fundamental mechanisms in the brain without commercial objectives; the work will be published freely in the scientific literature; and the ethical and scientific guidelines of the University will be observed." The institute's director, Erminio Costa, added that the five initial areas of investigation for the institute's staff, all Georgetown faculty, would be basic subjects such as synaptic communication, gap junctions, the mechanisms of anxiety and depression, the aging process, and opiate dependence.[55] But there was a certain commercialization of medical research taking place in the decade, which the joint ventures of medical centers and industrial corporations suggested. The eighties also marked the rise of university researchers' securing patents for their discoveries and sharing in the profits realized by their successful utilization commercially.[56] In 1983 Georgetown medical researchers applied for twenty-eight patents; in 1976 they had applied for only one.[57]

In 1984 the National Library of Medicine (NLM) designated the Dahlgren Memorial Library as one of four institutions in the country to be a strategic planning site for an integrated academic information management system. Funding from the NLM enabled the library to develop a digital biotechnology and biomedical knowledge network that made multiple information resources available to a dispersed community of users in homes, offices, laboratories, and clinics.[58]

By 1988, John Griffith reported that the center was making "steady progress" as a research institution. He pointed to the recent appointment of strong researchers as director of the Lombardi Center and as chairs of several departments. Expenditures for research, largely funded by grants and contracts, were up 30 percent from 1987, to $48.5 million. But much more needed to be done, he concluded, before Georgetown could become one of the nation's "premier biomedical research institutions."[59]

Faculty Practice Plans in Effect

The university administration had been calling for faculty practice plans since 1965. The accrediting committees of the American Medical Association (AMA) and AAMC had, since 1969, urged that the university implement such plans. The board of directors had approved guidelines for instituting such plans in 1974. Ostensibly they were intended to increase the attraction of the Georgetown University Medical Center to potential faculty members by giving them the opportunity to increase their income beyond their set salaries. But an equally important, if not more important, reason for instituting the plans was to provide much-needed revenue for the school and departments to use for education and research. The plans were to apply to all full-time geographical physicians in the clinical departments. Base salary was to be ideally at the 80th percentile level of the AAMC rankings. Clinical income would provide part of this base salary. Departments would establish what portion of clinical income physicians could retain beyond the portion being used to supplement their base salary. Despite much opposition within the medical center to any faculty practice plan that would include current tenured faculty, the general plan adopted in 1977 exempted only faculty who had been at Georgetown for approximately twenty years or more.[60] Faculty practice plans rapidly became a major source of funding for the Medical School. In 1980, when eight plans were in effect, over one-fifth of faculty practice income went to the support of departments within the school.[61] By 1984, when there were thirteen plans, the size of support increased. At the end of the decade, faculty practice accounted for over 25 percent of university revenue.[62] Medical education and research at Georgetown had become economically very dependent on clinical practice.

Medical School

With the expiration of the DC Health Manpower Act in 1977 as well as the termination of the Physicians' Augmentation Act, tuition for the Medical School the following year leapt from $6,800 to nearly $12,000, giving the Medical School the dubious distinction of charging the highest tuition in the country. Attempts to secure new forms of federal subsidy failed. In time, the revenue from faculty practice offset, to some extent, the loss of the federal subsidy, but medical education at Georgetown remained the most expensive in the country. Until the mid-eighties Georgetown suffered little drop-off in applications. Georgetown continued to lead the country in medical school applications. In 1982 there were more than 7,800 applications for the 205 available places in the entering class.[63] By 1984 the high tuition began to have an impact. Enrollment remained steady through the eighties, but by the end of the decade 25 percent of the students the school was taking on were not being accepted anywhere else. By 1989, when tuition stood at $22,500, 70 percent of the medical students at Georgetown needed financial aid; for most of them it came in the form of nonuniversity loans, which left many students with debts of $100,000 or more upon their graduation. On average, medical students were graduating with more than $74,000 in debt.[64]

The Changing World of Medical Care

In the latter seventies, the cost of medical care began to soar. One source of rapidly growing expense was malpractice insurance. In 1976 the premium for such insurance for Georgetown hospital increased by 600 percent, to nearly $3 million.[65] Another cause was the expensive medical technology that was increasingly needed for the intensive and aggressive therapy in which Georgetown as a tertiary care center specialized. But utilization of hospital facilities continued to increase as well, providing a steadily growing base of revenue. From 1975 to 1980, the total of patient days in the hospital, the number of beds used, and the use of the emergency room and clinics all increased, whereas the number of hospital personnel remained relatively steady.[66] In 1980 the hospital realized its highest occupancy rate in its history. The greatest increase among the inpatients were those with severe and complicated illnesses, who accounted for more than 130,000 patient days of intensive care, a telling sign of how Georgetown hospital had become primarily a tertiary care center.[67] The following year, 1980–81, the number of patient days grew to 152,000.[68] To expand its outpatient capacity, a new ambulatory department was created in 1979, where clinical patients could receive general medical care as they would in a private practice.

In the middle 1980s, when health care costs were increasing four times faster than the inflation rate, there was a fundamental change in health care reimbursement. Medicare led the way in this transformation. As medical costs soared, the government changed the method of reimbursing doctors and hospitals for their services. Instead of the virtually guaranteed fee-for-services system that had governed the administration of Medicare from its inception, a "prospective payment" mechanism now became the standard method of reimbursement. In this system Medicare paid a set fee determined by the patient's diagnosis, which had to fit within the 467 diagnosis-related groups (DRGs) that Medicare administrators had set up. For Medicare patients, the fee would no longer be set by the doctor or hospital but by an external agent, the reviewer for Medicare. The insurer, not the medical authorities, now controlled the process. For Georgetown, where Medicare paid one-third of patient fees, this change had profound consequences.[69] And the consequences became even more ominous by the end of the decade, when most private insurers imposed similar payment systems.[70]

The impact on the culture of hospitalization was immediate. A new position of director of management systems was established in anticipation of the complex management that the new reimbursement process would require. Efficiency was now the shibboleth of health care, and the rapid handling of inpatients was the core of efficiency. Hospitals needed to have a larger volume of patients that they could "throughput" from admission to discharge as expeditiously as possible. A critical way in which hospitals secured more patients was to form affiliations with community hospitals, which could refer their more critical or complex cases to the teaching hospitals. The formation of affiliate networks by teaching hospitals was one crucial factor in their ability to keep their budgets in the black through the eighties. In 1986 the board of directors authorized the hospital to establish a corporation with Fairfax

Hospital Association, for the purpose of managing an integrated system of community hospitals in Northern Virginia, in which Georgetown would be the hub.[71] Another was the maintenance of the indirect graduate education payment in which hospitals with medical schools received additional payments from Medicare and other insurers to subsidize their education and research.[72] A third factor was the expansion of emergency and ambulatory care services. To underscore its new importance, emergency medicine was made a separate department in 1987. The augmentation of ambulatory care service was a major reason for the decision to build a new clinical science building in which the medical faculty could have offices and facilities for the treatment of outpatients. In May 1986 ground was broken for the Pasquerilla Health Care Center, a $16.5 million, nearly 150,000-square-foot complex. Completed in April 1988, the health care center housed the Faculty Practice Group, the Center for Sight, clinics, and the departments of medicine, surgery, obstetrics and gynecology, pediatrics, and neurology.

Controversial Restructuring

One of the consequences of the financial pressures created by the changing landscape of medical care was a major restructuring of the administration of the medical center itself in the spring of 1989. Vice President Griffith announced a centralization of authority: Hereafter all decision making regarding the center would be done in the executive vice president's office. Three days later Milton Corn, who had succeeded John Henry as dean in 1984, feeling stripped of his essential powers as dean, submitted his resignation. The bylaws of the Medical School's constitution stipulated that the dean had full appointment and budgetary powers, powers that the president had effectively undercut by putting all authority in Griffith's hands. Many faculty at the center felt that this was just the latest of the president's "heavy-handed" administrative style. "The way in which this was handled," commented one member, "communicates a sense of . . . lawlessness at this university." The problem at the core of the controversy, another professor offered, was the essential autonomy of the department heads, who ran their departments "as personal fiefdoms." The dean had no real authority over them, and the executive vice president had only veto power. To deal with departmental financial deficits and appointments, Griffith needed more authority.[73] The board of directors' Committee on Medical Center Affairs, from their examination of the reorganization, was convinced that it would also enable the executive vice president to act as a more effective promoter and coordinator of expanded research among the medical faculty.[74] Like the controversy over the reform of the graduate programs six years earlier, structural change in the medical center hardly seemed likely if the administration strictly observed due process. So the president simply acted.

The Dental School: An Irreversible Decision

During the Healy years, the Dental School leadership matched that of any segment of the university. In deans David Beaudreau (1977–81) and Philip Hazen (1983–90) the school had two nationally recognized leaders in dental education. Their sterling credentials and heroic efforts to maintain enrollment at one of the nation's largest dental schools, while modernizing its curriculum and developing its faculty, proved at last to be insufficient in preventing the deteriorating national dental conditions from claiming the school as one of the victims of downsizing.

Under Dean Beaudreau a new Department of Occlusion was established, an area of specialization that was becoming prominent within the profession at the same time that it was assuming an important place in the predoctoral curriculum of most dental schools. The study and treatment of occlusion, the way the upper and lower teeth come together, was now seen as an integral part of any adequate training of students to provide comprehensive patient oral health care. The creation of a Department of Occlusion was part of an overall plan to restructure the curriculum, from a block-oriented system in which faculty taught their clinical specialties, respectively, to a comprehensive care curriculum that integrated the various aspects of oral pathology and treatment according to carefully prepared stages. By 1982 the comprehensive patient care approach had been introduced into three of the four years of the predoctoral program.[75]

Stanley P. Hazen, dean of the Dental School, 1983–90. (*Apollonian*, 1986)

By 1980 the American Association of Dental Schools (AADS) was becoming concerned about the deteriorating state of the profession and its impact on those considering a career in dentistry. Preventive dentistry, with its emphasis on flossing and the use of fluoride in water systems, had greatly reduced the number of people, especially in the younger cohorts of the population, who needed corrective dental care. As dental needs diminished, so did dental practice in general, and dentistry became a much less attractive profession. Compounding this were two other troubling realities: the shrinking pool of eighteen- to twenty-four-year-olds in the general population, who were projected to decline by nearly 25 percent in the next decade, and the ending of federal capitation grants for dental students. As the eighties began, AADS officials confronted the alarming drop in applications to dental schools by 40 percent over the past five years.[76] "It seems apparent to me," the executive director of AADS reported in 1980, "that the eighties will be a period of retrenchment for dental education."[77]

As early as 1978 the status of the school had been a concern for Timothy Healy. He asked newly appointed dean David Beaudreau to provide figures showing how Georgetown compared in its admission standards with other schools, what the comparative success rate of their graduates in national and state boards was, and how many students Georgetown was taking who were accepted by no other dental school. Beaudreau responded with figures that showed Georgetown (in 1976) had accepted students whose Dental Aptitude Test scores were considerably higher than the national average but whose GPAs were slightly lower than the national average. He had more sobering results from Georgetown dental graduates' performance in state board examinations. In 1976 Georgetown had the second highest failure rate (17%) among comparable dental schools in state board exams in 1976, and far above the national average (12%). As for the percentage of those accepted only by Georgetown, Beaudreau had to confirm Healy's suspicion that that number was increasing. Indeed, it was rapidly increasing, from 38 percent in 1974–75 to 71 percent by 1977–78.[78]

Healy apparently chose not to pursue the matter further, but Beaudreau clearly got the message: Increase the number of applicants and improve their quality. He set up an aggressive marketing and recruitment strategy to "identify, attract and enroll the most qualified dental applicants." The admissions staff, by monitoring the applications, tagged and contacted frequently the best applicants. The dean also combined the Offices of Admissions and Financial Aid to expedite the process of matching available aid to an applicant's need.[79] Beaudreau felt confident that this new approach would result in Georgetown's moving into the top five private dental schools. In 1979–80, Georgetown did rank first in one category: number of applications received.[80] However, over the next two years there was a dramatic decline of more than 25 percent in applications, leading to the fear that they would fail to find sufficiently qualified students to fill the classes of 1987 and beyond.[81] By 1983 there was an encouraging sharp turnaround in the percentage of accepted applicants who were accepted nowhere else. Ninety-eight percent of the 152 students who entered their first year at the school in 1983 had been accepted at other dental schools.[82] But the number of applicants continued to decline, as did the GPAs and Dental Aptitude Test scores of those who enrolled.

Beaudreau's successor, Philip Hazen, committed the school to even more intensive, creative, and broader recruiting. On-site visits by Georgetown recruiters were stepped up beginning in 1984, not only to traditional feeder schools in the Northeast, but to promising markets in the South and Southwest as well. At the same time, the school attempted to exploit an under-tapped market—the international student community. In 1984 Georgetown recruiters visited ten countries in Europe, the Middle East, and Asia seeking applicants. Their goal was to enroll twenty foreign students per year, but they never came anywhere near that number. They began, like the Medical School, an early acceptance program with the College of Arts and Sciences, through which the school accepted college applicants at the end of their sophomore year. The students would complete their four undergraduate years to gain their BS, but they would have the early assurance of a place in a dental school, a promise, Dental School officials thought, that would tend to sway Georgetown undergraduates to commit to the school. A more radical form of an early admission program was the joint degree programs worked out in 1983–84 between the Dental School and eight colleges in the Northeast, mostly traditional feeder schools, by which high school seniors would be selected by a committee composed of college and Georgetown Dental School representatives. The students would then do three years of undergraduate work at the respective college. At the end of their junior year, those with a GPA of 3.0 or better would be admitted to the Dental School for a regular term of four years. By 1986 joint degree students made up over 40 percent of the entering class. Finally, in the spring of 1985, a five-year program was begun for those who failed to qualify for normal admission.

Despite all these special programs, by the latter eighties both the quantity and quality of applicants were down. Applications declined by 35 percent between 1982 and 1986, greater than the national average of 26 percent, and the average GPA of those who enrolled dropped below 3.0. Between 1975 and 1986, there had been a 70 percent reduction in applications, from 3,926 to 1,180. The worsening performance of Georgetown graduates on the state and national boards was one sign of their deteriorating academic character. In 1976, 17 percent failed their state boards; in 1982 one-fifth of the dental graduates had failed at least one part of the national boards; four years later the number had climbed to 22 percent, more than twice the national average.[83] By 1986 enrollment at Georgetown had declined to 570, a 9 percent drop from the beginning of the decade, far less than most dental schools had experienced in the eighties but still a loss of more than $800,000 in revenue that the school would have had with full enrollment.[84] At the same time, a self-study of the school's educational program funded by the Pew Foundation concluded that the present program was weak and outdated in preparing students for the profession.[85]

John Griffiths, executive vice president for medical center affairs, 1986–96. (*Grand Rounds*, 1993)

"I suspect that dentistry in a sense is a dying profession," President Healy wrote to the superior general of the Jesuits in 1985, "and that over the next decade Georgetown will have to question seriously whether or not it wishes to continue dental education."[86] That questioning, in fact, came the following year, when John Griffith became executive vice president for health sciences and revived, probably at Healy's direction, the examination of the Dental School's viability that President Healy had initiated but did not pursue in 1978. The shortfall in school revenue from declining enrollment caught his attention. Aware of the projection that the already dwindling pool of applicants for dental education would get progressively smaller in the coming years,

Griffith ordered Price Waterhouse to do a financial study of the school's prospects over the next five years. As he grimly announced to the executive faculty of the school in November 1986, the school was "marginal at best," given the current trends, and they had to face up to "a problem that has been building over the past few years."[87] The following month the auditing firm reported that on its present course the Georgetown University School of Dentistry could expect to have escalating deficits that would reach $3.5 million by 1992. The board of directors charged the school with preparing a plan over the next six weeks for a reorganization of the school that would enable it, with a reduced enrollment yet on a self-sustaining budget, to prepare a dental student to be a "modern oral health care practitioner."[88]

As it happened, the Pew Memorial Trust had earlier in 1986 chosen the school as one of twenty-one dental schools to develop strategies for meeting the demographic and financial challenges that were facing institutions of dental education in the immediate future. Utilizing the preliminary report that this committee had already prepared, the Dental School faculty developed a five-year plan, from 1987 to 1992. The plan called for a reduction in class size from 156 to 100 by 1990, with admission standards set at a minimal 2.75 GPA and 4/4 on the Dental Aptitude Test. There was to be a reduction in clinical departments from thirteen to seven, with a corresponding reduction in faculty, from eighty-eight to sixty-four by 1991. At the same time, there would be an expansion of the graduate program to offset the loss in revenue from the smaller predoctoral program. With the increased emphasis on graduate education, all full-time faculty would be expected to engage in research and publication, with a minimum of one paper a year. The plan recommended the institution of a faculty practice plan. Dental clinic hours would be greatly increased to accommodate a much larger number of patients. Special clinics would be established for complex problems.[89]

There seemed hope, in the late winter of 1987, that the school had survived. When the officers of the faculty senate during a regular meeting with the president expressed their concern about the future of the dental clinic should the school be closed and asked Healy whether he was planning to shut the school down, he answered, "Absolutely not—precisely because of the clinic."[90] At the mid-March meeting of the board of directors, John Griffith assured the Committee on Medical Center Affairs that the school was not going to be closed.[91] At the full board meeting later that day, Griffith was shocked when Healy, in presenting the issue of the Dental School, made the recommendation that the board vote to accept no new admissions to the school and to phase it out over the next three years, a recommendation the board ratified. The sharp decline in the quantity and quality of dental school applicants, as well as the increasing burden of debt that dental graduates were taking with them from Georgetown, were the critical factors in Healy's brief for closing the school. "Georgetown University," a press release stated, "feels that it would be irresponsible to maintain its dental program."[92]

The dental faculty was angry, feeling that the board had not even taken their plan into consideration but had made its decision to close the school simply on the Price Waterhouse projections of soaring deficits, based on current conditions.[93] The students were outraged at the announcement. They began daily demonstrations outside the executive vice president's office. On Friday, April 10, some four hundred dental students and supporters staged a march from the school to the Healy Building. Carrying signs such as "God saves, Healy invests," and "Let My People Drill," they held a rally in Healy Circle at which the president of the school's student council announced that they were filing a suit in DC Superior Court to block the university from carrying out the closure. At a special meeting of the faculty senate in May, members decried, not the decision to close, but the unconstitutional manner in which the decision was reached. Once again the president had ignored the statutes of the constitution of the senate that called for "full Faculty participation in matters of general University interest by sharing responsibility with the University Board of Directors and Administration in the conduct of University affairs."

Nearly a year to the day later, Judge Eugene N. Hamilton of the DC Superior Court issued an injunction prohibiting any further action by the university to close the Dental School on the grounds that the board of directors had failed in their obligation to refer the question to the faculty senate before making their decision.[94] Hamilton added that it was clear to him that the school, at least through 1987, had not been operating with a deficit and that all projections of future losses were just estimates.[95] The relief for the faculty and students was brief. In July a three-judge appeal panel unanimously overturned the injunction; in its opinion, the court noted that the Commission on Dental Accreditation of the ADA had endorsed the university's decision to phase out the Dental School.[96] The phase-out went forward and was completed in May 1990 when the last class graduated. For the first time in its two centuries the university had closed one of its schools.

International Involvement and University Responsibility

From the late seventies through the eighties, there was an increasingly international air to the experience of Georgetown students. Foreign students made up a growing percentage of those enrolled. By 1989 they numbered about 10 percent. The study abroad office, established in 1974, when the university had a handful of study abroad programs, was overseeing some thirty-four programs, in countries ranging from Argentina to Vietnam, by 1989. In 1979 the university was given a villa in Fiesole, Italy, where it established a semester program for college juniors in the classics, fine arts, and history. By the 1980s, more than one-quarter of Georgetown students were spending at least one semester abroad.[97]

Beginning in December 1979 Georgetown medical faculty members, medical students, and nurses volunteered to spend six months in ministering to Southeast Asian refugees in camps in Hong Kong, Malaysia, Singapore, and Thailand. Dr. John Collins Harvey led the first team to Thailand; other teams followed throughout 1980 and into 1981. A parallel program, the Indonesian refugee aid internship, was begun by International Programs to send recent graduates to refugee camps and receiving centers to work with relocating and settling refugees. In 1981, Otto Hentz, SJ, at the initiative of several graduating seniors, started a program to send a dozen recent graduates, "Los Gringos," to work on community projects in Nicaragua. That program would continue through the eighties, although they were forced by international tensions from Nicaragua to Peru in the mid-eighties, before returning to Nicaragua. In that decade Georgetown became the home of the International Jesuit Volunteer Corps.

President Healy became personally involved in the political and military crisis in El Salvador. In September 1977 he made a visit there to investigate conditions that the church was facing in that country. While there he signed an agreement with the Universidad Centro Americana, a Jesuit institution, that included the offer to house the university's research institute at Georgetown. When Archbishop Romero was assassinated in El Salvador in the spring of 1980, in a homily at a memorial mass on campus Healy talked about the complacency of Americans "for the ease with which we forget the majority of our fellow Christians south of the border, for the terrible cruelty that we allow to be worked in the name of our government, and even worse in the name of our profits."[98]

In the spring of 1979 students at Georgetown began to urge that the university divest itself of all holdings in companies that did business in South Africa. The president utilized the Committee on Investments and Social Responsibility to weigh the ethics of the South African holdings, which, according to critics, was nearly one-tenth of the university's endowment (it was actually somewhat larger).[99] The faculty/administrative committee recommended that the university limit its investments to companies that were subscribing to the Sullivan principles (on corporate responsibility in promoting social justice while doing business in South Africa), a step the board took in May 1985.[100] The university also resolved to divest itself of stock in any company selling arms to South Africa.[101] In 1986 a new student group, GU-SCAR (Student Coalition against Racism), organized at the beginning of April a campuswide simulation of the apartheid system that governed South Africa, with fountains and restrooms marked "White" and "Colored," whites asked to sit in the rear of classrooms, and so forth. Ten days later they set up a Freedom College on the steps of White-Gravenor as a teach-in to heighten awareness of the need for the university to totally divest its holdings from companies doing business in South Africa. In a manifesto announcing the teach-in, GU-SCAR explained, "We . . . have decided, after years of fruitless negotiations . . . that action speaks louder than words and for this reason have occupied White Gravenor. . . . In solidarity with [the youth of South Africa] we have decided that there will be no business as usual at this University. Our action is intended to more fully dramatize and press our demands of TOTAL DIVESTMENT!"[102] For nearly two weeks Freedom College continued without incident. Then, on Thursday afternoon, April 24, GU-SCAR members placed a shanty on the lawn in front of White-Gravenor as part of a rally and left the structure standing afterward. Early on Friday morning, the shanty was taken down by university police and thirty-five students arrested by District of Columbia police for refusing to abandon the site. As the police corralled the protesters, students shouted, "GU, you know, South African stocks have got to go," and "The people, united, will never be defeated."[103]

Outrage swept the campus, including the faculty, some of whom had offspring among those arrested. Hundreds of students rallied on White-Gravenor steps to protest the arrests. The Georgetown University Student Association condemned the action. The vice president for student affairs, John DeGioia, explained that he had ordered the destruction of the shanty out of fear that it would trigger violence on campus, as had happened at Dartmouth, Penn State, and other places where shanties had been erected as protest gestures. In response to a petition from members of the faculty, Jo Ann Moran Cruz, faculty senate president, called a general meeting of the faculty to which she invited university administrators to explain why they had had the students arrested.[104] About 110 faculty turned out in McNeir Hall on May 14 for the meeting that lasted more than two and a half hours. President Healy, who had been reluctantly persuaded to fly back to the university to address the concerns of the faculty, spoke at great length about the workings of the university's investment policy and the steps he had taken to begin a possible divestiture, including seeking the advice of the bishops of South Africa. He refused to take any questions about the destruction of the shanty and the arrest of students. For that he turned over the podium to De-Gioia, who for the next hour was grilled by faculty members, who were furious that the president had passed the buck to his administrator, who gamely responded to the angry questions. In the end the faculty passed a resolution that expressed regret at the way the administration had handled the demonstration and called for all charges, criminal as well as internal disciplinary ones, to be dropped.[105] They eventually were.

At its first meeting the following academic year, the board voted to begin the process of divesting. As Healy explained in calling for the vote, the South African Catholic bishops had, ironically, in May issued a pastoral letter that essentially urged the economic pressure of divestment in companies doing business in South Africa.[106] As the *Washington Post* noted, Georgetown, the oldest Catholic university in the country, had become the first to follow the bishops' urging and support divestiture.[107] The faculty senate formed a Committee on Protests and Demonstrations that concluded that discourse and "the untrammeled expression of ideas and information" was at the heart of a university's being. Free speech was central to the life of a university and had to be so honored by all, including students, faculty, and administration.[108]

"Complexities and Ambiguities of Great Scope and Meaning"

Georgetown, Timothy Healy remarked in 1988, "has made longer and swifter strides toward establishing itself in the mainstream of American higher education, in fact in the headwaters of that mainstream, than any other Catholic college or university in America." But, he went on, that academic progress, striking as it was, was not enough. "It is vital that Georgetown develops . . . a viable way to marry secular excellence with its religious tradition."[109] Adopting the structures and norms of its secular counterparts to move Georgetown into the front currents of university life had in fact occurred along with a growing awareness and self-examination of its distinctive Catholic character. How to reappropriate that tradition in a vastly changed and changing demographic and intellectual landscape was the rub, as Healy well recognized. "The recognition of the essential secularity of the University," he wrote, "involves Catholics in complexities and ambiguities of great scope and meaning."[110] As he once admitted to his fellow Jesuits at Georgetown, "We have shown that we can be 'good' as a university, but we have yet to show that we can continue to be 'Catholic' and all that that means."[111]

One meaning of "Catholic" obviously related to the proportion of students, faculty, and administration that identified themselves as Catholic. The religious composition of Georgetown's student body, no longer overwhelmingly Catholic, at least at the undergraduate level when Healy became president, remained remarkably steady from the late seventies through the eighties, with Catholics representing about 60 percent of the undergraduate population. By 1988, Protestants made up a significant minority (about one-quarter of the undergraduates) and Jews a much smaller one (about 4%). Catholic graduate and professional students were in a distinct minority. At the faculty and administrative levels, Catholics were steadily decreasing below the 50 percent mark. Among the Jesuits at Georgetown, a slow decline set in during the period that, given the rapidly shrinking numbers of Jesuits nationally, threatened to become a precipitous one by the nineties. Georgetown benefited to some degree from the guidelines that the American Jesuit provincials issued in 1982 about the assignment of personnel in higher education. In assigning individual Jesuits, the guidelines directed, provincials should consider where the individual could accomplish the greater good, have the bigger influence.[112] The prestige that Georgetown was attaining as the leading Jesuit institution of higher education in America proved an attraction for Jesuit academicians and made a compelling case in many instances for qualified Jesuits, whether they were from Maryland or California, to join Georgetown's faculty. Still, the Jesuit presence at Georgetown began to shrink during the Healy years, most notably at the level of higher administration, but among the faculty as well.

Healy began to stress the need for inculcating faculty and administrators in the Jesuit tradition of spirituality and liberal education—the so-called Jesuit-lay collaboration. That was clearly one important way to remain vitally Catholic. "It seems to me that the Holy Ghost is sending us a clear message," he wrote in 1988. "We are either going to follow the teaching of the Vatican Council, or we will slide down the slow path to secularism. . . . There is no way that Georgetown will remain a Catholic and Jesuit institution unless we are willing to share and share deeply our religious heritage with these good and learned men and women." What Healy envisioned was the establishment of a Jesuit ministry to the faculty of Georgetown, both Catholic and non-Catholic, a ministry that would engage faculty in the Spiritual Exercises of Ignatius, the marrow of the religious heritage of Georgetown, as a way of making the faculty *seriatim* active participants in the perpetuation of Jesuit liberal education.[113] During Healy's last years at Georgetown, specific Jesuits were appointed to this ministry, and individuals and groups of faculty did begin to make the spiritual exercises.

Healy's notion of the Catholic-Jesuit university was not only that of the presence of a critical mass of Christian and Jesuit faculty within the larger university community but also a group that collectively would engage the full range of the Catholic intellectual tradition and bring its weight to bear on the teaching and research of the university. This group would incarnate in its teaching within the various disciplines Catholicism's distinguishing intellectual characteristics of contemplation (reflection on God and his creation as the highest human activity and the most direct experience of reality), a sacramental approach to the universe of knowledge that is both liberating and transforming by its recognition of the symbolic characteristics of nature, and the quest for intellectual unity and coherence in a universe that is at root one and comprehensible. This group would center the dialogue with other belief and cultural systems that need be at the heart of any university enterprise. It would also be a prophetic voice vis-à-vis the culture of the larger society, the policies of the state that governs it, and the larger church of which it is such a distinctive part. As such, it would be committed to participating in the remaking of the republic as well as of the church. Healy was adumbrating a mission for the Catholic university that David O'Brien would later develop in his *From the Heart of the American*

Church—a university that took seriously its unique intellectual tradition and used it to engage society, republic, and church.[114] It was a mission for which the president developed few programs or dedicated resources toward accomplishing, however, beyond the steps he took toward inculcating the Ignatian vision within the faculty.

Healy thought that there was a vibrant Catholic atmosphere on campus for the undergraduates, demonstrated by the heavily attended liturgies. He attributed that condition largely to the outreach of the Jesuit Community. A "great blessing," he wrote the Jesuit superior general in 1985, "is that the Jesuit Community is huge in its generosity, open in its facilities, and deeply and significantly involved with the life of this campus. The influence of the Jesuit Community in the life of Georgetown is significant and is deeply spiritual. I think we have more kids going to more Masses now than ever before in our history. . . . All told the Community . . . makes an incalculable contribution to the life of this University. . . . Every year two or three novices enter who have done their undergraduate work at Georgetown."[115]

Still he could not be shaken from his conviction that Georgetown, for all its deep religious tradition and identity, was essentially secular and autonomous in its being. When Rome issued a document concerning Catholic universities and faculties in 1983 that called local bishops to oversee Catholic institutions within their sees and to determine appointments and retention of those teaching religious subjects, Healy was one of the leaders of the opposition against the Vatican document, which he saw as a clear and distinct threat to the autonomy of Catholic institutions of higher education. In 1985, Healy, while on a trip to Paris, begged the cardinal archbishop of that city, a boyhood chum of Pope John Paul II, to intervene with his old friend to defuse this threat to Catholic higher education.[116] What influence Healy's plea had, if any, on the pontiff is unknown. Perhaps it played some part in the eventual decree on Catholic higher education that issued from the Vatican in 1989 that was much more modest in its declaration of the relationship between hierarchy and Catholic institutions of higher education, as it admitted that "a Catholic university possesses the autonomy necessary to develop its distinctive identity and pursue its proper mission" and "the responsibility for maintaining and strengthening the Catholic identity of the university rests primarily with the university itself."[117]

The religious identification of Georgetown did lead to a protracted legal fight between gay students at Georgetown University and the university administration. In 1980 the organization of Gay Students of Georgetown University brought suit against the university for its failure to grant them official recognition as a club and give them equal benefit, in other words violating the human rights law of the District of Columbia. In 1983 the District court upheld the first amendment rights of the university and turned down the plaintiffs, who appealed the case. Meanwhile, the university had adopted a new policy by which they would recognize certain clubs or organizations that were consonant with the university's mission. The granting of funds and other benefits would be consigned to the student government on the respective campuses of the university. In the fall of 1987 the District Appeals Court overturned the lower court and declared that, although the university did not have to recognize the group, it did have to give them equal benefits and access to facilities. Healy publicly announced that the university was ready to comply with the court's ruling, as it was already doing what the court ordered them to do. He apparently had second thoughts about this. As he told a group of faculty that he had called into his office in late December to discuss the matter, the decision was so muddled that it left open the possibility of leaving the university in a very compromised position down the road.[118]

Certainly there were external pressures on him to contest the decision. His personal counsel, Edward Bennett Williams, urged him to take the matter to the Supreme Court. The archbishop of Washington weighed in with his own call to fight this case to the end. Some thought the change of heart came about when Mayor Marion Barry refused to certify that Georgetown was now in compliance with the DC antidiscrimination laws, thus preventing the university from qualifying for $127 million in tax-exemption construction bonds that it badly needed. The university appealed to the Supreme Court to stay the Appeals Court ruling, but the highest court refused to do so. Finally, in March 1987, the board, at Healy's urging, agreed to drop the appeal with the understanding that the two sides would work out a modus vivendi. The Catholic community within and beyond Georgetown was very divided by the settlement, but as Healy indicated in his final letter about the matter, it was time to put Georgetown's community back together again.[119] Seven months later Congress ordered the District to change its antidiscrimination law to exclude matters of sexual orientation. Georgetown eventually—in 1989— got an authorization from the District to sell $237 million in bonds when Healy assured members of the city council that the university would continue to give equal treatment to gay groups, no matter what the fate of the District's antidiscrimination law.[120]

The Ethical Imperative and *haut en banc* Governance

Tim Healy stressed the ethical imperative that a Catholic university such as Georgetown had to honor through setting a moral example by its actions and public positions. Georgetown could not imagine itself in an intellectual world in which learning was divorced from doing. On a few occasions the president's own public actions seemed to fall short of his rhetoric, as when he made Henry Kissinger a university professor in 1977, resisting an organized student-faculty protest that claimed that Georgetown, on moral grounds, should deny Kissinger such an honor, given his record in the Nixon administration in the subversion of the Allende government in Chile, the deception of Congress about the bombing of Cambodia, and the warrantless wiretapping for which he had been responsible. Father Richard McSorley and Professor Dorothy Brown attempted to get the faculty senate to petition the president to explain his position in making the appointment, but their resolution narrowly failed. In November 1977 the student-faculty coalition Students Organized Against Kissinger (SOAK) secured the signatures of more than 450 students and 27 faculty for their petition to Healy. Initially the president agreed to meet with the leaders of the coalition to receive the petition but canceled the meeting three hours before the appointed time. A second attempt to present the petition the following month failed as well. "The issue we are raising," the petition stated, "is the propriety of bestowing upon [Kissinger] a symbolic honor on behalf of the entire Georgetown community, when the public record of his moral conduct is evidently in conflict with the professed ideals of this institution."[121] "We can't fire him because of politics," the president later explained to a student reporter.[122] He said nothing about the moral issues.

Despite his vehement denunciation of the Reagan administration's Central American policy as well as its budget cuts, in 1981 he proposed that the board invite Reagan to be the commencement speaker and receive an honorary degree. If Reagan was unavailable, Jeane Kirkpatrick, a former Georgetown government professor, now ambassador to the United Nations, would be his backup. As it turned out, Reagan was not available and Kirkpatrick filled in. Kirkpatrick had become an object of criticism for her callous remarks about the murder of three nuns and a lay missionary in El Salvador. The rector of the Jesuit Community pleaded until the last day before commencement for Healy to substitute himself for Kirkpatrick as commencement speaker, but the president refused, basically putting his personal friendship with Kirkpatrick over all else. Kirkpatrick received the honorary degree and gave the address. Many students and faculty wore white armbands in protest. Some students and faculty stood with their backs to the ambassador when she gave her address. Seven years later, at the convocation that formally began Georgetown's bicentennial celebration, Reagan finally received his degree. Again there was an organized student protest.[123] The student government association president, who was supposed to be a speaker at the event, boycotted it. Reagan, after a few perfunctory compliments to the university, used the occasion to deliver an apologia for the actions of his administration over the past eight years.

As these three events suggest, relations between the president's administration and significant portions of the rest of the Georgetown community, particularly the faculty, were often less than ideal. Promoting "amicable and effective relationships between the faculty and the administration" was the one feature of the ideal profile of a president that Timothy Healy failed to meet. The handling of the graduate program review was one cause of faculty resentment of the administration. Healy's unilateral appointment of university professors, the handling of the South African protests, the closing of the

Dental School, and the reorganization of the medical center were still others. One dean, mentioned earlier, resigned in protest when Healy reorganized the Medical School; faculty members resigned from search committees when they became convinced that the president had cooked the search. In 1985 a faculty survey showed the frustration clearly enough: 78 percent of the faculty thought they should have a larger role in the governance of the institution. And yet they may have resented the aloofness, the *haut en banc* governance, and the less than collegial relationship between faculty and president, but it was significant that when there was a search for his successor, no calls were made this time, unlike in 1976, for widening the search beyond the Society of Jesus. Deep down there was respect for, even perhaps an appreciation of, what this president had accomplished in his baker's dozen of years at Georgetown.

"Learning, Faith, and Freedom"

Planning began in 1982 to celebrate the university's bicentenary in 1989. In 1984 Charles Currie, SJ, a former member of the chemistry department and past president of two Jesuit institutions of higher education, was named director of bicentennial operations. Shortly afterward, Bicentennial House opened on O Street with a staff of six that planned and coordinated the more than one hundred events that were held in celebration of the bicentenary, beginning in September 1988 and extending through September 1989. In 1986 planners chose the theme "Learning, Faith, and Freedom" as the organizing principle for the bicentennial activities. As President Healy explained in his welcoming remarks at the opening convocation in October 1988, the theme had "three motifs: the learning that has graced this place for two hundred years; the freedom which this nation has granted us to be ourselves and in defense of which we have helped to prepare thousands of its citizens; and finally, the faith in God that has built us every brick and is still the inspiration of our being."[124]

An estimated thirty-five thousand faculty, staff, alumni, parents, friends, and visiting scholars took part in the events, held not only on campus and other sites in the Washington area (Washington National Cathedral, the Kennedy Center) but also in cities across the nation as well as in Costa Rica, Chile, France, and Italy. The celebration opened with the bicentennial convocation on a sunlit October Saturday before six thousand people gathered on Healy lawn to see President Reagan receive an honorary degree and the Librarian of Congress, James Billington, deliver the main address. That evening, at Constitution Hall, Georgetown parents Michael Eisner and Cliff Robertson, past parent Bob Hope, and alumna Pearl Bailey led the "Salute to Georgetown," which was simulcast to alumni audiences in thirty-seven cities around the country. The following day, on Healy lawn, Father Walter Burghardt, SJ, gave the homily at the bicentennial mass in which he urged his listeners to view the year ahead as a time for reflection on "the beauty and the burden" of a Georgetown education, "that began modestly with John Carroll, has grown in awareness through two hundred years[,] and God willing, will reach fresh heights in Georgetown's third century."

One of the objectives of the bicentennial was to reflect the international and intercultural character of the university. Three events that particularly achieved this were the two international folk festivals that marked the beginning and closing of the bicentenary, and the Intercultural Festival of the Performing Arts, which involved eighteen productions over a six-month period in the 1988–89 academic year. The first folk festival began with a parade led by Jack the Bulldog and the children of Holy Trinity School in French and Spanish costumes that came up O Street through Healy gates, where forty-nine artisans and craftsmen, twenty-three performing artists, and thirty-seven food groups entertained and exhibited their wares. Such a success was the festival that it was repeated eleven months later as part of the closing weekend of the bicentennial. The intercultural festival featured theatrical productions in fifteen languages staged by the language departments of the School of Languages and Linguistics at various venues on campus and elsewhere.

Another objective of the bicentennial—to reach out to Georgetown's local community—was perhaps best realized in the documentary project "Black Georgetown Remembered." Conceived by Valerie Babb of the English department, the project resulted in both a video (by David Powell) and a book, which traced the evolution of the African American community in Georgetown from the late eighteenth century to the late twentieth. Interviews with surviving black Georgetowners highlighted the shattering impact that urban

Georgetown University Jesuit Community, 1980.

(*Ye Domesday Booke,*)

renewal had on the community from the 1930s through the 1950s, leaving a black Georgetown that existed in memory only. The half-hour film premiered in the Bunn Intercultural Center auditorium on February 10, 1989; through television and private showings, it subsequently had a wide circulation in the greater metropolitan region and beyond.[125]

The director of the bicentennial noted that, in the numerous conferences and symposia held throughout the fifteen-month celebration, Georgetown faculty took a much more active role than their predecessors had during the 175th celebration, "a reflection of the increased stature of our faculty."[126] Among the many conferences were four that had a focus on the French Revolution, the two hundredth anniversary of which was also in 1989. Several other conferences honored Georgetown's international heritage, such as one on health care for refugees and displaced persons, another on parliamentary democracy in the third world, and one on management and the global marketplace. The Georgetown Center for Liturgy and Spirituality held a colloquium on liturgical renewal in America for the twenty-fifth anniversary of the Vatican Council's Constitution on the Liturgy. A two-day symposium involving noted Catholic scholars and public figures discussed the state of American Catholic intellectual life. Before and over the course of the bicentennial, seventeen faculty members met monthly in a seminar to present and discuss papers on various aspects of the Georgetown experience. The papers were published as *Georgetown at Two Hundred: Faculty Reflections on the University's Future* (1990), which was one of seventeen volumes published by Georgetown University Press and other scholarly presses as a result of the various projects of the bicentennial.

"Salute to Georgetown" at the Kennedy Center, October 1989. (Georgetown University Archives)

Bicentennial medals, sculpted by Don Everhart, were awarded to various dignitaries throughout the year, including the superior general of the Society of Jesus, Peter Hans Kolvenbach, SJ, the archbishops of Baltimore and Washington, five Nobel laureates, forty-three senators and representatives with ties to Georgetown, the alumni governors of Delaware (Michael Castle) and Arkansas (William Clinton), Justice William Brennan and alumnus Justice Antonin Scalia, President Oscar Arias of Costa Rica, and many other distinguished scholars, artists, and leaders.

On January 23, 1989, two hundred years to the day when John Carroll received the deed to the property on which the first building of his academy was being constructed, the postmaster general, Anthony M. Frank, formally issued a U.S. postal card depicting Healy Hall, the first of "15 million birthday cards," as Frank put it, that would grace every post office in the nation.[127] The design of the card was by an alumnus and fine arts faculty member, John Morrell (**C** 1973). A month later brought the Musical Celebration of Religious Freedom at the Washington Cathedral. Cliff Robertson narrated the celebration that included the reading of historical texts interspersed with classical and folk songs performed by the Washington Choral Arts Society and the Georgetown Gospel Choir. Bishop John T. Walker of the Episcopal Diocese of Washington, Rabbi Joshua Haberman, and Father Timothy Healy gave brief reflections. For alumni reunion week in June 1989 there was the Bicentennial and Grand Reunion Ball, held at newly renovated Union Station, where four thousand alumni, faculty, staff, and friends partied in five ballrooms with bands playing music from a distinctive era in each.

The bicentennial ended its year-long celebration with a National Symphony Orchestra Concert at the Kennedy Center on Saturday, September 23. Conductor Mstislav Rostropovich led the orchestra in an all-American program, highlighted by Aaron Copland's *Lincoln Portrait,* narrated by S. Fitzgerald Haney, president of the Georgetown Student Association. The following day there was a closing liturgy, again on Healy lawn, with William Richardson, SJ, the homilist, reflecting on the distinctiveness of Georgetown.

"Thou knowest not his wrastling"

In the middle of the bicentennial year, in February 1989, Timothy Healy wrote to the Georgetown University community that he had long planned to announce his retirement as president at the end of the observance of the bicentenary in the fall of 1989, with the intention of leaving office at the end of the 1989–90 academic year. "Events," he went on, "have a way of overtaking plans." The trustees of the New York Public Library had asked him to become its president. He had accepted their offer and would, at sixty-five, be stepping down at the end of the current year. "I made my decision fully aware of the great deal of unfinished business that faces" the university, he owned. "Long ago I learned that no one, certainly not me, is irreplaceable."[128]

In his final report to the university community in 1989, Tim Healy acknowledged that he had not yet brought Georgetown into that small and very special circle of great universities. "As we close our second century," he reflected, "strengthening doctoral studies leaps out as the first imperative for our third. Past and present success in collegiate, legal and medical training and research provide the model to make Georgetown complete its being—to add the doctoral research faculties that will make us what the nation's capital much needs, a great University." He ended by quoting his favorite poet, John Donne: "To each of us is spoken the warning, 'Thou knowest this man's fall; thou knowest not his wrastling.' Our own falls," he added, "have yet to reach the tolerant gaze of chroniclers."[129] If there were falls in Tim Healy's time at Georgetown, there was much more "wrastling" that changed the university in many, many ways for the better and brought it to the brink of becoming a great institution. He truly was a transforming figure—on the shape of its campus, the profile of its student body and faculty, and the sixfold increase in its endowment; by his leadership and vision; by involving the university for the first time in a major way in the life of the District; and in giving Georgetown an unprecedented visibility and voice in American higher education. As Dorothy Brown summed up Healy's years at Georgetown, "Father Healy came to us with a proven record of leadership in higher education. He brought a vision of remarkable clarity and force. Georgetown was to be a leader among American universities. In 1989, we are . . . and it happened on his watch."[130]

Timothy S. Healy, SJ, 1980s.

(Georgetown University Archives)

EPILOGUE

"A Weight to Our Establishment"

Georgetown is a Catholic and Jesuit, student-centered research university . . . founded on the principle that serious and sustained discourse among peoples of different faiths, cultures, and beliefs promotes intellectual, ethical, and spiritual understanding. We embody this principle in the diversity of our students, faculty, and staff, our commitment to justice and the common good, our intellectual openness, and our international character. An intellectual community dedicated to creating and communicating knowledge, Georgetown provides excellent undergraduate, graduate, and professional education in the Jesuit tradition— for the glory of God and the well-being of humankind.

MISSION STATEMENT, 2001

Renewing Georgetown

The university officially closed its bicentennial celebration and opened its third century with the inauguration of its forty-seventh president on Saturday, September 23, 1989. Leo O'Donovan, SJ, a graduate of the College of Arts and Sciences, class of 1956, was the first alumnus to become president since Alphonsus Donlan in 1912. In his inaugural address, O'Donovan laid out what he thought Georgetown needed to do "to fulfill its promise as a truly great university." Most of all it needed to maintain "the sort of

Joseph Durkin, SJ, a Georgetown presence for nearly sixty years, 1944–2003.

imaginative recollection in which we have engaged during our Bicentennial celebration." For Georgetown to remain true to itself (a prerequisite for becoming a great university), it had to turn its attention to the question of its central purpose, a purpose that the university's institutional memory revealed to be closely bound up with its catholic, and Catholic, character. Georgetown had to confront creatively the challenges—intellectual, academic, physical, financial—that it faced. It had to find ways to contribute to the cooperative pursuit of global goals that an evermore interdependent world was forcing upon nations. As a means to achieve this contribution, governance at Georgetown had to become participatory to the extent that there would be regular consultation "at every level and in every major case." Above all, Georgetown had to remain committed to being "a community of inquirers" in which the faculty would "constitute the heart of that community." In short, as Georgetown began its third century, the university community's prime task was not to discover, not to invent, but to renew that institution.[1]

The Middle States team that visited the university in the spring of 1993 found an institution "coming of age." The past decade had been a very progressive one for Georgetown that culminated in a significant increase in the size and quality of the faculty, an increasingly selective pool of student applicants, a winnowing of graduate programs, higher visibility and an elevated reputation, and admittance into a superior peer, COFHE. This growth meant tension, the main line of which involved the emergence of a comprehensive arts and sciences research university from the undergraduate teaching institution in the Jesuit tradition that Georgetown had been, with its emphasis on the *cura personalis* that was expected to mark the teacher's relation to the stu-

Leo O'Donovan, SJ, the first alumnus in more than seventy years to serve as Georgetown's president, 1989–2001.

dent. There was also palpable tension that resulted from the university's passage from an era of perceived plenty to one in which resources were increasingly constrained by shrinking sources of support. The team's recommendations included an examination of the current structure of schools on the main campus to test their intellectual and economic feasibility.

A year later the provost issued a white paper that essentially restructured undergraduate education at Georgetown. The School of Languages and Linguistics became a part of the College of Arts and Sciences; all of the former's departments and programs, with the exception of linguistics (which became part of the graduate school), would now be directed by the dean of the college. Economics, government, and history, three departments that at times had had a conflicted relationship with the dean of the School of Foreign Service to whom they reported, now were transferred under the jurisdiction of the college dean as well. An unanticipated by-product of the academic reorganization was a new structure for faculty participation in main campus governance. In reaction to the fait accompli that the provost had presented to them, the faculty took decisive action to secure an appropriate role in future decision making by gaining university recognition for a main campus executive committee, which would serve in the same capacity in relation to the executive vice president as the executive councils did for the deans. This ensured that no major academic change affecting the main campus would be implemented without the approval of the executive committee, which consisted of fifty-four representatives from the main campus departments and programs and from the caucus of the faculty senate. Faculty involvement in the governance of the central academic community of the university had finally reached the level sought by the original organizers of the faculty senate thirty years earlier.

Under President O'Donovan's direction, a new master plan for the main campus was developed that provided a cohesive profile for the campus by extending the campus's architectural core that the Healy building and its quadrangle defined and that would integrate naturally with the community's urban context by situating small-scale buildings on a grid that extended the existing city streets through the campus and bisected with traditional academic quadrangles and pedestrian pathways.[2] The development of a new master plan was one factor in the university's decision to not add any new buildings on the main campus between 1989 and 2001. Another factor was to address the crisis of deteriorating buildings that had resulted from the policy from the previous two decades of deferring maintenance. A third factor was the university's inability to secure further tax-exempt bonds to finance new construction projects.

In 1997 the Taxpayer Relief Act repealed the $150 million cap on tax-exempt bonds that had hampered universities such as Georgetown to pursue building projects. With the repeal, the university at last was able to fund the construction of the southwest quadrangle; at nearly $170 million, it was the largest construction project in university history, and it added 1 million square feet of residential space to the main campus by providing housing for 780 students in three connected residence halls and for the Jesuit Community in a four-story apartment building. A two-story dining facility for students was also built. The university could now house more than 90 percent of its undergraduates on campus.

In the fall of 2005, the Royden B. Davis, SJ, Performing Arts Center opened, which incorporated a renovated Ryan Administration Building and an extension to the west. Its first theatrical production took place in November. The center houses two small theaters that seat 230 and 100 persons, respectively; faculty offices; several classrooms; scene and costume shops; and performers' dressing rooms. Three years later the university completed the new home for the McDonough School of Business, which is located to the immediate southwest of the Leavey Center. The five-story, double-wing, $100 million facility, named for Rafik B. Hariri, the former prime minister of Lebanon and father of the current prime minister, Saad Hariri (**B** 1992), provides lecture halls, conference and seminar rooms, a 400-seat auditorium, common areas, and offices for administration, faculty, and staff.

Administration and Faculty

A notable characteristic of the O'Donovan administration was the unprecedented proportion of women who held leadership positions, continuing a trend over the past quarter century in which women had come to have a central place in the life of the institution at its various levels. By the end of O'Donovan's administration, women occupied many of the top administrative positions, including Dorothy Brown as provost, Jane Genster as vice president and general counsel, Jo-Ann Henry as vice president for human resources, Nicole Mandeville as vice president and treasurer, Judith Areen as executive vice president for law center affairs, and Jane McAuliffe as dean of Georgetown College.

In the last two decades of the twentieth century, Georgetown, countering the national trend, increased its full-time faculty on the main campus by 55 percent; by 2001 the 646 full-time members represented nearly three-quarters of the faculty. By 2005 there were 90 endowed positions. The percentage of women on the main campus faculty continued to grow; by 2001, women, who had constituted only one-quarter of the faculty in 1981, made up nearly 40 percent of faculty ranks. Minority faculty increased as well; there were more than 200 minority faculty (15.4%) among the university's nearly 1,300 members, and most of them were associated with the medical center. As a result of the overall increase in faculty, by 2000 the student-faculty ratio on the main campus had dropped to 10:1. In its 2001 report on Georgetown, the Middle States team found that the main campus had "an excellent and highly dedicated faculty who had a very serious commitment to intellectual purpose," in both teaching and research, and were "sensitive to student needs."[3] One indicator of the rising quality of the faculty was the awarding of seven Guggenheim Fellowships to members across the university from 1994 to 2005.

During the O'Donovan years, research and development funding increased by 119 percent, most of this centered at the medical center, particularly in the area of biomedical research. On the main campus there was a modest growth in the grant funding that faculty received for research. In 1997 grant money totaled $14 million; the Public Policy Institute received the largest grant of $4 million. Throughout the first fifteen years of its third century, the university consistently ranked from seventeenth to twenty-third among research universities in the nation.

Institutes and centers proliferated at the university in the 1990s and 2000s. Notable among these was the Georgetown Public Policy Institute created in 1990. Within its first two decades the institute had a faculty that numbered nearly one hundred and had become the largest recipient of sponsored research funds on the main campus; in addition, its public policy master's program ranked among the best ones in the nation. The Center for Muslim-Christian Understanding was established in 1993 to sponsor courses, research, and conferences that focused on the relationship between Christians and Muslims. In 2006 a $20 million gift from a member of the Saudi royal family provided for the endowment and expansion of the operations of the center. In honor of the benefactor, the center was renamed the Prince Alwaleed bin Talal Center for Muslim-Christian Understanding. During the same period, a quartet of centers for area studies—Germany and western Europe, Latin America, Australia and New Zealand, and Eurasia and eastern Europe, respectively—opened.

Graduate and Professional Education

In the late 1980s, the graduate school adopted a policy of promoting professional master's programs to support the doctoral programs that the administration had targeted for excellence. Certain master's programs, such as those in national security studies, business administration, and public policy, flourished, but in practice they did not provide the financial undergirding for the doctoral programs to achieve distinction.

In the first decade of the new century the school moved into two new areas of advanced education in the disciplines of physics and theology. To support the new program in industrial and applied physics, the university opened an advanced electronics laboratory that designed and produced microchips. Theology entered the world of doctoral education in 2006 with the establishment of a program in religious pluralism. By exploring two specific religious traditions, doctoral students investigated how various religions have dealt with diversity in theological reflection, ethical discourse, and religion and culture.

Despite these developments, by the first decade of the twenty-first century, the university still produced no doctoral programs that ranked in the top twenty, with the exception of linguistics. Many of the programs had improved markedly, some dramatically, over the previous fifteen years, which is an indication of how steep the climb was to reach the top tier. At the master's level, perhaps because programs often involved newer fields of study, ascent was a less challenging prospect; several master's programs, particularly the master in business administration, the master in public policy, and the master of science in foreign service, cracked the top grouping in national rankings of their respective fields.

Under Vice President Judith Areen, the law center completed the ascent begun by her predecessors over the previous four decades. It continued to add distinguished members to the ranks of the center's faculty. Full-time faculty at the law center expanded by 51 percent during the period and became a more significant force in publishing monographs as well as law review articles. The establishment of the Federal Legislation Clinic, the International Women's Human Rights Clinic, and the Office of Public Interest and Community Service solidified Georgetown's position as the national leader in clinical education; the outreach of the various clinical programs, one administrator noted, represented the equivalent of the largest public service firm in the country.[4] The law center completed its campus with the construction of a wing for McDonough Hall, a residence hall, and an academic and fitness facility. "Today, beyond a doubt," one law faculty member asserted, "GULC has the best law campus in the country."[5] By the mid-nineties the law center was the largest law school in the country and had reached the top-ten tier in a national ranking of law schools. It marked the first time that any school other than the traditional ten had breached the top bracket of law schools.

Judith Areen, executive vice president for law center affairs, 1989–2004. (Photo by Susie Fitzhugh. Courtesy of Georgetown University Law Center.)

John Griffith, as executive vice president for health sciences and executive dean of the medical school, had pledged to make research a higher priority in the mission of the medical center. That commitment delivered impressive results. Under Griffith's leadership, the Lombardi Cancer Center became a major international center for research as well as for cancer care. Griffith was also responsible for establishing centers and institutes that specialized in health care research, especially in the areas of bioethics and genetics. Two building additions at the center reflected the new emphasis: the perinatal center provided facilities for obstetrics and neonatal research as well as for state-of-the art care of mothers and infants, and the Biomedical Research Building, which opened in 1995, housed projects that attracted more than $100 million in grant support annually.[6] An early catalyst for increased research in the center came in 1990 with the $8 million gift from Frank and Sylvia Pasquerilla. In 1997 the center received what was then the largest private gift in the history of the university when Virginia Toulmin, a member of the board of regents and the widow of the owner of a pharmaceutical company (who was the grandson of Warwick Evans, first graduate of the medical school), created a charitable remainder trust worth $62 million to support biomedical research. Georgetown had risen to the top third of academic medical centers in the amount of funding for research from outside grants.

Undergraduate Education

For its undergraduate programs, Georgetown entered the ranks of the most selective institutions in the nation when it lowered its admission rate from 29 percent in 1991 to 21 percent in 2001, even as the pool of applicants continued to grow yearly. The geographical distribution of undergraduates became more balanced, with many more students from Florida, Illinois, Texas, and California entering Georgetown. Ethnic diversity continued to increase as well. By 1994, minorities constituted nearly one-quarter of the incoming class. Asian Americans led the way at 10 percent, African Americans followed at 7 percent, then Hispanic Americans at 6 percent, and Indigenous Americans at 1 percent, a ranking that remained virtually constant for the rest of the decade. From the mid-nineties on, Arab and Arab-American Muslim students became a notable part of the student population.

As selectivity increased, the academic qualifications of those admitted rose accordingly. By 2000, admitted undergraduates had the highest academic profile in Georgetown's history. Among peer institutions, Georgetown had become more selective than Columbia, Duke, and MIT and was close behind Dartmouth, Brown, and Yale. That Georgetown's students continued to know extraordinary success in garnering prestigious fellowships and other awards was one strong indication of their ascending quality. By 2006, Georgetown could claim twenty-two Rhodes scholars among its graduates and twenty Mellon fellowships. Fifteen Georgetown students had also won George C. Marshall fellowships. In the nineties Georgetown produced more Luce Scholars than all but two universities, and it led the nation in the number of Mitchell Scholars.

The four undergraduate schools—arts and sciences, foreign service, business, and nursing—all took major steps to improve the education they could offer to the unprecedentedly qualified students they were attracting. For the college, the priorities became the strengthening of the areas of the fine arts and sciences. A strong increase of faculty for the arts led to the creation of the Department of Art and Art History and the Department of Performing Arts, with a corresponding broad expansion in the range of offerings. In the sciences the establishment of the Sony Scholars Programs strengthened and expanded courses for nonmajors. Physics and biology both introduced distinct tracks or concentrations for their majors. Anthropology became an independent department.

For all departments within the college, the administration promoted smaller courses and seminars designed to challenge students intellectually. The School of Foreign Service also put more emphasis on small-scale education, most notably by the establishment of proseminars for its first-year students. The school also realized an unprecedented international outreach with the establishment of satellite campuses in Turkey and Qatar. The Business School nearly doubled its full-time faculty during the nineties, a reflection, in part, of the growing role of graduate education within the school. The concentration of resources on graduate education enabled the master of business administration program to reach elite status. (By 2003 it ranked fourteenth in the nation.) Fund-raising for the school increased dramatically, culminating with the gift of $30 million by an alumnus, Robert Emmett McDonough (SFS 1949), for whom the school was renamed.

No school in the period transformed itself more than the nursing school. Under the leadership of two visionary and resourceful deans, Elaine Lawson and Bette Rusk Keltner (later Bette Jacobs), the school boldly reinvented itself by diversifying the school's mission beyond nursing to include other important areas of health care. Four new departments within the school reflected the expanded mission: health care management and policy, human science, international health, and professional nursing. New master's programs were initiated in health care. Fund-raising reached new heights of success when goals of $2 million were oversubscribed by the turn of the century. Intensive recruitment of PhDs to staff the new programs led to an unprecedentedly qualified and talented faculty. St. Mary's Hall was radically renovated in 2003–4 to become a state-of-the-art home for the school. By the first decade of the twenty-first century, the school was becoming highly selective in admitting students (23% by 2006), had forty-five, full-time faculty, and was ranked in the top twenty-five nursing schools in the nation.

Identity

During the early nineties a university-wide discussion began about the institution's identity. Out of that process emerged a consensus that Georgetown's Jesuit and Catholic character was fundamental to its self-understanding. The president subsequently charged a task force with developing a strategic plan for cultivating that identity. It laid out four principal objectives for the university to be faithful to its Catholic and Jesuit heritage: (a) to foster "a full and vigorous dialogue about contemporary Catholic thought across a wide range of academic disciplines"; (b) to be a pioneer in "infusing learning with ethical and spiritual purpose"; (c) "to cultivate an institutional ethos of civic engagement and civil discourse that . . . encourages the Catholic and Jesuit objectives of dialogue, of service to the least advantaged in our own and the world's societies, and of contribution to social justice and the common good"; and (d) to conduct its own affairs in a way consistent with the "ethical and spiritual ideals of social justice and the common good."[7] More specific recommendations included the maintenance of the Jesuit presence at the university, a greater cultivation of Georgetown's Catholic and Jesuit intellectual heritage through the establishment of a research center for Catholic thought, the development of a graduate program in theology, and the adoption of a mission statement that clarified the institution's aims and objectives.[8]

In 2001, a year and a half after the task force's report, and decades after the university had inaugurated the quest to define itself, Georgetown finally had a succinct but comprehensive statement of what it is and what it aims to do:

Georgetown is a Catholic and Jesuit, student-centered research university. Established in 1789 in the spirit of the new republic, the University was founded on the principle that serious and sustained discourse among people of different faiths, cultures, and beliefs promotes intellectual, ethical, and spiritual understanding. We embody this principle in the diversity of our students, faculty, and staff, our commitment to justice and the common good, our intellectual openness, and our international character. An intellectual community dedicated to creating and communicating knowledge, Georgetown provides excellent undergraduate, graduate, and professional education in the Jesuit tradition—for the glory of God and the well-being of humankind.

"Part of Georgetown's greatness," President O'Donovan observed in releasing the mission statement, "is the very breadth of our calling. . . . At our University, we balance teaching and research, the secular and the spiritual, liberal arts and professional education, the national and the international, tradition and innovation. . . . With these aspirations, Georgetown has become a truly distinct national institution."[9]

Georgetown's identity was no longer dependent on its president being a Jesuit. In the spring of 2001, the board of directors elected John DeGioia as Georgetown's forty-eighth president. The forty-three-year-old DeGioia had earned two degrees at Georgetown (AB 1979, PhD [Philosophy] 1995) and had risen through several positions (assistant to the president, dean of student affairs, chief administrative officer for the main campus) to become senior vice president in 1998, in which position he had been responsible for university-wide operations. He had played a key role in negotiating the partnership between the

John J. DeGioia, president of Georgetown University, 2002–present.

medical center and Med Star, by which the latter took responsibility for the operation of Georgetown Hospital. Now the board determined that he was the person best fit to lead the university into the twenty-first century.

At his inauguration at Constitution Hall on October 14, 2001, Jesuits from across the country and beyond, including former presidents Campbell and O'Donovan as well as the Maryland provincial, underscored the continuity of mission that endured amid the passing of leadership from Jesuit to layman. In his address, new president DeGioia declared, "This is a moment in which we appreciate the tradition that animates this university. I believe at the deepest level of reality of our tradition is a spirituality with a deep resonance with the mission of a university. . . . Our tradition calls us to engage. And engage deeply with the tensions and conflicts, the questions and challenges [of the age]."[10] That living tradition was now entering a new era.

A Passing and the Weight of an Establishment

In late May 2003, Father Joseph Durkin died a few days after his one hundredth birthday. He had joined the faculty in 1944 and had served the university just shy of six decades, longer than any other individual in the course of its two plus centuries, including Father James Curley, who had been his counterpart for Georgetown's first century. As Curley's life nearly equaled the span of Georgetown's first century, Durkin's had filled most of its second century and beyond. Both men witnessed great change at Georgetown in the years they spent there, with Durkin's share more substantial than Curley's. If the Georgetown of James Curley had evolved from a small struggling college to something less than a university, that of Joseph Durkin grew from being a nominal university into finding purchase as an elite institution of higher education in the United States.

In many ways Joseph Durkin embodied the best of what the university had continued to be or had become since the middle of the twentieth century: an excellent teacher, long remembered by the thousands of students he engaged in the classroom; a caring mentor at both the graduate and undergraduate levels who personified the Jesuit tradition of *cura personalis;* a prolific scholar who was one of the pathsetters in the university's development of research and publication as core elements of its mission; a priest actively engaged well beyond his official retirement in the pastoral care of students, through retreats, sacraments, prayer services, and counseling; and a member of the university community who took a dedicated role in Georgetown's new dimension—its social outreach—through his prison and literacy ministries within the metropolitan area.

When Durkin arrived at Georgetown in the waning days of World War II, the university consisted of a loose collection of underpopulated schools with a war-shrunken enrollment hovering under 1,500 (the population had been

2,500 in 1941). Georgetown then comprised an undistinguished liberal arts college, a quasi-professional school of foreign service, a nursing diploma program, a graduate school in the first stage of formation, and three professional schools that were still proprietary in spirit, if not in structure. It was a regional, homogeneous semi-university in all of its components. Jesuits had a monopoly on the top administrative positions and were a close majority of the faculty on the main campus. There was a near absence of the religious, national, and international diversity that had historically distinguished Georgetown as an institution. The only African Americans on any of the three campuses were on the maintenance and serving staffs. Outside the nursing program there were virtually no women among students, faculty, or the administration. The schedule and discipline for undergraduates were closely akin to a seminary's. The university had a minuscule endowment, and, apart from the School of Foreign Service, it had little or no academic distinction. Its greatest national reputation was in sports: in track, football, and basketball. It was isolated from the Washington community but had growing connections with the federal government, particularly the military.

By the time Father Durkin died sixty years later, the institution had been almost totally transformed. University enrollment now totaled nearly thirteen thousand. The four undergraduate schools that had evolved from the college, the School of Foreign Service, and the nursing program now all enjoyed a ranking within the top twenty-five for their selectivity of students and the quality of their programs. There had been a remarkable recovery and expansion of diversity, not only among students, but among faculty and administration as well. Racial minorities, which were practically nonexistent in the 1940s, now made up one-quarter of the students. Women, confined to the nursing program in 1944, made up one-half the university student population in 2003. Women also composed nearly 40 percent of the faculty and occupied many of the highest administrative positions within the university. The Jesuits, who had dominated the administrative ranks during World War II, had one chief administrator by 2003: the vice president for ministry and mission. Of the two professional schools that had survived, the law school now stood within the top twelve of its peers; the medical school, although beset with extremely serious financial problems, had a highly respected academic standing and had achieved cutting-edge status for its research and experiments in certain fields. The graduate school had made perhaps the least progress over the past six decades, but even here there were programs, at both the master's and doctoral levels, that were competitive with the best in the country. The faculty across the university had been gaining in stature and accomplishments since the 1980s, as attested by the substantial body of faculty research and publications as well as the growing number of prestigious awards. The endowment, although still much too small for an institution with Georgetown's aspirations, had grown to $1 billion, a size unimaginable in the 1940s. The university at last had both a national and an international academic presence, thanks in significant part to the research centers that Georgetown had established since the 1960s. It was no longer unknown in its own city. Through its outreach programs on the main campus and the incomparable clinical services that the law center and medical center offered, Georgetown had become a very good citizen of the Washington, DC, community.

On the surface, the greatest continuity seemed to be Georgetown's stature on the intercollegiate sports scene. But considering the breadth of Georgetown's prominence within a spectrum of men's and women's college athletic competition today—ranging from basketball, sailing, and track to crew, golf, and lacrosse—its very temporary fame in football and basketball in the 1940s paled in contrast. Finally, it no longer took its character for granted, but had at last formally articulated its character and mission within its Jesuit and Catholic traditions. In that mission statement was an implicit commitment to continue to work to renew Georgetown as a vital institution of higher education, to continue what it had at last become: the preeminent Catholic university in the nation.

John Carroll had remarked in 1790 that the choice of the Georgetown area for the site of the federal capital would give "a weight to our establishment" that he had not really anticipated when he chose to locate his academy on a hill outside the town. Georgetown's history has certainly borne out Carroll's prescience about the importance of Washington for the school's development. But that history has also shown that factors other than location have given gravitas to the university that slowly developed from the academy that Carroll founded. In truth, one can argue that Washington began to be a distinct advantage in the building of the university's image and status only in the 1960s. Place became but one element among many in a synergistic process that accounted for Georgetown's rise.

The centralizing vision and execution of Edward Bunn, the recruiting genius of Paul McNally and Harold Jaeghers, the brick-by-brick development of the law center under Paul Dean, Gerard Campbell's crafting of the structure of a modern university, Byron Collins's extraordinary ability to secure federal funding for the university, Timothy Healy's presence in the academic and intellectual communities that gave Georgetown unprecedented visibility and leadership in these worlds, the teaching and scholarship of so many individual faculty in the spirit of Joe Durkin, the remarkably enduring coaching success of John Thompson and Frank Gagliano—they all made a difference in Georgetown's remarkable growth over the past six decades. Beyond those individual contributions was a collective factor that certainly played a part in the university's modern success—the enduring community, that sense of belonging to a very special place for seeking and learning that has managed to survive as the university profoundly changed in the course of the twentieth century. All these elements together have made Georgetown the distinctive university it is at the close of the second decade of its third century.

APPENDIX A

Student Enrollments, 1963–90

ACADEMIC YEAR	COLLEGE	MEDICAL	LAW	DENTAL	NURSING	SFS	SLL	SBA	GRAD
1963–64	1,531	423	1,160	368	271	916	748	557	1,168
1964–65	1,564	393	1,220	369	327	967	770	567	1,284
1965–66	1,618	445	1,272	390	331	912	685	553	1,470
1966–67	1,627	451	1,300	389	286	908	658	511	1,461
1967–68	1,652	438	1,232	369	294	956	601	477	1,461
1968–69	1,662	438	1,253	352	274	984	741	516	1,510
1969–70	1,730	471	1,273	413	296	969	753	571	1,449
1970–71	1,811	529	1,554	431	293	925	578	598	1,355
1971–72	1,946	638	1,921	482	345	918	655	640	1,310
1972–73	2,098	704	2,195	474	392	1,025	812	702	1,338
1973–74	2,145	789	2,320	489	425	1,118	772	792	1,422
1974–75	2,088	748	2,463	509	525	1,117	832	909	1,348
1975–76	2,101	818	2,449	577	562	1,148	897	957	1,548
1976–77	2,045	810	2,448	566	541	1,081	739	891	1,560
1977–78	2,125	829	2,726	572	570	1,162	722	907	1,317
1978–79	2,052	833	2,685	583	526	1,142	690	859	1,539
1979–80	2,063	847	2,706	579	508	1,206	739	877	1,799
1980–81	2,091	844	2,701	600	462	1,201	701	838	1,881
1981–82	2,108	843	2,743	615	438	1,195	740	922	1,959
1982–83	2,124	835	2,616	624	432	1,177	709	912	1,906
1983–84	2,111	841	2,622	629	423	1,160	742	944	1,918
1984–85	2,131	845	2,657	621	407	1,205	713	1,053	1,803
1985–86	2,166	849	2,690	616	365	1,266	694	1,044	1,808
1986–87	2,269	854	2,654	600	331	1,177	661	1,023	1,852
1987–88	2,302	843	2,580	412	266	1,230	701	1,026	1,824
1988–89	2,374	841	2,529	266	227	1,217	720	1,039	1,709
1989–90	2,346	808	2,579	133	205	1,224	773	1,038	1,752

APPENDIX B

Presidents of the University, 1952–2010

Edward B. Bunn, SJ, 1952–64

Gerard Campbell, SJ, 1964–68

*Edward Quain, SJ, 1969

Robert Henle, SJ, 1969–76

Timothy Stafford Healy, SJ, 1976–89

Leo O'Donovan, SJ, 1989–2001

John J. DeGioia, 2001–

*Served as acting president

Deans of the College of Arts and Sciences, 1957–2010

Joseph A. Sellinger, SJ, 1957–64

Thomas R. Fitzgerald, SJ, 1964–67

Royden B. Davis, SJ, 1967–89

Robert Lawton, SJ, 1989–99

Jane Dammen McAuliffe, 1999–2008

Chester Gillis, 2008–

APPENDIX D

Deans of the Graduate School, 1960–2010

James B. Horigan, SJ, 1960–67

Rocco E. Porreco, 1967–73

Donald G. Herzberg, 1973–81

Richard B. Schwartz, 1981–98

Joseph Serene, 1998–2001

David W. Lightfoot, 2001–6

Timothy A. Barbari, 2006–

APPENDIX E

Deans of the Medical School, 1963–2010

John C. Rose, 1963–74

John P. Utz, 1974–79

John Bernard Henry, 1979–84

Milton Corn, 1984–89

William Maxted, 1989–98

Carolyn Rabinowitz, 1998–2002

Stephen Ray Mitchell, 2002–

APPENDIX F

Deans of the Law School/ Executive Vice Presidents for Law Center Affairs, 1955–2010

Deans

Paul R. Dean, 1955–69

Adrian S. Fischer, 1969–74

Executive Vice Presidents for Law Center Affairs

Adrian S. Fischer, 1974–76

David J. McCarthy, 1976–83

Robert Pitofsky, 1983–89

Judith Areen, 1989–2004

T. Alexander Aleinikoff, 2004–10

APPENDIX G

Deans of the Dental School, 1950–90

Clemens V. Rault, 1950–66

Charles B. Murto, 1966–79

David E. Beaudreau, 1979–82

*Robert J. Taylor, 1982–83

Stanley P. Hazen, 1983–90

*Served as acting dean

APPENDIX H

Deans of the School of Nursing and Health Studies, 1963–2010

Ann Douglas, 1963–67

*Rose A. McGarrity, 1967–68

Sr. Rita Marie Bergeron, OSB, 1968–78

*Rose A. McGarrity, 1978–80

Elizabeth Hughes, 1980–86

Alma S. Woolley, 1986–92

Elaine L. Larson, 1992–98

*Judith Ann Baigis, 1998–99

Bette Rusk Jacobs, 1999–2010

*Served as acting dean

APPENDIX I

Deans of the School of Foreign Service, 1962–2010

William E. Moran Jr., 1962–66

Joseph S. Sebes, SJ, 1966–68

Jesse Mann, 1968–70

Peter F. Krogh, 1970–95

Robert Gallucci, 1995–2009

Carol Lancaster, 2009–

Deans of the School of Languages and Linguistics, 1962–95

Robert Lado, 1962–74

*Francis P. Dineen, SJ, 1967–69

James E. Alatis, 1974–95

* Served as acting dean

APPENDIX K

Director/Deans of the School of Business Administration, 1960–2010

Directors

Raymond Pelissier, 1960–64

Deans

*Joseph S. Sebes, SJ, 1964–65

Harry P. Guenther, 1965–69

Eugene K. Snyder, 1969–72

Edward M. Kaitz, 1972–76

*Joseph Pettit, 1976–77

Ronald Smith, 1977–86

Robert S. Parker, 1986–97

Christopher Puto, 1998–2002

John Mayo, 2002–4

*Reena Aggarwal, 2004–5

George G. Daly, 2005–

* Served as acting dean

Deans of the School of Summer and Continuing Education (School of Continuing Education), 1963–2010

Rocco E. Porreco, 1963–67

Jesse Mann, 1967–68

Joseph Pettit, 1969–81

Michael J. Collins, 1981–2003

Robert J. Thomas, 2003–5

Robert L. Manuel, 2006–

Academic Vice Presidents/ Executive Vice Presidents for the Main Campus, 1955–2010

Academic Vice Presidents

Brian A. McGrath, SJ, 1955–67

Thomas Fitzgerald, SJ, 1967–73

Aloysius Kelley, SJ, 1973–74

Executive Vice Presidents for the Main Campus

Aloysius Kelley, SJ, 1974–79

J. Donald Freeze, SJ, 1979–91

*Richard B. Schwartz, 1991–92

Patrick Heelan, SJ, 1992–95

*Richard B. Schwartz, 1995–96

William Cooper, 1996–98

Dorothy M. Brown, 1998–2002

James J. O'Donnell, 2002–

* Served as acting executive vice president

Executive Vice Presidents for Medical Center Affairs/Executive Vice President for the Health Sciences, 1963–2010

Executive Vice Presidents for Medical Center Affairs

Mark H. Bauer, SJ, 1963–68

Matthew McNulty, 1968–86

Executive Vice President for the Health Sciences

John Griffith, 1986–96

Sam Wiesel, 1996–2003

Daniel D. Sedmak, 2003–4

*J. Richard Gaintner, 2004–5

Howard J. Federoff, 2005–

* Served as acting executive vice president

Regents of the Law, Foreign Service, Languages and Linguistics, and Business Schools, 1961–68

Regent of the Law School

Brian A. McGrath, 1961–68

Regent of the School of Foreign Service

Joseph Sebes, SJ, 1962–66

Regent of the School of Languages and Linguistics

Frank Fadner, SJ, 1962–68

Regent of the Business School

Joseph Sebes, SJ, 1961–68

APPENDIX P

Georgetown University Buildings by Construction Date, 1964–2007

Main Campus

1965	Harbin Hall
1966	Darnall Hall
1970	Heating and Cooling Plant
1971	Joseph Mark Lauinger Memorial Library
1976	Henle Village
1978	Energy Plant
1979	Village A
1980	Yates Field House
1982	Bunn Intercultural Center
1983	Alumni Square (Village B)
1987	Village C
1989	Leavey Center
2002	McCarthy Hall
2002	Kennedy Hall
2002	Reynolds Family Hall
2002	O'Donovan Dining Hall
2002	Wolfington Hall (Jesuit Community)
2005	Royden B. Davis, SJ, Performing Arts Center
2007	Rafik B. Hariri Building (McDonough School of Business)

Medical Center

1970	Dahlgren Medical Library
1971	Dental Clinic (post-1990: Building D)
1972	Preclinical Science
1972	Marcus J. Bles Building (Child Development and Diagnostic Clinic)
1972	Basic Science Building
1976	Concentrated Care Center
1982	Lombardi Cancer Center
1988	Pasquerilla Health Care Center
1989	Research Resource Facility
1995	New Research Building

Law Center

1971	Bernard McDonough Hall
1989	Edward Bennett Williams Law Library
1993	Bernard and Sarah M. Gerwirz Student Center
1997	East Wing, Bernard McDonough Hall
2004	Georgetown Sport and Fitness Center
2004	Eric E. Hotung International Law Building

About the Author

Robert Emmett Curran is professor emeritus of history at Georgetown University. He was born in Baltimore, Maryland, and attended the College of Holy Cross, where he received a BA with honors in history. He later received an MA in history from Fordham University before earning a PhD in history from Yale University. In addition to writing numerous journal articles and chapters and reviews, Curran has published three books: *Michael Augustine Corrigan and the Shaping of Conservative Catholicism in America, 1878–1902*; *American Jesuit Spirituality: The Maryland Tradition, 1634–1900*; and *The Bicentennial History of Georgetown University, 1789–1889*. After teaching at Georgetown for more than thirty years, he now lives with his wife, Eileen, in Richmond, Kentucky, where his nonacademic interests include running, playing the banjo, and choral singing.

Notes

CHAPTER 1

1. Andrew Greeley, "The Problems of Jesuit Education in the United States" (unpublished paper, Jesuit Education Association Meeting, Chicago, April 10–11, 1966).
2. Daley to Bunn, Baltimore, June 24, 1963, Bunn Papers.
3. Gerard Campbell, SJ, interview, January 5, 1987; Pat Markun, "Father Campbell Reflects on Fifty Years as a Jesuit," *Holy Trinity News* 4 (September 10, 1989): 1–4.
4. Gerald Grant, "New GU Head Is Ivy League Product," *Washington Post,* August 9, 1964, B-13.
5. Interview with Thomas Fitzgerald, SJ, April 1984. In an address to the university community in 1967, Campbell noted that "tradition, however glorious, is useless, even detrimental, if it serves as an anchor; it is of inestimable value as a rudder. And the first to rise up and condemn us, should we keep our gaze anywhere but forward, would be those very forebears whom we would dishonor by resting on *their* laurels. For if we are heirs of the past, we are no less the trustees and brokers of the future. . . . She has to adapt, to examine, to restate, to alter her methods and her machinery, while holding fast to fundamental principle and purpose." Founder's Day address, April 9, 1967, Gerard Campbell Papers, GUA. As president he clearly felt a duty to do just that.
6. Campbell interview.
7. Ibid.
8. Edward J. Sponga, SJ, "Statements Prepared in Response to QQ Raised by Reverend Father General in His Letter of November 27 . . . to Father Edward J. Sponga, Maryland Province Provincial," Jesuit Community Papers, GUA.
9. The externalization of board membership and the introduction of lay members to boards was a development that had gathered momentum among Catholic institutions of higher education in the early 1960s. By 1965 about one-fifth of all Catholic colleges and universities had laypersons on their boards. Within the American Jesuit sphere, Fordham and Saint Louis were making the same transition as Georgetown in the mid-1960s. Martin J. Stamm, "The Laicization of Corporate Governance of Twentieth Century American Catholic Higher Education," *Records of the American Catholic Historical Society of Philadelphia,* 84 (March–December 1983): 81–99.
10. Statements Prepared in Response to Questions Raised by Reverend Father General in his Letter of November 27, 1967 to Father Edward J. Sponga, Maryland Province Provincial, December 5, 1967, Jesuit Community Papers, GUA.
11. October 22, 1966, Minutes of the Board of Directors, 550, GUA.
12. Thurston Davis, SJ, was the editor; Paul Harbrecht the provincial; and P. C. Lauinger, Raymond Reiss, and Col. Irving Solomon the three laymen.

13. The corporation itself, originally composed exclusively of Jesuits, had two laymen as members by the early seventies. This ratio of Jesuit to lay representation on the corporation continued for the next three decades.

14. Campbell interview.

15. John J. McGrath, *Catholic Institutions in the United States: Canonical and Civil Law Status* (Washington, DC: Catholic University Press of America, 1968), 33, 37.

16. "Proposed Separation of the Office of Rector and the Office of President at Georgetown University, Preliminary Draft prepared for the Georgetown Community Council, July 11, 1967," Jesuit Community Papers, GUA.

17. Joint Task Force Committee on Community-University Relations of the Jesuit Community and Georgetown University, March 13, 1968, Jesuit Community Papers, GUA; December 18, 1968, Minutes of the Board of Directors.

18. Charles J. Foley to John McGee, March 17, 1969, Jesuit Community Papers, GUA.

19. Preliminary Draft prepared for Georgetown Community Council, July 11, 1967, Georgetown University Jesuit Community Archives.

20. *Academic Vice President News*, October 7, 1967 (hereafter *AVP News*), Academic Vice President/Provost (hereafter AVP), GUA.

21. December 2–4, 1963; March 13-15, 1964, Minutes of the Board of Directors.

22. Thomas Fitzgerald interview.

23. Ibid.

24. Hugh David Graham and Nancy Diamond, *The Rise of American Research Universities: Elites and Challengers in the Postwar Era* (Baltimore: Johns Hopkins University Press, 1997), 102, 115.

25. *Mid/Week Report*, July 24, 1973.

26. October 10, 1974, Faculty Senate Minutes, GUA.

27. January 9, 1970, Minutes of the Board of Directors.

28. Thomas Fitzgerald interview.

29. Carl Abbot, *Political Terrain: Washington, D.C., from Tidewater Town to Global Metropolis* (Chapel Hill: University of North Carolina Press, 1999), 135.

30. July 10–12, 1973, Minutes of the Board of Directors; Hugh D. Graham, *The Uncertain Triumph: Federal Education Policy in the Kennedy and Johnson Years* (Chapel Hill: University of North Carolina Press, 1984), 91–93; Roger Geiger, *Research and Relevant Knowledge: American Research Universities since World War II* (New York: Oxford University Press, 1993), 269.

31. *Mid/Week Report*, June 25, 1974.

32. Dean's Report, September 1, 1968, to September 1, 1969, Graduate School, GUA.

33. *Washington Post*, March 4, 1967.

34. Seth P. Tillman, *Georgetown's School of Foreign Service: The First Seventy-five Years* (Washington DC: Georgetown University, Edmund A. Walsh School of Foreign Service, 1994), 61–63.

35. *Mid/Week Report*, January 14, 1975.

36. Ibid., November 27, 1973.

37. Ibid., October 8, 1974.

38. *AVP News*, December 14, 1966.

39. Ibid., October 7, 1967.

40. February 7–8, 1969, President's Council, Minutes of the Board of Regents, GUA.

41. December 4, 1970, President's Council, Minutes of the Board of Regents.

42. February 2, 1973, Minutes of the Board of Directors; *Mid/Week Report*, May 15, 1973.

43. *AAUP Bulletin*, August 1975, 144.

44. Revised Preliminary Report, February 7, 1975, Senate Committee on Faculty Salaries, Faculty Senate, GUA.

45. Ibid., 30.

46. Ibid.

47. Campbell interview.

48. September 17, 1965; March 10, 1967, Minutes of the Board of Directors; March 18–19, 1967, Minutes of the Board of Regents; "Remarks of Professor Valerie Earle

on the Occasion of the 25th Anniversary of the University Faculty Senate, May 11, 1993," in *University Senate News,* November 1994, 4. The initial division of membership was thirty from the main campus, of whom two had to be from the nursing faculty; thirteen from the medical and dental faculty; and seven from the law faculty. In 1971 the membership was enlarged to seventy-five, with the main campus having forty-five members, the medical center twenty, and the law center ten.

49. *AVP News,* September 20, 1974, 3–4.

50. October 22–23, 1965; May 1–2, 1966; Minutes of the President's Council, 221-5, GUA.

51. Elizabeth Prelinger, "'From Her Spires and Steeples Beaming': Mission and Image in Bricks and Stone," in *Georgetown at Two Hundred: Faculty Reflections on the University's Future,* ed. William C. McFadden, SJ (Washington, DC: Georgetown University Press, 1990), 345.

52. The multipurpose use was originally to be for five years. It was nearly two decades before the entire building was dedicated to library use.

53. Lewis B. Mayhew, "Higher Education in the Seventies: Growth or Decline," Address given at Georgetown University, February 26, 1974, AVP, GUA.

54. *Georgetown University: Its Impact on the Nation's Capital* (Washington, DC: Georgetown University, 1966).

55. October 9, 1966, Minutes of the President's Council, 221-5, GUA.

56. February 25, 1967, Minutes of the Board of Directors.

57. May 19, 1967, Minutes of the Board of Directors.

58. Gerard Campbell, Summary Report of the President, June 1967, Campbell Papers.

59. October 6–7, 1967, President's Council, Minutes of the Board of Regents.

60. January 4, 1968, Minutes of the Board of Directors.

61. Campbell to the Chancellor et al., January 8, 1968, President' Office, Dean, CAS, GUA.

62. September 13-14, 1968, President's Council, Minutes of the Board of Regents.

63. October 18, 1968, Minutes of the Board of Directors.

64. May 23, 1969, Minutes of the Board of Directors, Executive Council, GUA.

65. April 30–May 1, 1965, Minutes of Advisory Council, Dean, CAS, GUA.

66. *AVP News,* December 14, 1966; May 8, 1970, Minutes of the Board of Directors, Executive Council.

67. William C. McFadden, "'Catechism at 4 for All the Schools': Religious Instruction at Georgetown," in *Georgetown at Two Hundred: Faculty Reflections on the University's Future,* ed. William C. McFadden (Washington, DC: Georgetown University Press, 1990), 158–60.

68. Ibid., 158–61.

69. Dorothy M. Brown, "Learning, Faith, Freedom, and Building a Curriculum: Two Hundred Years and Counting," in *Georgetown at Two Hundred: Faculty Reflections on the University's Future,* ed. William C. McFadden (Washington, DC: Georgetown University Press, 1990), 86.

70. T. Fitzgerald, Talk delivered before the East Campus Student Council, December 1967, AVP, GUA.

71. *AVP News,* February 28, 1969.

72. Brown, "Learning, Faith, Freedom, and Building a Curriculum," 94.

73. A survey of College of Arts and Sciences student grades from 1967 to 1974 showed that grades had generally increased. In that period only two departments—biology and chemistry—had remained the same or showed a decrease. All other departments had shown either modest or substantial increases. The dean conducting the survey concluded that the "grading scale tends to remain conservative in departments which have required courses for the largest part of their offerings (e.g. biology and chemistry). . . . Inflation has been highest in those departments whose courses are mainly electives for non-majors." Richard Sullivan to Executive Council, January 16, 1976, Executive Council, Dean, CAS, GUA.

74. Greeley, "Problems of Jesuit Education in the United States," 10, 23–24.

75. Among the other signers were Theodore Hesburgh, Thomas Fitzgerald, and Robert Henle. Indeed, administrators from Georgetown, Notre Dame, Fordham, and Saint Louis dominated the meeting. Statement on the Nature of the Contemporary Catholic University by Members of the North American Region of the International Federation of Catholic Universities Meeting, Land O'Lakes, Wisconsin, July 21 through July 23, 1967, Campbell Papers.
76. August 6–8, 1968, Minutes of the Board of Directors.
77. "Georgetown's Characteristics and Goals," November 21, 1969, Henle Administration, box 1, folder 13, 10-02, GUA.
78. April 10, 1970, Minutes of the Board of Directors.
79. Dean's Report, 1968, Graduate School, GUA.
80. Dean's Report, September 1, 1968, to September 1, 1969, Graduate School, GUA.
81. February 14, 1967, Minutes of Advisory Council, 1967, SLL, GUA.
82. September 11, 1970, President's Council, Minutes of the Board of Regents.
83. Graham, *Uncertain Triumph,* 90.
84. Dean's Report, 1970, Graduate School, GUA.
85. Rocco Porreco, "The Georgetown Graduate School: Past, Present and Future," January 13, 1971, Graduate School, GUA.
86. Ibid.
87. Ibid.
88. Fitzgerald to Main Campus Deans, "Faulkner Meeting," June 15–16, 17, 1971, Henle Administration, box 1, folder 15, 10-02, GUA.
89. Confidential Report of Committee on Future of Astronomical Studies at Georgetown University, n.d., Astronomy, Dean, CAS, GUA.
90. December 15, 1967, Minutes of the Board of Directors.
91. February 2, March 8, 1968, Minutes of the Board of Directors.
92. December 10, 1971, Minutes of the Board of Directors.
93. *Mid/Week Report,* March 20, 1973.
94. John McGrath, "The Graduate School: From There to Where?" *Georgetown Today* (*GT*), September 1974, 13–15; "Profiles," *GT,* January 1976, 20.
95. "A Degree Program for 'Personal Fulfillment,'" *GT,* May 1974, 14.
96. Pam Ginsbach, "A Piece of Unfinished Business: A Personal Renaissance," *GT,* September 1975, 12–13.
97. Henle, *Personal Record,* 3:28.
98. John Rose interview, December 18, 1986.
99. John Rose interview with Ginsbach, 1976.
100. T. Byron Collins interview, September 27, 1972.
101. July 17–19, 1967, Minutes of the Board of Directors.
102. Campbell to the Members of the Full-Time Faculty, January 8, 1968, President's Office, Dean, CAS, GUA.
103. December 15, 1967, Minutes of the Board of Directors.
104. Rose interview with Ginsbach, 1976; John C. Rose, Chairman, Final Report, Committee on Separate Incorporation of the Medical Center, June 1, 1968, Medical Center, GUA.
105. Matthew McNulty interview, November 5, 1993.
106. *Georgetown University News* (hereafter cited as GU News), April 22, 1970; William R. Ayers et al., "Impact of High Tuition on Medical School Applicants and Enrollees," *Journal of Medical Education* 56 (October 1981): 796. Georgetown's grant was the fourth largest in the nation, behind those to the universities of Minnesota and Indiana and to Baylor. May 15, 1970, President's Council, Minutes of the Board of Regents.
107. "Dean's Report, 1972–73," *Georgetown Medical Bulletin* (November 1973): 13.
108. "22 Million Dollars in One Decade," *Georgetown Medical Bulletin* 29 (August 1975): 13–19.
109. Rose interview, December 18, 1986.
110. September 14, 1973, Minutes of the Board of Directors, Executive Committee.
111. *GU News,* June 16, 1976.

112. Kenneth M. Ludmerer, *Time to Heal: American Medical Education from the Turn of the Century to the Era of Managed Care* (New York: Oxford University Press, 1999), 234.

113. Ibid., 223–24.

114. John Rose to Departmental and Division Chairs, June 1964, Medical School, GUA.

115. J. D. McCarthy et al., "Council on Medical Service: Conclusions and Recommendations," n.d., Medical School, GUA, cited in Patricia Barry, *Surgeons at Georgetown: Surgery and Medical Education in the Nation's Capital, 1849–1969* (Franklin, TN: Hillsboro Press, 2001), 267.

116. Rose to Robert J. Coffey, January 4, 1965, Medical School, GUA.

117. Campbell to Rose, March 23, 1965, Medical School, GUA.

118. Barry, *Surgeons at Georgetown,* 271.

119. "Faculty Practice Plan, Preliminary Proposal," January 1967, Henle Administration, box 1, cited in Barry, *Surgeons at Georgetown,* 271.

120. Barry, *Surgeons at Georgetown,* 271–72.

121. "From the Dean," *Georgetown Medical Bulletin* (August 1966): 3, cited in Barry, *Surgeons at Georgetown,* 278.

122. Barry, *Surgeons at Georgetown,* 280.

123. GU News, February 18, 1972.

124. *Mid/Week Report,* January 6, 1976.

125. *GU News,* September 23, 1976.

126. September 12, 1975, Minutes of the Board of Directors.

127. Other schools' increases in enrollment were fairly minuscule compared to Georgetown's. For example, Duke in 1970 raised the quota for its entering class from 86 to 104, and Michigan increased its class size from 225 to 237. Ludmerer, *Time to Heal,* 271.

128. Ibid., 273, 295.

129. Ibid., 250.

130. Schools of Medicine, Dentistry, and Nursing, Number of Black Students Enrolled in the Schools 1970–1971 to 1975–76, Medical School, GUA.

131. Ludmerer, *Time to Heal,* 253.

132. Campbell to Faculty and Administrators of Georgetown University, December 2, 1965, Dental School, Chancellor Bunn Papers, box 14, GUA.

133. *GU News,* April 13, 1971.

134. Rault to T. B. Collins, SJ, August 11, 1964, Dental School, GUA.

135. Minutes of the President's Council, May 1–2, 1965, 221-5, GUA.

136. Senior Class to Dean, May 18, 1970, Dental School, GUA. Five years earlier a graduating senior had complained to President Campbell that it was a "shameful disgrace" that one-third of the graduating class did not get their diplomas. Terrence Murphy to Campbell, June 11, 1965, Dental School, GUA.

137. Special Faculty Meeting, May 19, 1970, Dental School, GUA.

138. *Washington Evening Star,* April 26, 1972, B-4.

139. C. B. Murto to Members of the Student Body, April 27, 1972, Dental School, GUA.

140. Lynn Dunson, "Dental School Boycott Is Off," *Washington Star,* May 10, 1972.

141. Robert J. Taylor, Chair, "Final Report: Special Ad Hoc Committee to Evaluate Clinic Education Programs," July 5, 1972, Dental School, GUA.

142. Evaluation Report, Commission on Accreditation of Dental and Dental Auxiliary Educational Programs, American Dental Association, May 7, 1975, Dental School, GUA.

143. "Shaping a Medical Center: The McNulty Years," *Georgetown Magazine* (hereafter GM), Summer 1986.

144. "Dean's Report, 1971–72," *Georgetown Medical Bulletin* (November 1972): 15–16.

145. *GU News,* July 15, 1971.

146. *GU News,* January 29, May 8, 1973.

147. Daniel Altobello interview, February 26, 1987.

148. *Washington Post,* July 1968.

149. E. A. Quain, Chair, Presidential Search Committee, September 12, 1968, Board of Directors, GUA.

150. *Hoya,* November 14, 1968.
151. Valerie Earle to [Members of the Faculty], October 31, 1968, President's Office, Dean, CAS, GUA.

CHAPTER 2

1. Thomas Fitzgerald interview.
2. June 29–July 1, December 10, 1971, Minutes of the Board of Directors, 550.
3. May 21, 1973, Minutes of the Board of Directors, 550.
4. Henle to the University Community, May 15, 1973, Henle Papers.
5. Houston, aware that Georgetown had had five vice presidents for finance in ten years, suggested to Henle that they break up the positions (finance and business), with Houston taking over finance and Altobello the business responsibilities. George Houston interview, January 23, 1985.
6. James Shannon interview, June 9, 1983.
7. Haller to Board of Directors, October 16, 1970, Henle Papers, GUA.
8. R. J. Henle, SJ, *A Personal Report: Georgetown University, 1969–1976* (June 1979), 1:1.
9. January 9, 1970, Minutes of the Board of Directors, 550.
10. Annual Report, 1969–70, Henle Papers.
11. October 6, 1969, Minutes of the Board of Directors, 550.
12. October 23, 1971, Minutes of the Board of Directors, 550.
13. March 19, 1971; March 16, 1973, Minutes of the Board of Directors, 550.
14. Henle to Members of the University Community, February 3, 1971, President's Office, CAS, GUA.
15. Henle to Members of the Faculty, "Faculty Finances," February 6, 1970, Henle, Chancellor Bunn Papers, box 13.
16. December 10, 1971, Minutes of the Board of Directors, 550.
17. January 22, 1971, Minutes of the Board of Directors, 550. James Kelly had made it clear that they had a choice of increasing enrollment substantially or reducing faculty by fifty positions. "I am proud of the fact," Houston later commented, "that we never eliminated a faculty position in the budget process; we never froze faculty or staff salaries; they increased every year." Houston interview.
18. The administration did not want to announce publicly a large deficit lest it negatively impact fund-raising. October 12, 1973, Minutes of the Board of Directors, 550.
19. October 20, 1972, Minutes of the Board of Directors, 550.
20. January 22, 1971, Minutes of the Board of Directors, 550.
21. *Faculty Senate News* 3 (November 1974).
22. Dan Ernst et al., *The First 125 Years: An Illustrated History of the Georgetown University Law Center* (Washington, DC: Georgetown University Law Center, 1995), 168; Georgetown Law Weekly, February 28, 1973.
23. "Law Center, Hilltop Administration Clash Over GULC Budget, Surplus," *GT,* May 1973, 18.
24. Ernst et al., First 125 Years, 170.
25. *Georgetown Law Weekly,* October 17, 1973, 1–2.
26. Sherman Cohn interview, November 23, 2005.
27. Ernst et al., *First 125 Years,* 170.
28. Cohn interview, November 23, 2005.
29. Edith Ray Saul to Patrick A. O'Boyle, February 2, 1966, Chancellor Bunn Papers, box 5.
30. Bunn to O'Boyle, February 15, 1966, Chancellor Bunn Papers.
31. Memorandum from George S. Roper, October 4, 1967, Chancellor Bunn Papers, box 15.
32. In a sense, the university suffered the consequences of urban renewal coming to the Georgetown area too early for it to reap the opportunities that other urban universities did in renewal projects during the sixties and seventies. In 1959,

Congress amended the Housing Act to subsidize universities in the acquisition of property in areas near them that had been designated for urban renewal. More than seventy-five institutions of higher education, such as the University of Pennsylvania, utilized this legislation to expand their campuses during the early sixties. By then Georgetown had completed its urban renewal or gentrification that had begun in the 1930s. At least the university evaded the moral stigma that plagued the institutions that expanded through the large-scale uprooting of poor, overwhelmingly black, communities. See Margaret Pugh O'Mara, *Cities of Knowledge: Cold War Science and the Search for the Next Silicon Valley* (Princeton, NJ: Princeton University Press, 2005), 78–79. Of course, as noted in chapter 9 of volume 2, the university had participated in the displacement of black residents that had occurred in Georgetown during the 1940s and 1950s.

33. "Archbold Estate Property," Chancellor Bunn Papers, box 3, fold A; January 22, 1971, Minutes of the Board of Directors, 550.
34. February 19, 1971, Minutes of the Board of Directors, Executive Committee, 550.
35. April 21, 1971, Minutes of the Board of Directors, Executive Committee, 550.
36. March 10, 1972, Minutes of the Board of Directors, 550.
37. April 21, 1971, Minutes of the Board of Directors, Executive Committee, 550.
38. January 23 and March 19, 1976, Minutes of the Board of Directors, Executive Committee, 550.
39. "Office of the President," October 10, 1969, Chancellor Bunn Paper, box 13; October 20, 1972, Minutes of the Board of Directors, 550.
40. Henle, *Personal Report,* 1:4.
41. Ibid., 3:14.
42. August 4–6, 1970, Minutes of the Board of Directors, 550.
43. October 22, 1971, President's Council, Minutes of the Board of Regents.
44. July 10–12, 1973, Minutes of the Board of Directors, 550; Patricia Alberger, "'All the People Dwell Together,'" *Georgetown,* March 1974, 4–7.
45. May 24, 1966, Minutes of the Board of Directors, 550.
46. David S. Cloud, "Georgetown Wins Friends and Funds on Hill," *Congressional Quarterly* (June 4, 1988): 1502–5.
47. April 5, 1968; November 7, 1969; August 4–6, 1970, Minutes of the Board of Directors, 550.
48. Quain had become acting president in February when Campbell had been unable to remain in office beyond the end of January 1969. June 9, 1969, Minutes of the Board of Directors, 550.
49. January 9, 1970, Minutes of the Board of Directors, 550.
50. October 9, 1966, Minutes of the President's Council, 221-5.
51. October 18, 1968, Minutes of the Board of Directors, 550.
52. July 10–12, 1973, Minutes of the Board of Directors, 550.
53. John McGrath, "Georgetown University Endowment: 'Long Way to Go,'" *Georgetown,* September 1973, 15.
54. Henle, *Personal Report,* 1:2–3
55. Memo of Egan, "Highlights of Georgetown Development Operations November 1963 to December 1966," Development, GUA; March 18–19, 1967, President's Council, Minutes of the Board of Regents.
56. November 18, 1966, Minutes of the Special Meeting of the Board of Directors, 550.
57. Timothy S. Healy, SJ, Eulogy at the Washington Cathedral, October 15, 1985, Timothy Healy Papers, GUA.
58. Campbell to Directors et al., December 5, 1968, President's Office, Dean, CAS, GUA.
59. December 16, 1968, Minutes of the Board of Directors, 550.
60. December 5–6, 1969, President's Council, Minutes of the Board of Regents; March 6, 1970, Minutes of the Board of Directors, Executive Committee, 550; March 20–21, 1970, Minutes of the Board of Regents.
61. December 5-6, 1969, President's Council, Minutes of the Board of Regents.
62. President's Report, 1969–70, GUA.

63. Ibid.

64. October 23, 1970, Minutes of the Board of Directors, 550; April 21, 1971, Minutes of the Board of Directors, Executive Committee, 550.

65. October 11, 1974, Minutes of the Board of Directors, 550.

66. July 17–19, 1967, Minutes of the Board of Directors, 550.

67. October 20, 1972, Minutes of the Board of Directors, 550.

68. The dean was Peter Krogh of the School of Foreign Service. December 15, 1972, Minutes of the Board of Directors, 550. About one-fifth of the institutions of higher education had collective bargaining contracts for faculty by the middle seventies. Graham, *Uncertain Triumph*, 88.

69. December 15, 1972, Minutes of the Board of Directors, 550.

70. Graham, *Uncertain Triumph*, 87.

71. February 2, 1973, Minutes of the Board of Directors, 550.

72. April 5, 1973, Minutes, Executive Faculty, Dean, CAS, GUA.

73. April 5, 1973, Executive Council Minutes, Dean, SFS, GUA.

74. Report of the Presidential Ad Hoc Committee on Tenure of Georgetown University, April 11, 1974, Henle Papers.

75. Henle to Committee, November 21, 1975, Henle Papers.

76. April 2, 1974, Minutes, Faculty Senate, GUA.

77. Report of the Presidential Ad Hoc Committee on Tenure of Georgetown University, April 11, 1974, Henle Papers.

78. In 1966 the university, at the initiative of the faculty, approached TIAA about the possibility of Georgetown faculty's participating in their retirement benefits program. In the spring of 1967, the university began a switch-over to TIAA/CREF, with the university contributing 5 percent of a faculty member's salary to the plan and Georgetown's own retirement plan being phased out. April 21, 1967, Minutes of the Board of Directors, 550. By 1974 the university had increased its contribution to the fund to 10 percent and decreased the employee's from 5 percent to 2 percent. December 13, 1974, Minutes of the Board of Directors, 550.

79. Henle to Members of the Faculty Senate, February 19, 1975; Memorandum from Henle to the Chancellor of the Medical Center et al., January 28, 1975, President's Office, Dean, CAS, GUA.

80. Faculty Senate, Dash and Penniman, In re: Grievance filed by Rev. Gerard F. Yates, SJ, May 20, 1976, GUA.

81. Yates died of a heart attack three years later, a month after he cut the ribbon for the opening of the new athletic facility named for him.

82. Charles Deacon interview, May 18, 2006.

83. *AVP News*, August 9, 1971.

84. Deacon interview.

85. *Chronicle of Higher Education*, February 10, 1975; *Mid/Week Report*, March 19, 1974.

86. David Cuttino et al., "New Student Survey," October 2, 1975, Henle Administration, box 1, folder 19.

87. Campbell interview.

88. Fitzgerald to Patricia Rueckel, October 29, 1968, Dean, CAS, GUA.

89. Royden Davis interview, May 19, 1986.

90. Memorandum, Fitzgerald to Board of Directors, August 5, 1969, Henle Administration, box 1, folder 1, 10-10.

91. Susan L. Poulson, "From Single-Sex to Coeducation: The Advent of Coeducation at Georgetown, 1965–75," *United States Catholic Historian* 13 (Fall 1995): 117–37.

92. Henle to Victor K. Scavullo, February 26, 1971, Henle, Chancellor Bunn Papers, box 13.

93. Admissions Annual Report, 1968–69, 6–7, cited in Poulson, "From Single-Sex to Coeducation," 127.

94. Poulson, "From Single-Sex to Coeducation,"127; John R. Thelin, *A History of American Higher Education* (Baltimore: Johns Hopkins University Press, 2004), 346–47.

95. Poulson, "From Single-Sex to Coeducation," 117–18.

96. "Data Presented for Consideration of the Commission on Institutions of Higher Education, Middle States Association of Colleges and Secondary Schools," November 1, 1970, Middle States' Self-Evaluation, Dean, CAS, GUA.

97. Annual Report, 1969–70, August 1970, Henle Administration, box 1, folder 31.

98. December 15, 1972, Minutes of the Board of Directors, 550. Two years later women made up nearly 40 percent of the college population.

99. Anne D. Sullivan, "Interracial and Intercultural Education at GU," in *Georgetown at Two Hundred: Faculty Reflections on the University's Future,* ed. William C. McFadden, SJ (Washington, DC: Georgetown University Press, 1990), 205.

100. Jesse Mann, "Black Experience," *Georgetown Record,* March 14, 1980.

101. *AVP News,* 1968.

102. Ibid., September 9, 1968.

103. Annual Report, 1969–70, August 1970, Henle Administration, box 1, folder 31.

104. "A Proposal Regarding the Recruitment and Admission of Minority/Poverty Students by Charles A. Deacon and Joseph A. Chalmers, September 11, 1970," Henle Administration, box 1, folder 32, 10-20.

105. Deacon interview.

106. "Georgetown's Changing Image," *GT,* March 1973, 5.

107. March 20–21, 1970, Davis Report, President's Council, Minutes of the Board of Regents.

108. Theology and philosophy took the biggest hits in the process, as these two disciplines, which had dominated the old curriculum, saw their hours reduced from twelve to six, clearly a recognition that they were not the synthesizing and apologetic instruments they had traditionally been considered to be. Dorothy Brown interview, December 16, 1986.

109. March 20–21, 1970, President's Council, Minutes of the Board of Regents.

110. "College Curriculum Revisions," [1969], Curriculum Committee, Dean, CAS, GUA; Curriculum Committee, [December 1969], Dean, CAS, GUA; Brown, "Learning, Faith, Freedom, and Building a Curriculum," 91–92.

111. Brown, "Learning, Faith, Freedom, and Building a Curriculum," 93.

112. Davis interview, March 24, 1986.

113. Daniel Bell, *The Reforming of General Education: The Columbia College Experience in Its National Setting* (New York: Columbia University Press, 1966), 51.

114. "Statement of Definitions and Beliefs," November 1966, Nursing, GUA.

115. Interview with Douglas, in Alma S. Woolley, *Learning, Faith, and Caring: History of the Georgetown University School of Nursing, 1903–2000* (Washington, DC: Georgetown University School of Nursing, 2001), 110.

116. Woolley, *Learning, Faith, and Caring,* 132.

117. Ibid., 143.

118. Thomas Fitzgerald to members of the Board of Directors, January 9, 1969, Nursing, GUA.

119. Interview with Ann Douglas in Woolley, *Learning, Faith, and Caring,* 109.

120. Patricia Alberger, "Nursing Is 'Getting It All Together,'" *GT,* September 1973, 4–8.

12 1. *Mid/Week Report,* March 13, 1973.

122. Rose McGarrity interview by Pam Ginsbach, n.d.

123. Woolley, *Learning, Faith, and Caring,* 140.

124. "Organization and Administration," Nursing, 1969–71, GUA; McGarrity interview, November 30, 1988.

125. Culliton to Campbell, January 26, 1965, SBA, 1965, GUA.

126. Guenther, in 1968, visited several universities in Lebanon, Libya, and Saudi Arabia. *Georgetown Record,* March 1968.

127. May 15, 1970, President's Council, Minutes of the Board of Regents; Henle, *Personal Report,* 3:23.

128. Othmar Winkler interview, September 26, 1986.

129. Houston interview.

130. "Quigley Probes Possibilities for F.S. Curriculum Reform," *Hoya,* November 16, 1967.

131. "SFS Losing Identity," *Hoya*, April 28, 1967.
132. *Hoya*, May 9, 1968.
133. Dean's Annual Report, 1968–69, SFS, 1957–76, GUA.
134. Jesse Mann interview, April 22, 1986.
135. "Growing Concern over the Future of the School of Foreign Service," SFS, 1968 folder, GUA.
136. Mann interview.
137. *Hoya*, January 15, 1969.
138. Don Panzera, Friends of the SFS, 1969 folder, GUA; *Hoya*, September 19, 1969.
139. "Fr. Yates Answers 'Friends of SFS,'" *Hoya*, March 20, 1969, 15.
140. *Hoya*, February 20, 1969.
141. March 21, 1969, Minutes of the Board of Directors, 550.
142. Henle address at F.S.S. Meeting, November 10, 1969, SFS, 1969 folder, GUA.
143. Henle address at F.S.S. Meeting, November 10, 1969, SFS, 1969 folder, GUA.
144. *Hoya*, February 19, 1970.
145. The meeting was held without the presence of at least three faculty who would have voted against the measure.
146. Mann interview. A month later the faculty senate went on record, 25–8, as opposing any 50-50 composition in executive committees. *Hoya*, March 20, 1970.
147. Henle to the Members of the University Community, February 26, 1970, SFS, 1957–76, 1970 folder, GUA.
148. Henle, *Personal Report*, 3:22.
149. September 18, 1970, Minutes of the Board of Directors, Executive Committee, 550.
150. *Hoya*, December 10, 1970 and February 18, 1971; Mann interview.
151. May 22, 1972, Minutes of the Board of Directors, 550.
152. Kelly to Henle, June 24, 1974, Henle Papers, box 1, folder 9.
153. Cohn interview, November 19, 2005.
154. Ibid., November 29, 2005.
155. Ibid., November 19, 2005.
156. "Proposed Tuition and Faculty Salary Increases," December 15, 1966, Law School, 1966, GUA; January 18, 1974, Minutes of the Board of Directors, 550.
157. "University Will Study Rehabilitation Project," *Georgetown Spectator*, July 27, 1967; John Fialka, "GU Use Space 'Directive' in Crime-War Lab," *Washington Star*, February 3, 1968.
158. Samuel Dash to Campbell, April 23, 1968, Law School, 1968, GUA.
159. Dean's Report, 1961–62, cited in Wallace Mlyniec, *Construction Notes: Transforming a Campus in Washington, D.C.* (Garrett Park, MD: On This Spot Productions, 2006), 83–84.
160. Cohn interview, November 19, 2005.
161. Raymond C. Brophy to T. B. Collins, January 28, 1965, Chancellor Bunn Papers, box 14.
162. Mlyniec, *Construction Notes*, 86.
163. Ibid., 87–88.
164. January 22, 1971, Minutes of the Board of Directors, 550.
165. The ratio at Yale was 11.9:1, at Stanford 15.3:1, 16.8:1 at NYU, and 23.8:1 at Columbia. *GT*, May 1973, 18.
166. Memorandum, "Report on the 1968–69 Law Center Budget," Dean to Faculty Committee on Finance, May 17, 1968, Law School, 1968, GUA.
167. Ernst et al., *First 125 Years*, 174.
168. Paul R. Dean to Chad Hickey, "Draft statement for release by the dean to the Georgetown Law Weekly re Negro student proposal," January 10, 1968, Law School, 1968, GUA.
169. April 5, 1968, Minutes of the Board of Directors, 550.
170. Ernst et al., *First 125 Years*, 170–71.
171. Ibid., 172.
172. Student Bar Association Annual Report, 1966–67, Law School, GUA.
173. Dean to Decanal Staff, February 20, 1967, Law School, 1967, GUA.

174. Wallace J. Mlyniec, "The Intersection of Three Visions—Ken Pye, Bill Pincus, and Bill Greenhalgh—and the Development of Clinical Teaching Fellowships," *Tennessee Law Review* 64 (Summer 1997): 974.
175. Wallace Mlyniec interview, April 12, 2006.
176. "Dean's Report to the Alumni of GULC," 1966–68, June 30, 1968, 34–38, Law School, GUA.
177. Pam Ginsbach, "Juvenile Clinic: Helping Neglected Children," *GT*, November 1974, 4–7.
178. Pam Ginsbach, "Lessons in a Courtroom," *GT*, September 1973, 13–14.
179. Cohn interview, November 19, 2005.
180. *GT*, May 1973, 23.
181. John G. Hervey, ABA, to the Approved Schools, September 4, 1964, Law School, 1964, GUA.
182. Dean to Campbell, April 19, 1967, Law School, GUA.
183. Paul R. Dean to Members of the Decanal Search Committee, September 30, 1968, Law School, 1968, GUA.
184. Ernst et al., *First 125 Years*, 153.
185. Bulletin issued on Law Day, 1969, "The Georgetown University Law Center and Federal Service," Law School, 1969, GUA.
186. Ernst et al., *First 125 Years*, 166.
187. David R. Papke, "The Legal Profession and Its Ethical Responsibilities: A History," in *Ethics and the Legal Profession*, ed. M. Davis and F. Elliston (Buffalo, NY: Prometheus, 1986), 44, in Monica Fuertes, "A Historical Perspective of Ethics in Legal Education with a Focus on Georgetown Law" (unpublished paper, 1993), 9.
188. Fuertes, "Historical Perspective of Ethics," 19.
189. Ibid., 19.
190. April 25, 1975, Minutes of the Board of Directors, Executive Committee, 550; *Mid/Week Report*, April 1, 1975.
191. Cohn interview, November 23, 2005.

CHAPTER 3

1. Joseph Epstein, "It's Only Culture," *Commentary*, November 1983, 61, cited in Russell Jacoby, *The Last Intellectuals: American Culture in the Age of Academe* (New York: Basic Books, 1987), 113–14.
2. "Address by Rev. Gerard J. Campbell, SJ," Fall Faculty Convocation, October 7, 1967, Campbell Papers.
3. J. A. Panuska, SJ, et al., December 2, 1965, Dean, CAS, GUA.
4. Robert Henle, Inaugural Address, in University Reform: U.S., 1970; *A Symposium on the Occasion of the Inauguration of Robert J. Henle, S.J., as 45th President of Georgetown University, October 7, 1969* (Washington, DC: Georgetown University Press, 1970), 41–55.
5. October 6–7, 1967, President's Council, Minutes of the Board of Regents.
6. August 6–8, 1968, Minutes of the Board of Directors, 550.
7. January 9, 1970, Minutes of the Board of Directors, 550.
8. Campbell interview.
9. Main Campus Planning and Building Committee, Robert Judge, SJ, to Subcommittee on Housing, March 24, 1970, Dean, CAS, GUA.
10. Main Campus Planning and Building Committee, "Construction of New Residence Halls," appendix to a letter from Fitzgerald to Henle, May 15, 1970, CAS, GUA.
11. *Hoya*, March 3, 1972.
12. August 13, 1973, Minutes of the Board of Directors, Executive Committee, 550; September 14, 1973, Minutes of the Board of Directors, 550.
13. Poulson, "From Single-Sex to Coeducation," 131.
14. Joseph P. Joyce, "Corridor Jesuit: 'An Older Friend,'" *GT*, May 1973, 6.

15. Susan L. Poulson, "A Quiet Revolution: The Transition to Coeducation at Georgetown and Rutgers Colleges, 1960–1975" (diss., Georgetown University, 1989), 94.
16. "College Makes Case for Parietal Hours," *Hoya,* December 14, 1967, in Poulson, "Quiet Revolution," 94–95.
17. April 5, 1968, Minutes of the Board of Directors, 550.
18. Rueckel to University Housemasters and Resident Assistants, February 20, 1970, GUA, cited in Poulson, "Quiet Revolution," 98.
19. Poulson, "Quiet Revolution,"98.
20. July 11–13, 1972, Minutes of the Board of Directors, 550.
21. July 10–12, 1973, Minutes of the Board of Directors, 550.
22. "Student Government Suit in Limbo," *Hoya,* January 25, 1974, 2, cited in Poulson, "Quiet Revolution," 101.
23. Raymond Schroth interview, July 28, 1985.
24. Robert Judge interview, July 30, 1987.
25. "Sex at Georgetown," *Ye Domesday Booke* (hereafter *YDB*), 1975, 92–97.
26. Statement of Edmund G. Ryan, SJ, November 24, 1972, President's Office, Dean, CAS, GUA.
27. Washington Star, September 26, 1968.
28. Schroth interview. The two Jesuit advisors were John Ford of the Weston Theologate (Massachusetts) and Patrick Haran of Holy Cross College.
29. Schroth interview.
30. *Hoya,* May 2, 1968.
31. "The Hidden World of Campus Drugs," *Hoya,* May 2, 1968.
32. *Hoya,* September 2, 1973.
33. "Drugs," *YDB,* 1975, 114–17; "Alcoholism at Georgetown," *YDB,* 108–13.
34. Schroth interview.
35. Lois Kopala, "A Student's Work Is Never Done," *GT,* January 1973, 13–15.
36. Henle, *Personal Report,* 2:32.
37. Edward Geary, SJ, to Campbell et al., September 27, 1965, Student Personnel, Dean, CAS, GUA.
38. Fitzgerald to Edward A. Geary, SJ, September 29, 1965, Student Personnel, Dean, CAS, GUA.
39. *Hoya,* September 26, 1968.
40. James Walsh, SJ, "Is Religion Dead at Georgetown?" *GT,* July 1976, 3–4.
41. Susan Poulson, "Bill Clinton's Georgetown," unpublished paper, 1995; *Hoya,* March 10, 1966.
42. Pisinski interview in Craig Goldblatt, "'Look beyond the Campus, to America Itself': Student Activism at Georgetown University during the 1960s and the Founding of the *Georgetown Voice*" (unpublished paper, 1988), 22–24.
43. Schroth interview.
44. *Hoya,* November 12, 1970.
45. Ibid., November 19, 1970.
46. "Hoya Debaters: First in the Nation for Third Year," *GT,* March 1974, 16.
47. Joyce Shelby, "Debate: 'A Verbal Chess Match,'" *GT,* September 1974, 6–12.
48. October 15, 1971, Minutes of the Board of Directors, 550.
49. Carol Sack Campion (**C** 1972), letter to Leisz, April 4, 1986.
50. March 19, 1976, Minutes of the Board of Directors, 550.
51. March 26, 1975; March 9, 1976, Minutes, Faculty Senate.
52. May 17, 1976, Minutes of the Board of Directors, 550.
53. March 19, 1971, Minutes of the Board of Directors, 550.
54. Lois Kopala, "A Former Homecoming Queen: Black, Proud and Angry," *GT,* July 1972, 15.
55. *GT,* March 1973, 32.
56. "United They Stand: Student Groups for Minorities at Georgetown," *GT,* March 1973, 15–18.
57. "Anti-Semitic Incident Believed Over," *Hoya,* February 25, 1966, 2.
58. "It Was the Winter of Discontent," *GT,* March 1972.

59. *Georgetown,* January 1975, 22.

60. Deacon interview.

61. Jim Mullay, "Through the Hoops," *GM,* Fall 1997, 29–31.

62. *Hoya,* February 7, 1975.

63. Fran Connors, "Basketball: A Whistle Away from Victory," *GT,* May 1975, 23–24.

64. Phil Marcelo, "Lacrosse Evolves from Club to Contender," *Hoya,* Special lacrosse edition, Spring 2005, 12–13.

65. *Hoya,* October 3, 1968.

66. Ibid., January 15, 1969.

67. Ibid.

68. *Hoya,* December 12, 1968.

69. Ibid., February 13, 1969.

70. Ibid., May 14, 1965, 2, cited in Rose Marie L. Audette, "Everything in Moderation: Social Activism and University Reform, Georgetown University, 1960–1970" (honors thesis, Georgetown University, 1981), 27–28.

71. February 26, 1964, report, Sodality, GUCAP, Student Development, GUA.

72. "Georgetown Reaches Out: GUCAP and a Sense of Mission," *Georgetown,* Winter 1965, 2, cited in Audette, "Everything in Moderation," 34.

73. *Hoya,* October 15, 1964, cited in Audette, "Everything in Moderation," 39.

74. Audette, "Everything in Moderation," 38.

75. February 25, 1966, Minutes of the Board of Directors, 550.

76. "GU Students Join Civil Rights Activity," *Hoya,* March 26, 1965, cited in Audette, "Everything in Moderation," 42.

77. "Hoyas Participate in Selma Maneuvers," *Hoya,* April 1, 1965, 3, cited in Audette, "Everything in Moderation," 42.

78. "GUCAP to Travel to Grenada, MS for SCLC Boycott," *Hoya,* December 15, 1966; "GUCAPers Go South to Enlist Negro Vote," *Hoya,* April 13, 1967, cited in Audette, "Everything in Moderation," 65.

79. "Fr. Gelson Outlines Unionization Views," *Hoya,* March 7, 1968.

80. "Labor Union Rejected by Campus Workers," *Hoya,* September 18, 1969, in Audette, "Everything in Moderation," 79.

81. *Washington Post,* April 4, 1968, cited in Audette, "Everything in Moderation," 75.

82. Interview, January 29, 1981, in Audette, "Everything in Moderation," 75.

83. Howard Gillette, *Between Justice and Beauty: Race, Planning and the Failure of Urban Policy in Washington, DC* (Baltimore: Johns Hopkins University Press, 1995), 169.

84. John Murphy cited in Ernst et al., *First 125 Years,* 156.

85. "U Responds to Needs of Strife-Torn City," *Georgetown Record,* April 1968, in Audette, "Everything in Moderation," 76.

86. Jesse Mann, "Black Experience," *Georgetown Record,* March 14, 1980.

87. Dexter L. Hanley, SJ, "The Baccalaureate Sermon Given at the One Hundred and Sixty-Ninth Annual Commencement and Baccalaureate Mass, Sunday, June 9, 1968," AVP, GUA.

88. *AVP News,* July 2, 1968.

89. "US Viet Nam Policy Favored in Confab; Students Give Flag," *Hoya,* October 21, 1965; "600 Rally Round Viet Nam Policy, Denounce 'Doves,'" *Washington Star,* October 17, 1965, cited in Audette, "Everything in Moderation," 55–56.

90. *Hoya,* February 25, 1966.

91. Audette, "Everything in Moderation," 59.

92. "Dovish Group Blasted by Hawkish Marchers," *Hoya,* October 26, 1967, in Audette, "Everything in Moderation," 84.

93. *AVP News,* April 2, 1968.

94. Ibid., September 12, 1968.

95. "Investigation of Students for a Democratic Society, Part 1-A (Georgetown University), Hearings before the Committee on Internal Security House of Representatives, Ninety-First Congress, June 3 and 4, 1969" (Washington, DC: U.S. Government Printing Office, 1969), cited in Audette, "Everything in Moderation," 95.

96. *AVP News,* October 28, 1968.

97. "Tropaia, 1969," Dean, CAS, GUA.

98. Goldblatt, "Founding of the *Georgetown Voice*," 27–28.

99. Ad Hoc Committee of the Regents, n.d., President's Council, GUA.

100. Audette, "Everything in Moderation," 101–3.

101. *Hoya*, May 1, 1968.

102. Published statement, July 1969, Henle Papers.

103. Audette, "Everything in Moderation," 85.

104. *Hoya*, May 2, 1968, cited in Audette, "Everything in Moderation," 85.

105. *Hoya*, editorial, February 13, 1969.

106. *AVP News*, September 15, 1969, 9–14; Audette, "Everything in Moderation," 108.

107. May 8, 1970, Minutes of the Board of Directors, 550. The university did sever ties with one military group on campus, the 352nd Civil Affairs Reserve Unit that had been originally set up at Georgetown in the 1950s as part of the university's contribution to the Cold War effort, with Georgetown faculty teaching the group skills they would use for occupying and governing other countries. In announcing the university's decision to cease sponsoring the unit, Henle noted that the group, initially an integral part of the university, had now become a rent-free occupier of space on campus, which the university could no longer afford.

108. Memorandum, Fitzgerald to Board of Directors, August 5, 1969, Henle Papers, box 1, folder 1, 10-10. In a Harris poll conducted in May 1970, nearly 60 percent of American students believed that the United States had become "a highly repressive society, intolerant of dissent." *The Report of the President's Commission on Campus Unrest* (Chicago: Avon Books, 1971), 216.

109. *Hoya*, September 18, 1969.

110. Audette, "Everything in Moderation," 113–14.

111. Henle to Directors et al., October 17, 1969, Misc. Memoranda, President's Office, Dean, CAS, GUA.

112. *Hoya*, October 10, 1969; Audette, "Everything in Moderation," 116.

113. "Moratorium Day in Washington, 1969," *Hoya Review*, October 23, 1969, 2–6, cited in Audette, "Everything in Moderation," 118.

114. Ernst et al., *First 125 Years*, 156.

115. Audette, "Everything in Moderation," 120–21.

116. Main Campus Planning and Building Committee Report, November 11, 1969, Chancellor Bunn Papers, box 13; February 19, 1971, Minutes of the Board of Directors, Executive Committee, 550.

117. "Student Dissenters Disrupt Q's Civilization Class," *Hoya*, February 13, 1970. Quigley showed up to the next class accompanied by a German shepherd.

118. "Henle to Continue Campus Interviews," *Hoya*, March 20, 1970, cited in Audette, "Everything in Moderation," 134.

119. *Hoya*, March 20, April 16, 1970.

120. *AVP News*, April 2, 1970.

121. The seven demands of the strikers were (a) a university condemnation of the invasion of Cambodia, (b) amnesty for those on academic probation for disrupting ROTC classes, (c) no academic credit for ROTC, (d) an investigation into university governance, (e) the resignation of the dean of men, (f) an investigation into the working conditions of the university's nonacademic personnel, and (g) the university's commitment to reduce its pollution of the atmosphere.

122. Ciancaglini interview, March 7, 1981, cited in Audette, "Everything in Moderation," 137.

123. Audette, "Everything in Moderation," 139.

124. *Hoya*, May 8, 1970.

125. "Law Center Faculty Resolution," May 6, 1970, Law School, GUA; Ernst et al., *First 125 Years*, 158.

126. *AVP News*, May 18, 1970.

127. Brown interview, December 12, 1986; Fitzgerald to Deans, May 18, 1970, Henle Papers, box 1, folder 14.

128. May 8, 1970, Minutes of the Board of Directors, Executive Committee, 550; Henle to Georgetown Parents, May 26, 1970, President's Office, Dean, CAS, GUA; *AVP News*, May 18, 1970.
129. *AVP News*, May 18, 1970.
130. *Report*, 46.
131. May 8, 1970, Minutes of the Board of Directors, Executive Committee, 550; Henle to Victor K. Scavullo, February 26, 1971, Chancellor Bunn Papers, Henle.
132. Henry Briefs interview, October 10, 1986.
133. Brown interview, December 12, 1986.
134. Valerie Earle, Orientation of New Faculty, Manresa, September 1970, GUA.
135. "This Week in Review," *New York Times*, July 27, 1970.
136. Zebot to Colleagues, July 27, 1970, author's copy.
137. "Agenda for Georgetown," 1, September 3, 1970, author's copy.
138. Ibid., 5, November 3, 1970.
139. The faculty signees included Louis Dupré, George Farr, Victor Ferkiss, James Lambert, Jesse Mann, Thomas McTighe, Rocco Porrecco, William McFadden, and Roger Slakey.
140. "Agenda," 7, February 2, 1971.
141. Ibid., 8, February 25, 1971.
142. March 19, 1971, Minutes of the Board of Directors, 550.
143. *AVP News*, May 18, 1970.
144. Ibid., September 4, 1970.
145. October 23, 1970, Minutes of the Board of Directors, 550.
146. Brown interview, December 16, 1986.
147. "Student Lethargy," *Hoya*, October 15, 1970, 4.
148. *Hoya*, April 22, 1971.
149. Ibid.
150. Fitzgerald interview; Judge interview; Emergency Committee to the Faculty, Students and Employees of Georgetown University, May 4, 1971, Henle, Chancellor Bunn Papers, box 13.
151. Ernst et al., *First 125 Years*, 158–59.
152. October 22, 1971, President's Council, Minutes of the Board of Regents.
153. March 10, 1972, Minutes of the Board of Directors, 550.
154. *Hoya*, April 22, 1971.
155. Ibid., April 28, 1972.
156. Ibid., September 3, 1972.
157. Mark J. Gleason Jr. "Students Serving Students: A History of Students of Georgetown, Inc." (unpublished paper, 1987).
158. *Hoya*, January 18, 1974.
159. Ibid., January 26, 1973.
160. *Mid/Week Report*, February 8, 1973.
161. *Hoya*, March 30, 1973.
162. "Positions Change," *Georgetown*, July 1972, 20.
163. The role that Fitzgerald played in directing the university's response to the student strike in May 1970 and in creating a fait accompli for the president in the form of the faculty vote to close the university apparently did not sit well with Henle. When he later accused Fitzgerald of not being a "team member," he probably had the May events in mind. His exclusion of Fitzgerald from the emergency committee that he set up to deal with any possible crisis in the following spring was a clear sign of Fitzgerald's fall from grace.
164. *Mid/Week Report*, September 18, 1973.
165. *Hoya*, December 7, 1973; January 18, 1974.
166. George Behan, "Fr. Henle Plans to Stay in Office," *Hoya*, February 8, 1974.
167. June 8, 1970, Minutes of the Board of Directors, 550.
168. Personal and confidential memorandum from Edmund G. Ryan to Henle, March 5, 1974, Edmund Ryan Papers, GUSC.
169. Ibid.

170. March 15, 1974, Minutes of the Board of Directors, 550.

171. April 19, 1974, Minutes of the Board of Directors, Executive Committee, 550.

172. Henle to Joseph Sweeney, SJ, April 30, 1974, GUA.

173. Personal and confidential memorandum, April 1, 1974, Ryan Papers.

174. May 20, 1974, Minutes of the Board of Directors.

175. Curran diary, April 12, 1974, author's possession.

176. Altobello interview.

177. Houston interview, January 23, 1985.

178. Fitzgerald interview.

179. Sherman Cohn, quoted in *Hoya,* April 19, 1974, 9.

180. *Hoya,* April 19, 1974, 4.

181. Ken Zemsky, *Hoya,* April 19, 1974, 7.

182. April 19, 1974, Minutes of the Board of Directors, Executive Committee.

183. Ibid.

184. Thirty-three Jesuits of the Georgetown Community to Board of Directors, May 11, 1974, author's copy.

185. May 21, 1974, Minutes of the Board of Directors.

186. Statement of Edmund Ryan to the Board, May 21, 1974, Ryan Papers, GUA.

187. Curran diary, May 21, 1974.

188. July 12–13, 1974, Minutes of the Board of Directors, 550.

189. *Faculty Senate News* 3 (November 1974), Faculty Senate, GUA.

190. May 19, 1975, Minutes of the Board of Directors, 550.

191. Julia Montgomery Walsh, cited in Curran diary, June 12, 1975.

192. Altobello interview.

193. *Mid/Week Report,* September 16, 1975.

194. May 17, 1976, Minutes of the Board of Directors, 550.

CHAPTER 4

1. The other two finalists were Thomas Fitzgerald, former academic vice president, and Robert Mitchell, a former member of the board of directors.

2. Curran diary, April 14, 1976.

3. "Presidential Search Committee Profile of Desired President," *Mid/Week Report,* February 17, 1976.

4. Dorothy Brown, quoted in *Georgetown Magazine,* Summer 1989, 11–12.

5. Royden Davis, SJ, quoted in Mary Carroll Johansen, "Davis Reflects on Georgetown Life," *Hoya,* May 2, 1986.

6. Martha Duffy, "New Page for an Old Bookworm," *Time,* May 28, 1990.

7. *Mid/Week Report,* January 19, 1977.

8. Dave Cannella, "What They Don't Want You to Hear: How G's WGTB 90.1 FM Died," *Voice,* January 26, 1989.

9. As James Walsh, a former member of the station's board of review reported to the faculty senate, "Reliable estimates of total costs for running a university station such as Georgetown fix on $40,000 annually, given proper management, not the $100,000 quoted. More than half this amount—as has been shown in recent years—can be raised by public contributions. Quality broadcasting, furthermore, generates grants. Indeed, given proper management, in the long run there is no reason why the station could not be self-supporting." WGTB-FM, 1975–1978: A Report to the Faculty Senate, Georgetown University," [May 1978].

10. Ibid.

11. May 5, 1978, Minutes, Faculty Senate.

12. Ibid.

13. Dennis John Lewis, "Alliance Challenges WGTB-FM Transfer," *Washington Star,* July 29, 1978.

14. Cannella, "What They Don't Want You to Hear." The FCC finally approved the transfer of the license in the late winter of 1978. March 14, 1980, Minutes of the Board of Directors, 550.

15. President's Annual Report, 1979, GUA.

16. Quoted in *Hoya,* April 28, 1989.

17. *GM,* November–December 1980, 6.

18. Ibid.

19. *GM,* March–April 1981, 18.

20. "Studies in Success," *Washington Post,* January 7, 1984.

21. Eugene Sloan, "Georgetown Plans Its Architectural Future: Rigorous Building Will Forge a New Look for the University," *Hoya,* January 31, 1989.

22. "Cityscape: The Inside Story; A Look at Georgetown's New Leavey Center," *Washington Post,* November 19, 1988.

23. April 22, 1977, Minutes of the Board of Directors, 550.

24. March 25, 1977, Minutes of the Board of Directors, 550.

25. Vincent Fuller to John Hamilton, Esq., June 14, 1977, Georgetown Visitation Archives (hereafter GVA).

26. Hamilton to Mother M. Philomena Tisinger, Superior, September 11, 1978, GVA.

27. May 5, 1978, Minutes of the Board of Directors, 550.

28. Hamilton to Lewis Ferguson III, November 29, 1978, copy, GVA.

29. According to John Rose and Michael Klemmer, Raymond Brophy, a realtor, was brought into the board meeting by George Houston to give his appraisal of the value of the property. Brophy asserted that the property was not worth the $4.5 million asking price, that it would not be commercially developed at that price, and that the university could very likely acquire it later at a much lower price. Rose interview, December 18, 1986.

30. January 19, 1979, Minutes of the Board of Directors, 550.

31. April 22, 1977, Minutes of the Board of Directors, Executive Committee, 550.

32. Jo Ann Moran Cruz interview, July 16, 2007.

33. December 9, 1983, Minutes of the Board of Directors, Executive Committee, 550.

34. Altobello interview.

35. July 8-9, 1977, Minutes of the Board of Directors, 550.

36. *Mid/Week Report,* February 8, 1978.

37. Ibid., December 17, 1976.

38. May 11, 1979, Minutes of the Board of Directors, 550; December 14, 1979, Minutes of the Board of Directors, Executive Committee.

39. December 5, 1980, Minutes of the Board of Directors, 550.

40. *GM,* January–February 1982, 31.

41. *Annual Report 1982,* 31, Healy Papers.

42. *Annual Report 1980–81,* 27, Healy Papers.

43. Michael Feinstein, "Chasing Carroll's Dream," GM, July–August 1982, 14.

44. *The Georgetown University Campaign,* n.d., 3, University and Alumni Relations, GUA.

45. As Joseph Sellinger, SJ, happily reported to the board in October 1983, "That [judgment] may have been true three years ago, . . . [but] today it [is] absolutely false." October 21, 1983, Minutes of the Board of Directors, 550.

46. October 18, 1984, Minutes of the Board of Directors, 550.

47. Geiger, *Research and Relevant Knowledge,* 312.

48. April 14, 1989, Minutes of the Board of Directors, 550.

49. By 1988 faculty practice plans at the medical center were producing about one-quarter of the university's income. Tuition and fees accounted for approximately 45 percent of revenue. Within the three-campus budgeting, however, the main campus was still 81 percent dependent on tuition, the law center 89 percent. "Report of the Vice President for Financial Affairs and Treasurer," *Chronicle,* November 1988, Special issue.

50. June 6, 1985; March 20, 1986, Minutes of the Board of Directors, 550.

51. December 10, 1987, Minutes of the Board of Directors, Executive Committee and the Finance Committee, 550. A law was indeed passed later that year by the Congress that put a limit of $150 million on the amount of tax-exempt bonds that a private institution could issue.

52. *New York Times,* June 16, 1988.

53. December 11, 1986, Minutes of the Board of Directors, 550.

54. Graham and Diamond, *Rise of American Research Universities,* 179.

55. Geiger, *Research and Relevant Knowledge,* 320–21.

56. October 1, 1981, Minutes of the Board of Directors, 550.

57. Kevin Greene, "Swallows to Capistrano: The Georgetown-Government Talent Exchange," GM, September–October 1981, 13–16.

58. Gwendolyn Mikell, "Catholic Diversity, Pluralism, and Interracial/Intercultural Education," in *Georgetown at Two Hundred: Faculty Reflections on the University's Future,* ed. William C. McFadden (Washington, DC: Georgetown University Press, 1990), 224–25.

59. *Hoya,* April 29, 1988, 1.

60. Mikell, "Catholic Diversity," 229.

61. Stuart L. Rich, Director, OIR, "MC Planning Committee Survey of Faculty Attitudes and Opinions," May 14, 1985, Office of Institutional Research (OIR), GUA.

62. Talk of James Devereux to members of the Georgetown Jesuit Community, March 25, 1987.

63. Heidi Fritschel, "Treasures in the Stacks," *GM,* Honor Roll 1986, 2–7.

64. Judith A. Pezza, "The Evolution of Admissions," *Georgetown Magazine,* Summer 1989, 17–18.

65. "Georgetown University Undergraduate Admissions by Type of High School Attended," OIR, GUA. The author is grateful to Joseph Pettit for this information.

66. John J. DeGioia, "The Three 'Lands' of Timothy Healy," *Washington Post,* January 1, 1993.

67. *Hoya,* April 29, 1988, 1.

68. At the undergraduate level, white Americans constituted 74.7 percent of enrollment, African Americans made up 7.4 percent, Asian Americans made up 4.6 percent, and Hispanic Americans made up 4.5 percent. Foreign undergraduate students made up 8.7 percent.

69. Pettit to Healy, "Geographic Diversity of Freshmen," July 17, 1987, Healy Papers.

70. Nicole Wong, "Admissions Sets 'Goals' for Student Diversity," *Hoya,* March 25, 1988.

71. Deidre Carmody, "Georgetown Seen as Making Gains by Reaching Out to Needy Students," *New York Times,* February 13, 1989.

72. Report of the Provost's Task Force on the Academic State of the Main Campus, April 1981, AVP, GUA.

73. Brown, "Learning, Faith, Freedom, and Building a Curriculum," 96–97.

74. "Working Paper on Georgetown's Core Curriculum," *University Senate News,* October 1985.

75. "Report of the Core Review Committee," January 21, 1987, AVP/Provost, GUA.

76. Edited transcript of the third General Faculty Meeting on the Core Curriculum Proposal, February 19, 1987, AVP/Provost, GUA.

77. Brown, "Learning, Faith, Freedom, and Building a Curriculum," 101–2.

78. "Report of the Committee to Review 4/4-5/5 Options," February 6, 1990, AVP/Provost, GUA.

79. Survey of Graduating Seniors, 1985, OIR, GUA.

80. Healy to Kolvenbach, January 19, 1985, Healy Papers.

81. Undergraduate Alumni Outcomes Survey, 1988, Office of Institutional Research.

82. Dean's Report, 1993, cited in Tillman, *Georgetown's School of Foreign Service,* 79.

83. Tillman, *Georgetown's School of Foreign Service,* 65–66.

84. Interview with Allen Goodman, September 23, 1993, cited in Tillman, *Georgetown's School of Foreign Service,* 76.

85. Dean's Annual Report, 1991, cited in Tillman, *Georgetown's School of Foreign Service,* 73.

86. Houston interview.

87. *AVP News,* January 11, 1977.

88. Annual Report 1982, 11; Annual Report, 1983, 16, SBA, GUA; *GM,* January–February 1981, 11.

89. *GM,* Spring–Summer 1988, 2.
90. Ibid., July–August 1982, 20.
91. Dean's Annual Report, 1983, 17, SBA, GUA.
92. *GT,* September–October 1983, 14–16; Winkler interview.
93. Winkler interview.
94. *Georgetown Record,* April 9, 1980.
95. Dean's Report, 1979–80, 13–15, cited in Woolley, *Learning, Faith, and Caring,* 155.
96. Woolley, *Learning, Faith, and Caring,* 172–74.
97. Ibid., 174.
98. Annual Report, 1983, 24, Nursing School, GUA.
99. Woolley, *Learning, Faith, and Caring,* 165.
100. Ibid., 153; *GM,* May–June 1982, 21–22.
101. Hughes to Chancellor McNulty, July 8, 1982, Nursing, GUA, cited in Woolley, *Learning, Faith, and Caring,* 166.
102. Woolley, *Learning, Faith, and Caring,* 167.
103. Ibid., 168.
104. Ibid., 169.
105. Ibid.
106. Ibid., 184.
107. Judith A. Allen, secretary of the Board of Review, to John F. Griffith, March 29, 1988, Nursing School, GUA, cited in Woolley, *Learning, Faith, and Caring,* 185.
108. Woolley, *Learning, Faith, and Caring,* 187.
109. Ibid., 194.
110. Ibid., 195–96.
111. Ibid., 205.
112. Evidence for this is found in the growing number of graduates who became nurse practitioners, either in private practice, such as Maureen Riley (1978), for the United States government; Jennifer Grise (1980) at the U.S. embassy in Ghana; and Patricia Connery-Ducharme (1987) at the U.S. embassy in Singapore, or as staff members of hospitals, such as Kathleen McKernan Naughton (1978) at Johns Hopkins Hospital. Laura Peterson (1982) went on to earn a medical degree from Dartmouth.
113. Alan Fogg and Rod Kuckro, "Heat Is on Res-Life as Ex-RAs Smolder," *Hoya,* March 25, 1977.
114. Briefs interview.
115. "Report from the Student Life Policy Committee in response to the hearings concerning Residence Life," June 1977, Student Development, GUA.
116. August 29, 1978, Minutes, Steering Committee, Faculty Senate, GUA.
117. Patricia Rueckel to Emmett Curran, January 28, 1977, author's possession.
118. Memorandum from P. Rueckel, Chair of the Residential College Study Group to T. S. Healy, "Phase I of the Study Group Completed," April 12, 1977, Student Development, GUA.
119. William R. Stott Jr. et al., for the Living/Learning Program Planning Committee, to Dear Colleague, May 15, 1978, Student Development, GUA.
120. *GM,* July–August 1980, 28.
121. "Debate at Georgetown: A Tradition for 158 Years," *Community Matters,* March 1988, 10–12.
122. *GM,* March–April 1984, 9–10.
123. Scott Walter, "The Devil Disguised as a Spirit of Light: The Stewards Society of Georgetown College, 1982–1989" (unpublished paper).
124. Joe Rand, "The Stewards: Fact and Fiction," Voice, February 8, 1988.
125. Ibid.
126. *Hoya,* February 9, 1988.
127. "Secrecy Serves No One," *Hoya,* February 9, 1988.
128. "John J. DeGioia to Undergraduate Students," *Community Matters,* March 1988, 5.
129. Joe Rand, "More Thoughts on the Society of Stewards," *Voice,* February 11, 1988.
130. Chris Reid, "Steward Alumni Vote to Alter Secrecy Policy," *Hoya,* April 19, 1988.

131. *Hoya,* May 2, 1989, 1.

132. *Voice,* September 28, 1989.

133. "The Stampede to Drug Testing," *Washington Post,* August 31, 1986.

134. "Alcohol & Drug Policy," August 1987, Student Development, GUA.

135. Ibid.

136. Ibid.

137. Casey Anderson, "GUPS Makes Arrest in Drug Investigation," *Hoya,* February 12, 1988.

138. "Watching for Signals," *Hoya,* February 12, 1988.

139. *Community Matters,* March 1988, 4.

140. The four had current and past connections. Gavitt had coached John Thompson at Providence and was on the basketball committee of the East Coast Athletic Conference with Rienzo. Crouthamel had been Gavitt's fraternity brother at Dartmouth. Carnesecca had taught with Rienzo at Saint Ann's Academy in New York City.

141. Francis Rienzo interview, November 14, 2005.

142. Adam Himmelsbach, "Hoyas' First Thompson Era Has Long Life on the Payroll," *New York Times,* March 3, 2006.

143. *GM,* May–June 1982, 13.

144. Roland Lazenby, *Georgetown: The Championships and Thompson* (Washington, DC: Full Court Press, 1984), 99.

145. *GM,* July–August 1980, 32.

146. Ibid., July–August 1982, 26.

CHAPTER 5

1. T. S. Healy, "Contemplation in Education," Faculty Convocation Address, November 21, 1981, Healy Papers.

2. Geiger, *Research and Relevant Knowledge,* 271.

3. "Self-Evaluation Report for the Middle States Association of Colleges and Schools," October 1981, 21, AVP, GUA.

4. January 25, 1977, Minutes, Faculty Senate, GUA; "Recommendations of the Educational Affairs Committee," Spring 1979, Faculty Senate, GUA.

5. Remarks of Aloysius Kelley, SJ, October 21, 1983, Minutes of the Board of Directors, 1983, 550.

6. November 10, 1978, Minutes of the Board of Directors, 550.

7. Hope Rogers, "A Design for the 80s: Streamlining Georgetown's Graduate School," *GM,* September–October 1983, 9.

8. Cited in Rogers, "Design for the 80s," 9–10.

9. Richard B. Schwartz, "The Georgetown Graduate School in 1989," in *Georgetown at Two Hundred: Faculty Reflections on the University's Future,* ed. William C. McFadden, SJ (Washington, DC: Georgetown University Press, 1990), 286.

10. "A Proposal to Establish a Center for Immigration Policy and Refugee Assistance at Georgetown University," November 1980, CIPRA, GUA.

11. Quoted in Paul Findley, *They Dare to Speak Out: People and Institutions Confront Israel's Lobby* (Westport, CT: Lawrence Hill Books, 1985), 196.

12. Ibid., 199.

13. October 12, 1979, Minutes of the Board of Directors, 550.

14. Sandra Reeves, "The Think Tank on the Potomac," *GM,* July–August 1980, 6–19.

15. Ibid.

16. Abshire vehemently denied that the center was an ideological incubator for the Reagan revolution. "We've got a large umbrella," he insisted, pointing out that two prominent Democrats, Robert Strauss and Lane Kirkland, both served on CSIS's advisory board. The role of the center, he asserted, "was indeed to help policymakers get beyond ideological . . . preconceptions and see problems in long-range, interdisciplinary perspective." To Abshire, CSIS was an effort "to be a bridge between the world of ideas and the world of action." James Lardner,

"Thick & Think Tank," *Washington Post,* September 21, 1982; James Allen Smith, *Strategic Calling: The Center for Strategic and International Studies, 1962–1992* (Washington, DC: Center for Strategic and International Studies, 1993), 138.

17. As part of the separation, the university transferred $10 million in endowment funds, which had been raised by CSIS, to the newly independent center. George Houston, *Annual Report,* 1987, 3, Healy Papers.
18. May 5, 1978, and September 15, 1978, Minutes of the Board of Directors, 550.
19. Cohn interview, November 19, 2005.
20. Ernst et al., *First 125 Years,* 179.
21. Ibid., 186.
22. "Class Entering in 1987," Office of Admissions, Law School, GUA.
23. Cohn interview, November 19, 2005.
24. *USA Today,* October 23, 1987.
25. Quoted in George Berry, "Georgetown University Law Center," *GM,* November–December 1981, 8.
26. Ernst et al., *First 125 Years,* 176.
27. Ibid., 184.
28. Ibid., 185.
29. March 19, 1987, Minutes of the Board of Directors, 550.
30. Dean Robert Pitofsky to Law Center Alumni and Alumnae, June 15, 1989, cited in Mark Tushnet, "Catholic Legal Education at a National Law School: Reflections on the Georgetown Experience," in *Georgetown at Two Hundred: Faculty Reflections on the University's Future,* ed. William C. McFadden (Washington, DC: Georgetown University Press, 1990), 323.
31. October 17, 1985, Minutes of the Board of Directors, 550.
32. March 21, 1985, Minutes of the Board of Directors, 550.
33. Ibid.
34. Mlyniec, *Construction Notes.*
35. December 14, 1979, Minutes of the Board of Directors, 550.
36. Ibid.
37. Geiger, *Research and Relevant Knowledge,* 320.
38. *GM,* January–February 1982, 21.
39. May 11, 1979, Minutes of the Board of Directors, 550; February 13, 1980, Minutes of the Board of Directors, Executive Committee, 550.
40. Danielle Dubas, "The Vincent T. Lombardi Cancer Research Center," *GM,* March–April 1982, 10–11.
41. Danielle Dubas, "Cancer: Unraveling the Mystery," *GM,* March–April 1982, 2–9.
42. October 17, 1985, Minutes of the Board of Directors, 550.
43. *Chronicle,* May 1987, 2–3.
44. Ibid., December 1988, 8.
45. Ibid., 9–10.
46. March 20, 1986, Minutes of the Board of Directors, 550.
47. John Griffith, "Why Research," *Chronicle* (December 1988), 2–3.
48. Graham and Diamond, *Rise of American Research Universities,* 122.
49. Ibid., 130.
50. *GM,* Summer 1987, 7.
51. Dan Davis, "AIDS," *GM,* Winter 1988, 14–16, 36–39.
52. Geiger, *Research and Relevant Knowledge,* 299.
53. Ibid., 302.
54. Ibid., 304.
55. *GM,* Winter 1986, 18.
56. Geiger, *Research and Relevant Knowledge,* 317; Ludmerer, *Time to Heal,* 342.
57. *Annual Report,* 1983, 22, Healy Papers.
58. *GM,* Spring 1989, 3–4.
59. Griffith, "Why Research," 2–3.
60. Thomas Macnamara, Chair, Medical Center Senate Caucus to Faculty, School of Medicine Clinical Departments et al., December 21, 1977.

61. October 16, 1981, Minutes of the Board of Directors, 550.
62. "Report of the Vice President for Financial Affairs and Treasurer," *Chronicle,* November 1988.
63. *GM,* January–February 1982, 21.
64. *Chronicle,* December 1988, 5; *Georgetown,* Winter 1989.
65. October 15, 1976, Minutes of the Board of Directors, 550.
66. May 9, 1980, Minutes of the Board of Directors, 550.
67. *GM,* Annual Report, January–February 1981, 16.
68. *GM,* January–February 1982, 20.
69. Hope Rogers, "What Are the Options? Controlling the High Cost of Health Care at Georgetown's Hospital," *GM,* November–December 1983, 7–9.
70. Ludmerer, *Time to Heal,* 351.
71. December 11, 1986, Minutes of the Board of Directors, 550.
72. Ludmerer, *Time to Heal,* 352–53.
73. *Hoya,* April 18, 1989, 1, 5.
74. April 14, 1989, Minutes of the Board of Directors, 550.
75. Beaudreau to Healy, July 31, 1980; and Dean's Report, 1980–81, 45–46, Dental School, GUA; *GM,* January–February 1982, 22.
76. Eric Solomon, "Applicant Trends: Past, Present and Future," 1980 Deans' Conference, Monterey, CA, Dental School, GUA.
77. Report of the Executive Director, Presented at the 1980 Deans Meeting in Monterey, CA, Dental School, GUA.
78. Healy to Beaudreau, February 27, 1978; and Beaudreau to Healy, March 14, 1978, Dental School, GUA.
79. Eleanor Nealon, "Dental School: Meeting the Challenges of the 80s," *GM,* October 1980, 4–5.
80. Dean's Report, 1979–80; and Beaudreau to Healy, July 31, 1980, Dental School, GUA.
81. In 1975 there had been nearly sixteen thousand applications to dental schools. A decade later there were a bit more than six thousand. By 1990 it was estimated that there would be, at most, 1.3 applicants for every available position nationally, a very unacceptable ratio. "Report to the Council of Deans on Applicants & Enrollment," by Eric S. Solomon, Assistant Executive Director for the Association of American Dental Schools Application Service and Resources, January 13, 1988, Executive Faculty Meeting Minutes, App. D, Dental School, GUA.
82. September 7, 1983, Executive Faculty Meeting Minutes, Dental School, GUA.
83. September 8, 1982 and September 2, 1986, Executive Faculty Meeting Minutes, Dental School, GUA.
84. "Demographic Data Update," ADA, December 16, 1988, Dental School, GUA; October 22, 1986, Executive Faculty Meeting Minutes, Dental School, GUA.
85. "Strengths and Weaknesses of the School," Dean's Alumni Council Workshop, April 10, 1986, Dental School, GUA.
86. Healy to Kolvenbach, January 17, 1985, Healy Papers.
87. November 12, 1986, Executive Faculty Meeting Minutes, Dental School, GUA.
88. December 11, 1986, Minutes of the Board of Directors, Executive Committee; December 15, 1986, Executive Faculty Meeting Minutes, Dental School, GUA.
89. Plan for School of Dentistry, Fiscal Years 1987–92, Dental School, GUA.
90. Moran Cruz interview.
91. Ibid.
92. March 19, 1987, Minutes of the Board of Directors, 550; GU Press Release, March 23, 1987, author's copy.
93. April 1, 1987, Executive Faculty Meeting Minutes, Dental School, GUA.
94. At the trial, the university presented a deposition by President Healy that he had consulted with the appropriate faculty before making the recommendation to close to the board. Senate officers Jo Ann Moran Cruz and Jack Murphy in their testimony swore that Healy had not consulted them or any other officer of the senate. Moran Cruz interview.

95. *Hoya*, May 27, 1988.
96. *GM*, Summer 1989, 3–4. Indeed, Georgetown was only one of five dental schools to close their doors in the late eighties.
97. From 1977 to 1983, there was a steep increase in the number of undergraduates doing a semester abroad, although the proportion of students doing so differed sharply among schools. In the college, the percentage rose from 9.6 percent to 15.2 percent, in nursing from 1 percent to 24.1 percent, in the School of Foreign Service from 33 percent to 40.2 percent, and in the School of Languages and Linguistics from 66.2 percent to 69.2 percent. Only the Business School remained static at 13 percent.
98. Homily at Memorial Mass, March 29, 1980, *Georgetown Record,* April 9, 1980.
99. By 1986, at least, the university had stock holdings in forty-five corporations that did business in South Africa. These holdings had a market value of $28.6 million, about 16 percent of the university total endowment. *GM,* Honor Roll, 1986, 13.
100. *Chronicle,* special issue, May 15, 1985.
101. May 10, 1985, Minutes, Faculty Senate, GUA.
102. GU-SCAR to All Faculty, April 12, 1986, GUA.
103. John J. DeGioia to Members of the Georgetown University Community, April 29, 1986, GUA; Mary Carroll Johansen and Chris Donesa, "University Shuts Down Freedom College Protest," *Hoya,* May 2, 1986.
104. Jo Ann Moran, President, Faculty Senate, to all Faculty, May 1, 1986, Faculty Senate, GUA.
105. *University Senate News,* May 3, 1986, Faculty Senate, GUA.
106. May 15, 1986, Minutes of the Board of Directors, Executive Committee, 550; September 19, 1986, Minutes of the Board of Directors.
107. Marjorie Hyer, "GU Votes S. African Divestment," *Washington Post,* September 23, 1986.
108. "Report on Speech and Expression on the Main Campus at GU," *Community Matters,* special issue, January 1989, 1–2.
109. Timothy Healy, "The Laity of the Future," *Annual Report,* 1988, Healy Papers.
110. "The Doing of Truth," *Annual Report,* 1983, 3.
111. Comments at a Jesuit Community meeting, April 2, 1987, in Curran diary, April 8, 1987.
112. U.S. Jesuit Conference, *The Jesuit Mission in Higher Education* (Washington, DC: Association of Jesuit College and Universities, 1982).
113. Healy to Rudolph Brenninkmeijer, June 27, 1988, Healy Papers.
114. T. S. Healy, SJ, "God's Better Beauty," *Annual Report,* 1984; David J. O'Brien, *From the Heart of the American Church: Catholic Higher Education and American Culture* (Maryknoll, NY: Orbis Books, 1994), 110ff.
115. Healy to Kolvenbach, January 17, 1985, Healy Papers.
116. Edwin Yoder, "Tim Healy's Spirit and Grace Will Be Missed by Those Friends Touched by the Jesuit," *Philadelphia Inquirer,* January 9, 1993.
117. John Paul II, *Ex corde ecclesiae,* August 15, 1990, in *American Catholic Higher Education: Essential Documents, 1967–90,* ed. Alice Gallin, OSU (Notre Dame, IN: University of Notre Dame Press, 1992), 429–30.
118. Healy felt that the university had a good chance of getting the decision clarified, if not reversed, with the Supreme Court. Most of the faculty he had summoned for their views thought that he should be satisfied with what he had already won: the right not to recognize. Curran diary, December 21, 1987.
119. Healy to the Members of Georgetown's Faculty and Alumni, March 28, 1988, Healy Papers.
120. *Washington Post,* February 24, 1989.
121. Bettina Bergo et al., Petition to the President from SOAK, November 22, 1977, author's copy.
122. Molly Moore, "'No Apologies' Comments by Healy," *Voice,* September 20, 1978, 4.
123. A handbill, distributed to the thousands streaming onto Healy lawn for the convocation, read, in part, "Today Ronald Reagan is receiving a G.U. degree. Does

he deserve this honor? The Reagan administration has compiled the worst civil rights record of any recent president. . . . His administration has drastically cut federal student aid and reduced the education budget. . . . While Reagan has allocated billions of dollars for S.D.I. research, he has ignored the urgency of A.I.D.S. which has already taken 41,000 lives. While Reagan has cut aid and eliminated programs that provide vital social services, he has continually pushed for an increased military budget. Only 3 years after he took office 5 million more women and children dropped below the poverty level. . . . Does the G.U. administration have no shame?" Sponsored by a coalition of GU students and student groups.

124. Charles L. Currie, SJ, *For the Record: Georgetown in Its Bicentennial Year* (Washington, DC: Georgetown University Press, 1990), 8.
125. Ibid., 26.
126. Ibid., 18.
127. Ibid., 68.
128. Healy to All Members of the Faculty and Administration, February 23, 1989, Healy Papers.
129. Timothy Healy, "The Hill, the River, the City: A Meditation on the Bicentennial," *Annual Report,* 1989, 10–11, Healy Papers.
130. Georgetown, Summer 1989, 11.

EPILOGUE

1. Inaugural address of Leo J. O'Donovan, SJ, September 23, 1989.
2. Main Campus Master Plan," http://facilities/georgetown.edu/architect/masterplan.html.
3. Evaluation Report by Middle States Visiting Team, March 24–27, 2002, 6.
4. Ernst et al., *First 125 Years,* 198.
5. Sherman Cohn interview, November 20, 2005.
6. *Blue & Gray,* May 1–14, 1995, 1.
7. "Report of the Task Force on Georgetown's Catholic and Jesuit Identity," May 1999.
8. Task Force on Georgetown's Catholic and Jesuit Identity, Final Report and Recommendations, October 1998.
9. O'Donovan to Friends, October 5, 2000.
10. "Inaugural Address," *GM,* Winter 2002, 21–23.

Selected Bibliography

PRIMARY SOURCES

Archives

Georgetown University Jesuit Community Archives
  Memorials of Provincial Visitations
Georgetown University Special Collections
  Edmund Ryan, SJ, Papers
  Georgetown University Archives
    Academic Vice President/Provost
    Academic Vice President Newsletters
    Reports of the Inspections of Georgetown University by the Middle States
        Association of Colleges and Secondary Schools
    Bicentennial
    Chancellor Bunn Papers
    College of Arts and Sciences
      Dean
      Executive Faculty
    Dental School
      Dental Faculty Minutes
    Development/University and Alumni Relations
    Edward Bunn, SJ, Papers
    Faculty Senate
      Minutes
      Reports
    Gerard Campbell, SJ, Papers
    Graduate School
      Dean
    Jesuit Community Papers
    Joseph Havens Richards, SJ, Letterbooks, 14 vols., 1888–98
    Joseph Havens Richards, SJ, Papers
    Law School
      Dean
      Office of Admissions
    Main Campus Planning Committee
    Medical School
      Correspondence
      Reports and Statistics
    Minutes of the Board of Directors, 1797–1989
    Minutes of the Board of Regents

Minutes of the President's Council
Office of Institutional Research
President's Office
   Henle Administration
Robert Henle, SJ, Papers
School of Business Administration
School of Foreign Service
   Dean
   Executive Faculty
School of Languages and Linguistics
School of Nursing and Health Studies
Student Development
Timothy Healy Papers
University and Alumni Relations
Georgetown Visitation Archives

Newspapers

Georgetown Law Weekly
Hoya
New York Times
Voice
Washington Evening Star
Washington Post
Washington Star

Magazines and Bulletins

AAUP Bulletin
Blue and Gray
Chronicle of Higher Education
[Georgetown] *Chronicle*
Community Matters: Newsletter of the Office of Student Affairs
Faculty Senate News
Georgetown
Georgetown Magazine
Georgetown Medical Bulletin
Georgetown Record
Georgetown Spectator
Georgetown Today
Georgetown University News
Mid/Week Report
University Senate News
Ye Domesday Booke

Books

Bell, Daniel. *The Reforming of General Education: The Columbia College Experience in Its National Setting.* New York: Columbia University Press, 1966.

Currie, Charles L., SJ. *For the Record: Georgetown in Its Bicentennial Year.* Washington, DC: Georgetown University Press, 1990.

Gallin, Alice, OSU, ed. *American Catholic Higher Education: Essential Documents, 1967–90.* Notre Dame, IN: University of Notre Dame Press, 1992.

Georgetown University: Its Impact on the Nation's Capital. Washington, DC: Georgetown University, 1966.

Henle, R. J., SJ. *A Personal Report: Georgetown University, 1969–1976.* Vol. 1, *Financial Problems and Progress in Relation to Its Academic and Educational Mission;* Vol. 2 *Projections and Recommendations beyond Mandate '81, Phase 1;* Vol. 3, *Planning at Georgetown University.* June 1976.

Langan, John P., SJ, ed. *Catholic Universities in Church and Society: A Dialogue on Ex Corde Ecclesiae*. Washington, DC: Georgetown University Press, 1993.

O'Brien, David J. *From the Heart of the American Church: American Catholic Higher Education and American Culture*. Maryknoll, NY: Orbis Books, 1994.

The Report of the President's Commission on Campus Unrest. Chicago: Avon Books, 1971.

University Reform: U.S., 1970; A Symposium on the Occasion of the Inauguration of Robert J. Henle, S.J., as 45th President of Georgetown University, October 7, 1969. Washington, DC: Georgetown University Press, 1970.

Articles

Alberger, Patricia. "All the People Dwell Together." *Georgetown*, March 1974, 4–7.

———. "Nursing Is Getting It All Together." *Georgetown*, September 1973, 4–8.

Ayers, William R., et al. "Impact of High Tuition on Medical School Applicants and Enrollees." *Journal of Medical Education* 56 (October 1981): 791–802.

Berry, George. "Georgetown University Law Center." *Georgetown Magazine*, November–December 1981.

Cannella, Dave. "What They Don't Want You to Hear: How G's WGTB 90.1 FM Died." *Voice*, January 26, 1989.

Carmody, Deidre. "Georgetown Seen as Making Gains by Reaching Out to Needy Students." *New York Times*, February 13, 1989.

Cloud, David S. "Georgetown Wins Friends and Funds on Hill." *Congressional Quarterly* (June 4, 1988): 1502–5.

Connors, Fran. "Basketball: 'A Whistle away from Victory.'" *Georgetown Today*, May 1975, 23–24.

DeGioia, John J. "The Three 'Lands' of Timothy Healy." *Washington Post*, January 1, 1993.

Dubas, Danielle. "Cancer: Unraveling the Mystery." *Georgetown Magazine*, March–April 1982, 2–9.

Duffy, Martha. "New Page for an Old Bookworm." *Time*, May 28, 1990.

Feinstein, Michael. "Chasing Carroll's Dream." *Georgetown Magazine*, July–August 1982.

Fialka, John. "GU Use Space 'Directive' in Crime-War Lab." *Washington Star*, February 3, 1968.

Fritschel, Heidi. "Treasures in the Stacks." *Georgetown Magazine*, 1986, 2–7.

Ginsbach, Pam. "Juvenile Clinic: Helping Neglected Children." *Georgetown Today*, November 1974, 4–7.

———. "Lessons in a Courtroom." *Georgetown Today*, September 1973, 13–14.

———. "A Piece of Unfinished Business: A Personal Renaissance." *Georgetown Today*, September 1974, 13–15.

Grant, Gerald. "New GU Head Is Ivy League Product." *Washington Post*, August 9, 1964.

Greeley, Andrew. "The Problems of Jesuit Education in the United States." Unpublished paper, Jesuit Education Association Meeting, Chicago, April 10–11, 1966.

Greene, Kevin. "Swallows to Capistrano: The Georgetown-Government Talent Exchange." *Georgetown Magazine*, September–October 1981, 13–16.

Johansen, Mary Carroll. "Davis Reflects on Georgetown Life." *Hoya*, May 2, 1986.

———, and Chri Donesa. "University Shuts Down Freedom College Protest." *Hoya*, May 2, 1986.

Joyce, Joseph P. "Corridor Jesuit: 'An Older Friend.'" *Georgetown Today*, May 1973.

Kopala, Lois. "A Former Homecoming Queen: Black, Proud and Angry." *Georgetown Today*, July 1972.

———. "A Student's Work Is Never Done." *Georgetown Today*, January 1973, 13–15.

Lewis, Dennis John. "Alliance Challenges WGTB-FM Transfer." *Washington Star*, July 29, 1978.

Mann, Jesse. "Black Experience." *Georgetown Record*, March 14, 1980.

Marccelo, Phil. "Lacrosse Evolves from Club to Contender." *Hoya*, Special lacrosse edition, Spring 2005, 12–13.

Markun, Pat. "Father Campbell Reflects on Fifty Years as a Jesuit." *Holy Trinity News* 4 (September 10, 1989): 1–4.

McGrath, John. "Georgetown University Endowment: 'Long Way to Go.'" *Georgetown,*
     September 1973.
———. "The Graduate School: From There to Where?" *Georgetown Today,* September
     1974, 13–15.
Moore, Molly. "'No Apologies' Comments by Healy." *Voice,* September 20, 1978.
Mullay, Jim. "Through the Hoops." *Georgetown Magazine,* Fall 1997, 29–31.
Nealon, Eleanor. "Dental School: Meeting the Challenges of the 80s." *Georgetown
     Magazine,* October 1980, 4–5.
Pezza, Judith A. "The Evolution of Admissions." *Georgetown Magazine,* Summer 1989,
     17–18.
Rand, Joe. "The Stewards: Fact and Fiction." *Voice,* February 9, 1988.
Reeves, Sandra. "The Think Tank on the Potomac." *Georgetown Magazine,* July–August
     1980, 6–19.
Rogers, Hope. "A Design for the 80s: Streamlining Georgetown's Graduate School."
     Georgetown Magazine, September–October 1983, 9–10.
———. "What Are the Options? Controlling the High Cost of Health Care at George-
     town's Hospital." *Georgetown Magazine,* November–December 1983, 7–9.
Scott, Walter. "'The Devil Disguised as a Spirit of Light': The Stewards Society of
     Georgetown College, 1982–1989." Unpublished paper, n.d.
Shelby, Joyce. "Debate: 'A Verbal Chess Match.'" *Georgetown Today,* September 1974,
     6–12.
Sloan, Eugene. "Georgetown Plans Its Architectural Future: Rigorous Building Will Forge
     a New Look for the University." *Hoya,* January 31, 1989.
Walsh, James, SJ. "Is Religion Dead at Georgetown?" *Georgetown Today,* July 1976, 3–4.
Wong, Nicole. "Admissions Sets 'Goals' for Student Diversity." *Hoya,* March 25, 1988.
Yoder, Edwin. "Tim Healy's Spirit and Grace Will Be Missed by Those Friends Touched by
     the Jesuit." *Philadelphia Inquirer,* January 9, 1993.

Interviews

(*Unless otherwise noted, all interviews are by the author*)

Altobello, Daniel. February 26, 1987.
Briefs, Henry. October 10, 1986.
Brown, Dorothy. December 12, 16, 1986.
Campbell, Gerard, SJ. January 5, 1987.
Cohn, Sherman. November 19, 20, 23, 29, 2005.
Collins, T. Byron, SJ. September 27, 1972. [by Joseph Durkin, SJ]
Cruz, Jo Ann Moran, July 16, 2007.
Davis, Royden, SJ. March 24, May 19, 1986.
Deacon, Charles. May 18, 2006.
Fitzgerald, Thomas, SJ. April 1984.
Houston, George. January 23, 1985.
Judge, Robert, SJ. July 30, 1987.
Mann, Jesse. April 22, 1986.
McGarrity, Rose. November 30, 1988.
McGarrity, Rose, n.d. [by Pam Ginsbach]
McNulty, Matthew. November 5, 1993; August 17, 1994.
Myniec, Wallace. April 12, 2006.
Rienzo, Francis. November 14, 2005.
Rose, John. December 18, 1986.
Rose, John. 1976. [by Pam Ginsbach]
Schroth, Raymond, SJ. July 28, 1987.
Shannon, James. June 9, 1983.
Winkler, Othmar. September 26, 1986.

SECONDARY SOURCES

Books and Articles

GENERAL

Abbot, Carl. *Political Terrain: Washington, D.C., from Tidewater Town to Global Metropolis.* Chapel Hill: University of North Carolina Press, 1999.

Geiger, Roger. *Research and Relevant Knowledge: American Research Universities since World War II.* New York: Oxford University Press, 1993.

Gillette, Howard. *Between Justice and Beauty: Race, Planning and the Failure of Urban Policy in Washington, DC.* Baltimore: Johns Hopkins University Press, 1995.

Graham, Hugh D. *The Uncertain Triumph: Federal Education Policy in the Kennedy and Johnson Years.* Chapel Hill: University of North Carolina Press, 1984.

Graham, Hugh David, and Diamond, Nancy. *The Rise of American Research Universities: Elites and Challengers in the Postwar Era.* Baltimore: Johns Hopkins University Press, 1997.

Horowitz, Helen Lefkowitz. *Campus Life: Undergraduate Cultures from the End of the Eighteenth Century to the Present.* Chicago: University of Chicago Press, 1987.

Jacoby, Russell. *The Last Intellectuals: American Culture in the Age of Academe.* New York, Basic Books, 1987.

Ludmerer, Kenneth M. *Time to Heal: American Medical Education from the Turn of the Century to the Era of Managed Care.* New York: Oxford University Press, 1999.

Marsden, George M. *The Soul of the American University: From Protestant Establishment to Established Nonbelief.* New York: Oxford University Press, 1994.

O'Mara, Margaret Pugh. *Cities of Knowledge: Cold War Science and the Search for the Next Silicon Valley.* Princeton, NJ: Princeton University Press, 2005.

Thelin, John R. *A History of American Higher Education,* Baltimore: Johns Hopkins University Press, 2004.

GEORGETOWN UNIVERSITY HISTORY AND RELATED DOCUMENTS

Audette, Rose Marie L. "Everything in Moderation: Social Activism and University Reform, Georgetown University, 1960–1970." Honors thesis, Georgetown University, 1981.

Barry, Patricia. *Surgeons at Georgetown: Surgery and Medical Education in the Nation's Capital, 1849–1969.* Franklin, TN: Hillsboro Press, 2001.

Brown, Dorothy M. "Learning, Faith, Freedom, and Building a Curriculum: Two Hundred Years and Counting." In *Georgetown at Two Hundred: Faculty Reflections on the University's Future,* ed. William C. McFadden, 79–108. Washington, DC: Georgetown University Press, 1990.

Ernst, Dan, et al. *The First 125 Years: An Illustrated History of the Georgetown University Law Center.* Washington, DC: Georgetown University Law Center, 1995.

Findley, Paul. *They Dare to Speak Out: People and Institutions Confront Israel's Lobby.* Westport, CT: Lawrence Hill Books, 1985.

Fuertes, Monica. "A Historical Perspective of Ethics in legal Education with a Focus on Georgetown Law." Unpublished paper, 1993.

Gleason, Mark J., Jr. "Students Serving Students: A History of Students of Georgetown, Inc." Unpublished paper, 1987.

Goldblatt, Craig. "'Look beyond the Campus, to America Itself': Student Activism at Georgetown University during the 1960s and the Founding of the *Georgetown Voice.*" Unpublished paper, 1988.

Hanley, Thomas O'Brien, SJ, ed. *The John Carroll Papers.* 3 vols. Notre Dame, IN: University of Notre Dame Press, 1976.

Himmelsbach, Adam. "Hoyas' First Thompson Era Has Long Life on the Payroll." *New York Times,* March 3, 2006.

Lazenby, Roland. *Georgetown: The Championships and Thompson.* Washington, DC: Full Court Press, 1984.

McFadden, William C., SJ, ed. *Georgetown at Two Hundred: Faculty Reflections on the University's Future.* Washington, DC: Georgetown University Press, 1990.

McLaughlin, J. Fairfax. *College Days at Georgetown, and Other Papers*. Philadelphia, 1899.

McNamara, Patrick. "Edmund A. Walsh, S.J., and Catholic Anti-Communism in the United States, 1917–1952." Dissertation, Catholic University of America, 2003.

Mikell, Gwendolyn. "Catholic Diversity, Pluralism, and Interracial/Intercultural Education." In *Georgetown at Two Hundred: Faculty Reflections on the University's Future*, ed. William C. McFadden, 213–36. Washington, DC: Georgetown University Press, 1990.

Mlyniec, Wallace. *Construction Notes: Transforming a Campus in Washington, D.C.* Garrett Park, MD: On This Spot Productions, 2006.

———. "The Intersection of Three Visions—Ken Pye, Bill Pincus, and Bill Greenhalgh—and the Development of Clinical Teaching Fellowships." *Tennessee Law Review* 64 (Summer 1997).

Poulson, Susan L. "Bill Clinton's Georgetown." Unpublished paper, 1995.

———. "From Single-Sex to Coeducation: The Advent of Coeducation at Georgetown, 1965—1975." *United States Catholic Historian* 13 (Fall 1995): 117–37.

———. "'A Quiet Revolution: The Transition to Coeducation at Georgetown and Rutgers Colleges, 1960–1975." Dissertation, Georgetown University, 1989.

Prelinger, Elizabeth. "'From Her Spires and Steeples Beaming': Mission and Image in Bricks and Stone." In *Georgetown at Two Hundred: Faculty Reflections on the University's Future*, ed. William C. McFadden, 335–53. Washington, DC: Georgetown University Press, 1990.

Schwartz, Richard B. "The Georgetown Graduate School in 1989." In *Georgetown at Two Hundred: Faculty Reflections on the University's Future*, ed. William C. McFadden, 281–91. Washington, DC: Georgetown University Press, 1990.

Shea, John Gilmary. *Memorial of the First Centenary of Georgetown College, D.C. Comprising a History of Georgetown University*. Washington, DC: P. F. Collier, 1891.

Smith, James Allen. *Strategic Calling: The Center for Strategic and International Studies, 1962–1992*. Washington, DC: Center for Strategic and International Studies, 1993.

Stapleton, John F. *Upward Journey: The Story of Internal Medicine at Georgetown, 1851–1981*. Washington, DC: Georgetown University Medical Center, 1996.

Sullivan, Anne D. "Interracial and Intercultural Education at GU." In *Georgetown at Two Hundred: Faculty Reflections on the University's Future*, ed. William C. McFadden, 201–12. Washington, DC: Georgetown University Press, 1990.

———, ed. *Women of Georgetown College: The First Quarter Century*. Washington, DC: Georgetown College, 1995.

Tillman, Seth P. *Georgetown's School of Foreign Service: The First Seventy-five Years*. Washington, DC: Georgetown University, Edmund A. Walsh School of Foreign Service, 1994.

Tushnet, Mark. "Catholic Legal Education at a National Law School: Reflections on the Georgetown Experience." In *Georgetown at Two Hundred: Faculty Reflections on the University's Future*, ed. William C. McFadden, 321–34. Washington, DC: Georgetown University Press, 1990.

Woolley, Alma S. *Learning, Faith, and Caring: History of the Georgetown University School of Nursing, 1903–2000*. Washington, DC: Georgetown University School of Nursing, 2001.

Jesuit and Catholic Educational History

Gleason, Philip. *Contending with Modernity: Catholic Higher Education in the Twentieth Century*. New York: Oxford University Press, 1995.

Leahy, William P., SJ. *Adapting to America: Catholics, Jesuits, and Higher Education in the Twentieth Century*. Washington, DC: Georgetown University Press, 1991.

McGrath, John J. *Catholic Institutions in the United States: Canonical and Civil Law Status*. Washington, DC: Catholic University Press of America, 1968.

Stamm, Martin J. "The Laicization of Corporate Governance of Twentieth Century American Catholic Higher Education." *Records of the American Catholic Historical Society of Philadelphia* 84 (March–December 1983): 81–99.

U.S. Jesuit Conference. *The Jesuit Mission in Higher Education*. Washington, DC: Association of Jesuit Colleges and Universities, 1982.

Index

Martin, Anita, 96
Martin, Bill, 222
Martin, Cheryl English, 95
Martin, Steve, 221
Martinez, Luis, 132
Martire, Daniel E., 15
Martyak, Anthony, 45
Mask and Bauble Dramatic Society, 213
Massimino, Rollie, 224
Mathias, Charles, 93
Matthews, Wesley, 12, 15
McAndrews, Lawrence, 236
McArdle, Patrick, 127
McAuliffe, Jane, 276
McAuliffe, Terry, 245
McBride, J. Nevins, 176
McCabe, Douglas, 12, 202
McCabe, Patrick, 225
McCahill, Eugene P., 176
McCarthy, Anne Derwinski, 198
McCarthy, David: and civil rights
    movement, 139; and Law Center,
    96, 103, 106, 240–44, 246
McCarthy, Gene, 140
McClatchy, J. D., 80
McClure, Joe, 228
McCormack, Malcolm, 54, 66, 161
McCormick, Jamie, 141
McCormick, Richard, 16, 17
McCourt, Frank, 82
McDermott, Jim, 134
McDonald, Jackson, 200
McDonald, Perry, 224
McDonald, William, 12, 16
McDonough, Bernard, 97
McDonough, Robert Emmett, 279
McDonough Hall, 98, 99
McDonough School of Business, 275
McElroy, William, 12, 15
McGarrity, Rosemary, 82–83, 85
McGee, Jack, 127, 128
McGovern, George, 154
McGovern, James, 245
McGovern, Terrence, 82
McGowan, Gerald S., 94
McGrath, Brian, 7, 10, 23
McGreevey, James, 245
McGuire, Patricia, 104, 246
McHenry, Donald, 185
McKelvey, Tara, 198
McKeown, Elizabeth, 13
McKeown, Margaret, 104
McKithen, Aubrey, 224, 225
McMahon, Brian, 187
McNally, Paul, 284
McNamara, Christopher, 81
McNamara, Robert M., 104

McNeill, John, 184
McNelis, Brian, 225
McNelis, Paul, 184
McNulty, Matthew, 36–38, 48–49, 161,
    178, 208
McSorley, Richard, 138, 144, 145, 266
Meagher, Ria, 228
Medical Center: administration of,
    36–37; community outreach,
    48–49; Concentrated Care Center,
    38–39; enrollment, 37–38; faculty
    development, 39–43; faculty
    practice plans, 251–52; federal
    funding for, 37–38; growth of,
    34–49; Hospital, 48–49; Lombardi
    Cancer Center, 38–39; Medical
    School and, 14, 43–45, 252, 293;
    research, 247–51; restructuring of,
    254; separate incorporation of,
    35–36. See also Dental School;
    Nursing School
Medical-Dental Manpower Bill of the
    District of Columbia, 37
Med Star, 281
Mellon fellowships, 191, 279
Memorial Lemon Day, 155
Mendoza, Ricardo, 132
Meredith, Eleanor, 133
Meridien Hall, 113
Mermel, Virginia, 206
Merrill, Steve, 104
Metzger, Stanley, 241
Meyers, Erik, 131
Middle States Association of Colleges
    and Secondary Schools, 10, 234,
    235, 274, 276
Millemann, Michael, 104
Milliken, Jane, 133
minorities: and affirmative action, 12;
    as faculty, 12, 24, 32, 96, 185–86;
    student organizations, 125–26.
    See also specific minority groups
Minority Affairs Office, 76
Mitchell Scholars, 279
Moliski, Ken, 136
Monet, Alice Babcock, 80
Montero, Alfredo, 132
Montoya, Joseph M., 105
Moore, Julia, 94
Moran, Theodore, 200
Moreland, Jeff, 133
Morgan, Dayton, 23
Morial, Marc, 245
Morrell, John, 270
Morris, Michele, 13
Mortara, Michael P., 95
Mott, Randy, 102
Mourning, Alonzo, 224

Mujal-Leon, Eusabio, 184
Mujica, Barbara, 13
Mull, Stephen D., 200
Mulledy Building, 8
Mullen, Christine, 225
Mullen, Peter, 246
Murkowski, Lisa, 197
Murphy, Donn, 213
Murphy, G. Ronald, 14
Murphy, Jack, 59, 96, 99
Murphy, Molly, 228
Murray, Douglas J., 95
Murtaugh, George, 126
Murto, Charles B., 37, 46
Mushkin, Selma, 13, 15
Mlyniec, Wallace, 98

N
National Aeronautics and Space
    Administration (NASA), 28
National Cancer Institute (NCI), 38,
    248, 249, 250
National Capital Planning Commission,
    10, 20
National Center for Export-Import
    Studies (NCEIS), 202
National Collegiate Athletic Association
    (NCAA), 130, 133–36, 220–22
National Committee for Fund-Raising
    for Athletics, 230
National Council for the Georgetown
    University Campaign, 181
National Defense Education Act of
    1958 (NDEA), 29
National Endowment for the
    Humanities, 187
National Heart and Lung Institute of
    NIH, 49
National Institute of Citizens for
    Education in the Law, 101
National Institutes of Health (NIH), 15,
    28, 42, 143, 250
National League of Nursing, 208
National Library of Medicine (NLM),
    251
National Science Foundation (NSF),
    28, 143
National Street Law Institute, 101
Native Americans: in Medical School,
    45; as students, 99–100, 279
Natsios, Andrew, 81
NCAA. See National Collegiate Athletic
    Association
NCEIS (National Center for
    Export-Import Studies), 202
NCI. See National Cancer Institute
NDEA (National Defense Education
    Act of 1958), 29